International Organizations as Self-Directed Actors

This exciting new text illustrates and advances the argument that international organizations (IOs) need to be taken seriously as actors in world affairs.

Bringing together an international line-up of distinguished contributors, the text examines recent theories that suggest how IOs are able to set their own policies and implement them in meaningful ways. The chapters review these theoretical positions and then present a series of case studies which focus on how these theories play out when IOs are charged with solving global problems, including development, peacekeeping and environmental policy coordination.

Examining and analyzing both positive and negative examples of this independence, this text is a valuable resource on the topic of the internal workings of IOs, providing the richest and most focused book so far dealing with the capacity of IOs for independent action in international politics. It is essential reading for all students of international organizations.

Joel E. Oestreich is Associate Professor at Drexel University, Philadelphia. He has published on the human rights policies of UN agencies, the moral responsibilities of the World Bank, and various other human rights issues.

Routledge Global Institutions Series

Edited by Thomas G. Weiss
The CUNY Graduate Center, New York, USA
and Rorden Wilkinson
University of Manchester, UK

About the series

The Global Institutions Series is designed to provide readers with comprehensive, accessible, and informative guides to the history, structure, and activities of key international organizations as well as books that deal with topics of key importance in contemporary global governance. Every volume stands on its own as a thorough and insightful treatment of a particular topic, but the series as a whole contributes to a coherent and complementary portrait of the phenomenon of global institutions at the dawn of the millennium.

Books are written by recognized experts, conform to a similar structure, and cover a range of themes and debates common to the series. These areas of shared concern include the general purpose and rationale for organizations, developments over time, membership, structure, decision-making procedures, and key functions. Moreover, current debates are placed in historical perspective alongside informed analysis and critique. Each book also contains an annotated bibliography and guide to electronic information as well as any annexes appropriate to the subject matter at hand.

The volumes currently published are:

64 International Organizations as Self-Directed Actors (2012)
A framework for analysis
edited by Joel E. Oestreich (Drexel University)

63 Maritime Piracy (2012)
by Robert Haywood and Roberta Spivak (One Earth Future Foundation)

62 UNHCR: The Politics and Practice of Refugee Protection (2nd edition, 2012)
by Alexander Betts (University of Oxford), Gil Loescher (University of Oxford), and James Milner (Carleton University)

61 International Law, International Relations, and Global Governance (2012)
by Charlotte Ku (University of Illinois)

60 Global Health Governance (2012)
by Sophie Harman (City University, London)

59 The Council of Europe (2012)
by Martyn Bond (University of London)

58 The Security Governance of Regional Organizations (2011)
edited by Emil J. Kirchner (University of Essex) and Roberto Domínguez (Suffolk University)

57 The United Nations Development Programme and System (2011)
by Stephen Browne (FUNDS Project)

56 The South Asian Association for Regional Cooperation (2011)
An emerging collaboration architecture
by Lawrence Sáez (University of London)

55 The UN Human Rights Council (2011)
by Bertrand G. Ramcharan (Geneva Graduate Institute of International and Development Studies)

54 The Responsibility to Protect (2011)
Cultural perspectives in the Global South
edited by Rama Mani (University of Oxford) and Thomas G. Weiss (The CUNY Graduate Center)

53 The International Trade Centre (2011)
Promoting exports for development
by Stephen Browne (FUNDS Project) and Sam Laird (University of Nottingham)

52 The Idea of World Government (2011)
From ancient times to the twenty-first century
by James A. Yunker (Western Illinois University)

51 Humanitarianism Contested (2011)
Where angels fear to tread
by Michael Barnett (George Washington University) and Thomas G. Weiss (The CUNY Graduate Center)

50 **The Organization of American States (2011)**
Global governance away from the media
by Monica Herz (Catholic University, Rio de Janeiro)

49 **Non-Governmental Organizations in World Politics (2011)**
The construction of global governance
by Peter Willetts (City University, London)

48 **The Forum on China-Africa Cooperation (FOCAC) (2011)**
by Ian Taylor (University of St. Andrews)

47 **Global Think Tanks (2011)**
Policy networks and governance
by James G. McGann (University of Pennsylvania) with Richard Sabatini

46 **United Nations Educational, Scientific and Cultural Organization (UNESCO) (2011)**
Creating norms for a complex world
by J.P. Singh (Georgetown University)

45 **The International Labour Organization (2011)**
Coming in from the cold
by Steve Hughes (Newcastle University) and Nigel Haworth (University of Auckland)

44 **Global Poverty (2010)**
How global governance is failing the poor
by David Hulme (University of Manchester)

43 **Global Governance, Poverty, and Inequality (2010)**
edited by Jennifer Clapp (University of Waterloo) and Rorden Wilkinson (University of Manchester)

42 **Multilateral Counter-Terrorism (2010)**
The global politics of cooperation and contestation
by Peter Romaniuk (John Jay College of Criminal Justice, CUNY)

41 **Governing Climate Change (2010)**
by Peter Newell (University of East Anglia) and Harriet A. Bulkeley (Durham University)

40 **The UN Secretary-General and Secretariat (2nd edition, 2010)**
by Leon Gordenker (Princeton University)

39 Preventive Human Rights Strategies (2010)
by Bertrand G. Ramcharan (Geneva Graduate Institute of International and Development Studies)

38 African Economic Institutions (2010)
by Kwame Akonor (Seton Hall University)

37 Global Institutions and the HIV/AIDS Epidemic (2010)
Responding to an international crisis
by Franklyn Lisk (University of Warwick)

36 Regional Security (2010)
The capacity of international organizations
by Rodrigo Tavares (United Nations University)

35 The Organisation for Economic Co-operation and Development (2009)
by Richard Woodward (University of Hull)

34 Transnational Organized Crime (2009)
by Frank Madsen (University of Cambridge)

33 The United Nations and Human Rights (2nd edition, 2009)
A guide for a new era
by Julie A. Mertus (American University)

32 The International Organization for Standardization (2009)
Global governance through voluntary consensus
by Craig N. Murphy (Wellesley College) and JoAnne Yates (Massachusetts Institute of Technology)

31 Shaping the Humanitarian World (2009)
by Peter Walker (Tufts University) and Daniel G. Maxwell (Tufts University)

30 Global Food and Agricultural Institutions (2009)
by John Shaw

29 Institutions of the Global South (2009)
by Jacqueline Anne Braveboy-Wagner (City College of New York, CUNY)

28 International Judicial Institutions (2009)
The architecture of international justice at home and abroad
by Richard J. Goldstone (Retired Justice of the Constitutional Court of South Africa) and Adam M. Smith (Harvard University)

27 The International Olympic Committee (2009)
The governance of the Olympic system
by Jean-Loup Chappelet (IDHEAP Swiss Graduate School of Public Administration) and Brenda Kübler-Mabbott

26 The World Health Organization (2009)
by Kelley Lee (London School of Hygiene and Tropical Medicine)

25 Internet Governance (2009)
The new frontier of global institutions
by John Mathiason (Syracuse University)

24 Institutions of the Asia-Pacific (2009)
ASEAN, APEC, and beyond
by Mark Beeson (University of Birmingham)

23 United Nations High Commissioner for Refugees (UNHCR) (2008)
The politics and practice of refugee protection into the twenty-first century
by Gil Loescher (University of Oxford), Alexander Betts (University of Oxford), and James Milner (University of Toronto)

22 Contemporary Human Rights Ideas (2008)
by Bertrand G. Ramcharan (Geneva Graduate Institute of International and Development Studies)

21 The World Bank (2008)
From reconstruction to development to equity
by Katherine Marshall (Georgetown University)

20 The European Union (2008)
by Clive Archer (Manchester Metropolitan University)

19 The African Union (2008)
Challenges of globalization, security, and governance
by Samuel M. Makinda (Murdoch University) and F. Wafula Okumu (McMaster University)

18 Commonwealth (2008)
Inter- and non-state contributions to global governance
by Timothy M. Shaw (Royal Roads University)

17 The World Trade Organization (2007)
Law, economics, and politics
by Bernard M. Hoekman (World Bank) and Petros C. Mavroidis (Columbia University)

16 A Crisis of Global Institutions? (2007)
Multilateralism and international security
by Edward Newman (University of Birmingham)

15 UN Conference on Trade and Development (2007)
by Ian Taylor (University of St. Andrews) and Karen Smith (University of Stellenbosch)

14 The Organization for Security and Co-operation in Europe (2007)
by David J. Galbreath (University of Aberdeen)

13 The International Committee of the Red Cross (2007)
A neutral humanitarian actor
by David P. Forsythe (University of Nebraska) and Barbara Ann Rieffer-Flanagan (Central Washington University)

12 The World Economic Forum (2007)
A multi-stakeholder approach to global governance
by Geoffrey Allen Pigman (Bennington College)

11 The Group of 7/8 (2007)
by Hugo Dobson (University of Sheffield)

10 The International Monetary Fund (2007)
Politics of conditional lending
by James Raymond Vreeland (Georgetown University)

9 The North Atlantic Treaty Organization (2007)
The enduring alliance
by Julian Lindley-French (Center for Applied Policy, University of Munich)

8 The World Intellectual Property Organization (2006)
Resurgence and the development agenda
by Chris May (University of the West of England)

7 The UN Security Council (2006)
Practice and promise
by Edward C. Luck (Columbia University)

6 Global Environmental Institutions (2006)
by Elizabeth R. DeSombre (Wellesley College)

5 Internal Displacement (2006)
Conceptualization and its consequences
by Thomas G. Weiss (The CUNY Graduate Center) and David A. Korn

4 **The UN General Assembly** (2005)
by M. J. Peterson (University of Massachusetts, Amherst)

3 **United Nations Global Conferences** (2005)
by Michael G. Schechter (Michigan State University)

2 **The UN Secretary-General and Secretariat** (2005)
by Leon Gordenker (Princeton University)

1 **The United Nations and Human Rights** (2005)
A guide for a new era
by Julie A. Mertus (American University)

Books currently under contract include:

The Regional Development Banks
Lending with a regional flavor
by Jonathan R. Strand (University of Nevada)

Millennium Development Goals (MDGs)
For a people-centered development agenda?
by Sakiko Fukada-Parr (The New School)

Peacebuilding
From concept to commission
by Robert Jenkins (The CUNY Graduate Center)

UNICEF
by Richard Jolly (University of Sussex)

The Bank for International Settlements
The politics of global financial supervision in the age of high finance
by Kevin Ozgercin (SUNY College at Old Westbury)

International Migration
by Khalid Koser (Geneva Centre for Security Policy)

Human Development
by Richard Ponzio

Religious Institutions and Global Politics
by Katherine Marshall (Georgetown University)

The Group of Twenty (G20)
by Andrew F. Cooper (Centre for International Governance Innovation, Ontario)
and Ramesh Thakur (Balsillie School of International Affairs, Ontario)

The International Monetary Fund (2nd edition)
Politics of conditional lending
by James Raymond Vreeland (Georgetown University)

The UN Global Compact
by Catia Gregoratti (Lund University)

Institutions for Women's Rights
by Charlotte Patton (York College, CUNY) and Carolyn Stephenson (University of Hawaii)

International Aid
by Paul Mosley (University of Sheffield)

Global Consumer Policy
by Karsten Ronit (University of Copenhagen)

UN Industrial Development Organization (UNIDO)
by Stephen Browne (FUNDS Project)

The Changing Political Map of Global Governance
by Anthony Payne (University of Sheffield) and Stephen Robert Buzdugan (Manchester Metropolitan University)

Coping with Nuclear Weapons
by W. Pal Sidhu

Global Sustainability
by Tapio Kanninen

Private Foundations and Development Partnerships
by Michael Moran (Swinburne University of Technology)

Decolonization, Sovereignty, and the African Union
by Martin Welz (University of Konstanz)

Feminist Strategies in International Governance
edited by Gülay Caglar (Humboldt University of Berlin), Elisabeth Prügl (Graduate Institute of International and Development Studies, Geneva), Susanne Zwingel (SUNY Potsdam)

The International Politics of Human Rights
edited by Monica Serrano (Colegio de Mexico) and Thomas G. Weiss (The CUNY Graduate Center)

For further information regarding the series, please contact:

Craig Fowlie, Publisher, Politics & International Studies
Taylor & Francis
2 Park Square, Milton Park, Abingdon
Oxford OX14 4RN, UK
+44 (0)207 842 2057 Tel
+44 (0)207 842 2302 Fax
Craig.Fowlie@tandf.co.uk
www.routledge.com

International Organizations as Self-Directed Actors
A framework for analysis

**Edited by
Joel E. Oestreich**

Taylor & Francis Group

LONDON AND NEW YORK

First published 2012
by Routledge
2 Park Square, Milton Park, Abingdon, Oxon, OX14 4RN

Simultaneously published in the USA and Canada
by Routledge
711 Third Avenue, New York, NY 10017

Routledge is an imprint of the Taylor & Francis Group, an informa business

© 2012 selection and editorial matter, Joel E. Oestreich; contributors, their contributions

The right of Joel E. Oestreich to be identified as editor of this work has been asserted by him in accordance with the Copyright, Designs and Patent Act 1988.

All rights reserved. No part of this book may be reprinted or reproduced or utilised in any form or by any electronic, mechanical, or other means, now known or hereafter invented, including photocopying and recording, or in any information storage or retrieval system, without permission in writing from the publishers.

Trademark notice: Product or corporate names may be trademarks or registered trademarks, and are used only for identification and explanation without intent to infringe.

British Library Cataloguing in Publication Data
A catalogue record for this book is available from the British Library

Library of Congress Cataloging in Publication Data
International organizations as self-directed actors : a framework for analysis / edited by Joel E. Oestreich.
 p. cm. – (Routledge global institutions series)
 Includes bibliographical references and index.
 1. International agencies. 2. International organization. 3. International agencies–Case studies. 4. International organization–Case studies. I. Oestreich, Joel E.
 JZ4839.I59 2012
 341.2–dc23
                        2011039484

ISBN 13: 978-0-415-78290-6 (hbk)
ISBN 13: 978-0-415-78291-3 (pbk)
ISBN 13: 978-0-203-12378-2 (ebk)

Typeset in Times New Roman
by Taylor & Francis Books

Printed and bound in Great Britain by
CPI Antony Rowe, Chippenham, Wiltshire

Contents

List of illustrations	xv
List of contributors	xvi
Foreword	xix
List of abbreviations	xxi

Introduction 1
JOEL E. OESTREICH

PART I
The United Nations Secretariat 27

1 The UN Secretary-General and self-directed leadership: development of the democracy agenda 29
KIRSTEN HAACK AND KENT J. KILLE

2 The roots of UN post-conflict peacebuilding: a case study of autonomous agency 60
MARGARET P. KARNS

PART II
Intergovernmental organizations 89

3 The anatomy of autonomy: the case of the World Bank 91
SUSAN PARK AND CATHERINE WEAVER

4 UNHCR, autonomy, and mandate change 118
ALEXANDER BETTS

5 Changing actors and actions in the global fight against AIDS 141
CHRISTER JÖNSSON

6 Disaggregating delegation: multiplying agents in the
  international maritime safety regime   168
  KENDALL W. STILES

7 Not just states or the Secretary-General, but also staff: the
  emergence of UNOPS as a new UN organization   195
  DENNIS DIJKZEUL

PART III
Expanding the argument   **219**

8 ASEAN as an informal organization: does it exist and does it
  have agency? The emergence of the ASEAN secretariat   221
  BOB REINALDA

9 New types of organizations and global governance in the
  twenty-first century: the case of ICANN   241
  JAMES P. MULDOON, JR

10 Conclusion   264
   JOEL E. OESTREICH

   Index   270

Illustrations

Box

2.1 Post-conflict peacebuilding tasks　　　　　　　　　　63

Table

6.1 Disaggregation of agent functions　　　　　　　　　169

Figures

6.1 Actor powers in policy advocacy　　　　　　　　　183
6.2 Actor powers in policy adoption　　　　　　　　　183
6.3 Actor powers in rule supervision　　　　　　　　　184
9.1 Network of Internet governance organizations　　　251
9.2 ICANN structure in 1999 and 2009　　　　　　　　253

Contributors

Alexander Betts is Hedley Bull Research Fellow in International Relations at the University of Oxford. He is author of *Protection by Persuasion: International Cooperation in the Refugee Regime* (2009) and editor of *Global Migration Governance* (2011). His research focuses on the international politics of asylum and migration, international institutions and global governance, and the international relations of Africa.

Dennis Dijkzeul is Professor of Conflict and Organization and Executive Director of the Institute for International Law of Peace and Armed Conflict at Ruhr University Bochum. He is also Adjunct Professor at the School of International and Public Affairs of Columbia University. His main research interests are humanitarian studies and the management of international organizations and humanitarian action.

Kirsten Haack is Senior Lecturer in International Politics at Northumbria University. She is the author of *The United Nations Democracy Agenda: A Conceptual History* (2011) and has published on international organization studies as a field of study, ideas and the UN system, and leadership by the UN Secretary-General.

Christer Jönsson is Professor Emeritus of Political Science at Lund University, and a member of the Royal Swedish Academy of Sciences. His research interests include diplomacy, international negotiation, transnational networks, and international organization. He is co-author of *Essence of Diplomacy* (2005), and co-editor of *Transnational Actors in Global Governance* (2010).

Margaret P. Karns is Professor Emerita of Political Science at the University of Dayton. She is co-author with Karen A. Mingst of *International Organizations: The Politics and Processes of Global Governance* (2009) and *The United Nations in the 21st Century*

Contributors xvii

(2012). She has also written on the subjects of peacekeeping, the United States and multilateral institutions, and global governance.

Kent J. Kille is Associate Professor of Political Science at The College of Wooster. He is the author of *From Manager to Visionary: The Secretary-General of the United Nations* (2006), and editor of and contributor to *The UN Secretary-General and Moral Authority: Ethics and Religion in International Leadership* (2007).

James P. Muldoon, Jr is Senior Fellow with the Center for Global Change and Governance, Rutgers University. He is the author of *The Architecture of Global Governance: An Introduction to the Study of International Organizations* (2003) and co-editor of *The New Dynamics of Multilateralism: Diplomacy, International Organizations, and Global Governance* (2010). His research focuses on multilateral diplomacy, the United Nations, and the challenges of global governance in the twenty-first century.

Joel E. Oestreich is Associate Professor of Political Science at Drexel University. He is the author of *Power and Principle: Human Rights Programming in International Organizations* (2007). He has also published on the rights of indigenous peoples, children's rights, and the moral responsibilities of international organizations.

Susan Park is a Senior Lecturer of International Relations at the University of Sydney. She is the author of *World Bank Group Interactions with Environmentalists* (2010). Susan has co-edited a collection on the International Monetary Fund and the World Bank (2010), and has published on constructivist accounts of change in international organizations.

Bob Reinalda is Senior Researcher at the Institute for Management Research at Radboud University Nijmegen, the Netherlands. He has published the *Routledge History of International Organizations* (2009) and edited the *Ashgate Companion to Non-State Actors* (2011). He is an editor of IO BIO, the *Biographical Dictionary of Secretaries-General of International Organizations*.

Kendall W. Stiles is Professor of Political Science and International Relations Program Director at Brigham Young University. He is the co-author of *International Norms and Cycles of Change* (2008) and co-editor of *Cooperating without America* (2009). He writes on international law and institutions.

Catherine Weaver is Associate Professor at the LBJ School of Public Affairs and Distinguished Scholar at the Robert S. Strauss Center for International Security & Law at the University of Texas at Austin. She is the author of *Hypocrisy Trap: the World Bank and the Poverty of Reform* (2008) and co-editor of *International Political Economy: Debating the Past, Present, and Future* (2010). She has published widely on the organizational culture, behavior, and reform of international organizations, and the politics of transparency and accountability in international development aid.

Foreword

The current volume, dealing with an idea that has recently captured the global public policy Zeitgeist, is edited by Joel E. Oestreich and is the third in what we anticipate will be a growing number of longer research volumes in our "global institutions" series that examine crucial global problems and possible global policies and solutions. *International Organizations as Self-Directed Actors: A Framework for Analysis* consists of specialized and critical case studies demonstrating the underappreciated contribution by international organizations to contemporary global governance. While for some time international relations scholars have made way for non-state actors in their theoretical and applied analyses, intergovernmental organizations, as the creation of states, are still mainly considered as essentially dependent upon the whims and dictates of the member states that pay the bills. This volume probes the extent to which such organizations themselves can create the space to maneuver. In point of fact, the collective argument here adds up to substantial evidence of an independent ability to influence normative, policy, and operational agendas with examples drawn from international peace and security, human rights, and development.

Our research volumes are intended to complement the shorter, definitive guides to the most visible institutional components of what we know as "global governance," which comprise the core of our series and sit alongside volumes that offer authoritative accounts of the issues and debates in which international organizational entities are embroiled. We now have more than 60 books that act as key references for the most significant global institutions and the evolution of the challenges that they face. Our intention has always been to provide one-stop shopping for all readers—students (both undergraduate and postgraduate), interested negotiators, diplomats, practitioners from nongovernmental and intergovernmental organizations, and interested parties alike—seeking information about most prominent institutional aspects of global governance.

The new research stream incorporates lengthier single and co-authored as well as edited volumes by knowledgeable analysts. The logic is simple—we want to provide a platform that allows authors to push the envelope on important topics linked to global institutions but that are not covered in depth in our definitive guides. The research stream is thus a perfect companion to the shorter volumes. Indeed, seven of the nine institutions that figure in the individual case studies of this compilation are the main subjects in complete volumes in the series,[1] and virtually all of the others in the series are relevant to the main parts of this volume.

Ideally, *International Organizations as Self-Directed Actors* and future volumes in the research stream will be used as complementary readings in courses in which specific titles in the series are pertinent. Our aim is to enable topics of importance to be dealt with exhaustively by specialists as well as enabling collected works to address issues in ways that bring more than the sum of the individual parts, while at the same time maintaining the integrity of the Global Institutions Series.

As always, we look forward to comments from our readers.

Thomas G. Weiss, The CUNY Graduate Center, New York, USA
Rorden Wilkinson, University of Manchester, UK
September 2011

Note

1 See in this Routledge series the following titles: for chapter 1, Leon Gordenker, *The UN Secretary-General and Secretariat* (2010); for chapter 2, Robert Jenkins, *Peacebuilding* (forthcoming); for chapter 3, Katherine Marshall, *The World Bank* (2008); for chapter 4, Alexander Betts, Gil Loescher, and James Milner; for *UNHCR: The Politics and Practice of Refugee Protection (2012)*; for chapter 5, Franklyn Lisk, *Global Institutions and the HIV/AIDS Epidemic* (2010); for chapter 8, Mark Beeson, *Institutions of the Asia-Pacific* (2009); and for chapter 9, John Mathiason, *Internet Governance* (2009).

Abbreviations

ACABQ	Advisory Committee on Administrative and Budgetary Questions
ACC	United States Administrative Committee on Coordination
AFTA	ASEAN Free Trade Area
AIP	ASEAN Industrial Projects
AOC	Affirmations of Commitment
APEC	Asia-Pacific Economic Cooperation
APT	ASEAN Plus Three
ARF	ASEAN Regional Forum
ARPA	Advance Research Projects Agency
ARV	antiretroviral
ASEAN	Association of Southeast Asian Nations
ASO	AIDS service organization
CAS	Country Assistance Strategy
CCM	Country Coordination Mechanism
ccTLD	country code top-level domain
CEPT	Common Effective Preferential Tariff
CIAV	International Support and Verification Commission
DDSMS	Department for Development Support and Management Services
DfID	Department for International Development
DIESA	Department of International Economic and Social Affairs
DIP	Department of International Protection
DNS	domain name system
DoC	Department of Commerce
DoD	Department of Defense
DOS	Department of Operational Services
DPKO	Department of Peacekeeping Operations
EC	European Commission

ECB	UN System Chief Executives Board for Coordination
ECOSOC	Economic and Social Council
ERC	Committee on ICANN Evolution and Reform
ESSD	Environmentally and Socially Sustainable Development
EU	European Union
FDI	foreign direct investment
FMLN	Farabundo Martí National Liberation Front
FSI	Flag State Implementation Committee
GAC	Governance and Anti-Corruption
GAO	General Accounting Office
GAP	Government Accountability Project
GATT	General Agreement on Tariffs and Trade
GFATM	Global Fund to Fight AIDS, Tuberculosis and Malaria
GMC	Global Management Committee
GPA	Global Programme on AIDS
gTLD	generic top-level domain
HIV/AIDS	Human Immunodeficiency Virus/Acquired Immune Deficiency Syndrome
HRBA	human rights-based approach
IAAG	Inter-agency Advisory Group
IAB	Internet Activities Board, later renamed Internet Architecture Board
IANA	Internet Assigned Numbers Authority
IASC	Inter-Agency Standing Committee
IAVI	International AIDS Vaccine Initiative
ICANN	Internet Corporation for Assigned Names and Numbers
ICASO	International Council of AIDS Service Organization
ICCB	Internet Configuration Control Board
ICJ	International Court of Justice
ICM	Internet Content Management Registry
ICNRD	International Conference of New and Restored Democracies
ICT	Information and Communications Technology
IDA	International Development Association
IDP	internally displaced person
IEG	Independent Evaluation Group
IETF	Internet Engineering Task Force
IGP	Internet Governance Project
ILC	International Law Commission
ILO	International Labour Organization
IMB	International Maritime Bureau
IMF	International Monetary Fund

IMO	International Maritime Organization
INF	Infrastructure
INT	Department of Institutional Integrity
IO	international organization/ intergovernmental organization
IOM	International Organization for Migration
IP	Internet Protocol
IR	international relations
IRTF	Internet Research Task Force
ISOC	Internet Society
ISPS	International Ship and Port Facility Security
ITU	International Telecommunication Union
MDB	multilateral development bank
MDGs	Millennium Development Goals
MIC	middle-income country
MIT	Massachusetts Institute of Technology
MOU	Memorandum of Understanding
MSC	Maritime Safety Committee
MSC	Maritime Security Council
NAC	National HIV/AIDS Council
NATO	North Atlantic Treaty Organization
NGO	nongovernmental organization
NSFNET	National Science Foundation Network
NSI	Network Solutions, Inc.
NTIA	National Telecommunications and Information Agency
NWG	Network Working Group
OAS	Organization of American States
OECD	Organisation for Economic Co-operation and Development
OED	Operations Evaluation Department
ONUCA	United Nations Observer Group in Central America
ONUSAL	United Nations Observer Mission in El Salvador
OPE	Office for Project Execution
OPS	Office for Project Services
PA	principal-agent
PED	Project Execution Division
PLWHA	people living with HIV/AIDS
PMC	Post Ministerial Conference
PPP	public-private partnership
PREM	Poverty Reduction and Economic Management
QACU	Quality Assurance and Compliance Unit
QAG	Quality Assurance Group
RFP	Request for Proposals
SARS	severe acute respiratory syndrome

SDN	Sustainable Development Network
SOLAS	Safety of Life at Sea Convention
SWAPO	South West Africa People's Organization
TCP/IP	Transmission Control Protocol/Internet Protocol
TLD	top-level domain
TNC	transnational corporation
TRP	Technical Review Panel
UN	United Nations
UNAIDS	Joint United Nations Programme on HIV/AIDS
UNCLOS	United Nations Convention on the Law of the Sea
UNCTAD	United Nations Conference on Trade and Development
UNDP	United Nations Development Programme
UNEP	United Nations Environment Programme
UNESCO	United Nations Educational, Scientific and Cultural Organization
UNFPA	United Nations Population Fund
UNGA	United Nations General Assembly
UNGASS	United Nations General Assembly Special Session on AIDS
UNHCR	United Nations High Commissioner for Refugees
UNICEF	United Nations Children's Fund
UNODC	UN Office on Drugs and Crime
UNOPS	United Nations Office for Project Services
UNSG	United Nations Secretary-General
UNTAC	United Nations Transitional Authority in Cambodia
UNTAG	United Nations Transition Assistance Group
USG	Under-Secretary-General
WFP	World Food Programme
WHO	World Health Organization
WTO	World Trade Organization

Introduction

Joel E. Oestreich

- **Ontology of international organizations**
- **Two approaches to international organizations**
- **Definitional questions**
- **IOs and issues**
- **Structure of cases**
- **Case selection and organization of chapters**

The goal of this book is to provide empirical examples of the ways in which international organizations (IOs) can be meaningful, independent actors in international relations. A central issue it seeks to explore—can IOs "act"?—might seem a bit odd to many readers. After all, IOs, like all organizations, act every day in a thousand different ways. The World Trade Organization (WTO) rules on trade disagreements; the North Atlantic Treaty Organization (NATO) makes decisions about military policy; the United Nations Educational, Scientific and Cultural Organization (UNESCO) decrees picturesque towns to be World Heritage Sites. IOs act all the time, and their actions sometimes have serious real-world consequences—they can help national economies, intervene in civil conflicts, and draw tourists to remote parts of the world. Yet in most mainstream approaches to international relations (IR) theory, IOs are not really thought of as actors at all. Rather, these theories assume that it is states that act, working through the IOs they create. This assumption is made by traditional Realists, who see IOs as essentially meaningless bodies in a world of state actors, and also by many branches of Liberal theory, which assume that IOs influence world politics as loci of social norms and expectations, but not as agents with their own wants and desires, and the ability to act on them.

Until fairly recently, these assumptions have meant that IR theory has produced few studies that relate what actually happens within IOs to IR theory in general. Some newer approaches, however, have gone a long way to challenge these assumptions. The purpose of this book is to explore the nature of international organizations, and in particular their ability to act on their own, in ways not dictated or perhaps even foreseen by the states that create them. It seeks to present a wide-ranging picture of IO action, bringing together work being done in a number of theoretical areas—including principal-agent (PA) theory, "constructivist" or sociological theories, and elements of Realism and its offshoots—to present an overview of when and how IOs are able to act on their own in the international system. It also wants to ask what it really means to act independently. We will begin with a set of hypotheses (set out later in this chapter) about what factors enable or constrain independence, and then use case studies to show how these factors "play out" in the real world of IOs. By presenting so many cases together that open the "black box" of IO decision-making in a way that ties theory to practice, we hope to help both scholars and practitioners better understand what actually happens within IOs.

Each case examines a particular example of an IO performing as an independent, meaningful actor (more on this below) in the international system, or, in the presented counter-examples, failing to act as one when some capacity for independence might otherwise have been expected. Careful examination of the internal workings of IOs and their interaction with the international environment will show the processes by which IOs are able to play a productive role in international politics. The contributors are well cognizant of the limitations of IOs: we understand that IOs are often severely constrained in their powers, particularly when their actions go against the wishes of important states, and we don't suggest that states can't control IOs when they really want to. Still, a growing body of literature takes seriously the notion that IOs can be independent, and, when conditions are met, serious actors in the international system.

This volume does not in itself claim to want to "prove" the validity, or expand the scope, of any particular theoretical model of IO autonomy and independence. The authors do not limit themselves to any single body of theoretical material on IO decision-making, but instead feel free to see what is most useful from the various ways that IOs have been examined in the IR literature. This does not equal chaos, or a lack of rigor. Rather, we are trying to see what facets of IO activity are best described by what set of theories, and how those theories might be used in combination to paint a broader, more nuanced portrait of IO activity than any single approach. We aim for no larger, "general" theory of IOs or some sort of consensus model of IO action. Instead, we want to explore how various theories illuminate different aspects of

IO performance and action, and to discover how the most complete possible picture of IOs might be put together. Different approaches help us to understand different aspects of IO decision-making, performance, and interests.

Ontology of international organizations

Do IOs "exist" at all in world politics? In a world of states that primarily relate to each other one-on-one, this can be a controversial question. It is possible to give IOs the status of "social facts," mediating the behavior of others but not themselves existing independently of states (Johnston 2001). This applies primarily to informal modes of organization, for example "regimes" (Krasner 1983), but one can, in a way, see even formal IOs the same way—it is not the IOs that really exist, it is the states that make them up. We reject this approach as both factually incorrect and also not particularly useful; however, to do so, it is important to understand where IOs fit in the larger universe of international institutions, since much confusion stems from the tendency of theorists to use "institutions" and "organizations" interchangeably.

The study of international organizations is often subsumed under the wider category of international institutions. International relations theorists often ask themselves whether institutions matter in IR, yet institutions can take many forms, and even the word institution is often thrown about with little effort at definition. In the sense used by "English School" scholars such as Hedley Bull, as well as that familiar to sociologists, institutions are not necessarily specific organizations, but are "a set of habits and practices shaped towards the realization of common goals ... [they] symbolise the existence of an international society that is more than the sum of its members [and] ... give substance and permanence to their collaboration in carrying out the political functions of international society" (Bull 1977). In Bull's definition, an "institution" could be any patterned behavior within international society that has a certain legitimacy within the community of states.

John Duffield (2007) shows that the notion of institutions has also been used in three different, somewhat more specific senses within the IR literature. First, institutions can mean formal international organizations—what Duffield refers to as the "traditional" definition of an institution as an ongoing, organized, generally accepted body of people and rules. Second, the term can be used in the rationalist sense as referring to sets of rules that states follow out of a larger sense of self-interest. Rules shape behavior by replacing the desire for short-term gain with a belief in the possibility of longer-term benefits through structured interactions. Third, there is the "constructivist sociological" notion of institutions as sets of norms, followed by states not (only) because of rational self-interest but (also) because of their ability to shape state identities and through a "logic of appropriateness" (Duffield 2007).

We focus here on the first definition, emphasizing institutions as established, legitimate organizations. As Susan Park (2006) explains in a comprehensive study, there was some work being done before the 1990s that began to view IOs as more than ways for states to bring about converging expectations (e.g. Cox and Jacobson 1973; Haas 1990). Until then, the main theoretical approach to IOs suggested that they were set up by states to solve coordination problems, or embodied regimes that were actually formed by state interaction. However, it was in the years after 1990 that this new approach began to really develop some momentum. The impetus for this increasing attention to IOs was the development of "constructivist" IR theory, with its focus on the creation and diffusion of norms in the international system. While Realists assume that state interests can be defined simply as the maximization of relative power within the international system, constructivists began to ask how international norms could define and redefine what states want and, just as importantly, how they go about getting it. These norms, in the right circumstances, could take concrete form as IOs. The overall understanding by international relations scholars of how international organizations work, and how they fit into international politics, has grown by leaps and bounds in recent years. Several of these studies (e.g. Ness and Brechin 1988) have reviewed the relative neglect of international organizations as organizations by the international relations theoretical literature. The point has been to take seriously the internal workings of IOs, both as worthy of study in their own right, and as capable of having an effect in the wider sphere of international politics.

This book will start with the basic premise that IOs matter in international politics—that they have an effect on state behavior and state identities beyond the purely rational/instrumental one of coordinating action towards commonly identified goals. Now, at one level it might not be necessary to qualify our assertion that IOs "matter" in this way. We might simply point out that IOs act all the time in the conventional sense, as shown above. The question of whether IOs have a real, important effect on international politics is meaningful only if one accepts the realist premise that only the actions of states, and particularly powerful states, really matter; that the rest is just background noise against the foreground of power politics. Nevertheless, the authors here share the belief that IOs make a difference in world politics, and that they themselves have an effect independently (sometimes) of the states that create them.

For the millions affected by their efforts, the discussion over the right way to approach IOs in IR theory is, exactly, theoretical: it appears divorced from everyday practice. The Realist denial of the "importance" of IOs is based on the presumption that only the highest realm of politics—that interested in the national security of major powers— really matters in world politics. It is not at all clear that even this assumption is valid. For example, IOs matter in peacekeeping: even if the general terms of peacekeeping are dictated by the major powers, the exact form of peacekeeping, and a great deal of its efficacy, depends on how it is implemented on the ground (O'Neill 2005). Similarly, the role of IOs in defining what is "development" and how it is best practiced has been well considered (Jolly *et al.* 2004). Whether or not this affects the major industrial powers—and one can certainly argue that it does—it affects a lot of people, and shapes how world politics is conducted at other levels than that of national security. The quotidian world of IOs appears to require further study, and to be tied into the larger questions of international theory.

Two approaches to international organizations

Our ontological position, then, is that IOs exist independently of states, and have an effect of their own that makes them matter in various ways. But what, exactly, do IOs do, and why do they do it? Two approaches have come to dominate thinking about how IOs function as autonomous actors: broadly, those that depend on "principal-agent theory," and focus on contracting arrangements between states and IOs; and those that draw from constructivist IR theory, and view IOs as bureaucracies formed within the broader social framework of international society. Each of these approaches tries to categorize modes of IO action and make some predictions about why IOs do what they do. To be fair, plenty of literature about IOs simply takes for granted the importance of IOs and examines their inner workings, without caring greatly about the larger theoretical implications. The two more theoretical approaches often use such works as sources of empirical information.

Principal-agent theory and IOs as actors

The principal-agent approach to IO independence begins with the notion of a delegating contract between states and IOs. IOs are taken to be important, useful facts of international life. States create IOs to serve certain purposes—providing information, solving collective action problems, conferring legitimacy, etc.—and delegate to them certain powers necessary for them to perform their function effectively. States remain the central fact and most important actors of international politics: IOs become their servants, "hired," in a sense, to perform tasks that states feel they can't perform themselves, or that would be too costly to perform without a coordinating body. Delegation involves a contract between states—the principals—and IOs—the agents. The agent's job is to pursue the interests of the principal in a manner specified in the initial contract, and subject to revision in succeeding forms of that contract (Hawkins et al. 2006).

Principal-agent (PA) analysis becomes most interesting when one recognizes the ways in which the interests of the principal and that of the agent might diverge. Agents are hired to serve the interests of their masters but it is assumed that they will actually act in their own self-interest, or, if the agent is an organization, the self-interest of the individuals who make it up (Kiewiet and McCubbins 1991: 24–25). The key element of design in IOs, then, as in any such organization designed to serve principals who are not themselves running the organization (such as shareholders to a corporation, or politicians to a government bureaucracy), is to design an organization in such a way as to bring the interests of the agents into alignment with the interests of the principals. In other words, the agent must know that his or her own interests will be served by serving the interests of his or her principal. If the interests of the agents and principals are aligned, then presumably the relationship can be carried out to mutual satisfaction. Principals should build into the relationship adequate means for overseeing the actions of the agent (Brehm and Gates 1997: 25–46). Agents who deviate from their task—that is, from serving the interests of the principal—in the name of their own interests, can be caught and either reprimanded or replaced by others.

On the other hand, agents find "slack" when oversight is lax, or when organizations are not well designed to bring their interests into line with those of their principals. In particular, agents can exploit asymmetric information to carve out for themselves the ability to operate with some independence and to pursue their own interests (Kiewiet and McCubbins 1991: 25–26). PA theory begins with the assumption that agents will, when possible, pursue their own interests and not necessarily those of their principals. Instead, bureaucrats will further their own careers, and seek to increase the budgets and influence of their own organizations (Moe 1996: 458–59). Asymmetric information allows bureaucrats within organizations to find ways to pursue their own interests.

Still, principals such as states have incentives to delegate tasks to these bureaucrats, even in the knowledge that some agency slack is inevitable. Foremost among these reasons is the inability or unwillingness of principals to manage large, complex tasks directly; bureaucracies and other large organizations must be built to pursue such tasks (Berle and Means 1932). Principals can find some utility in delegating tasks to others; it can make certain jobs more palatable by having someone do it at arm's length. Smart principals make decisions to delegate even when they know that delegation is not perfect, although they will do so carefully and after designing the delegation contract as best they can.

Principal-agent analysis, as it has been applied to IR theory, has focused more on means of control than on actual goals; there is relatively little theorizing about what an independent IO would actually do when it finds enough slack. Work has tended to focus on delineating the conditions under which an agent will be able to act with discretion or in a self-interested manner, and has taken interests as being endogenously given and largely self-evident. Principal-agent theory and work on bureaucratic behavior suggests that the primary goal of bureaucracies is their own expansion: expansion of budgets, of powers, and of existence over time. Individuals within an organization are expected to behave in the same way on the personal scale: they will seek to increase their own authority, advance their careers, expand their budgets and mandates (Brehm and Gates 1997: 15).

A PA approach would expect to see agents (in this case, international organizations and their staff) have a greater range of independent action when they are able to exploit asymmetric information to their advantage. IOs would also have greater independence when the delegating contract is vaguely written, or when it is in the interests of the principals to give the agent greater "slack" or leeway to make decisions. A largenumber of principals, or principals that differ substantially on their policy preferences, can be exploited by agents in order to follow preferred policies. These would tend, in the first instance, to increase the influence and important of the IO, and consequently its budget and powers; and second, policies that fit the ideological preferences of IO staff or conform to their own way of thinking about how to tackle the issues in front of them. So, there is a great deal more theoretical thought about how agents can find slack for themselves, but somewhat less about what they do with that, other than simply pursue their own interests.

8 Joel E. Oestreich

Constructivist theory and IOs as actors

A second vein of thought has been part of the broader constructivist approach to IR, using insights from sociology to theorize about the nature of an international community. Here states are taken to be engaged in a constant process of learning and interacting, a set of intersubjective relationships where interests are not given but developed through a process of learning and institutionalizing behaviors. Within such a community, states create international organizations for the same reason that bureaucracies are created within the domestic realm: to rationalize the management of a complex world through the creation of organizations and the application of expertise. Constructivists recognize in PA theory a powerful tool for understanding the distinction between state actors and IOs, and for finding insights into why IOs are structured as they are; however, they then move beyond the purely rationalist approach to understanding actions and interests, by incorporating insights into bureaucratic behavior, socialization, and culture, among other factors.

Constructivist work on IO, most notably that of Barnett and Finnemore (1999, 2004), has focused on the bureaucratization of world politics and the ways in which large international organizations are able to use knowledge and expertise, as well as their capacity for organized behavior, to influence state behavior. Bureaucracies are an inevitable result of a social situation that requires creation of institutions to bring order (Weber 1947). Internally, IOs are not perfect machines, flawlessly carrying out the desires of their creators, but instead are subject to the same dysfunctional behavior as any other large organization. They are given some power and authority which they are expected to use responsibly, yet they often fail to do so, and the resulting outcome might be quite different from what was expected. Externally, IOs will sometimes use their control over bureaucratic power and resources to influence state behavior through a number of different mechanisms. States rely on IOs to perform certain functions, and give them power and authority. States then find themselves engaged in an intersubjective relationship with these IOs and inevitably find their own interests affected by this relationship, as their own identity shifts. The "power" of an IO comes not from the more traditional trappings of state power, but from their ability as bureaucracies to manipulate these mechanisms, and to claim authority through expertise.

IOs' power and influence, then, is largely in the realm of ideas; constructivists, taking ideas seriously, are able to trace the source of IO influence as well as the means of IO independence. States are forced, in a sense, to defer to these collections of knowledge because of the inability of states to consistently oversee their operations in a meaningful way. This deference carves out for IOs greater autonomy. One can see places where this concept of IOs overlaps with PA theory; both presume that states create IOs to solve complex problems of coordination, and that IO power comes from application of expertise to these complex problems.

Constructivist literature on IOs, by its nature, makes few specific predictions about exactly what IOs will want or how they will act. As with constructivist theory in general, the approach to IOs is more a methodology than a predictive set of hypotheses. However, some conclusions can be drawn from work done in this area. Weaver and Leiteritz, for example, have used constructivist and PA approaches to look at reform and decision-making at the World Bank. They conclude that organizational culture plays a vital role in the ability of IOs to change (or not change); whatever the principals might want, the internal dynamics of an organization and the environment in which it operates have important influences over outcomes and actions (Weaver and Leiteritz 2005). This comports well with work by the current author, who found organizational culture and the training of individual staff to have an effect on the implementation of human rights norms (Oestreich 2007).

Along with having their own corporate or bureaucratic culture, IOs serve as conduits for globalized or globalizing ideas; they pick up, internalize, and disseminate ideas that are part of their operating environment, when those ideas seem to match with the mandate of the bureaucracy. Elizabeth Prugl (1999), for example, demonstrates the process by which IOs serve as conduits for ideas about women and work; Finnemore, ideas regarding the proper structure of states towards science bureaucracies (Finnemore 1996); Haas (1989), regarding environmental ideas. In a constructivist world view interests are not determined by a simple calculation of rational self-interest; rather, self-interest can change depending on the ideas and beliefs held by individual or collective actors. States, for example, can choose to act to advance their relative power or to advance other goals (e.g., environmental protection) depending on how they view their larger interests. Similarly, actors in an international organization or the organization itself have their own beliefs which shape how they pursue their goals. These might change over time, for example through the influence of epistemic communities.

A constructivist approach to IO independence does not by itself reject the PA assumption of self-interested actors pursuing their goals when they are able to find slack from their principals; it does, however, introduce other reasons for action besides self-aggrandizement, and suggest a more complex interaction between agents and principals. Constructivist theory, first of all, assumes that IOs will act like bureaucracies; they will use their resources to organize information, rationalize complex issues, and impose routines on otherwise complicated matters. Bureaucracies are assumed to be rational, but their interests are not always externally given; rather, they have preferences of their own which conform to their own prejudices, and might change over time. A constructivist approach generally takes bureaucracies to be "open systems," interacting with their environment and picking up both resources and ideas from it (Scott 1992). To understand how IOs are independent and what they do with that independence, it is important to look at the environment within which they operate. They will, certainly, take direction from states, but they will also pick up ideas from nongovernmental organizations (NGOs), civil society, and other international actors and influences. These will be reflected in IO preferences. IOs might seek to both use and expand their authority, which is not necessarily the same as saying that they want to increase power and resources. IOs have authority through their control over information and the deference shown to them as experts in a particular field, and they will use this authority to pursue their interests as they define them.

Strengths and weaknesses of each approach

Each of the two approaches brings strengths and weaknesses to the understanding of IO independence. PA theory is the more rationalist approach, and generates more testable hypotheses. By holding one set of interests (those of the agent) as given, and allowing variation in principal interests, it is possible to look for variations in policy outcomes that will conform to simple theoretical propositions. Different hypotheses about the ability of principals to control agents, and under what circumstances that control breaks down, are easy to pose and analyze. PA theory brings important parsimony to analyzing IOs.

On the other hand, constructivist theories try to present a more nuanced understanding of how IOs function and of their place in a larger international community. It does have difficulty presenting itself as a testable set of hypotheses about which one can gather unambiguous data. Instead, it presents more of a lens which one can train on the processes within organizations, allowing a careful examination of their operations. Constructivists don't hold interests as given; indeed, a key element of constructivist theory is the examination of where interests come from and how they are influenced by exogenous factors. This is less parsimonious than theories that take interests as given and assume that actors behave to rationally pursue them, but with the benefit of increased subtlety of explanation. Along with this examination of interest formation, constructivist theory fills in one of the important gaps of PA theory, already noted above: it tells us something about what IOs actually do with their independence, not just from where that independence comes.

We see each body of work as complementary, helping in different ways to fill out the broader picture of how IOs work and what they do. Rather than seek a single theory that is some sort of synthesis of the two competing approaches (or three, since we must include the insights of realism as well), we want to show how the two approaches complement each other and help illuminate different aspects of the same problem. Because we are being so broad in our approach, it is vitally important to carefully define the terms we are using and the units of analysis at which we will look. We turn to that in the next section.

Definitional questions

What does it mean to act?

The authors of this volume have struggled a surprising amount with the question of what it actually means for an IO to act, and to act independently. This is a key concept, around which much of the rest of our argument turns. A fuller exploration of this concept, and its difficulties, follows here.

The primary challenge we faced, in establishing the premises of this book, was distinguishing truly independent matters from delegated discretion (Haftel and Thompson 2006). From the discussion of principal-agent theory in particular, it should be clear that when states create IOs they don't expect to dictate every single action; rather, principals create a contract that delegates to their agents certain tasks, and a range of discretion within which to carry out those tasks. They might create the International Monetary Fund (IMF) to maintain a stable currency regime, and, through an initial contract, give it a certain amount of discretion (but not unlimited discretion) to carry out that task on a day-to-day basis. The authors of this volume have paid attention to showing that in the cases under study IOs are not just doing something that wasn't specifically tasked to them, but also are acting outside any reasonable notion of delegated discretion. In some cases there will be actual state resistance to proposed policies. Where this is the case, we have been careful to highlight the nature of state resistance, and how IOs were able to overcome that resistance. Indeed, the tactics employed by IOs to overcome state resistance form a key element of many chapters.

Beyond this, in the workshop from which this volume springs we established a two-step notion of what agency would mean in these cases. To understand why we felt this necessary, it is useful to recall why there is a debate at all over this question. Again, some Realists dismiss IOs as being too weak to have an impact on the *realpolitik* affairs of powerful states. The issue isn't whether IOs act independently of states—Realists don't need to deny that—but whether their actions have any real effect on how states pursue their interests. To act—or, more accurately, to be an "actor"—in world politics would therefore mean the ability to perform in a way that actually makes a difference. On the other hand, a neo-realist or institutionalist interpretation of IO independence actually assumes that IOs do not have an independent set of policies, but merely reflect the desires of states themselves (Keohane 1984, 1988). Presumably states, or the powerful states that "matter," would not create such organizations without some assurance that these organizations will only do what they are supposed to do. The assumption is that IOs don't have ideas of their own, or at least, that if they do, those ideas cannot be effectively translated into action, because states have effective ways of overseeing those IOs.

Both of these approaches to denying that IOs are meaningful international actors have a different definition of acting in mind: effectiveness on the one hand, actual independence on the other. Each set of assumptions has been questioned by the literature on IO agency in recent years. The constructivist approach has looked at the ability of IOs to actually affect the behavior of states through the creation and dissemination of norms (e.g., Whitworth 1994). Drawing also on organizational theory perspectives, it has shown that IOs are able to create ideas themselves and to pressure states, even the most powerful ones, to act in accordance with those ideas (March and Olsen 1998). At the same time, principal-agent theory has paid less attention to the effects of IO policy-making, and more to the ways in which IOs are able to distance themselves from the desires of states; acting here means independence, and the focus has tended to be on the conditions that allow independence rather than what IOs do with it.

The authors of this volume assume that the most useful definition of acting is one that combines these insights. Without the assertion that IOs do something meaningful and important, the examination of their independence is pointless: why should we care? However, if we assume that when they appear to be acting they are actually only doing what states ask of them (e.g., if we assume that the World Bank has undertaken the Social Development approach of recent years solely because of prompting from member states rather than from an interplay of internal and external forces), then the IOs are the wrong unit of analysis. The key, then, is to demonstrate a two-step process: the determination by an IO to follow a particular course of action not dictated to it by its members; and the actual carrying out of that action in a way with meaningful results to the international system.

The picture that will emerge is a sense of IO action that combines both the PA and constructivist meanings, as well as a more traditional liberal notion of IOs as important loci of international cooperation, creating a definition closer to what is meant in everyday parlance. From PA theory, there is the sense that IOs are independent, that they have the ability, in certain circumstances, to create follow through on their own preferences. Case study research will also allow a more detailed examination of the source of these preferences. From constructivist theory, there is the idea that these actions matter, that they have some real effect on the conduct of international politics. To be sure, many of the authors have made clear that they see substantial restrictions on the independence of IOs, and consider them to be agents in only certain circumscribed ways. An important part of fleshing out the definition of agency, then, is to remove the "all or nothing" character of general statements, and to see exactly where these limitations are.

Who acts?

The authors of these case studies assume that it is ultimately people who act, and that to understand the activities of IOs we must know something about the people within them. As we reject the realist assumption that IOs do not matter, and also the assumption that preferences are exogenously given to international actors, we further reject that it is not necessary to know anything about the people who actually make up international organizations. IOs are comprised of individuals, and both a PA approach and a constructivist one show us the importance of understanding the interests, beliefs, and roles of the individuals who make up IOs. When we talk, then, about IOs "acting" or showing a level of independence, we are of course talking about decisions made by the staff of those IOs, or, at other times, state delegates, acting in ways not foreseen by those who had sent them there.

The question of "who acts," however, is more complex than it might first seem. We reject that there is any single, parsimonious explanation of IO activity, and instead seek to understand the complexity that goes into decision-making. This much should be clear by now to the reader. It is also true that IOs themselves do not always speak with one voice. Bureaucratic theories of state action understand that large, complex organizations cannot be reduced to a single decision-maker or a single set of actions; different branches act in different ways, and sometimes according to different logics. Actions might be attributed to executive heads, to members of the bureaucracy lower down the chain of command unbidden by the chief executive of the organization, or even by a bureaucracy as a whole, without a specific decision-making instance, as when a bureaucratic culture shifts and standard procedures are changed. What matters is the outcome: the production of policies that are new, innovative, and effective. Each case will be careful in examining who made decisions, what factors went into that person's decision, and how they were enabled or constrained by their institutional environment. We reject the sole focus on institutions as a whole, and understand that the "black box" must be opened up down to the individual level.

Types of IO action

What types of IO actions can we expect to see? First, it is important to remember that we are focusing in this project on a particular notion of action; that is, independent action, or activities that show the ability of IOs to innovate without direction from states. For the sake of conceptual clarity it is important to focus on activities that seem to actually contradict state preferences, or at least go well beyond what states had expected and wanted from their surrogates in IOs. Within those limitations, what sorts of decisions might we expect from IOs, and how might they be affected by our theoretical approach?

One useful starting point is the taxonomy of decision-making suggested by Cox and Jacobson in 1973's *The Anatomy of Influence* (Cox and Jacobson 1973: chapter 1). The authors suggest seven forms of decision-making:

- Representational decisions, affecting membership and representation;
- Symbolic decisions, which "test how opinions are aligned" with "no practical consequences in the form of actions."
- Boundary decisions, concerning an "organization's external relations with other international and regional structures" regarding scope, cooperation, and other interactions.

Introduction 15

- Programmatic decisions about the distribution of resources for various operational purposes, and the use of budgets.
- Rule-creating decisions, defining rules and norms regarding relevant issues.
- Rule-supervisory decisions, "concern[ing] the application of approved rules by those subject to them," for example, gathering information about state compliance with labor or nuclear proliferation rules by those IOs charged with their supervision.
- Operational decisions, which "relate to the providing of services by the organization or the use of its resources in accordance with approved rules, policies, or programs."

Of these seven (presented in the same order that Cox and Jacobson present them) we might say that the first two are the least likely to concern the authors. Representational decisions are usually the exclusive province of states; membership decisions are essentially never delegated to IOs but are kept at the level of the oversight body. Symbolic decisions, on the other hand, might be made at various levels of an organization, but fail to satisfy our two-step definition of "acting"—that is, both exhibiting independence and having a practical effect on outcomes. Of the remaining five we would expect varying opportunities for independence, for example Cox and Jacobson (1973: 382) suggest that executive heads are more involved with boundary decisions than any other set of decisions. Rule supervisory decisions are also unlikely to figure substantially, since states will chafe at having rules enforced on them by IOs (although there are exceptions, notably the WTO).

IOs and issues

One important question raised by the authors of this volume was whether, to study IO action, it was best to focus on a specific IO, or to focus on a specific set of problems and how IOs were able to approach it. Which approach would capture the important variables? A series of workshops involving many of the represented authors determined that it was impossible to structure these cases around either a particular organization by itself, or a particular issue or set of issues. Rather, the question of how organizations approach particular problems must be taken as a cohesive whole—the organization and the issue must be two sides of the same coin, forming an example of self-directed policy-making in a particular set of circumstances conducive to such autonomy or independence. Thus, each case here begins with a description of both which organization (or organizations) is being studied, and what policy problems it faces in the particular case study.

An organization as large and complex as the IMF, the United Nations (UN) Secretariat, or the UN High Commissioner for Refugees (UNHCR), cannot have its actions reduced to a simple set of central directives; bureaucracies are complex systems that have many different subsystems, priorities, and desires. To understand the activities of such organizations it is necessary to understand which part or parts of them are engaged in solving a particular problem. The nature of the problem itself, of course, is also an important variable, for a variety of reasons spelled out below. Problems are often given to sub-units of an IO rather than engaging the central structure of the IO management. Or issues might "bubble up" from below; by the time these issues engage the interest of senior managers (and states), they may already have influenced the activities of the IO or influenced lower-level personnel in a way that predisposes top managers and states to take one approach over another—a form of "path dependence," which requires understanding the interaction of issues and organizations. Neither a focus on organizations not on issues, by itself, can fully explain the course of events.

The interaction of organizations and issues also says a great deal about the ability of organizations to act on their own volition—each case will, in a sense, be a unique interaction of both. In this sense, many previous works on IO self-direction have been flawed in their exclusive focus on one or the other, rather than both. For example, some work on IO adaptation has looked closely at the size of the organization or the complexity of its bureaucratic structure. It has tended to see the capacity for self-direction in the control of the IO over information and the difficulty that states have keeping tabs on such far-flung and complex institutions. Others have looked exclusively at the nature of issues; complicated issues, or those that seem remote from the core interests of states, are presumed to garner more room for maneuver by IOs than others might. Our approach hopes to bring both insights, and others, into a more complex (albeit less parsimonious) view of the nature of IO self-direction.

Relevant factors of independence: organizations and issues

From the discussion above, it should be clear that one strand of thinking by the authors concerns the nature of an IO itself and how that nature relates to its relative ability to act in a self-directed way. Authors have kept in mind at times the need to delineate those features

Introduction 17

of IOs themselves that tend to add to their ability to act in this way. It is worth here laying out some of the basic factors, identified in a series of workshops, roundtables, and other forums, that have informed our research.

Organizational attributes

IO size and complexity. A central supposition of this project is that larger, more complex organizations will have greater capacity for independent action than smaller ones, or those in which the organizational structure is simpler to understand and to monitor. An early, seminal work on the separation of ownership from management, Berle and Means' (1932) *The Modern Corporation and Private Property*, noted how the growing size and complexity of modern corporations made it more difficult for owners to monitor the activities of managers. Berle and Means also noted that the tendency towards larger sized corporations meant that management itself was becoming a "profession," one which worked by its own set of rules and principles and which demanded a certain amount of deference from those who ostensibly employed them. It seems intuitively sensible that the same dynamics would be found within IOs, and both empirical and theoretical research appears to support this conclusion. Both key principal-agent works, and the sociological work of Barnett and Finnemore, look at factors such as size, complexity, and deference to figures with technical expertise, when considering the ability of IOs to act in self-directed ways.

Maturity/age of the IO. Closely related to the above point, we hypothesize that older, more mature IOs exhibit more independence than those that are newer. Organizations tend to evolve over time, and as they do so, they add new tasks which were not foreseen when they were first created. These tasks may be outside what was initially envisioned for the organization, and require new responses. Or, the approach to an initial task may evolve over time, for example, as the development of the Internet has required existing organizations like the International Telephone and Telegraph Union to redefine how it approaches its own mission (Drake 2000). States will often want to see existing organizations evolve, but it will not always be possible to supervise every aspect of that evolution. It may not even be clear to states that the organization is changing, if the change is sufficiently incremental; an IO such as the UN Children's Fund (UNICEF) might change from a service-delivery paradigm to a rights-empowering one without any single decision made to do so (Oestreich 1998). An evolutionary change might not have any one moment when there is a recognition that the IO is acting independently, yet the result might be a substantial change which was self-directed and unforeseen, and perhaps even unwanted by states parties. There is also evidence, as well as intuitive sense, that older, more established organizations will have greater authority as well as command more deference from states, and will find it easier to "chart their own course" as situations change.

Personal characteristics of IO staff. It has already been noted that an important lacuna in IO research has been a focus on the qualities of individuals. This remains an important characteristic of IOs that tends to be overlooked by the literature on IO self-direction. The reasons are fairly clear: in the interest of parsimonious and generalizable explanation, there is a strong tendency in the social sciences to remove individual characteristics from theory-making. People are quirky, unpredictable, and unique; it is not easy to generalize from any one person, or to use theory to predict how a person will act. Cortell and Peterson (2006) theorize on the nature of IO staffing as having important ramifications for IO slack; staff who see themselves as independent civil servants (rather than as instructed state representatives) will on the whole seek more independence, although they will be somewhat constrained at the same time by the desire to remain on the good side of their "employers." These factors interact with voting rules and other means of state control. We theorize here that, further, the qualities of leadership among staff—particularly, of course, top management—also affect the independence of IOs, as they maneuver among states to pursue their preferred policies.

Presence of IO networks. IOs do not work in isolation: they are parts of networks of organizations which build up over time to solve complex problems. Often, more than one organization has authority over an issue (sometimes many more, as in the case of economic development) and responsibilities have to be shared, apportioned, or fought over. Christer Jönsson (1993), for example, has shown how cooperation can be shaped by "interorganizational" dynamics, for example in the multi-agency response to the HIV/AIDS crisis. Similarly, Craig Murphy (2006) has documented the role of the UN Development Programme (UNDP) in coordinating among development agencies, leveraging its own expertise and shaping the development agenda, and giving a home to crucial development networks. Social networks might be made up of individuals, groups, organizations, or an entire society; participation in networks shapes actor behavior, both "constraining and enabling" actors and sets of actors within a system (Emirbayer and Goodwin 1994). The presence of networks helps IOs in at least two relevant

Introduction 19

ways. First, networks provide IOs with ideas and resources. IOs are, recall, "open systems" in our view, with their own internal logic but also open to their environment and able to take from it what they need. Networks form part of that environment and thus shape IOs, as well as providing IOs with resources and thus enhancing their capacity for self-directed action. Second, the presence of networks enhances IO capabilities by allowing them to work with similarly minded organizations and to coordinate activities, as Murphy has shown. Similar to NGO networks (Keck and Sikkink 1998) or epistemic communities (Haas 1992), IO networks and the interaction of IOs with other international non-state actors enable new forms of action and allow novel use of information.

Issue attributes

In addition to those factors identified as being part of the organization itself, other factors related to the issues being considered facilitate or constrain IO self-direction.

Issue complexity, and linkage with other issues. This is the corollary of the first point listed above. Complex issues, those requiring a high degree of scientific or other technical expertise, will by their nature tend to allow greater freedom for the IOs that deal with them. This is not necessarily the case, of course; for example, William Drake (2000) also showed how the International Telecommunication Union (ITU) was carefully monitored by states that perceived themselves to have important interests in the development of the international communication network, and later the Internet itself. In other areas, however—notably international development (Ayres 1983) and transboundary environmental issues (Haas *et al.* 1993)—this is easier to see. The tendency of epistemic communities to form around such issues is an important factor here, too, and these epistemic communities will enhance IO freedom through their own efforts to exploit the power and reach of networks, in this case networks of similarly trained experts in national capitals.

Lack of issue salience to states. States will likely exercise more control over IOs when those organizations are dealing with issues of greater importance to states, and less control when there is less importance. It is only to be expected that states will be unwilling to delegate much control to IOs when they feel that the issue touches directly on their security interests, broadly understood. This does vary within issue area: for example, some environmental issues (such as global warming) are seen as being directly important to the prosperity of states and their internal politics, while others will seem less so. Steven Krasner (1983) suggests in a study of regional development banks that institutions have greater freedom of action when their operations are considered peripheral by the major donors. That is, the primary contributors of funds are less likely to interfere in operations and policy when they are not directly affected by the way those funds are used. Other studies have made the same point more generally (Hazelzet 1998).

Lack of agreement among states over issues. This is the problem of preference heterogeneity, analyzed extensively in Hawkins *et al.* (2006), which has an important role in allowing agent "slack." IOs are able to play off principals against each other in order to pursue their preferred policies, and heterogeneity makes it more difficult for states to present to IOs a single, clear mission (Martin 2002). Staff, who will naturally have their own preferences, will be able to work for the passage of policies that fit their preferences if they can create coalitions of states to support them. As Martin shows, this also allows staff to better exploit asymmetries of information.

Structure of cases

To recap, our intention in this volume is to show the ability of IOs to act in independent ways, and to understand that ability in the context of the main theoretical currents examining IO decision-making. We will be specific about what sorts of decisions are involved; who made them; where they came from (in terms of interest formation); and what enabled or constrained the exercised independence. We will use various theoretical approaches to explain the decision in a larger context and to see how they help us to understand the usefulness of that theory. Each case study focuses on an example of IO action, and delineates the pathways of that action. We hope to approach these key questions in a systematic way. Our goal is to illuminate the strengths and weaknesses of the two approaches to IO agency, plus, where possible, to highlight the insights of more traditional (realist and institutionalist) approaches, where they are valuable in their own right.

Cases will begin by identifying both the issue under examination, and the organization or organizations being studied. Recall our assertion that neither can be studied in isolation; the interplay of the two is vital to understanding how IO independence plays out in the real world. So, we need to understand the nature of the issue itself: what is at stake? How did it come to be the province of the particular organization(s) being examined? Were they tasked with this issue in their original charter, or is it something they have come to handle as the organization or the issue itself (or both) has evolved? A brief historical background will help situate the issue within a larger context and bring up relevant factors that will influence later decisions.

Each case is, in a sense, the story of a decision: a decision by an organization to tackle a particular problem in a particular way. The cases will look at and describe exactly what sort of decision is being made, and who is making the decision. What is the unit of analysis we need to look at in terms of the actual decision-maker—is it an individual (and if so, where in the hierarchy is that individual?), a department, or a bureaucracy as a whole making a collective decision? What, also, was the pathway to making that decision effective? In some cases, a single person is able to change the direction of an organization or part of one. In other cases, people within a bureaucracy act according to bureaucratic logic. In Dennis Dijkzeul's case study, for example, decisions are made by individuals, but the role of each individual person tends to be subsumed into a larger logic of resource maximization and a bid for independence. People act, but they sometimes act more as parts of an organization than as individuals.

As we have said, IOs act every day in a thousand different ways; states give them specific direction on a few big goals or strategies, but by necessity defer to them on exactly how those goals will be reached or those strategies carried out. IOs, in the language of PA theory, have discretion, a circumscribed range of activity for deciding exactly how they should carry out their mandate. It is central to the success of this project that the authors look at how IOs act outside this delegated range of discretion, how they decide for themselves how to act. This might be against explicit state wishes, or, less severely but equally importantly, in a way that was not foreseen by states and importantly innovative, even if it is not exactly forbidden. In discussing the nature of IO action, it's important to identify what makes the case under study interesting; what happened that traditional rationalist theories of IOs are inadequate to understand it? Whether it's a case of actually pushing back against state desires, actively working to change state positions on an issue, or using discretion to set a new and unforeseen agenda, each case will be clear about what exactly happened to make the case interesting.

With this established, the case study will then "tell the story," that is, relate the events that led up to a particular decision. The empirical information will illuminate the way in which a decision was made—who made it, what factors led to this decision or course of action, and, where appropriate, how it might have gone differently. The factors that helped determine the outcome, and that show the validity of the conclusions drawn from it, are carefully detailed by each author. In particular, those factors that allowed the organization to act independently will be elucidated, and, at the same time, why the organization or those within it decided it was important for them to act in the way they did. These factors will be related back to the issues mentioned above—those related to the nature of the issue and the nature of the organization—along with which ones proved to be determinative, and to what extent they accord with the hypotheses presented about organizations and independence. Where appropriate we also look at the interaction of various factors.

Finally, each case relates the empirical material back to the basic hypotheses made by PA and constructivist theories. Authors use the empirical material to ask which theory, or what sort of combination of theories, best explains the outcome of the case. We will point out both where the theory helps to explain IO action, and also where there is need for more specification or the theory in fact falls down altogether. The relative strengths and weaknesses of each approach will be considered. The goal ultimately is to expand our knowledge of how IOs work on a day-to-day basis; what is the reality of IO action, of their internal processes, and their abilities free of state control? We seek ultimately to free the study of IO action from the purely theoretical, and bring an empirical richness to theory that has been lacking up until now.

Case selection and organization of chapters

This book, again, is not intended to "prove" any single theory, in the traditional social-science sense of the term. Rather, our goal is to examine the inner workings of international organizations, and to examine how existing theories help us to understand and categorize these workings. We have seen that there exists already a vibrant and growing literature, following several different theoretical models, on the independence of international organizations and their ability to act in ways that have real effects on the international environment. As such, cases are chosen not randomly or with the focus on "hard cases," but instead with an eye towards illuminating interesting aspects of IO independence. In an effort to probe the nature of IO activity we have tried to find a wide variety of organizations, and to see how they act in the widest possible range of issue areas. We recognize that the total range of IO actions is too broad, and the various combinations too numerous, to cover in their entirety.

We know that states often do insist on a certain type of behavior from IOs. It is not hard to come up with many stories of states dictating exactly what policies they want from IOs. We do not say that IOs are always independent, or even that they are able to act as they wish any time certain conditions are met. We do, however, propose that IO action is a serious issue, worthy of greater study and description. The theoretical literature has already set out some important models of IO behavior and IO influence in world affairs; we want to choose cases that are illustrative of how these models work in practice, and provide a set of empirical examples that allow comparison across issues.

The following chapters are organized into three sections. The first consists of two case studies of policy-making by the UN Secretariat, and in particular the Secretary-General. Whether a "secretary" or a "general" (as Kirsten Haack and Kent Kille puts it in their contribution), the office of the Secretary-General commands particular respect and has influence, obviously, over the entire UN system. Haack and Kille importantly examine the question of whether the UN should have a degree of autonomy, as well as looking at the origin of that autonomy. The following section expands our argument to look at other UN bodies. In the final section, we consider how much of the argument might be applicable to other, non-UN agencies. The conclusion will recap some of what was learned, and consider its overall meaning for IR theory.

Bibliography

Ayres, Robert L., *Banking on the Poor: The World Bank and World Poverty* (Cambridge, MA: M.I.T. Press, 1983).

Barnett, Michael N. and Martha Finnemore, "The Politics, Power, and Pathologies of International Organizations," *International Organization* 53, no. 4 (1999): 699–732.

——*Rules for the World: International Organizations and Global Politics* (Ithaca, NY: Cornell University Press, 2004).

Berle, Adolph A. and Gardiner C. Means, *The Modern Corporation and Private Property* (New York: The MacMillan Company, 1932).

Brehm, John and Scott Gates, *Working, Shirking, and Sabotage: Bureaucratic Response to a Democratic Public* (Ann Arbor, MI: University of Michigan Press, 1997).

Bull, Hedley, *The Anarchical Society* (London: MacMillan, 1977).

Cortell, Andrew P. and Susan Peterson, "Dutiful Agents, Rogue Actors, or Both? Staffing, Voting Rules, and Slack in the WHO and WTO," in *Delegation and Agency in International Organizations*, ed. Darren G. Hawkins, David A. Lake, Daniel L. Nielson, and Michael Tierney (New York: Cambridge University Press, 2006), 255–80.

Cox, Robert and Harold K. Jacobson, *The Anatomy of Influence* (Cambridge: Cambridge University Press, 1973).

Drake, William J., "The Rise and Decline of the International Telecommunications Regime," in *Regulating the Global Information Society*, ed. Christopher T. Marsden (London: Routledge, 2000), 124–77.

Duffield, John, "What Are International Institutions?" *International Studies Review* 9, no. 1 (2007): 1–22.

Emirbayer, Mustafa and Jeff Goodwin, "Network Analysis, Culture, and the Problem of Agency," *American Journal of Sociology* 99, no. 6 (1994): 1411–54.

Finnemore, Martha, *National Interests in International Society* (Ithaca: Cornell University Press, 1996).

Haas, Ernst B., *When Knowledge is Power: Three Models of Change in International Organizations* (Los Angeles: University of California Press, 1990).

Haas, Peter, "Introduction: Epistemic Communities and International Policy Coordination," *International Organization* 46, no. 1 (1992): 1–35.

——"Do Regimes Matter? Epistemic Communities and Mediterranean Pollution Control," *International Organization* 43, no. 3 (1989): 377–403.

Haas, Peter M. et al., *Institutions for the Earth: Sources of Effective International Environmental Protection* (Cambridge, MA: M.I.T. Press, 1993).

Haftel, Yoram Z. and Alexander Thompson, "The Independence of International Organizations," *Journal of Conflict Resolution* 50, no. 2 (2006): 253–75.

Hawkins, Darren G., David A. Lake, Daniel L. Nielson, and Michael Tierney, eds, *Delegation and Agency in International Organizations* (New York: Cambridge University Press, 2006).

Hazelzet, Hadewych, "The Decision-Making Approach to International Organizations: Cox and Jacobson's Anatomic Lesson Revisited," in *Autonomous Policy Making by International Organizations*, ed. Bob Reinalda and Bertjan Verbeek (New York: Routledge, 1998).

Johnston, Alastair I., "Treating International Institutions as Social Environments," *International Studies Quarterly* 45, no. 4 (2001): 487–515.

Jolly, Richard, Louis Emmerij, Dharam Gai, and Frédéric Lapeyre, *UN Contributions to Development Thinking and Practice* (Bloomington: Indiana University Press, 2004).

Jönsson, Christer, "International Organization and Co-operation: An Interorganizational Approach," *International Social Science Journal* 45, no. 3 (1993): 463–77.

Keck, Margaret E. and Kathryn Sikkink, *Activists Beyond Borders: Advocacy Networks in International Politics* (Ithaca, NY: Cornell University Press, 1998).

Keohane, Robert O., *After Hegemony: Cooperation and Discord in the World Political Economy* (Princeton, NJ: Princeton University Press, 1984).

——"International Institutions: Two Approaches," *International Studies Quarterly* 32, no. 4 (1988): 379–96.

Kiewiet, D. Roderick and Matthew D. McCubbins, *The Logic of Delegation: Congressional Parties and the Appropriations Process* (Chicago: University of Chicago Press, 1991).

Krasner, Stephen, *International Regimes* (Ithaca, NY: Cornell University Press, 1983).

March, James G. and Johan P. Olsen, "The Institutional Dynamics of International Political Orders," *International Organization* 52, no. 4 (1998): 943–69.

Martin, Lisa, "Agency and Delegation in IMF Conditionality," IMF Working Paper, 2002. Available at www.people.fas.harvard.edu/~llmartin/imfconditionality.html. Accessed April 2002.

Mearsheimer, John J., *The Tragedy of Great Power Politics* (New York: W.W. Norton, 2001).

Moe, Terry M., "The Positive Theory of Public Choice," in *Perspectives on Public Choice*, ed. Dennis C. Mueller (New York: Cambridge University Press, 1996), 455–80.

Murphy, Craig, *The United Nations Development Programme: A Better Way?* (New York: Cambridge University Press, 2006).

Ness, Gayl D. and Steven R. Brechin, "Bridging the Gap: International Organizations as Organizations," *International Organization* 42, no. 2 (1988): 245–73.

Oestreich, Joel, "UNICEF and the Implementation of the Convention on the Rights of the Child," *Global Governance* 4, no. 2 (1998): 183–99.

——*Power and Principle: Human Rights Programming in International Organizations* (Washington, DC: Georgetown University Press, 2007).

O'Neill, John T., *United Nations Peacekeeping in the Post-Cold War Era* (New York: Routledge, 2005).

Park, Susan, "Theorizing Norm Diffusion within International Organizations," *International Politics* 43, no. 3 (2006): 342–61.

Prugl, Elisabeth, *Global Construction of Gender* (New York: Columbia University Press, 1999).

Scott, Richard, *Organizations: Rational, Natural, and Open Systems* (Englewood Cliffs, NJ: Prentice Hall, 1992).

Weaver, Catherine and Ralf J. Leiteritz, "'Our Poverty is a World Full of Dreams': Reforming the World Bank," *Global Governance* 11, no. 3 (2005): 369–88.

Weber, Max, *The Theory of Social and Economic Organization* (New York: The Free Press, 1947).

Whitworth, Sandra, *Feminism and International Relations: Towards a Political Economy of Gender in Interstate and Non-Governmental Institutions* (New York: St Martin's Press, 1994).

Part I
The United Nations Secretariat

1 The UN Secretary-General and self-directed leadership
Development of the democracy agenda
Kirsten Haack and Kent J. Kille

- **Perspectives on the UN Secretary-General**
- **The UN democracy agenda**
- **Conclusion: potential for self-directed leadership**

According to the United Nations (UN) Charter the Secretary-General serves the member states as the "chief administrative officer" and the legal duties of the office outlined are very prescribed. Despite these limitations, the role played by the Secretary-General has often been extended in ways that assert the independence of the office and the UN beyond member-state control. The tension between these roles reflects the challenge to the state-centric view taken by many international relations scholars from theoretical approaches focusing on the independent agency of international organizations (IOs) and the self-directed leadership provided through these organizations that is the emphasis of this volume.

In terms of the framework of this volume, this opening chapter thus addresses the question "who acts?" at the individual level of the UN Secretary-General, as opposed to later chapters which detail particular UN agencies as a whole. As established in the introductory chapter, an examination of executive heads such as the Secretary-General is an important starting point since such leaders provide a key potential dimension for analyzing the possibilities, as well as the limitations, of international organizations acting in a self-directed manner. As set out under the "attributes of international organizations," with the focus on individual leadership this chapter is clearly able to speak to the personal characteristics of international organization staff, but the case analysis also seeks to move beyond a sole focus on the individual to consider the broader network connections within which the Secretary-General is operating.

This chapter first reflects on the potential leadership to be provided by the Secretary-General in global governance and the limits that are detailed in the existing scholarship on the office. The traditional debate in analyses of the Secretary-General is whether office-holders *can* or even *should* overcome challenges that impede their ability to provide independent leadership. Research has shown that focusing on the individual behind the office provides important insights into how the Secretary-Generalship has performed in practice. Recent studies of the office have touched on prospects for the Secretary-General to provide self-directed leadership, but this literature, except for work providing an increasing emphasis on the normative dimension of the office, has largely been divorced from theoretically grounded analysis that is present in the broader study of international organization.

The advantages of such a theoretically grounded approach are demonstrated by detailing the development of the UN democracy agenda by Secretaries-General Boutros Boutros-Ghali and Kofi Annan. The analysis highlights the importance of establishing an organizational discourse and general "UN approach," even where member states are not fully convinced and ready to change policy. As established in the introduction to this volume, tracking the development of an idea such as democracy within the UN allows for exploration and better understanding of both the origins of the idea within the organization and how this idea was translated into UN policy. In particular, the case of democracy in the UN sheds light on the level of issue salience to the member states and the implications that this had in practice. The case also probes how the Secretaries-General approached their decisions and were impacted by environmental constraints. The conclusion to the chapter reflects on the analysis and highlights the role of ideas and UN practices mediating the potential and limitations set by both principal-agent theory and constructivism in the study of international organizations as self-directed actors in general and reflects on the implications of this for the study of Secretary-General leadership.

Perspectives on the UN Secretary-General

The existing literature on the UN Secretary-General has been built around the longstanding debate over whether the office can, or should, operate as a "secretary" or as a "general." Yet, David Kennedy's sentiment rings true that, "Debates about the leadership of intergovernmental organizations return again and again to the same, unhelpful alternatives ... Ultimately, however, the strong-weak, leader-clerk debate is a red herring" (Kennedy 2007: 158–59). Thus, after reviewing the traditional studies of the Secretary-General, as well as efforts to extend the study of the individual behind the office in a more analytical fashion that helps to shed light on the ability and need to move beyond the simple secretary versus general approach, the discussion turns to considering how work on the Secretary-General could be meshed with recent theoretical advances in the literature on international organizations emphasized in this volume in order to provide a clearer view on what Secretary-General leadership means in this context.

Secretary versus general: the traditional analytical approach

Traditional analyses of the UN Secretary-Generalship most often relate to the ongoing debate over whether office-holders can overcome the challenges that impede their ability to provide independent leadership for the global community. Some studies place great emphasis on limiting factors external to the office, both organizational (James 1985; Franck and Nolte 1993; Kanninen 1995) and broader environmental dimensions (Jackson 1978; James 1993; Gordenker 1993; Rivlin 1993, 1995; Newman 1998), thereby downplaying the capability of office-holders penned in by such constraints. The duties outlined in the UN Charter certainly do not reflect great leadership expectations for the Secretary-General. Beyond the ability to "bring to the attention of the Security Council any matter which in his opinion may threaten the maintenance of international security" (Article 99), there is little in the Charter to suggest a strong role for the office. Despite the status of the Secretariat as one of the principal organs (Article 7), as mentioned in the introduction to this chapter the Secretary-General is relegated to serving as the "chief administrative officer" (Article 97), in addition to attending meetings and preparing an annual report for the General Assembly (Article 98), and appointing staff (Article 101).

The perspective of a Secretary-General being limited to the role of "secretary" can be seen in analyses of the election of current office-holder Ban Ki-Moon.[1] For example, Thorsten Benner (2007) looks to provide advice to Ban that builds upon his view of Annan's time in office. Benner argues that Annan was able to provide positive leadership in some areas, but generally struggled with management issues and faced great limits placed on the office by member states' obstructive disagreements, or at times apathy, and global challenges.[2] Similarly, while encouraging the Secretary-General to do what he can to push beyond serving solely as a secretary, James Traub's (2007) "Foreign Policy Memo" to Ban points to the limited autonomy and managerial expectations for Ban by the member states. The member states are portrayed as focused on their own clashing interests in a manner that precludes establishing harmony through the UN, so that the best a

Secretary-General can do is make the UN "work well enough so that they [members] continue to resort to it," and in the job of Secretary-General "it's easy to fail, and almost impossible to succeed" (74, 78).³ The pressures on Ban from external powers are well exemplified by a hearing in February 2007 where the members of the House of Representatives Committee on Foreign Affairs continually emphasized the organizational dimension of needed structural reforms. The ramifications of these expectations were made clear, with members of the committee already looking ahead to Ban's possible re-election (which stood five years away after only a month and a half on the job), with the Chair of the committee stating, "I hope we will find reason to recommend a second [term], based on his success in implementing meaningful and lasting reforms" (House of Representatives Committee on Foreign Affairs 2007: 3).

Other analysts stress the continual strong capabilities of the Secretary-General (for example, Bourloyannis 1990; Murthy 1995), thus pointing out a much easier road to strong leadership. A closer analysis of the role beyond the Charter reveals important capabilities that derive from administrative duties (Finger and Mungo 1975; Meron 1982; Szasz 1991; Ameri 1996; Sutterlin 2003), such as shaping and developing UN practices to present to the General Assembly or Security Council in response to global problems. Indeed, work within the Secretariat can provide an important base of support for a Secretary-General's activities, so that "each Secretary-General, in his own way and in his own political context, has had to push back repeated attempts to roll back Secretariat independence and agency" by states that wanted a weaker Secretariat (Myint-U and Scott 2007: 118). Office-holders also hold a central strategic political position within the organization that provides for an important potential avenue of influence (Buza 1962; Rikhye 1991; Dorn 2004) and a key public voice and range of activities that can allow them to impact the global agenda (Cordier 1961; Goodrich 1962; Cordovez 1987). In addition, in the realm of maintaining peace and security Secretaries-General may be involved with both independently initiated and mandated peaceful settlement of dispute missions as well as engagement with UN military peacekeeping interventions (Gordenker 1967; Elarby 1987; Boudreau 1991; Skjelsbaek 1991; Pasternack 1994; Brehio 1998), and can also draw on the resource of "groups of friends" formed to help resolve conflicts (Krasno 2003; Prantl and Krasno 2004; Whitfield 2007a, 2007b).

When these abilities for the office are viewed together, it presents a more impressive possibility for the Secretary-General to take on the role of "general" and lead in the international realm. At the same

Development of the democracy agenda 33

time, even when analysts note that there are opportunities for independent Secretary-General leadership and ideas, these are often placed within particular delimiting constraints that set out areas that cannot realistically be pursued. This is evident in the framework provided by Jeong-Tae Kim (2006), which details how the Secretary-General operates within the "legal sphere" bounded by the traditional division between the "dual mandate" of administrative and political roles. Within the legal sphere, a Secretary-General possesses a particular "role-scope" that is "determined by both his own conception of office and awareness of political settings" (72), but is bound within the "tolerance-scope" set by the degree of legitimacy and resources granted by the member states. The overlapping area of the role-scope and tolerance-scope provides the "available range for the Secretary-Generalship."[4] The notion of particular boundaries and scope of leadership capabilities is also stressed in Thomas Weiss and Peter Hoffman's "A Priority Agenda for the Next Secretary-General" (2006), which reports on four moderated meetings held in October and November 2006 and organizes the agenda suggestions into actionable (progress can be made relatively easily), achievable (progress will require strong and bold action but is attainable), and untenable (pressing these issues would be counter-productive due to their divisiveness or difficulty to achieve) categories. Thus, applied Secretary-General leadership is not required to make actionable progress, will be needed to press for achievable but difficult agenda items, and should not be wasted on untenable issues. They particularly encourage the Secretary-General to attend to Secretariat management issues, where he "could be more a 'general' than a 'secretary'" (Weiss and Hoffman 2006. 24–25).

Beyond objective considerations of what a Secretary-General *can* do while in office, there is the broader debate of what a Secretary-General *should* do with the position. This is a longstanding point of contention that pre-dates the creation of the UN Secretary-Generalship. The quiet and more subservient role played by the League of Nations' Secretary-General, Sir Eric Drummond, is often contrasted with the head of the International Labour Organization, Albert Thomas, and implications for the UN Secretary-General are drawn (Schwebel 1952; Alexandrowicz 1962; Fosdick 1972). This debate essentially revolves around to what degree analysts believe that an office-holder should seek to provide leadership distinct from the member states. For example, the work of James Barros (1979, 1983) makes it clear that he prefers a style of Secretary-General leadership that hews more closely to Drummond's because a more openly active approach will undermine the office in the eyes of the disgruntled member states.

Other analysts want to see Secretaries-General using the office's capabilities to the fullest extent in a courageous manner that promotes and defends UN values (Pechota 1972; UNA-USA 1986; Urquhart and Childers 1996; Ramcharan 1990a, 1990b; Claude 1993). Thus, while analysts such as Barros decry the model of Secretary-General provided by Dag Hammarskjöld, Sten Ask and Anna Mark-Jungkvist's volume *The Adventure of Peace: Dag Hammarskjöld and the Future of the UN* (2005) extols Hammarskjöld as an independent, visionary leader and focuses on the impact and guidance that his time as Secretary-General continues to have on ideals of leadership in the global arena. As one contributor notes, "Even today, when people are faced with international crises, it is to Hammarskjöld's words and actions that they turn for guidance. He has, in fact, become *the* model for international leadership" (Jones 2005: 193, original emphasis; see also Jones 1994, 2004). Oftentimes, the desire for such leadership is stressed as a need for the Secretary-General to act as a vital "moral authority" operating above and beyond state interests (Narasimhan 1988; Urquhart 1996; Nachmias 1993; Shimura 2001; Ramcharan 2002; Paepcke 2005). In this manner, the Secretary-General transcends simply serving the needs of the member states, or restraining him or herself to the bureaucratic realm, to reach out as an independent voice on behalf of the UN or, even more broadly, the global citizenry (Lentner 1965; Rovine 1970; van Boven 1991; Dorn 1999).

The Secretary-General as an individual

Questions revolve around the degree to which the individual behind the office matters as part of this debate over the Secretary-General's role. Recent research on Secretary-General leadership styles has closely linked personal traits to behavioral patterns while in office (Kille and Scully 2003; Kille 2006). In addition, with the Secretary-General often seen as a vital "moral authority," research has explored how the personal religious and moral values of an office-holder inform the political decisions taken while in office (Kille 2007). Overall, this research indicates that individual differences between office-holders can be a vital dimension for understanding how Secretaries-General handle their office. Put simply, certain individuals will be more predisposed than others to use their position to pursue strong, independent leadership, and without this individual level of understanding we will not be able to fully grasp the level of leadership provided by a Secretary-General.

At the same time, research on personal traits has shown that the contextual constraints highlighted in much of the Secretary-General literature cannot be readily dismissed. How exactly the external context is viewed by an office-holder varies according to their personal makeup, so it is necessary to move beyond simply outlining the constraints on the office to detail how a particular Secretary-General engages with these constraints.

Returning to the two-track issue of *can* a Secretary-General provide supranational leadership and *should* an office-holder pursue such a role, yes a Secretary-General can provide such leadership, but not every Secretary-General will seek to do so due to personal proclivities. Contextual limitations will also impede the ability of those so inclined, with the degree to which this occurs somewhat dependent on office-holders' personal capabilities. While some analysts argue that a Secretary-General should not undertake an independent stance out of the fear that this will undermine the capability of the Secretary-General, such leadership can be handled successfully with a capable reading of context by office-holders depending upon their personal traits and values. At the opposite end of the spectrum, those pressing the argument that a Secretary-General must stand forward as a key independent actor representing the voice of the world's people regardless of the situation need to better take into account the political realities faced by individual office-holders and reflect on their abilities in a more pragmatic manner.

The Secretary-General as a self-directed actor

Simon Chesterman (2007), in *Secretary or General? The UN Secretary-General in World Politics*, reflects the debate over the role of the Secretary-General through the very title of the book. As Chesterman explains in the introduction, "The tension between these roles—of being secretary or general—has challenged every incumbent ... A central question for each Secretary-General has been the extent to which he ... could pursue a path independent of the member states that appointed him."[5] These competing dual-role expectations of the Secretary-General are continually referenced by contributors throughout the book, although several of the authors seek to extend the categorizations. This includes Adekeye Adebajo categorizing the debate as between three metaphors—"the pharaoh," "the prophet," and "Pope"—and Kennedy encouraging more complex role categorization across and beyond notions of "leader," "clerk," and "policy entrepreneur."

As John Mathiason (2007) is careful to note in his study *Invisible Governance: International Secretariats in Global Politics*, the lack of attention paid to international public service in international relations theory is problematic. While Mathiason seeks to rectify this problem by reviewing and briefly drawing out what he perceives to be important theoretical applications, in particular using functionalist thinking, other studies of the Secretary-General, or the international secretariat more broadly, have not done so. Instead, the discussion of the Secretary-General's leadership prospects has largely been divorced from theoretically grounded analysis and the related literature largely treads over familiar ground without extending analytical thinking in new and engaging ways.

A key exception has been important developments in studying the normative dimension of Secretary-General leadership and the application of constructivist scholarship. Ian Johnstone, for example, concludes that "Ultimately, a Secretary-General's 'norm entrepreneurship' must be aimed at advancing the values embodied in the Charter in light of changing circumstances within the constraints of what the political traffic will bear" (Johnstone 2007: 138; see also Johnstone 2003). Recent work by Simon Rushton (2008) reinforces this approach by emphasizing the importance of being a norm entrepreneur to the independence and authority of the Secretary-General and tracking this in relation to Boutros-Ghali's efforts to promote democracy. Manuel Fröhlich (2002, 2005a, 2005b, 2007, 2008) traces both the roots and impact Dag Hammarskjöld's political ethics had on the handling of the office and the work of the UN in order to more closely explore "the connection between the private and the public man" (Fröhlich 2008: 10). His analysis shows how political ethics can serve as a "power resource" (Fröhlich 2008: 44).

Such work demonstrates the possibilities of developing further analytical insight by placing the study of the Secretary-General in conjunction with the important and growing theoretical literature examining international organizations as independent actors.[6] In light of these developments, it is possible to establish a more clearly theoretically grounded understanding and more focused conceptualization of what Secretary-General leadership means that is largely lacking in current studies of the office. In this manner we can better grasp the ways that Secretary-General leadership can be exercised through a carefully negotiated or mediated process between delegated authority and assumed authority as office-holders endeavor to shape new ways of understanding. Thus, the following analysis of the engagement of Secretaries-General Boutros Boutros-Ghali and Kofi Annan with the development of the democracy agenda through the UN demonstrates the value added to the understanding of the office by incorporating principal-agent and constructivist theorizing as outlined in the introduction to this volume.

The UN democracy agenda

The development of the UN democracy agenda shows how an idea that had been previously defined through ideology (such as liberal Western democracy versus socialist people's democracy) evolved into a UN concept and practice throughout the 1990s. This agenda was shaped in the rapidly changing global context of the post-Cold War world in response to emerging problems and challenges. Its foundations were laid in the 1980s by academia, development politics and the dynamics of the Third Wave (Huntington 1991) of democratization.

Research supported interest in an international norm of democracy by establishing what is widely called the first "empirical law in international relations" (Levy 1988: 662): the fact that democracies do not go to war with each other. Research further suggested that the guarantee of human rights is greater in democratic states (Davenport 1999). Legal scholars supported the creation of a democracy agenda by reconceptualizing democracy as a human right, or "democratic entitlement," based on the right to self-determination, the right to freedom of expression and the right to free and open elections (Franck 1992). A further impetus for the progress of the UN democracy agenda was the reintroduction or renewed emphasis of the importance of the state in development by both theory and practice. This followed the failure of the neoliberal market agenda and Structural Adjustment Programs to achieve development goals (Rapley 1996). It was now argued that democracy no longer needed a certain level of economic development to become sustainable, as modernization theorists had suggested (Lipset 1959). Instead, democracy was seen as compatible with any level of development as long as growth was sustained and benefits could be felt throughout society (Diamond 1992). Thus, the state and democracy became part of the development process.

While the end of the Cold War and with it the process of Third Wave democratization enabled a UN democracy agenda to become viable, it was the movement of the International Conference of New or Restored Democracies (ICNRD) that initiated the development of the democracy agenda. While both urgency and legitimacy for UN engagement with democracy were first hinted at during the 1980s as both Namibia and Nicaragua requested UN election observations, the 15 states that met in Manila in 1988 triggered the development process by requesting the UN to look into how the organization could support new and restored democracies (Dumitriu 2003). In February 1991 the General Assembly asked Secretary-General Javier Pérez de Cuéllar to report on measures undertaken by the UN so far and how these could be improved.

The Secretary-General responded that within the context of decolonization practice the UN had observed or supervised 31 referenda, plebiscites and elections since 1956 (United Nations Secretary-General 1991, A/46/609). Drawing on these (democratic) processes to establish independence in former colonial states, the Secretary-General now had to apply this UN assistance in existing sovereign states. With this change in application the two types of assistance that existed in 1991, election verification and election assistance, became seven by 1994.

The early lead taken by the General Assembly in the creation of a democracy agenda served as a trigger for the Secretary-General to develop practice, ideas and organizational capacity. This example supports the idea that agency of actors such as the Secretary-General to "investigate" options is delegated. However, the fact that the shape of the proposal—especially for an idea as conceptually complex and contested as democracy—is primarily determined by the Secretary-General and the practices available at the time and not by the member states, moves beyond such simple delegation models and fits with constructivist insights about the role of ideas. With his proposal the Secretary-General pre-structures discussion, manages understanding and creates meaning. A constructivist interpretation illuminates how the Secretary-General challenged the boundaries of his task by promoting a broader understanding of democracy. It was in this context that Boutros-Ghali entered office in 1992, supporting *and driving* the creation of the UN democracy agenda.

Boutros-Ghali's framework of ideas and UN practices for a New World Order

The fact that Boutros-Ghali did not merely operate within a changing context and understanding of democracy but that he contributed to this discourse and exercised leadership by promoting democracy and influencing its conceptualization could be seen right from the start of his term. In his acceptance speech the Secretary-General declared that democracy was a central element of his conception of international order and that he saw it as part of the UN's activity in working towards the goals of the UN Charter. He referred to the UN core values as "peace, development and *democracy*," not "peace, development and *freedom*" as outlined in the Charter. Boutros-Ghali declared that he wanted to emphasize the UN's role in "strengthening fundamental freedoms and democratic institutions which constitute an essential and indispensable stage in the economic and social development of nations" (Boutros-Ghali 2003b: 3).

In this he differed markedly from his predecessor, Pérez de Cuéllar, whose tenure may have spanned two very different world orders, the bipolar Cold War order and the emerging multi-polar order of the post-Cold War world, but who continued to be rooted very much in the former. As Pérez de Cuéllar's term in office was dominated by conflict and security issues of the Cold War world, his understanding of the place and shape of democracy within the normative and operational framework of the UN was a continuation of the ideas prominent in the Cold War context, i.e. democracy as a particular ideology. It was only in his memoirs that Pérez de Cuéllar equated freedom with democracy and wrote:

> If the United Nations is to lead in the pursuit of peace, it also must be able to promote the growth of democratic societies and encourage the development of economic well-being on which both democratic governance and peace ultimately depend. At the end of my second term as Secretary-General, this is what I saw as the major challenge facing national governments and the United Nations
> (Pérez de Cuéllar 1997: 18).

By contrast, Boutros-Ghali no longer saw democracy as an identifier of a particular ideology or political grouping (i.e. the West), but as a universal concept. Moreover, by stating that democracy was "an essential and indispensable stage" of development, Boutros-Ghali reinforced democracy's teleological character. In other words, Boutros-Ghali described from the outset a particular view of democracy's place in the canon of UN ideals, goals and practices, thereby shaping member states' understanding of democracy in a specific way. With this radically different vision of democracy he also set the tone for a "more active and assertive" (Rivlin 1996: 141) Secretary-Generalship, typical for what is described as a "visionary" leadership style (Kille 2006).

Analysts generally describe Boutros-Ghali as a cultured and intelligent person with a sharp expression and wit (Gordenker 2005), a man who was strongly influenced by classic liberal values and international law (Lang 2007). According to Lang, Boutros-Ghali was convinced that international lawyers like himself, and most of all UN Secretaries-General, ought to be the designers of conceptual foundations for global change and its consolidation (Lang 2007: 298). Following the picture of an intellectual politician, Charles Hill describes Boutros-Ghali as a writer with conviction, who believed that "policy was made by the written word, that texts make things happen in the realm of high diplomacy and statecraft" (Hill 2003: iii). His very personal agenda for leadership relied strongly on the three *Agendas for Peace* (1992), *Development* (1994), *Democratization* (1996), and to some extent the *Supplement to the Agenda for Peace* (1995), as well as speeches and other, non-UN publications. Hence, the Secretary-General had many tools of leadership available to him, which supported his aim to create a new intellectual framework for the UN to match its new, emerging role in the post-Cold War world (Boutros-Ghali 1999: 337). Boutros-Ghali had a very strong personal influence in the writing process of all of these, as his speechwriter Caroline Lombardo (2001) attests, and he acted as norm entrepreneur, challenging member states' views on how democracy should be defined and used in the context of the UN. While Boutros-Ghali clearly outlined his views on democracy from the outset, it was only after 1994 and the second Conference of New or Restored Democracies that he used his annual reports on democracy (Enhancing the Effectiveness of the Principle of Periodic and Genuine Elections and Support by the United Nations of the Efforts of Governments to Promote and Consolidate New or Restored Democracies) to elaborate on the concept of democracy and its relationship to the UN. The annual *Support* ... report in particular was an important avenue for the Secretary-General to express his views and his main idea: the triangulation of democracy with peace and development.

In his reports Boutros-Ghali stressed that democracy, peace and development are "indissolubly linked." The Secretary-General emphasized that democracies are more peaceful than non-democratic states, stressing either that "democracies never fight each other" (Boutros-Ghali 1993: 651) or that "governments which are responsive and accountable are likely to be stable and to promote peace" (Boutros-Ghali 2003a: 540). Echoing the logic of the Democratic Peace, Boutros-Ghali thus followed an emerging consensus among Western politicians.

Although he tried to be clear in his acceptance speech that democracy was neither a "magic potion" that cures all problems, nor that it would be a justification for intervention, the Secretary-General's own voice of caution soon subsided in the light of the challenges confronting the UN. Triangulation with core values of the UN therefore provided the justification for democracy to become a UN norm. It created a need for democracy within the stated purpose of the UN and shaped a particular view of what democracy is and what it does, namely to promote peace and support development.

In addition to this functional justification of democracy, the Secretary-General also sought to outline a normative-legal foundation for democracy. Although he sketched this foundation in several of his reports and speeches, he most clearly described this foundation in his *Agenda for*

Democratization. Central to the development of the democracy agenda was the reinterpretation of sovereignty as popular sovereignty. Although Boutros-Ghali admitted that the word democracy did not appear in the Charter, he stated:

> [W]ith the opening words of that document, "We the Peoples of the United Nations," the founders invoked the most fundamental principle of democracy, rooting the sovereign authority of the Member States—and thus the legitimacy of the Organization ... in the will of their peoples.
>
> (Boutros-Ghali 1996: para. 28)

From this it followed that democracy was fundamental to the organization, pointing to key principles such as self-determination and human rights as surrogates for democracy.

However, despite the Secretary-General's keen attempts to justify and promote democracy, he was aware of the limitations of this new agenda. Hence, in his annual reports the promotion of democracy was restrained by reassurances of sovereignty as he emphasized the processes of democratization over specific models of democracy (Boutros-Ghali 1996: para. 11). Indeed, without a broader framework of practice beyond election assistance, the UN would make no judgment about the substance of democracy, such as which institutions beyond elections were needed or which were better. As soon as the democracy agenda expanded beyond election assistance in the mid-1990s, this would no longer be the case.

Following this first impetus provided by both the ICNRD and states' requests for elections assistance, a second push for the democracy agenda emerged out of the changing political landscape and the role of the Secretary-General in maintaining peace and security. In 1992, as Boutros-Ghali assumed office, the political landscape had seen a rise in intra-state conflict. Since 1988 six peacekeeping missions had been established. These addressed national issues, primarily involving transition periods such as those in Angola, Namibia, Nicaragua and El Salvador. Encouraged by the successful intervention against the Iraqi invasion of Kuwait, the international community sought new solutions to the developing situations in Yugoslavia and Somalia, including the reconfiguration of existing conflict management tools. Thus, one of Boutros-Ghali's first tasks as Secretary-General was to revisit and revise the organization's framework for conflict management. In his *Agenda for Peace*, issued in June 1992, Boutros-Ghali acknowledged the unique changes that the Third Wave of democratization had brought about. He highlighted new forms of insecurity, primarily non-military in nature, as well as what he saw as the demise of absolute sovereignty. Following this, democracy assumed a key place and function in the *Agenda for Peace*. Boutros-Ghali saw elections and election monitoring as the means to enhance the promotion of all "formal and informal processes of political participation" to facilitate conflict solution (Boutros-Ghali 1992). Thus, democracy, or elections, became an integral part of peacekeeping missions and the political settlements underlying them.

However, in the early 1990s, where the relationship between the different aspects of peacekeeping, development and election assistance was concerned, peacekeeping missions were still developing. Unfortunately, elections held in this context did not always lead to the desired results. The Secretary-General used this opportunity to highlight the importance of good governance and governance support in the institutionalization of peace (United Nations Secretary-General 1995, A/50/60-S/1995/1). The practice of good governance, as used by the World Bank and the UN Development Programme (UNDP), addressed the structures and processes of (democratic) states beyond elections. Although intended to be a "neutral" practice that sought to promote open, transparent and, most of all, effective *governance*, the practice of *good governance* supported elections by providing a legal and political framework for democratic societies beyond the election event. This framework would, according to Boutros-Ghali, help address the causes of conflict and support the UN's goals of maintaining peace. Boutros-Ghali saw conflict as emerging out of political oppression, a lack of political participation, social injustice and economic grievances. This meant that causes of conflict were clearly structural, i.e. embedded in the foundations of the state. The (re)construction of the state after conflict could therefore address and resolve conflict. The practice of good governance could thus join election assistance in a package of post-conflict state reconstruction to help achieve peace.

Boutros-Ghali thus integrated the idea of democracy into existing practices while legitimizing it through new tasks and changes in those practices. He also reached out to other agencies of the UN system to bring together ideas and practices such as peacekeeping and good governance, thereby creating an interagency approach. Many of these ideas were left for Annan to put into practice and to institutionalize. However, before leaving office after only one term, Boutros-Ghali published his *Agenda for Democratization*, in an attempt to summarize, synthesize and develop a comprehensive vision of democracy at the UN.

The **Agenda for Democratization:** *a cautionary tale of visionary leadership*

The *Agenda for Democratization* was part of Boutros-Ghali's attempt to create his intellectual framework for the UN, a "holistic vision" of how the UN might contribute to a peaceful and stable international world after the end of the Cold War, and to enable the UN to meet emerging challenges. As such the agenda was intended to complete the preceding *Agenda of Peace* and *Agenda of Development*. All three were "formed in confrontation of theory with practice" (Russett 2003: 2065), envisaged to outline key principles that would define each area of activity. The Secretary-General understood that publishing the *Agenda for Democratization* would be "risky business" (Boutros-Ghali 1999: 320), yet he may have been unprepared for the response his attempt at leadership received. The Agenda was roundly rejected by states and UN civil servants alike. Boutros-Ghali's attempt at leadership in this area was as unwelcome as it was regarded inappropriate (Lombardo 2001). Indeed, in his memoirs Boutros-Ghali wrote that as the UN bureaucracy got wind of the Agenda, "its counterblast against this was of hurricane force" (Boutros-Ghali 1999: 320).

Unlike the *Agenda for Peace* and the *Agenda for Development*, which had been requested by the Security Council and the General Assembly, respectively, a mandate for this third Agenda was not forthcoming. Instead, Boutros-Ghali used opportunities such as the 1994 Gauer Lecture to flesh out his thoughts on "The United Nations and Democracy." According to Lombardo, the situation exploded in 1995 when the Secretary-General shared his thoughts with senior UN staff and heads of departments. Following a very negative reaction, the Secretary-General decided to publish only those elements of the Agenda that concerned operational dimensions. He published these elements as an introduction to the annual report *Support by the United Nations System of the Efforts of Government to Promote and Consolidate New or Restored Democracies*, as requested by the General Assembly. He then continued to revise his text, using his annual reports, speeches and publications to test his ideas with a wider audience (Lombardo 2001).

By November 1996 Boutros-Ghali sought renewed feedback from friends and acquaintances, who were generally more encouraging (Hill 2003). Already vetoed out of office by the United States, a move that Boutros-Ghali considered "a rejection of democracy" (Boutros-Ghali 1999: 318), he moved quickly in December 1996 to issue his *Agenda for Democratization* only days before his departure from the UN. Vociferous criticism was leveled at Boutros-Ghali by a number of member states. Member states criticized Boutros-Ghali's attempt at leadership. Considering the way in which the Secretary-General dealt with the *Agenda for Democratization*, that is, the lack of mandate and the decision to publish despite criticism, meant that even democracy promoters such as the United States did not welcome the Agenda. Related to this, some member states criticized the fact that the Secretary-General had addressed the idea of democracy in general. Authoritarian states in Asia, as well as some of their European allies argued that it was not for the UN to concern itself with democracy. Democracy, they argued, had no place in the international system because it was a culturally (i.e. Western) specific concept. As such, some Arab member states even accused Secretary-General Boutros-Ghali of having forgotten his own cultural roots (Russett 2003: 2067). Third, member states were incensed by the ideas brought forward concerning international democracy, or the democratization of the international system. This required a restructuring of the UN to ensure more democracy and sovereign equality between states irrespective of their relative power, the establishment of an international culture of democracy, and the inclusion of a number of new, non-state actors in international decision-making, such as nongovernmental organizations (NGOs).

Overall, it appears evident that the Secretary-General's attempt at leadership through the *Agenda for Democratization* failed to achieve its intended aims. As Rushton (2008) notes, the promotion of norms does not take place in a political vacuum, and thus the Secretary-General failed to achieve "his potential as an agent of democracy promotion" due to his inept use of leadership instruments and by ignoring his political environment. Visionary leaders like Boutros-Ghali challenge constraints, they "bend" the leadership tools available to them and do so "to the extreme in order to gain as much influence as possible without recognizing the danger of 'breaking' the tool" (Kille 2006: 59) or considering their audience.

However, Rushton's pessimistic conclusion of Boutros-Ghali's "failure" is misguided insofar as it determines the success of the democracy agenda on the basis of a single event, and judges national democracy in connection with international democracy. While the event of publication may have been unsuccessful in its intention, the promotion of national democracy was embedded in a broader process of agenda-setting—and it is here that leadership by the Secretary-General as the chief administrator took on its unique form. The Secretary-General wove the idea of democracy into the fabric of the UN, from its foundational goals to current issues and practices. Agencies and programs could pick up democracy to support, operationalize or implement their own policies

Development of the democracy agenda 45

and practices, while the Secretariat could draw on the same to further justify and legitimize the democracy agenda.

Once introduced the democracy agenda was intimately connected to the UN and therefore difficult to remove by resistant member states. Boutros-Ghali's successor, Kofi Annan, then created a legacy for the *Agenda for Democratization* by continuing Boutros-Ghali's norm entrepreneurship on *national* democracy and pursuing international democracy elsewhere. He thereby moved beyond the resistance of member states directed at Boutros-Ghali to further refine and broaden the meaning of UN democracy.

Kofi Annan: refinement of ideas and institutionalization through practice

Secretary-General Annan's strategy to develop the UN democracy agenda differed from Boutros-Ghali's insofar as he was able to build on the foundations laid by Boutros-Ghali, relying less on the development of ideas but increasingly on the development of UN practice. Annan merely needed to re-affirm the importance of democracy and continue its application and development in the field.

Although Annan emphasized that democracy was "dear to [his] heart" (United Nations Information Service 2001, SG/SM/7850), he did not afford democracy the same role in his acceptance speech as did Boutros-Ghali. Instead, he returned to the traditional triangle of peace, development and *freedom*. Although democracy may have lost somewhat in prominence in the Secretary-General's documents during Annan's term, the agenda became increasingly institutionalized. Institutionalization meant that more organizations, agencies and programs became concerned with democracy while existing programs extended their reach. Moreover, more member states increasingly supported and accepted the democracy agenda as they declared at the Millennium Summit to "spare no effort to promote democracy and strengthen the rule of law, as well as respect for all internationally recognized human rights and fundamental freedoms, including the right to development" (United Nations General Assembly 2000, A/RES/55/2: para. 24). By 2003 Annan stated that the promotion of democracy was "one of the main goals of the Organization for the twenty-first century" (United Nations Secretary-General 2003, A/58/392: para. 12).

Annan shared with his predecessor the understanding that democracy was more than just elections, and that institutions and values were just as important for the consolidation of democracy and the creation of a democratic society. More nuanced than his predecessor, Annan emphasized that it was *mature* democracies that do not fight each other and that only "states with open and accountable systems of government" would translate into a more peaceful world. From this it followed that the consolidation of democracy, and therefore an extension of UN practice, would be needed to ensure peace (Annan 2002: 135). This then justified a longer-term commitment for UN support and increased involvement of a variety of UN programs. It also emphasized that democracy was more than just elections.

In addition to a more nuanced understanding of democracy's benefits, it was the so-called "Kofi Doctrine" (Smith 2007: 305) that influenced the way in which democracy was shaped during Annan's Secretary-Generalship. This "doctrine" encapsulated the values of human dignity and the peaceful resolution of conflict. In theory this doctrine found expression in the concepts of human security and the Responsibility to Protect, which reconceptualized the individual's relationship to the state by emphasizing the role of the state as caretaker of individuals' well-being (International Commission on Intervention and State Sovereignty 2001; MacFarlane and Foong-Khong 2006). In practice, the doctrine raised questions about the UN's potential commitment to humanitarian interventions. As both concepts placed individual sovereignty over state sovereignty, neither of these concepts was recognized by member states beyond gross human rights violations and genocide.

Although Annan followed a less visionary leadership strategy than Boutros Boutros-Ghali, his impact on the democracy agenda was significant. Annan's leadership style has been identified as "strategic," a style that lies between the pro-active visionary style of Boutros-Ghali and the reserved, bureaucratic style of "managers" such as Kurt Waldheim (Kille 2006). Strategists are constraint respecters who seek to balance the demands of the office by neither unduly challenging set boundaries nor retreating within these boundaries. Following a strategic leadership style, Annan developed the democracy agenda through the integration of practices from different UN agencies, while diffusing the idea of democracy throughout the UN system. His goal to bring about a "quiet revolution" (Annan 1998) of good governance and cooperation shaped his first contribution to the democracy agenda and member states' understanding of democracy.

In his first report on democracy Annan connected back to Boutros-Ghali's leadership, describing his own report as a path "Towards an Agenda for Democratization." In drawing on Boutros-Ghali's Agenda, Annan called for "a new understanding of democratization" based on his conviction that "democratization and governance... are two key concepts which I believe should stand together" (UNSG 1997, A/52/513: para. 6). With this report Annan used his tools for administrative leadership to join up the existing practices of election assistance and governance support. In joining up these practices, Annan communicated to member-states a specific view of democracy: democracy was more than the event of legitimizing and selecting a government (i.e. elections) and instead emphasized that institutions, rights and processes are all important for a successful democracy.

The application of Annan's "quiet revolution" inside the UN administration also provided an important vehicle for the development of the democracy agenda through the institutionalization of a multi-disciplinary, inter-agency framework. The foundation for this framework was a list of eleven principles of good governance that the Subgroup on Capacity Building for Governance of the UN Administrative Committee on Coordination (ACC)[7] had drawn up in June 1997. These principles were based on the different approaches and experiences of various UN agencies involved in democracy support activities, which in 1998 included no fewer than 13 agencies (United Nations Secretary-General 1998, A/53/554). In October 2000 Annan formally created the practice of *democracy assistance* (United Nations Secretary-General 2000, A/55/489: para. 14), thereby defining democracy in extensive terms and opening the door for greater UN "intervention" in national affairs.

In addition to the joining up of practices, Annan's reform further included a reshaping of organizational structures and the introduction of new management systems and cultures. These reforms forced a rethinking of how practices, including democracy assistance, were executed. While innovations such as UNDP's Democratic Trust Fund in 2001 sought to focus and streamline assistance, it was Annan's reconceptualization of human rights as an organizational principle and practice that was critical in changing the democracy agenda. The democracy agenda was spread throughout the UN system by Annan's 1998 proposal to mainstream human rights. In his 1998 report to the Economic and Social Council the Secretary-General called for a human rights-based approach (HRBA) to be adopted as a fundamental principle for the execution of all activities carried out by UN agencies thereby reinforcing the "right to democracy". Following Sen's (1999) capability approach, the HRBA mirrored UNDP's development agenda, with both policies—development and human rights—following a two-pronged strategy of empowerment and capacity-building. The democratic process (in its broadest sense) was placed at the heart of this approach: "in a dynamic world, democratic processes and poverty reduction would continuously feed into strengthening the rights-based effort" (Ljungman 2005: 8). Establishing democracy as a human right changed the focus from democracy as a system to the political relationships of society. This thus brought "the people" back into the equation, reinforcing Annan's idea of people-centered politics.

Annan's people-centered politics, i.e. his focus on human dignity, contributed to the development of the democracy agenda by providing a framework of related ideas and practices, such as human development, human security and the responsibility to protect. Democracy and the democracy agenda could nestle in this framework, being at the same time informed by these ideas and practices, as well as informing them. While human security and the Responsibility to Protect largely remained at a conceptual stage, the idea and practice of human development as a central UN policy was institutionalized by Annan through the Millennium Development Goals (MDGs). While democracy did not play a part in the operationalization of the MDGs, Annan emphasized that democratic governance would play a crucial role in their implementation. By ensuring greater participation and accountability, democratic governance would further social progress and development. Moreover, better governance would enable countries to address minority issues through financial transfers. Therefore governance would also function more effectively as a conflict-prevention system (Annan 2000).

Thus, Annan did not significantly diverge from his predecessor's ideas, yet used very different tools and techniques to bring about the broadening of the UN democracy agenda. Instead of pushing the boundaries of his delegated authority by promoting unsolicited opinions he used administrative tasks through the operationalization of ideas and the definition of practice to shape, and extend, the meaning of UN democracy. In other words, he shaped the agenda by creating facts.

Conclusion: potential for self-directed leadership

The influence of the Secretary-General, his leadership in shaping an agenda, is evident in the cumulative development of a particular definition of democracy. The development of the democracy agenda showed a clear trajectory in which the idea and practice of democracy became increasingly institutionalized and broader in application. This was done by coupling new ideas with existing ideas or using operational tools as an avenue to expand the scope of both the idea and practice of democracy. Secretaries-General exercised norm entrepreneurship by framing democracy as embedded in the framework of the UN's core ideas of peace, development and human rights. To justify democracy as an appropriate idea for the UN as well as establish a degree of relevance for a UN democracy agenda, they needed to show that democracy assistance would solve a problem relevant to the UN. In responding to a changing environment both Secretaries-General used the opportunity to embed democracy in existing practices without creating radical changes.

The development of the democracy agenda through practice thus followed two distinct but related processes: first, the practice of democracy assistance was developed by restructuring and building on existing practices (election assistance, good governance), while legitimizing it through new challenges and tasks (peacekeeping, failed states). Second, the practice of democracy assistance was distributed across, or adopted by different institutions of the UN system. Central ideas and practices of these institutions, such as good governance and human rights, influenced the democracy agenda as much as they were influenced by it, in effect creating a system-wide agenda of democracy assistance. Resistance by member states was overcome by "repackaging" the controversial issue by disengaging national democracy from international democracy and by focusing on its operational dimension.

In shaping a UN practice that was responsive to the needs of the organization and to member states, both Secretaries-General contributed to how member states would view and understand democracy. They both insisted that democracy was more than just elections and sought to include a variety of state institutions in a definition of democracy. Consequently, over the course of 10 years, UN democracy practice changed from *election assistance* to *democracy assistance*. As a result, the meaning of democracy changed from a procedural, election-focused definition to a broader, more substantive view. This definition now included aspects of the efficiency and accountability of institutions, systems and processes, as well as the specification of outcomes, which could not be achieved by elections alone. By triangulating peace, development and democracy in both theory and practice, member states would be confronted with a different view of what constitutes peace and security, and how crises could be defined. By using these framing processes the Secretary-General "softened up" (Kingdon 2003: 201) the system, creating a favorable environment for the development of new or changed agendas. Indeed, this triangulation of ideas and practices may have contributed (or may in future contribute) to the actual or potential expansion of the Secretary-Generalship through its peace-related functions.

The case of the democracy agenda highlights the advances made in understanding self-directed leadership by the Secretary-General, yet also underlines Kennedy's (2007: 158) previously mentioned warning that "the strong-weak, leader-clerk debate is a red herring." A comparison between the two Secretaries-General underlines the opportunities and limitations for self-directed leadership by the Secretary-General. It shows both the impact of individual leadership styles in successful leadership, i.e. the limitations of pushing the boundaries set by delegated authority and the principal, as well as the relevance of constructivist norm entrepreneurship. At the same time it shows that a traditional reading of the UN Charter (focused on Articles 97 and 99) overlooks activities that are undertaken as part of these roles, which are not explicitly enumerated in the Charter. These activities offer a variety of opportunities for norm entrepreneurship through the operationalization of ideas. These activities are delegated in the broadest sense as they are part of the Secretary-General's main functions as chief administrator, while their substance, in the form of the content of the ideas in question as well as their operationalized form, is not.

The question of whether the Secretary-General *can* exercise leadership is answered in the positive. As Michael Barnett and Martha Finnemore emphasize, "understanding IOs as bureaucracies opens up an alternative view of regarding the sources of their autonomy and what they do with that autonomy" (Barnett and Finnemore 2004: 5). Indeed, the Secretary-General exercises leadership where ideas require definition and operationalization. In this the Secretary-General has an important interpretation and coordination function to define or clarify meaning for member states, and to manage the effectiveness of UN practice across different organizations, agencies and programs.

The question of whether the Secretary-General *should* exercise leadership in a functional sense similarly points towards the office's important role played in mediating between bureaucracy, member states and global values. A Secretary-General's unique position at the center of the UN system both allows and requires an office-holder to bring together ideas and practices from different sources to both shape agendas that further the values of the Charter and prevent potential clashes and redundancies between practices. Moreover, where complex and contested ideas such as democracy are concerned, the Secretary-General ought to provide guidance on appropriate or feasible interpretations, as well as mediate potential conflict over different interpretations. This re-emphasizes the moral authority dimension of Secretary-General leadership, where the office's ethical standing can imbue handling difficult conceptual debates with the backing from the perceived voice of the global citizenry above that of the member states. At the same time, the difficulties demonstrated through Secretary-General engagement with a controversial issue area such as democracy reveal the pragmatic limits to asserting such moral authority.

In conclusion, both constructivism and the principal-agent approach help to understand how self-directed leadership is exercised. While principals may trigger or legitimize the development of a new agenda, they do not or only rarely define the terms of this activity or indeed the shape of the practice or idea in question. Leadership by the Secretary-General is then a carefully negotiated process of communication, with ideas and practices playing an important role in mediating the potential and limitations set by both principal-agent theory and constructivism in the study of international organizations as self-directed actors. The implications for the study of the Secretary-General are clear: not only is there a need to further study both successful and unsuccessful attempts at leadership to better understand the context and conditions for leadership, but a greater understanding of the position of the Secretary-General within the UN system in his role of chief administrator is required to understand the potential for self-directed leadership.

Notes

1 Along with other published analyses, such as DiMaggio 2006, Urquhart 2006, UNA-USA 2006 and Keating 2007, there were also significant efforts to track and discuss the selection process through online forums such as www.unsg.org and www.unsgselection.org.
2 For more on Benner's analysis, see Benner 2006, and Benner and Luck 2007.
3 Traub also provides great detail on the tenure of Annan, which provides a basis for drawing such conclusions for Ban, in his book *The Best Intentions: Kofi Annan and the UN in the Era of American World Power* (Traub 2006; see also Traub 1998, 2004). In addition, see Stanley Meisler's *Kofi Annan: A Man of Peace in a World of War* (2007), and Meisler's (1995a, 1995b) earlier work.
4 Kim's arguments build upon the work of Jorge Viñuales (2005). Although Kim critiques Viñuales for "falling short of some hypothetical clearness," this is presented as a key area of work in discussing the relationship of legal and political constraints to the operation of the office, which is categorized by Kim as one of the three variables studied in the literature on the Secretary-General, along with political circumstances as an independent variable and personality and leadership as an independent variable. See also Viñuales (2006). Note that Roberto Lavalle (1990) also previously invoked the idea of a "political sphere."
5 For more of Chesterman's writing on the topic preceding this volume, see Chesterman 2005a, 2005b.
6 The preceding analysis of the Secretary-General as an individual also shows the value of drawing across international relations literatures beyond Secretary-General-specific work—including work done in the fields of foreign policy decision-making, ethics and international affairs, and religion

and international relations, but is limited by not tapping directly into the valuable international organization theoretical work being undertaken in the field.

7 Now the UN System Chief Executives Board for Coordination (ECB).

Bibliography

Adebajo, Adekeye, "Pope, Pharaoh, or Prophet? The Secretary-General After the Cold War," in *Secretary or General? The UN Secretary-General in World Politics*, ed. Simon Chesterman (New York: Cambridge University Press, 2007).

Alexandrowicz, Charles H., "The Secretary-General of the United Nations," *International and Comparative Law Quarterly* 11, no. 44 (1962): 1109–30.

Ameri, Houshang, *Politics of Staffing the United Nations Secretariat* (New York: Peter Lang, 1996).

Annan, Kofi, "The Quiet Revolution," *Global Governance* 4, no. 2 (1998): 123–38.

——"Two Concepts of Sovereignty," *The Economist*, 18 September 1999.

——*"We the Peoples": The Role of the United Nations in the 21st Century* (New York: UN Department of Public Information, 2000).

——"Democracy as an International Issue," *Global Governance* 8, no. 2 (2002): 135–42.

Ask, Sten and Anna Mark-Jungkvist, eds, *The Adventures of Peace: Dag Hammarskjöld and the Future of the UN* (New York: Palgrave Macmillan, 2005).

Barnett, Michael and Martha Finnemore, *Rules for the World: International Organizations in Global Politics* (Ithaca, NY: Cornell University Press, 2004).

Barros, James, *Office Without Power: Secretary-General Sir Eric Drummond 1919–1933* (Oxford: Clarendon Press, 1979).

——"The Importance of Secretaries-General of the United Nations," in *Dag Hammarskjöld Revisited: The UN Secretary-General as a Force in World Politics*, ed. Robert S. Jordan (Durham, NC: Carolina Academic Press, 1983).

Benner, Thorsten, "Over to You Ban Ki Moon," *International Herald Tribune*, 4 October 2006.

——"Filling Sisyphus's Shoes: The Annan Years and the Future of the United Nations," *Internationale Politik—Global Edition* 8 (2007): 76–82.

Benner, Thorsten and Edward C. Luck, "Making the Most of the Ban Years," *Spiegel Online*, 23 April 2007.

Boudreau, Thomas E., *Sheathing the Sword: The U.N. Secretary-General and the Prevention of International Conflict* (Westport, Conn.: Greenwood Press, 1991).

Bourloyannis, M. Christiane, "Fact-finding by the Secretary-General of the United Nations," *New York University Journal of International Law and Politics* 22, no. 4 (1990): 641–69.

Boutros-Ghali, Boutros, *An Agenda for Peace* (New York: United Nations, 1992).

———"An Agenda for Peace, One Year Later," *Orbis* 37, no. 3 (1993): 323–32.
———*An Agenda for Democratization* (New York: United Nations Department of Public Information, 1996).
———*Unvanquished: A U.S.-U.N. Saga* (New York: Random House, 1999).
———"Address to the American Publishers Association, Washington D.C., 1993," in *The Papers of United Nations Secretary-General Boutros Boutros-Ghali*, vols. 1–3, ed. Charles Hill (New Haven: Yale University Press, 2003a).
———"Oath of Office taken by Boutros-Ghali [in Arabic], 3 December 1991," in *The Papers of United Nations Secretary-General Boutros Boutros-Ghali*, vols. 1–3, ed. Charles Hill (New Haven: Yale University Press, 2003b).
Brehio, Alys, "Good Offices of the Secretary-General as Preventive Measures," *New York University Journal of International Law and Politics* 30, nos. 3–4 (1998): 589–643.
Buza, Laszlo, "The Position of the Secretary-General of the United Nations in International Law," *Questions of International Law* (1962): 5–23.
Chesterman, Simon, ed., *Secretary or General? The UN Secretary-General in World Politics* (New York: Cambridge University Press, 2007).
———"Duty Pulls Annan in Two Directions," *International Herald Tribune* 9 September 2005a.
———"Great Expectations: UN Reform and the Role of the Secretary-General," *Security Dialogue* 36, no. 3 (2005b): 375–77.
Claude, Inis L., "Reflections on the Role of the UN Secretary-General," in *The Challenging Role of the Secretary-General: Making "The Most Impossible Job in the World" Possible*, ed. Benjamin Rivlin and Leon Gordenker (Westport, Conn.: Praeger, 1993).
Cordier, Andrew W., "The Role of the Secretary-General," in *Annual Review of United Nations Affairs, 1960–1961*, ed. Richard N. Swift. (Dobbs Ferry, NY: Oceana Publications, 1961).
Cordovez, Diego, "Strengthening United Nations Diplomacy for Peace: The Role for the Secretary-General," in *The United Nations and the Maintenance of International Peace and Security*, UNITAR (Dordrecht: Martinus Nijhoff, 1987).
Davenport, Christian, "Human Rights and the Democratic Proposition," *Journal of Conflict Resolution* 43, no. 1 (1999): 92–116.
Diamond, Larry, "Economic Development and Democracy Reconsidered," in *Reexamining Democracy*, ed. Gary Marks and Larry Diamond (Newbury Park, Calif.: Sage Publications, 1992).
DiMaggio, Suzanne, "Selecting the Next Secretary-General," *Foreign Service Journal*, September 2006: 40–46.
Dorn, A. Walter, "The United Nations in the Twenty-First Century: A Vision for an Evolving World Order," in *World Order for a New Millennium: Political, Cultural, and Spiritual Approaches to Building Peace*, ed. A. Walter Dorn (New York: St Martin's Press, 1999).
———"Early and Late Warning by the UN Secretary-General of Threats to the Peace: Article 99 Revisited," in *Conflict Prevention from Rhetoric to Reality*,

Volume 1: Organizations and Institutions, ed. Albrecht Schnabel and David Carment (Lanham, MD: Lexington Books, 2004).

Dumitriu, Petru, "The History and Evolution of the New or Restored Democracies Movement," paper presented at the Fifth International Conference of New or Restored Democracies, Ulaan Bataar, Mongolia, September 2003.

Elarby, Nabil, "The Office of the Secretary-General and the Maintenance of International Peace and Security," in *The United Nations and the Maintenance of International Peace and Security*, UNITAR (Dordrecht: Martinus Nijhoff, 1987).

Finger, Seymour Maxwell and John F. Mungo, "The Politics of Staffing the United Nations Secretariat," *Orbis* 19, no. 20 (1975): 117–45.

Finnemore, Martha and Kathryn Sikkink, "International Norm Dynamics and Political Change," *International Organization* 52, no. 4 (1998): 887–917.

Fosdick, Raymond B., *The League and the United Nations After Fifty Years: The Six Secretaries-General* (Newtown, Conn.: Raymond B. Fosdick, 1972).

Franck, Thomas M., "The Emerging Right to Democratic Governance," *Journal of International Law* 86, no. 1 (1992): 46–91.

Franck, Thomas M. and Georg Nolte, "The Good Offices Function of the UN Secretary-General," in *United Nations, Divided World: The UN's Roles in International Relations*, ed. Adam Roberts and Benedict Kingsbury (Oxford: Clarendon Press, 1993).

Fröhlich, Manuel, "A Fully Integrated Vision: Politics and the Arts in the Dag Hammarskjöld-Barbara Hepworth Correspondence," *Development Dialogue* 1 (2002): 17–57.

——"Hammarskjöld and his Legacy," in *United Nations and Global Security*, ed. Magnus Lundgren and Henrik Holmquist (Stockholm: United Nations Association of Sweden, 2005a).

——"The Quest for a Political Philosophy of World Organisation," in *The Adventures of Peace: Dag Hammarskjöld and the Future of the UN*, ed. Sten Ask and Anna Mark-Jungkvist (New York: Palgrave Macmillan, 2005b).

——"The Ironies of UN Secretariat Reform," *Global Governance* 13, no. 2 (2007): 151–59.

——*Political Ethics and the United Nations: Dag Hammarskjöld as Secretary-General* (New York: Routledge, 2008).

Goodrich, Leland M., "The Political Role of the Secretary-General," *International Organization* 16, no. 4 (1962): 720–35.

Gordenker, Leon, *The UN Secretary-General and the Maintenance of Peace* (New York: Columbia University Press, 1967).

——"The UN Secretary-Generalship: Limits, Potentials and Leadership," in *The Challenging Role of the Secretary-General: Making "The Most Impossible Job in the World" Possible*, ed. Benjamin Rivlin and Leon Gordenker (Westport, Conn.: Praeger, 1993).

——*The UN Secretary-General and Secretariat* (London: Routledge, 2005).

Hill, Charles, ed., *The Papers of United Nations Secretary-General Boutros Boutros-Ghali*, vol. 1–3 (New Haven: Yale University Press, 2003).

House of Representatives Committee on Foreign Affairs, "The Future of the United Nations Under Ban Ki-Moon," hearing before the Committee on Foreign Affairs House of Representatives, 110th Congress First Session, Serial No. 110–17, 13 February 2007.

Huntington, Samuel P., *The Third Wave: Democratization in the Late Twentieth Century* (Norman: University of Oklahoma Press, 1991).

International Commission on Intervention and State Sovereignty, *The Responsibility to Protect* (Ottawa: International Development Research Centre, 2001).

Jackson, William D., "The Political Role of the Secretary-General Under U Thant and Kurt Waldheim: Development of Decline?" *World Affairs* 140, no. 3 (1978): 230–44.

James, Alan, "The Secretary-General: A Comparative Perspective," in *Diplomacy at the UN*, ed. G. R. Berridge and A. Jennings (New York: St Martin's Press, 1985).

———"The Secretary-General as an Independent Political Actor," in *The Challenging Role of the Secretary-General: Making "The Most Impossible Job in the World" Possible*, ed. Benjamin Rivlin and Leon Gordenker (Westport, Conn.: Praeger, 1993).

Johnstone, Ian, "The Role of the UN Secretary-General: The Power of Persuasion Based on Law," *Global Governance* 9, no. 4 (2003): 441–58.

———"The Secretary-General as Norm Entrepreneur," in *Secretary or General? The UN Secretary-General in World Politics*, ed. Simon Chesterman (New York: Cambridge University Press, 2007).

Jones, Dorothy V., "The Example of Dag Hammarskjöld: Style and Effectiveness at the UN," *The Christian Century* 111 (1994): 1047–50.

———"The World Outlook of Dag Hammarskjöld," in *Ethics and Statecraft: The Moral Dimension of International Affairs*, ed. Cathal J. Nolan. (Westport, Conn.: Praeger, 2004).

———"International Leadership and Charisma," in *The Adventures of Peace: Dag Hammarskjöld and the Future of the UN*, ed. Sten Ask and Anna Mark-Jungkvist (New York: Palgrave Macmillan, 2005).

Kanninen, Tapio, *Leadership and Reform: The Secretary-General and the UN Financial Crisis of the Late 1980s* (The Hague: Kluwer Law International, 1995).

Keating, Colin, "Selecting the World's Diplomat," in *Secretary or General? The UN Secretary-General in World Politics*, ed. Simon Chesterman (New York: Cambridge University Press, 2007).

Kennedy, David, "Leader, Clerk, or Policy Entrepreneur? The Secretary-General in a Complex World," in *Secretary or General? The UN Secretary-General in World Politics*, ed. Simon Chesterman (New York: Cambridge University Press, 2007).

Kille, Kent J., *From Manager to Visionary: The Secretary-General of the United Nations* (New York: Palgrave Macmillan, 2006).

———, ed., *The UN Secretary-General and Moral Authority: Ethics and Religion in International Leadership* (Washington, DC: Georgetown University Press, 2007).

Kille, Kent J. and Roger M. Scully, "Executive Heads and the Role of Intergovernmental Organizations: Expansionist Leadership in the United Nations and the European Union," *Political Psychology* 24, no. 1 (2003): 175–98.

Kim, Jeong-Tae, "The UN Secretary-General 'Walking a Two-Scope Rope': An Analytic Approach to the Secretary-Generalship," *Korea Review of International Studies* 9, no. 2 (2006): 65–88.

Kingdon, John W., *Agendas, Alternatives and Public Policies* (New York: Longman, 2003).

Krasno, Jean, "The Group of Friends of the Secretary-General: A Useful Leveraging Tool," in *Leveraging for Success in United Nations Peace Operations*, ed. Jean Krasno, Bradd C. Hayes, and Donald C.F. Daniel (Westport, Conn.: Praeger, 2003).

Lang, Anthony F. Jr, "A Realist in the Utopian City: Boutros Boutros-Ghali's Ethical Framework and its Impact," in *The UN Secretary-General and Moral Authority. Ethics & Religion in International Leadership*, ed. Kent J. Kille (Washington, DC: Georgetown University Press, 2007).

Lavalle, Roberto, "The 'Inherent' Powers of the UN Secretary-General in the Political Sphere: A Legal Analysis," *Netherlands International Law Review* 37, no. 1 (1990): 22–36.

Lentner, Howard H., "The Diplomacy of the United Nations Secretary-General," *Western Political Quarterly* 18, no. 3 (1965): 531–50.

Levy, Jack, "Domestic Politics and War," *Journal of Interdisciplinary History* 18, no. 4 (1988): 662.

Lipset, Seymour Martin, "Some Social Requisites of Democracy: Economic Development and Political Legitimacy," *American Political Science Review* 53, no. 1 (1959): 69–105.

Ljungman, Cecilia M., "Applying a Rights-Based Approach to Development: Concepts and Principles," paper presented at The Winners and Losers from Rights-Based Approaches to Development conference, Manchester, 2005.

Lombardo, Caroline E., "The Making of *An Agenda for Democratization*: A Speechwriter's View," *Chicago Journal of International Law* 2, no. 1 (2001): 253–66.

MacFarlane, S. Neil and Yuen Foong-Khong, *Human Security and the UN: A Critical History* (Bloomington: Indiana University Press, 2006).

Mathiason, John, *Invisible Governance: International Secretariats in Global Politics* (Bloomfield, Conn.: Kumarian Press, 2007).

Meisler, Stanley, "Dateline U.N.: A New Hammarskjöld?" *Foreign Policy* 98 (1995a): 180–97.

——*United Nations: The First Fifty Years* (New York: Atlantic Monthly Press, 1995b).

——*Kofi Annan: A Man of Peace in a World of War* (Hoboken, NJ: John Wiley and Sons, 2007).

Meron, Theodor, "The Role of the Executive Heads," *New York University Journal of International Law and Politics* 14 (1982): 861–69.

Murthy, C.S.R., "The Role of the UN Secretary-General Since the End of the Cold War," *Indian Journal of International Law* 35 (1995): 181–96.

Myint-U, Thant and Amy Scott, *The UN Secretariat: A Brief History* (New York: International Peace Academy, 2007).

Nachmias, Nitza, "The Role of the Secretary-General in the Israeli-Arab and the Cyprus Disputes," in *The Challenging Role of the Secretary-General: Making "The Most Impossible Job in the World" Possible*, ed. Benjamin Rivlin and Leon Gordenker (Westport, Conn.: Praeger, 1993).

Narasimhan, C.V., *The United Nations: An Inside View* (New Delhi: Vikas Publishing House, 1988).

Newman, Edward, *The UN Secretary-General From the Cold War to the New Era: A Global Peace and Security Mandate?* (New York: St Martin's Press, 1998).

Paepcke, Henrike, *Another U.N. Secretary-General Soon Decapitated?*, DIAS Analysis 14 (Dusseldorf: Dusseldorf Institute for Foreign and Security Policy, 2005).

Pasternack, Scott, "The Role of the Secretary-General in Helping to Prevent Civil War," *New York University Journal of International Law and Politics* 26, no. 4 (1994): 701–59.

Pechota, Vratislav, "The Quiet Approach: A Study of the Good Offices Exercised by the United Nations Secretary-General in the Cause of Peace," in *Dispute Settlement Through the United Nations*, ed. K. Venkata Raman (Dobbs Ferry, NY: UNITAR-Oceana Publications, 1972).

Pérez de Cuéllar, Javier, *Pilgrimage for Peace. A Secretary-General's Memoir* (New York: St Martin's Press, 1997).

Prantl, Jochen and Jean E. Krasno, "Informal Groups of Member States," in *The United Nations: Confronting the Challenges of a Global Society*, ed. Jean E. Krasno (Boulder, Col.: Lynne Rienner, 2004).

Ramcharan, Bertram G., "The Office of the United Nations Secretary-General," *Dalhousie Law Journal* 13 (1990a): 742–57.

——"The History, Role and Organization of the 'Cabinet' of the United Nations Secretary-General," *Nordic Journal of International Law* 59, no. 2/3 (1990b): 103–16.

——"The Secretary-General and Human Security: Good Offices and Preventive Action," in *Human Rights and Human Security* (The Hague: M. Nijhoff, 2002).

Rapley, John, *Understanding Development: Theory and Practice in the Third World* (Boulder, Col.: Lynne Rienner, 1996).

Rikhye, Indar Jit, "Critical Elements in Determining the Suitability of Conflict Settlement Efforts by the United Nations Secretary-General," in *Timing the De-Escalation of International Conflicts*, ed. Louis Kriesberg and Stuart J. Thorson (Syracuse, NY: Syracuse University Press, 1991).

Rivlin, Benjamin, "The Changing International Climate and the Secretary-General," in *The Challenging Role of the Secretary-General: Making "The Most Impossible Job in the World" Possible*, ed. Benjamin Rivlin and Leon Gordenker (Westport, Conn.: Praeger, 1993).

———"The UN Secretary-Generalship at Fifty," in *The United Nations in the New World Order: The World Organization at Fifty*, ed. Dimitris Bourantonis and Jarrod Wiener (New York: St Martin's Press, 1995).

———"Boutros-Ghali's ordeal: leading the United Nations in an age of uncertainty," in *A United Nations for the Twenty-first Century: Peace, Security and Development*, ed. Dimitris Bourantonis and Marios Evriviades (The Hague: Kluwer Law International, 1996).

Rovine, Arthur W., *The First Fifty Years: The Secretary-General in World Politics 1920–1970* (Leyden: A.W. Sijthoff, 1970).

Rushton, Simon, "The UN Secretary-General and norm entrepreneurship: Boutros Boutros-Ghali and democracy promotion," *Global Governance* 14, no. 1 (2008): 95–110.

Russett, Bruce, "Afterword," in *The Papers of United Nations Secretary-General Boutros Boutros-Ghali*, ed. Charles Hill (New Haven: Yale University Press, 2003).

Schwebel, Stephen M., *The Secretary-General of the United Nations: His Political Powers and Practice* (New York: Greenwood Press, 1952).

Sen, Amartya, *Development as Freedom* (Oxford: Oxford University Press, 1999).

Shimura, Hisako, "The Role of the UN Secretariat in Organizing Peacekeeping," in *United Nations Peacekeeping Operations: Ad Hoc Missions, Permanent Engagements*, ed. Ramesh Thakur and Albrecht Schnabel (New York: United Nations University Press, 2001).

Simma, Bruno, *The Charter of the United Nations: A Commentary*, Vol. 1 (Oxford: Oxford University Press, 2002).

Skjelsbaek, Kjell, "The UN Secretary-General and the Mediation of International Disputes," *Journal of Peace Research* 28, no. 1 (1991): 99–115.

Smith, Courtney B., "Politics and Values at the United Nations: Kofi Annan's Balancing Act," in *The UN Secretary-General and Moral Authority. Ethics & Religion in International Leadership*, ed. Kent J. Kille (Washington, DC: Georgetown University Press, 2007).

Sutterlin, James S., *The United Nations and the Maintenance of International Security: A Challenge to Be Met* (Westport, Conn.: Praeger, 2003).

Szasz, Paul C., "The Role of the U.N. Secretary-General: Some Legal Aspects," *New York University Journal of International Law and Politics* 24, no. 1 (1991): 161–98.

Traub, James, "Kofi Annan's Next Test," *New York Times Magazine*, 28 March 1998.

———"Traveling with Kofi Annan: Diplomatic Theater in Nairobi and Dar Es Salaam," *Slate*, 22 November 2004. Available at: slate.msn.com/id/2110040.

———*The Best Intentions: Kofi Annan and the UN in the Era of American World Power* (New York: Farrar, Straus, and Giroux, 2006).

———"The FP Memo," *Foreign Policy* 158 (2007): 74–78.

United Nations Association of the United States of America, *Leadership at the United Nations: The Roles of the Secretary-General and the Member States* (New York: UNA-USA, 1986).

———*Selecting the Next UN Secretary-General* (New York: UNA-USA, 2006).

United Nations General Assembly, *United Nations Millennium Declaration* (General Assembly resolution A/RES/55/2), 18 September 2000.

United Nations Information Service, "War Less Likely between Mature Democracies, says Secretary-General" (UN Press Release SG/SM/7850), 19 June 2001.

United Nations Secretary-General, *Support by the United Nations system of the efforts of Governments to promote and consolidate new or restored democracies* (Report of the Secretary-General, UN document A/55/489), 13 October 2000.

———*Enhancing the Effectiveness of the Principle of Periodic and Genuine Elections* (Report of the Secretary-General, UN document A/46/609), 19 November 1991.

———*Supplement to An Agenda for Peace: Position Paper of the Secretary-General on the Occasion of the Fiftieth Anniversary of the United Nations* (UN document A/50/60-S/1995/1), 25 January 1995.

———*Support by the United Nations system of the efforts of Governments to promote and consolidate new or restored democracies* (Report of the Secretary-General, UN document A/58/392), 26 September 2003.

———*Support by the United Nations system of the efforts of Governments to promote and consolidate new or restored democracies* (Report of the Secretary-General, UN document A/53/554), 29 October 1998.

Urquhart, Brian, "The Role of the Secretary-General," in *U.S. Foreign Policy and the United Nations System*, ed. Charles William Maynes and Richard S. Williamson (New York: W.W. Norton, 1996).

———"The Next Secretary-General: How to Fill a Job With No Description," *Foreign Affairs* 85, no. 5 (2006): 15–22.

Urquhart, Brian and Erskine Childers, *A World in Need of Leadership: Tomorrow's United Nations, A Fresh Appraisal* (Uppsala, Sweden: Dag Hammarskjöld Foundation, 1996).

van Boven, Theo, "The Role of the United Nations Secretariat in the Area of Human Rights," *New York University Journal of International Law* 24, no. 1 (1991): 69–107.

Viñuales, Jorge E., *The U.N. Secretary General between Law and Politics: Towards an Analytical Framework for Interdisciplinary Research* (Geneva: Graduate Institute of International Studies, 2005).

———"Can the UN Secretary-General Say 'No': Revisiting the 'Peking Formula'," *Bepress Legal Series*, Working Paper 1478, 2006.

Weiss, Thomas G. and Peter J. Hoffman, "A Priority Agenda for the Next UN Secretary-General," *Dialogue on Globalization*, Occasional Paper number 28 (New York: Friedrich-Ebert-Stiftung, 2006).

Whitfield, Teresa, *Friends Indeed? The United Nations, Groups of Friends, and the Resolution of Conflict* (Washington, DC: United States Institute of Peace Press, 2007a).

———"Good Office and 'Groups of Friends'," in *Secretary or General? The UN Secretary-General in World Politics*, ed. Simon Chesterman (New York: Cambridge University Press, 2007b).

2 The roots of UN post-conflict peacebuilding
A case study of autonomous agency
Margaret P. Karns

- What is peacebuilding?
- The roots and evolution of the idea of UN post-conflict peacebuilding
- Merging two root systems: *An Agenda for Peace*
- Analyzing the roots of UN post-conflict peacebuilding
- Conclusion

On 31 January 1992 the United Nations (UN) Security Council held an extraordinary summit meeting at the level of heads of state and government. It was the first such meeting ever and was convened to consider "The responsibility of the Security Council in the maintenance of international peace and security ... [in] timely recognition of the fact that there are new favourable international circumstances under which the Security Council has begun to fulfill more effectively its primary responsibility for the maintenance of international peace and security" (United Nations Security Council 1992, S/23500).

It was an extraordinary time. The UN had already played important roles in ending the Iran–Iraq war, the Soviet intervention in Afghanistan, Namibia's successful transition to independence, the peace process in Central America, the enforcement action that secured Iraq's withdrawal from Kuwait, and the intrusive effort to destroy its weapons of mass destruction. The UN was in the process of taking up its responsibilities for implementation of the Paris Peace Agreement in Cambodia. At the conclusion of the January 1992 summit, the council members asked Secretary-General Boutros-Ghali to prepare "his analysis and recommendations on ways of strengthening and making more efficient ... the capacity of the United Nations for preventive diplomacy, for peacemaking and for peace-keeping" (United Nations Security Council 1992, S/23500). He was given a 1 July deadline for the report.

When *An Agenda for Peace* was delivered on 17 June 1992, it included a number of sections that were not listed in that presidential statement.

Among them was "post-conflict peace-building." The former Secretary-General himself has since commented, "The most important idea in *The Agenda for Peace* is that 1) the process of peace is a continual process, 2) the prevention of conflict takes place both before and also after the conflict because it can have a relapse, 3) it is necessary to link urgency, rehabilitation, reconstruction and development in order to consolidate the peace (peace-building)." He added, "Coming back to the concept of 'peace-building' that I have developed, I would say, without false modesty, [that I] invented. This concept is extremely important."[1]

An Agenda for Peace is probably the closest thing to a bestseller that the UN has ever produced. It has been translated into 40 languages and has been the subject of academic as well as practitioner discussions. The short section on post-conflict peacebuilding represented an act of conceptual innovation by the Secretary-General and those who had aided in its drafting. The puzzle is where the core ideas about post-conflict peacebuilding originated that led Boutros-Ghali to invent the concept.

The large scholarly literature on the subject of peacebuilding, which is also sometimes referred to as nation- or state-building, has ignored this puzzle.[2] There is recognition that the earliest examples include the reconstruction of Germany and Japan following World War II and some aspects of the UN's operation in the Congo in the early 1960s (Dobbins *et al.*, 2005). Most of this literature, however, links peacebuilding to the Cold War's end and renewed hope for the UN that inspired the expansion of peacekeeping to new tasks, a series of innovative UN missions in the late 1980s and early 1990s, and the publication of Secretary-General Boutros-Ghali's *Agenda for Peace* in 1992. All of these are important. None, however, explains the intellectual roots of peacebuilding nor the agents—that is, who came up with key ideas.

This chapter uses both principal-agent (PA) theory and a social constructivist approach to identify and analyze the roots and branches of the concept of peacebuilding articulated in *An Agenda for Peace*. PA theory helps us understand how UN Secretaries-General, other senior UN officials, and the Secretariat as key actors were able to exercise varying degrees of autonomy or discretion—even independence—at important points. They were aided in this by a number of factors, including the personalities of particular leaders, and the complexity of the issues at hand. Meanwhile constructivism helps explain the importance of the ideas associated with the concept of post-conflict peacebuilding, the process by which those ideas evolved, and the role of changes in the international environment. Where PA theory assumes simple interest-seeking behavior by agents, in fact, Secretaries-General acted in far more complex ways.

What is peacebuilding?

Of the 48 peacekeeping operations the United Nations had undertaken between 1988 and 2008, 29 involved tasks now associated with the concept of post-conflict peacebuilding, the core ideas of which involve preventing renewed hostilities and aiding countries in building the foundations for long-term stability, including democratic polities. When the UN first undertook some of these tasks, the term peacebuilding had not yet been coined, however. There were serious questions regarding the authority for such tasks given state sovereignty and Article 2(7) of the UN Charter, which states: "Nothing contained in the present Charter shall authorize the United Nations to intervene in matters which are essentially within the domestic jurisdiction of any state." This provision has long been seen by both member states and the UN Secretariat as a relatively sharp line marking the divide between the sovereignty of states and the authority of the UN. Yet, in a short period of three-to-four years at the end of the 1980s and beginning of the 1990s, the UN Security Council authorized a series of peacekeeping operations involving tasks that clearly did cross that very line.

Peacebuilding activities signify the recognition that in societies rent by civil strife, failure to address root causes of conflict may lead to a new cycle of violence. Thus, "prevention and rebuilding are inextricably linked ... leading to the conclusion that formal agreement ending a civil war is meaningless unless coupled with long-term programs to heal the wounded society" (Weinberger 2002: 248; see also Leatherman *et al.* 1999).

Peacebuilding operations are complex, multi-faceted operations. Their specific contours depend on the nature of the conflict situation as well as the consensus and political will among those authorizing an operation. The majority of operations since the late 1980s have been UN-organized. It has become common to see long lists of military and civilian tasks associated with complex peacekeeping and peacebuilding operations (see Box 2.1 for a sample list). Such lists provide little sense of priorities and strategy, however.

Similarly, one study (Barnett *et al.* 2007: 44) found significant agreement "that peacebuilding is more than stability promotion; it is designed to create a positive peace, to eliminate the root causes of conflict, to allow states and societies to develop stable expectations of peaceful change." Some analysts argue that the very breadth of the concept now diminishes its utility. Hence, for analytical purposes, it is necessary to specify whether the focus is post-conflict peacebuilding or some broader set of situations. At the same time, it is essential to recognize that most armed conflicts do not conform to a neat, phased

Box 2.1 Post-conflict peacebuilding tasks

Creating the structures for the institutionalization of peace

Military tasks:

- Supervision of cease-fire (a task associated with traditional peacekeeping)
- Regroupment and demobilization of forces—regular military and paramilitary/militias
- Disarmament and destruction of weapons
- Reintegration of forces into civilian life
- Design and implementation of de-mining programs

Humanitarian relief tasks:

- Return and resettlement of refugees and displaced persons
- Provision of humanitarian assistance—food, water, shelter, medical aid ...

Administrative/governmental tasks:

- Supervision of existing administrative structures (government) or providing an interim/transitional civil administration
- Establishment of new police forces or retraining existing police

Democratization-related tasks:

- Design and supervision of constitutional, judicial, and electoral reforms (i.e. building new national institutions)
- Monitoring and promotion of human rights

(from *Supplement to Agenda for Peace*, 1995)

evolution where there is a clear end to violence and, therefore, a clear beginning to post-conflict activities.

The roots and evolution of the idea of UN post-conflict peacebuilding

The roots of Boutros-Ghali's concept of post-conflict peacebuilding spread out in several directions. One part of that root system lies in the long history of the UN's role in the process of decolonization that more than tripled the number of independent states in the world (and UN membership) in the space of less than 20 years after World War II. This root established precedents for certain kinds of UN activities undertaken with the support of the member states and under the authority of the Charter; it also gave a number of Secretariat members experience in those activities. A branch of that same root—the special problem of Namibia—created a number of important precedents. A second set of roots developed as a result of initiatives that Secretary-General Javier Pérez de Cuéllar took to end the conflicts in Central America and Cambodia in the late 1980s. These roots were nurtured by the changing international context associated with the Cold War's end and new enthusiasm among member states and the Secretariat for roles the UN could play in addressing threats to international peace and security. They also influenced the thinking of senior UN officials. The two root systems then merged in the process of drafting *An Agenda for Peace*.

Root system no. 1: precedents in the UN's role in the decolonization process

From the late 1940s to the 1970s the UN played a significant role in the process of decolonization that ended colonial rule throughout Africa, the Americas, Asia, and Oceania and brought more than 100 new states into being. Part of its role involved conducting 30 plebiscites and referenda in trust and other territories. As Beigbeder (1994) notes, that was not part of any democratizing mandate. The goal of the UN was to ensure that the self-determination process was reasonably free and fair. "UN monitoring of self-determination electoral processes," he adds, "was ... not adopted or accepted as a general rule, but only in specific cases" (Beigbeder 1994: 130). Nevertheless, the institutional experience that the UN gained in conducting plebiscites and referenda over more than 30 years proved valuable in the late 1980s when the third wave of democratization and innovative diplomacy led to the UN becoming actively involved in organizing, supervising, and monitoring elections in sovereign, independent states as part of post-conflict peacebuilding operations. This is the core of the first root.

West Irian and Congo

In two instances during the decolonization process, however, the UN did take on other types of roles that presaged responsibilities it would undertake in several post-Cold War, post-conflict situations. These constitute short branches on that tap root. The first was in West

Irian—or West New Guinea—the status of which was unresolved when the Netherlands granted Indonesia independence in 1949. A UN-brokered agreement in 1962 provided for it to serve as the Temporary Executive Authority to administer the territory for an interim period in 1962–63 prior to Indonesia assuming control, and a UN-monitored but not -organized vote no later than 1969 to permit the West New Guineans the choice of remaining with or severing their ties with Indonesia.

The UN undertook even broader responsibilities for a time in newly independent Congo. Within two months of the Congo's independence in June 1960, its government and economy had collapsed and one of its richest provinces, Katanga, had seceded. The tasks the UN took on included the restoration of law and order, securing the removal of Belgian forces, preventing Katanga's secession, providing public services, and establishing a new government. It was a messy, costly, and controversial operation. As Dobbins *et al.* (2005: 13) note, "Despite the United Nations' success in achieving its principal objectives, the experience of the Congo generated an enduring resistance within the Secretariat and among member states to peace enforcement and nation-building missions." Yet, the UN's role in The Congo also presaged tasks it took or in several post-Cold War operations.

Namibia: a special case

Namibia, a former German colony and League of Nations mandate known as South West Africa, which was administered by South Africa from 1920 until 1990, posed a very different type of challenge for decolonization. The process of bringing it to independence led to several important innovations in UN practice and ideas that influenced *An Agenda for Peace*. It was the only League mandate not to be granted either independence or trust territory status under the UN. Advisory opinions of the International Court of Justice (ICJ) in 1950, 1955, 1956, and 1971 affirmed the territory's unique status under international supervision of the UN as the successor to the League. This gave the UN itself a stake in seeing the problem resolved peacefully. In 1966 the General Assembly ended South Africa's mandate (Resolution 2145). In 1971, the ICJ affirmed a Security Council decision (Resolution 276/1970) that South Africa's presence in South West Africa (Namibia) was illegal (International Court of Justice 1971). From this point forward, Namibia was a special case of decolonization since it represented a situation that was recognized by the UN Security Council as a threat to international peace and security.

In the late 1970s Namibia was the subject of intense efforts by five major Western powers (the United States, United Kingdom, Federal Republic of Germany, Canada, and France), which formed the first contact group to work with the UN Secretariat to bring South Africa, the South West Africa People's Organization (SWAPO), and the Front Line states in southern Africa (Angola, Botswana, Lesotho, Mozambique, Zambia, Tanzania, and Zimbabwe) to an agreement (Karns 1987). The resulting agreement embodied in the 1978 Security Council Resolution 435 envisioned a significant UN role in the transition process. South Africa, however, blocked implementation, blaming in part the presence of Soviet-backed Cuban troops in neighbouring Angola.

Still, the planning for implementation proceeded within the UN Secretariat. In 1989, following agreement for withdrawal of Cuban troops, the UN Transition Assistance Group (UNTAG) was created in Namibia. UNTAG was deployed with the most ambitious, diverse mandate of any UN mission to that time. It included supervision of the ceasefire between South African and SWAPO forces; monitoring the withdrawal of South African forces from Namibia and the confinement of SWAPO forces to a series of bases; supervising the South African civil police force; securing the repeal of discriminatory and restrictive legislation; arranging for the release of political prisoners and the return of exiles; and creating conditions for free and fair elections, which were conducted by South Africa under UN supervision. With military and civilian personnel from 109 countries, UNTAG managed the process by which Namibia moved from South African rule to sovereign independence (Howard 2008; Paris 2004; Dobbins et al. 2005).

A key innovation was the pre-eminence of the civilian component and the coordinating role of Special Representative of the Secretary-General Martti Ahtisaari. UNTAG's role in aiding not only with elections but also with drafting a new constitution for a sovereign, democratic Namibia presaged future efforts to use post-conflict peacebuilding activities to create democratic governments. Other innovations included the creation of regional and district offices with various political functions; the UN civilian police force; and a public information office that provided unbiased news to Namibians (Thornberry 2004: 377–79).

In tracing the origins of post-conflict peacebuilding ideas, it is important to place Namibia chronologically first in the late 1970s when the Contact Group plan was negotiated, approved by the Security Council, and implementation planning undertaken by the Secretariat. Its precedents should then be considered secondarily in the context of the late 1980s when actual implementation took place. By viewing

Namibia's precedents in this way, it is possible to see how the thinking about the UN roles in Namibia influenced efforts by the UN Secretariat to develop ideas for peaceful settlements of other conflicts during the 1980s. One such set of conflicts were those in Central America.

Root system no. 2: ending conflicts in Central America— a Secretary-General's initiative

In the mid- and late 1980s the UN was involved in searching for a peaceful end to the conflicts that wracked the Central American region from the late 1970s until 1992.[3] The conflicts involved the outside intervention of both superpowers as well as Cuba but had their roots in a long history of authoritarian rule, injustice, human rights abuses, and poverty. Initially, Secretary-General Javier Pérez de Cuéllar acted without any mandate from the Security Council, but in collaboration with the Organization of American States (OAS). He recruited Peruvian diplomat Alvaro de Soto and UN staff member Francesce Vedrell to explore the possibilities in Central America, authorizing them to draft an inventory of services that the UN and OAS could provide "to complement and consolidate...the Contadora framework" worked out by four Central American Countries (Pérez de Cuéllar 1997: 401). These became part of the Arias Plan of February 1987 and the Esquipulas II Declaration of August 1987 (de Soto 1999: 353–54). They included international verification of various undertakings including steps toward democratization and national reconciliation, separation of forces, demobilization and cantonment of combatants, observing borders, monitoring elections, and investigating allegations of human rights violations (Pérez de Cuéllar 1997: 400). Some of these drew from the Namibia plan. The major new elements were election monitoring and human rights investigation in sovereign states.

The Central American peace process, however, stalled until early 1989, when the foreign ministers of the five Central American countries requested that the Secretary-General draw up plans for an international military observer force and for the political aspects (i.e. elections and human rights monitoring) of the Arias Plan and Esquipulas II. These plans were endorsed by the Security Council in Resolution 537 (1989). The council subsequently endorsed the establishment of the International Support and Verification Commission (CIAV) and the UN Observer Group in Central America (ONUCA) as the military component.[4] The stage was set for implementation.

Nicaragua

In addition to monitoring elections, there were two major objectives relating to Nicaragua: verification of compliance with Esquipulas II and the demobilization, disarmament, repatriation, and reintegration of the Contra forces. In pursuing these three simultaneously, Pérez de Cuéllar notes:

> The United Nations entered new and unknown terrain ... More flexible limits were established for the involvement of the United Nations in domestic developments within a Member state. New approaches were developed for bringing governments into negotiations with insurgent groups. Perhaps most important, the United Nations accepted and carried out a responsibility to strengthen democratic institutions and to monitor compliance with accepted human rights norms within a country. Article 2, paragraph 7... gained a new and broad interpretation.
>
> Pérez de Cuéllar (1997: 404–5)

In short, the UN's involvement in Nicaragua set a number of important precedents. The military and civilian observer units were tiny by peacekeeping standards (260 unarmed military observers and 100 civilian observers). Nonetheless, ONUCA established "an important precedent for the control by the United Nations of developments *within* a country's sovereign jurisdiction—in this case, control over the utilization of its territory" (Pérez de Cuéllar 1997: 409).

For the UN to monitor Nicaragua's election process—a matter so clearly within a sovereign state's jurisdiction—it was necessary to surmount the hurdle of Article 2(7) of the UN Charter. Pérez de Cuéllar (1997: 412) noted that "Previous requests to monitor elections in Member states had always been refused, the United Nations having only assisted in the conduct of elections as part of the decolonization process. To oversee the electoral process in a sovereign state would take the United Nations into uncharted and, I thought, potentially treacherous waters." What made the difference in his mind and, importantly, for the General Assembly was the context—an international agreement the goals of which the Assembly had previously endorsed, the importance attached therein to international verification of electoral processes in the region, and the explicit request of the Nicaraguan government for observers.

Nicaragua's elections in February 1990 came off largely without hitch and were certified as "free and fair" by the international observers. For the UN, its role in election monitoring in Nicaragua initiated a practice that has become commonplace when, as former Secretary-General Pérez de Cuéllar (1997: 413) notes, "democracy is very widely accepted in principle as the desirable form of government."

The negotiations with the government of El Salvador and leaders of the Farabundo Martí National Liberation Front (FMLN) required still more innovative services from the UN to bring peace to that Central American country. Although there were negotiations in 1988 and 1989, only in January 1990 did the two parties declare their desire for peace and request assistance from Secretary-General Pérez de Cuéllar in mediating an agreement.

El Salvador

A major shortcoming of the 1987 Esquipulas plan laying out principles to address the Central American crisis was the absence of a credible way to bring in insurgent and other groups. In a further illustration of initiative, Secretary-General Pérez de Cuéllar had spoken out strongly to this effect in Guatemala in May 1989 and wrote to the Central American leaders in December 1989 immediately prior to a summit in Costa Rica saying that there was a "need for a visible and viable mechanism for bringing guerrilla groups into the effort to solve the conflicts in the region" (de Soto 1999: 358). His representative, Alvaro de Soto, in fact met with FMLN leaders, at their request, in order to discuss a possible UN involvement in ending the war in El Salvador and how verification could be implemented once a settlement was reached.

In describing the negotiations that ensued, de Soto (1999: 574) wrote: "The goal of this effort is not merely to stop the fighting, but to establish conditions that will ensure that once fighting stops, it will not resume ... because the root causes of the war are being addressed ... It follows that a cease-fire is not likely to come about without agreement on profound changes in El Salvador ... There is no such thing as instant peace in a conflict of this nature." In short, the negotiations were a much more ambitious undertaking than those in Nicaragua and involved a series of agreements over an 18-month period between May 1990 and January 1992. The scope of the final peace agreement was unprecedented, requiring the government of El Salvador to undertake reforms of its judiciary, military, and economy, to institute human rights protections and submit itself to a truth commission process. It has been called "a negotiated revolution" (Karl 1992: 150).

As Call (2002: 402–3) notes, "El Salvador's civil war was unusual in the degree to which human rights were a prominent element of the national discourse surrounding the war and of international debate about the war." The human rights provisions were the most distinctive part of the peace agreement and represented de Soto's solution to problems in negotiations on the armed forces.[5] The ideas for monitoring human rights violations, rebuilding the police force, reforming the judiciary, monitoring implementation, and a truth commission were drawn from human rights experts and de Soto himself. It was a clear case of agent discretion and independence being accepted by principals more concerned about getting a peace agreement than thinking through the precedents it would set. Regarding the truth commission, "No one," de Soto says, "had fundamental objections, but I have always wondered why the government agreed."[6] Commenting on its significance for the UN, Pérez de Cuéllar states in his memoir:

> It was and remains an intrusive operation, going far beyond the monitoring of elections. Since it was undertaken with the consent of the lawful government and of the other major elements in the political life of El Salvador, I do not believe it constituted an infringement on the country's sovereignty. It accords with those provisions of the UN Charter that clearly define respect for human rights as a matter of international concern.
> (Pérez de Cuéllar 1997: 426)

The UN's relative success in El Salvador is attributed to the "ripeness" of the situation at the time of the negotiations which enabled the UN to play a key role not only in negotiating the peace agreements themselves but also in the implementation process. Comparing the settlement, Doyle and Sambanis (2006: 205) note, however, "the Salvadoran parties were more prepared to make peace than the Cambodian parties ... [as a result] ONUSAL [the United Nations Observer Mission in El Salvador] was asked to do relatively less than UNTAC [the United Nations Transitional Authority in Cambodia]."

Root system no. 3: the UN's ambitious role in Cambodia

In October 1991 the Agreements on a Comprehensive Political Settlement of the Cambodia Conflict were signed in Paris with strong US, Soviet, Chinese, and Vietnamese support. The agreements ending the 20-year civil war in Cambodia "charged the UN—for the first time in its history—with the political and economic restructuring of a member state as part of the building of peace under which the parties were to institutionalize their reconciliation."[7]

The 1992 Security Council mandate for the UN Transitional Authority in Cambodia (UNTAC) called for up to 22,000 military and civilian personnel. They were to supervise the ceasefire and disarming and demobilizing forces, administer the country for an 18-month transition period, monitor the police, promote respect for human rights, assist in the return of 370,000 Cambodian refugees from camps in Thailand, organize the 1993 elections that returned civil authority to Cambodians, and rehabilitate basic infrastructure and public utilities. As then Secretary-General Boutros Boutros-Ghali observed, "Nothing the UN has ever done can match this operation."[8]

The idea for this expansive UN role is variously attributed to Australia's foreign minister Gareth Evans, Cambodia's Prince Sihanouk, and US Congressman Stephen Solarz (Evans 2001: 237, 240). Because parts of this role drew in the UN's then very recent experience in Namibia, Marrack Goulding (2002: 250), then Under-Secretary-General for political affairs responsible for peacekeeping, later characterized the UN's role in Cambodia as "the child of UNTAG."

In describing the Cambodian settlement and the UN's role, former Secretary-General Pérez de Cuéllar (1997: 465) comments, "For more than four decades, the Permanent Members had been reluctant to give the United Nations any independent authority at all. Now they seemed prepared to have it administer a whole country, a task that was, in my view, inappropriate and beyond its capacity." The UN's new responsibilities clearly took it into the uncharted terrain of a sovereign state's domestic jurisdiction. Small wonder that the Secretary-General had concerns on both legal and practical grounds.

The UN conducted what was widely viewed as a successful election in 1993, despite the boycott by the Khmer Rouge. It repatriated some 400,000 refugees and initiated a degree of civil political life (Peou 2002: 507). UNTAC was unable, however, to achieve a complete cease-fire, demobilize all forces, or complete its civil mission. It exercised only limited administrative or governmental functions. The election did not transform the country into a democracy. Cambodia, therefore, illustrates the difficulty of carrying out all aspects of a complex peacekeeping and peacebuilding mission.

Merging two root systems: *An Agenda for Peace*

When the members of the Security Council charged the Secretary-General with preparing a report on strengthening the UN's capacity for preventive diplomacy, peacemaking, peacekeeping, and dealing with areas of instability, there was no mention of peacebuilding. The puzzle is: who proposed the inclusion of peacebuilding and how those ideas were shaped. What emerges is the ability of a Secretary-General and senior officials in the UN Secretariat both to learn from past experience and to engage in conceptual innovation in the mode of autonomous agents.[9]

In early February 1992 Boutros-Ghali established a high-level working group composed of the five Under-Secretaries-General, with Petrovsky, Under-Secretary-General for Political Affairs, as Chair, to develop ideas for the report.[10] Alvaro de Soto, the Secretary-General's senior political advisor, recalls that Boutros-Ghali was reading an early draft during a joint trip to South America in April and asked, "Where is El Salvador in this? It doesn't fit the established categories. It's not peacemaking or peacekeeping. This is post-conflict and really is peacebuilding." De Soto says the term was coined by the Secretary-General in reference to "a set of political actions once the guns have fallen silent." It was, in de Soto's words, a moment of "conceptual epiphany" for Boutros-Ghali.[11] Virendra Dayal, who was also on the working group, relates, "Boutros said to me, 'I would rather like something on peace-building also. It is not included in the agenda. It is not included in the resolution itself, but it's a concept which I want to bring to the UN as my concept—peace-building'."[12] Working in secrecy, Dayal and former UN official James Sutterlin produced an entirely new draft which incorporated most of the ideas from the earlier one as well as additional suggestions.[13] The title came from a joint meeting of the two with Boutros-Ghali (Krasno 1998).

The section (VI) in *An Agenda for Peace* on "post-conflict peacebuilding" is relatively brief (five paragraphs), defining the latter as "comprehensive efforts to identify and support structures which will tend to consolidate peace and advance a sense of confidence and well-being among people." The text lists a number of tasks from disarming warring parties to monitoring elections, promoting human rights, and reforming governmental institutions to cooperative economic and social development projects. It also describes peacebuilding as "the construction of a new environment" and "the counterpart of preventive diplomacy." The report notes "a new requirement for technical assistance which the United Nations has an obligation to develop and provide when requested ... for the strengthening of new democratic institutions." Finally, the report avers, "the authority of the United Nations system to act in this field would rest on the consensus that social peace is as important as strategic or political peace."

The significance of *An Agenda for Peace* lay in the conceptual innovation that "post-conflict peacebuilding" represented and in the degree of change in the Secretary-General and other senior UN officials' thinking about the scope of the UN's legal authority for undertaking tasks within the domestic jurisdiction of member states. Thus, the report not only introduced post-conflict peacebuilding to UN lexicon and practice, but also endorsed a UN role in promoting and strengthening democracy and democratic institutions within member states (paragraph 81).

Following its presentation to the Security Council in late June 1992, the report was the subject of extensive discussion both by members of the council and by the General Assembly. Because these give us some insights into the reactions of UN member states—the principals in this story—they are examined further in the analytical section of the chapter.

Boutros-Ghali may have demonstrated the ability of the UN's Secretary-General to engage in an act of conceptual innovation, but he failed to follow through institutionally. "He issued no directive to give the lead to X in the Secretariat," de Soto notes. "DPKO [the Department of Peacekeeping Affairs] insisted on being in charge ... [and] many other agencies and programs jumped on the idea and came up with proposals for their own roles in peacebuilding."[14] Virendra Dayal has commented:

> I personally don't think that the fault was with *An Agenda* ... but I think in a way the exigencies of the moment pushed the UN, or the Secretary-General felt compelled, to go marching into situations for which neither the organization nor the membership were quite ready ... One can only say, "If only we had a little more time after *An Agenda for Peace* before all hell broke loose in the Balkans, and Somalia, and Rwanda, maybe we wouldn't have had such a rough time in dealing with these three horrible situations."[15]

The UN's ability or capacity to undertake complex peacebuilding operations and tasks depends on institutional developments—reforms in the Departments of Political Affairs and Peacekeeping, better coordination with various specialized agencies, and other key parts of the UN system. Some important reforms took place under Secretary-General Kofi Annan in the late 1990s and following the Brahimi Report in 2000. Only following the UN's 60th anniversary in 2005 was the Peacebuilding Commission approved to fill some of the institutional gap in managing post-conflict peacebuilding and thus far it has dealt only with a handful of situations.

Analyzing the roots of UN post-conflict peacebuilding

Both Boutros-Ghali and his predecessor, Javier Pérez de Cuéllar, demonstrated the ability of UN Secretaries-General to take initiatives.

The roles of Alvaro de Soto and Martti Ahtisaari in El Salvador and Namibia illustrate the flexibility and entrepreneurship that special representatives of the Secretary-General can also exercise. The Contact Group's proposal for a major UN role in Namibia as well as Australian Foreign Minister Gareth Evans' initiative in proposing that the UN provide transitional administration in Cambodia show how others can thrust new responsibilities on the UN which its Secretariat must then determine how best to carry out.

The types of decisions these individuals took can best be classified as boundary decisions, rule or norm-creating decisions, and operational decisions (according to the categories set forward by Cox and Jacobson (1973) and repeated in the Introduction to this volume). The boundary decisions in this case were decisions relating to state sovereignty and Article 2(7) of the Charter. They include decisions in the Namibian case to draft a constitution and to create conditions for free and fair elections; in the Nicaraguan case, to monitor elections in a sovereign state as part of an international agreement; in El Salvador to undertake human rights monitoring, organize a truth commission, and create a new national police force; in both Nicaragua and El Salvador, to bring insurgent groups into peace negotiations.

Norm-creating decisions included the decision to structure the Namibian transition in terms of steps toward creating a democracy, but several of the boundary decisions such as those on election and human rights monitoring also have programmatic elements. Certainly, the inclusion of peacebuilding in *An Agenda for Peace*—Boutros-Ghali's act of conceptual innovation—also should be classified as norm-creation inasmuch as it established a new standard for UN activity in the area of peace and security. Operational decisions in the Namibian case regarding the appointment of a special representative to coordinate the entire operation, both military and civilian components, set precedents that continue to this day.

How did UN members react to these decisions? Overall, the steps that led to the UN's post-conflict peacebuilding role have generated surprisingly little controversy. Secretaries-General have historically been quite conscious of the limits of their authority and autonomy. This has been particularly true with respect to crossing the line into matters within states' domestic jurisdiction. Pérez de Cuéllar, trained in international law, was quite sensitive to this. His memoir (Pérez de Cuéllar 1997) makes clear his concern about the limits Article 2(7) placed on what the UN could do in dealing with matters within the domestic jurisdiction of sovereign states. That included election monitoring, human rights monitoring, and other intrusive tasks. Of course, he was not alone. Reading the earliest resolutions of the General Assembly on "Enhancing the Effectiveness of the Principle of Periodic and Genuine Elections" in 1988, 1989, and 1990 is to see clearly the reservations and opposition of many countries to what they perceived as outside interference and compromise of the principle of non-intervention (Beigbeder 1994: 100–2). In de Soto's view, there was "a turning point ... a 'Dag moment' when people said 'let Javier handle it.' It was an indefinable yet propitious moment and Pérez de Cuéllar dared."[16] In PA theory terms, this qualifies as discretion granted by the principal (the General Assembly and Security Council in this case). Given the sensitivity of Secretaries-General to the limits of their autonomy and discretion, however, the "daring" part is also key here.

The statements of member states concerning *An Agenda's* section on peacebuilding provide some insight into the reactions of "the principals" to the new concept. Two small, developing countries, Bahrain and the Maldives, joined a number of developed countries (and long-time peacekeeping contributors) to endorse the concept. Bahrain, for example, called it "an important element in the future role of the Organization." The Maldives said, "Greater emphasis on the use of preventive diplomacy and post-conflict peace-building measures has never been more urgent" (United Nations Secretary-General 1999a). Many developing countries welcomed the report's reaffirmation of the state as the foundation of the UN and of the necessity of applying the Charter's principles (including the principle of non-intervention) "consistently" not "selectively" (United Nations Secretary-General 1999b). In sum, the remarks of member states evidence no opposition to post-conflict peacebuilding except insofar as interventions might contravene important Charter principles and/or resulted from decisions in the Security Council that were dominated by a few countries.

Were the actions, then, of the two UN Secretaries-General, their special representatives, and other senior UN officials contrary to what might be expected if we assume they are only diligent agents of member states, within the bounds of expected levels of discretion? Or were they showing an unexpected level of initiative?

The relevant factors for Secretary-General initiatives are the size and complexity of the UN as an organization, the UN's maturity, the personal characteristics of Secretaries-General and others, and the requirements of diplomacy to forestall or end conflicts. Briefly, the scope of the UN's operational activities means that the Secretariat plays a key role not only in carrying out those activities, but also in taking initiatives and making decisions. Bureaucracies matter, as Barnett and Finnemore in *Rules for the World* (2004) show. They articulate a set of points that help frame the analysis of the UN Secretary-General and Secretariat as important actors within the UN system and, in the context of this study, important actors with degrees of autonomy and authority.

> IOs [international organizations] do not simply pursue the mandates handed to them. Indeed, they probably could not do so, even if they wanted to … IO staff must transform these broad mandates into workable doctrines, procedures, and ways of acting in the world … States may actually want autonomous action from IO staff. Indeed, they often create an IO and invest it with considerable autonomy precisely because they are neither able nor willing to perform the IO's mission themselves. Once in place, the staff of IOs take their missions seriously and often develop their own views and organizational cultures to promote what they see as "good policy" or to protect it from states that have competing interests. And, of course, neither states nor IO staff can predict new challenges, crises, and exigencies that force IO staff to change their missions and their existing policies.
>
> (Barnett and Finnemore 2004: 5)

Because the UN is a 68+-year-old, it is certainly a "mature" organization and, hence, there is a long series of precedents for Secretary-General initiatives and independence. For example, Dag Hammarskjöld, the second Secretary-General (1953–61), demonstrated the Secretary-General's efficacy as an agent for peaceful settlement of disputes with his successful 1954–55 mediation of the release of eleven US airmen under the UN command in Korea who had been imprisoned by Communist China, which was then excluded from the UN. Hammarskjold's successor, U Thant articulated his view of the Secretary-General's independent role stating, "The Secretary-General must always be prepared to take an initiative, no matter what the consequences to him or his office may be, if he sincerely believes that it might make the difference between peace and war" (quoted in Young 1967: 284). As noted earlier, Pérez de Cuéllar set a precedent for including insurgent groups such as the Nicaraguan Contras and Salvadoran FMLN in peace negotiations. In short, over time, successive Secretaries-General have taken advantage of opportunities for initiatives, applied flexible interpretations of Charter provisions, and sought mandates from UN organs as necessary.

The personalities of individuals affect their willingness and ability to act independently and take initiatives. The Secretary-General's role historically has been most prominent with respect to matters of international peace and security where the Secretary-General is well placed to serve as a neutral communications channel and intermediary. Hence, the fourth factor—the character of an issue—is closely tied to personal characteristics in this case. As we have seen, member states have generally not constrained Secretaries-General from acting independently even when Security Council or General Assembly resolutions have condemned a party to a dispute. This is consistent with Hawkins and Jacoby's (2006: 200, italics in original) expectations regarding the strategies of IOs as agents, namely that "independent agent *strategies* can influence a *principal's decision to delegate* and the *agent's level of autonomy.*"

The authority and autonomy of the UN Secretary-General

The UN's Secretary-General and Secretariat have often been viewed as what might be called "classic agents" whose actions are guided and constrained by the provisions of the UN Charter and the mandates of UN organs which function as "collective principals" (Lyne *et al.* 2006). Yet, Article 99 of the Charter authorizes the Secretary-General "to bring to the attention of the Security Council any matter which in his opinion may threaten the maintenance of international peace and security." It thus provides the basis for Secretary-General autonomous authority and an important agenda-setting, problem-framing or problem-constituting role. In fact, both the Secretary-General and the UN's bureaucracy command authority to shape agendas and the ways issues are framed. Autonomy and discretion are important Secretary-General resources. Hawkins *et al.* (2006b: 8) define the former as "the range of independent action that is available to an agent and can be used to benefit or undermine the principal." Discretion is defined as "a grant of authority that specifies the principal's goals but not the specific actions the agent must take to accomplish those objectives ... Greater discretion often gives agents greater autonomy, but not always."

Secretary-General Javier Pérez de Cuéllar

In his 1989 report to the General Assembly, Pérez de Cuéllar noted the proliferation of new peacekeeping operations and the fact that some were "mainly concerned with the situation within the boundaries of a State ... [and included] a wider range of tasks, including the supervision of elections and monitoring of the implementation of complex agreements." He cautioned about the need for "a rigorous analysis of what the United Nations can, and cannot, do, and how it should do it" (Pérez de Cuellar 1991: 224–25). The 1990 report recognized that "To build peace and create conditions of stability in the world of the 1990s will require innovative responses to security challenges of a type radically different from those encountered in the past."

Through his exercise of the authority, autonomy, and discretion of the Secretary-Generalship and through those whom he empowered as his special and personal representatives, it is clear that Pérez de Cuéllar deserves considerable credit for fostering a number of new ideas about UN post-conflict peacebuilding roles. Given the lack of opposition to Pérez de Cuéllar's initiatives and new ideas, for example, his behavior exemplifies two of Hawkins and Jacoby's (2006: 207) four methods for agents: reinterpreting rules in "incremental steps [that] can then sum in substantial ways" and behaving "in ways that accord with the substantive preferences of principals but that develop procedural innovations." His successor exemplified still another of these methods when he articulated new ideas in *An Agenda for Peace*: namely, "Agents can ask principals to formalize a practice that agents have developed informally."

Secretary-General Boutros Boutros-Ghali

Boutros Boutros-Ghali pushed the boundaries of the Office of Secretary-General still further, but with a very different personality and personal style. Also trained in international law with a background as both scholar and diplomat, having served for many years as Egypt's Minister of State for Foreign Affairs, he was the first African Secretary-General. He took office at the peak of post-Cold War optimism regarding new roles for the UN and had the misfortune to serve as the conflicts in Somalia, Bosnia, and Rwanda engulfed the UN, leading to heavy criticism of the organization. As an activist Secretary-General, Boutros-Ghali prodded the member states, including the United States, to take action in Somalia when he thought they were paying more attention to the conflict in the Balkans. However, his arrogance contributed to an antagonistic relationship with the United States that led to his defeat for a second term in 1996—a principal's ultimate constraint on an errant agent.

Other entrepreneurial UN officials

In analyzing the roots of UN post-conflict peacebuilding, two other senior UN officials stand out. These are individuals who have seen beyond traditional diplomacy to end conflicts through negotiated agreements to envision and create new roles for the UN in building the foundations for long-term peace by addressing the roots of conflicts, especially those within states. They are Alvaro de Soto and Martti

Ahtisaari. As senior UN officials, they could be seen as agents either of the Secretary-General or the Security Council (or both). In the Central American and Namibian cases each exercised considerable independence and entrepreneurship. Particularly in El Salvador, de Soto's proposals on human rights monitoring, overseeing a truth commission, rebuilding the police and judiciary were evidence of his autonomy and norm-enterprenership.

Because of the unusual circumstances in which the plan for Namibia was negotiated and then put on hold for a decade, Martti Ahtisaari, who was appointed Special Representative in 1978, had almost a decade to design the operational plan for UNTAG. During that time, he and others visited Namibia and South Africa, met with SWAPO leaders in exile and South African officials in both Pretoria and Windhoek. One might be inclined to view Ahtisaari as an agent or expert authority with a certain amount of "slack" or discretion. Lise Howard (2008: 66), however, indicates that Ahtisaari pushed for "a massive active intervention by UNTAG to change the political climate in the country." Once the operation began, he expanded the number of district and regional offices to increase interaction with the local population and developed a public information program to "raise public consciousness of what UNTAG was doing and why, as he had 'essentially to build up and rely upon a moral authority rather than direct executive or enforcement powers'" (Howard 2008: 69). Howard credits Namibia's success in part to field-level organizational learning.

The "power" and expert authority of the UN Secretariat

The previous section focused on the delegation of discretion to IOs, and the ways in which entrepreneurial officials have used that discretion to shape the direction of their organization, but where did those ideas come from? How did officials know what they wanted? Principal-agent theory largely leaves that question under-defined, assuming that agents work for their own personal benefit or for the material benefit of their organization. However, social constructivism is a particularly valuable tool for analyzing how the UN as an organization and bureaucracy played a role in the evolution of post-conflict peacebuilding, and for understanding the formation of the interests of officials in certain situations. For example, social constructivism illuminates Boutros-Ghali's role in providing leadership for new thinking within the UN on peace and security, democratization, and development with the publication not only of *An Agenda for Peace*, but also *An Agenda for Development* (1995), and *An Agenda for Democratization* (1996). In coining the phrase post-conflict peacebuilding and insisting that it be included in *An Agenda for Peace* as well as in a number of areas, Boutros-Ghali exemplified the UN Secretary-General's role as a "norm entrepreneur" (Johnstone 2007).

Key to the development of new norms and ideas were the 30+ years of experience that the UN Secretariat gained in translating vague mandates for peacekeeping operations into reality. As it developed experience, it came to command expert authority in this field, one element of what Barnett and Finnemore (2004) term the "power" of IO bureaucracies. Security Council resolutions authorizing peacekeeping missions continued to be brief and vague until the 1990s when the Council moved to drafting detailed mandates. This left considerable discretion to the Secretariat for interpretation, albeit within a strongly shared understanding of the political nature of traditional peacekeeping missions.

Clearly, ideas were important to the evolution of the UN's role and at least some of these (though little is known about alternatives that got rejected) were accepted and institutionalized (Hiebert 2007: 460), creating new expectations about the types of roles the UN could play in post-conflict situations. As Wendt (1999: 114) notes, "Ideas can have causal effects independent of other causes like power and interests. However, ideas also have constitutive effects, on power and interest themselves." As either key individuals such as Alvaro de Soto and Martti Ahtisaari or others within the UN Secretariat elaborated peacebuilding ideas that got accepted and institutionalized, those ideas had their own causal effects and contributed to the UN developing new capacities such as electoral assistance that made possible subsequent choices by the Security Council and the Secretariat itself—i.e. more peacebuilding operations, more electoral assistance, and other tasks such as rebuilding police and judiciary functions. The expansion of tasks, however, required innovation, adaptation, and new types of expertise, some of which the UN bureaucracy was slow to acquire—consistent with classic bureaucratic behavior (Barnett and Finnemore 2004: 34–41).

Unquestionably, these operations would not have taken place and at least some of the ideas would not have flourished if it had not been for a permissive and changing international environment. The key question for this analysis is how individuals and their thinking were affected by system change.

Changes in the international system

In his 1987 *Report on the Work of the Organization*, Secretary-General Pérez de Cuéllar expressed eloquently the then unfolding awareness that major changes were underway in the international system. He wrote:

> Over the past year, in the midst of continuing regional strife and economic and social hardship, there have been occasions in which a great solidarity among nations was evident in addressing serious problems with global implications, within the multilateral framework of the United Nations ... It is as if the sails of the small boat in which all the people of the earth are gathered had caught again, in the midst of a perilous sea, a light but favourable wind.
>
> (Pérez de Cuéllar 1991: 136–37)

Yet neither the Secretary-General nor anyone else could foresee at the time how extensive those changes would be over the next several years. With the end of the Cold War, the Permanent Five (P-5) members of the Security Council were working together in ways they never had previously. There was clearly a new attitude toward the possibilities for the UN. In addition, the so-called third wave of democratization was then sweeping Latin America, Asia, and Africa; it would burst forth in Eastern and Central Europe in the fall of 1989. There was a growing sense that democracy could even be considered an emerging "right." Even before Nicaragua's 1990 election, there were requests from other countries for assistance in monitoring elections. At the 1990 General Assembly, President George H.W. Bush called for the creation of a UN election assistance unit.

Cedrick Thornberry captured some sense among those in the UN Secretariat of the significance of the events unfolding:

> In November 1989, after Namibia's elections, our Windhoek office was besieged by senior diplomats. They had been told by their capitals to visit UNTAG and beg, borrow or steal UNTAG's "Namibia Blueprint" for study, and for future peace-support operations. As the dust settled after the Berlin Wall had crashed down, there was a widespread conviction that, as the grip of rival super powers loosened, the organized international community would soon be required to provide answers to some difficult geo-strategic questions.
>
> (Thornberry 2004: 375)

Indeed, they would! Thus, the Cold War's end was marked not only by events in Central and Eastern Europe in late 1989 and 1990, but also by developments at the UN. When the Soviet Union joined the United

States and all but two of the other members of the Security Council to support a series of strong UN responses to Iraq's invasion of Kuwait in 1990 it was clear that an old order had ended and a new, as yet undefined, order would begin to take shape, one in which the UN would have a central place.

Yet, systemic changes cannot explain the emergence of new ideas and new roles, nor identify the agents responsible for those ideas and roles. To reiterate a point from Barnett and Finnemore (2004: 5), "Neither states nor IO staff can predict new challenges, crises, and exigencies that force IO staff to change their missions and their existing policies." The systemic changes associated with the Cold War's end helped to create an environment in which new ideas and roles became possible with the leadership and initiative of key individuals as well as the support of the UN's member states. Those changes also contributed to the spate of new, nasty conflicts, humanitarian crises, and failed states that by the mid-1990s led to the UN being overburdened by the Security Council's mandates for complex peacekeeping and peacebuilding operations for which the UN organizationally was ill-equipped and for which members were not forthcoming with adequate resources.

Conclusion

Without the initiatives and leadership of key individuals within the UN, it is likely that the outcomes in Namibia, Nicaragua, El Salvador, and Cambodia would have been quite different; it is probable that the conflicts would have dragged on longer and that if or when settlements were reached they might not have laid the same conditions for long-term, if not always perfect, peace. Without these initiatives, it is also probable that the ways in which other conflicts in the 1990s and more recently were addressed would have been substantially different since there would have been no precedents for the UN to undertake various military and civilian post-conflict peacebuilding tasks—whether in Bosnia, Kosovo, Sierra Leone, Democratic Republic of Congo, East Timor, or elsewhere.

It is important to note, however, that all of the steps taken were ad hoc in nature—initiatives devised to deal with particular situations. There was never a coordinated effort to create new capabilities and very little incentive (let alone time in most situations)—except in the Namibian case—to plan how to undertake new tasks, even after *An Agenda for Peace* was published. Ad hoc-ism continued. As an agent, the UN Secretariat is not the European Union (EU) Commission, and dealing with threats to peace and security is considerably different than promoting development or creating a common market. Pollack (1994) notes that the EU Commission was explicitly empowered by the founding Treaty of Rome to play an "engine" role in driving the process of integration and historically its initiatives have been key to that process. Still, this case study has illuminated the entrepreneurship of two Secretaries-General and other key officials as agents and norm entrepreneurs in what might be termed a "process of task expansion" not totally dissimilar from that in the EU.

The case study has also shown how both principal-agent theory and social constructivism are valuable to understanding these acts of conception in the development of post-conflict peacebuilding. Using a PA theory "lens" enhances our understanding of the UN as an independent actor in international politics and the nature of the UN Secretary-General, other senior officials, and the Secretariat's agency in exercising autonomy, discretion, and, occasionally, independence. Social constructivism illuminates the evolution of ideas and the organizational innovation and learning that took place over time as the Secretariat, with the acquiescence if not active support of member states, built on the precedents and knowledge gained during the decolonization process to develop new roles in organizing and monitoring elections, transitional administration, rebuilding institutions such as police and judiciary, monitoring human rights, and other tasks now associated with post-conflict peacebuilding.

Finally, this case study also illuminates the importance of organizational capacity for assessing the nature of conflict situations and meeting peacebuilding needs. If there is one lesson from more than 20 years of post-conflict peacebuilding, it is that no one size fits all. Each operation is unique because each conflict has distinctive characteristics and roots. It took time for the UN as an organization to learn this lesson, however. Although the Secretariat's capacity has since been enhanced, it remains limited. This raises serious questions about whether the UN truly has the institutional capacity—or can develop it—and whether the member states have the political will to support the long-term processes of peacebuilding in a number of very different and very difficult conflict situations that exist in today's world. A subject for further research is why the incentives—either for the Secretariat or for the Security Council members—have not been sufficient by now to do a better job of institutionalizing peacebuilding capabilities.

Notes

1 The Oral History Interview of Boutros Boutros-Ghali on 5 May 2001 in The Complete Oral History Transcripts of *UN Voices*, CDROM (New York: United Nations Intellectual History Project, 2007: 37). This particular interview was conducted in French. Translation by the author.

2 For discussion of this terminology, see Charles T. Call and Elizabeth M. Cousens, "Ending Wars and Building Peace: International Responses to War-Torn Societies," *International Studies Perspectives* 9, no. 1 (2008): 1–21.
3 For an account of the process, see Jack Child, *The Central American Peace Process, 1983–1991: Sheathing Swords, Building Confidence* (Boulder, Col.: Lynne Rienner, 2002). The ad hoc Contadora group was composed of Colombia, Mexico, Panama, and Venezuela.
4 The Security Council's decision on the commission is contained in a letter dated 28 August 1989 from the President of the Council to the Secretary-General (S/20856); the decision to create ONUCA is contained in Resolution 644 of 7 November 1989. The Council's approval of the proposed observer group composition was also conveyed via a presidential statement later in November 1989 (S/20892). It was the custom at that time for details of peacekeeping mandates to be contained in letters or reports of the Secretary-General to the Security Council, documents that are not readily accessed.
5 Author interview with Alvaro de Soto, 18 February 2008.
6 Author interview with Alvaro de Soto, 18 February 2008.
7 Michael W. Doyle, *UN Peacekeeping in Cambodia: UNTAC's Civil Mandate* (Boulder, Col.: Lynne Rienner, 1995), 26.
8 United Nations *Chronicle*, "The 'Second Generation': Cambodia Elections 'Free and Fair,' but Challenges Remain" (November–December 1993), 26.
9 This story has been pieced together from various sources including interviews in the UN Intellectual History Project, interviews by the author, and the unpublished biographical sketch of former senior UN official James S. Sutterlin entitled "A Quiet Revolutionary."
10 The five were: Vladimir Petrovsky, USG for Political Affairs; James Jonah, a second USG for Political Affairs; Marrack Goulding, USG for Peacekeeping; Jan Eliasson, USG for Humanitarian Affairs; and Richard Thornberry, USG for Administration and Management.
11 Author interview with Alvaro de Soto, 18 February 2008.
12 The Oral History Interview of Virendra Dayal (15 July 2002), in The Complete Oral History Transcripts of *UN Voices*, CDROM (New York: United Nations Intellectual History Project, 2007).
13 Sutterlin is credited by Krasno with the concept of peace enforcement as well as the inclusion of a recommendation that governments conclude Article 43 agreements and the idea of preventive deployment.
14 Author interview with Alvaro de Soto, 18 February 2008.
15 The Oral History Interview of Virendra Dayal (15 July 2002), in The Complete Oral History Transcripts of *UN Voices*, CDROM (New York: United Nations Intellectual History Project, 2007), 40.
16 Author interview with Alvaro de Soto, 18 February 2008.

Bibliography

Barnett, Michael, *Eyewitness to a Genocide: The United Nations and Rwanda* (Ithaca: Cornell University Press, 2002).
Barnett, Michael and Raymond Duvall, eds, *Power in Global Governance* (New York: Cambridge University Press, 2005).

Barnett, Michael and Martha Finnemore, *Rules for the World: International Organizations in Global Politics* (Ithaca: Cornell University Press, 2004).

—— "The Power of Liberal International Organizations," in *Power in Global Governance*, ed. Michael Barnett and Raymond Duvall (New York: Cambridge University Press, 2005), 161–84.

Barnett, Michael, Hunjoon Kim, Madalene O'Donnell, and Laura Sitea, "Peacebuilding: What is in a Name?" *Global Governance* 13, no. 1 (2007): 35–58.

Beigbeder, Yves, *International Monitoring of Plebiscites, Referenda and National Elections: Self-determination and Transition to Democracy* (Dordrecht, Netherlands: Martinus Nijhoff, 1994).

Berry, Ken, *Cambodia—From Red to Blue: Australia's Initiative for Peace* (Canberra: Unwin Hyman, 1997).

Boutros-Ghali, Boutros, *An Agenda for Peace: Preventive Diplomacy, peacemaking and peace-keeping* (New York: United Nations, 1992).

Call, Charles T., "Assessing El Salvador's Transition from Civil War to Peace," in *Ending Civil Wars: The Implementation of Peace Agreements*, ed. Stephen John Stedman, Donald Rothchild, and Elizabeth M. Cousens (Boulder, Col.: Lynne Rienner, 2002), 383–420.

Call, Charles T. and Elizabeth M. Cousens, "Ending Wars and Building Peace: International Responses to War-Torn Societies," *International Studies Perspectives* 9, no. 1 (2008): 1–21.

Checkel, Jeffrey T., "Tracing Causal Mechanisms," in Audie Klotz, ed. "Moving Beyond the Agent-Structure Debate," *International Studies Review* 8, no. 2 (2006): 362–70.

Cox, Robert and Harold K. Jacobson, *The Anatomy of Influence* (Cambridge: Cambridge University Press, 1973).

de Soto, Alvaro, "Ending Violent Conflict in El Salvador," in *Herding Cats: Multiparty Mediation in a Complex World*, ed. Chester A. Crocker, Fen Osler Hampson, and Pamela Aall (Washington: United States Institute for Peace, 1999), 345–85.

de Soto, Alvaro and Graciana del Castillo, "Obstacles to Peacebuilding," *Foreign Policy* 94 (1994): 69–93.

Dobbins, James, Seth G. Jones, Keith Crane, Andrew Rathmell, Brett Steele, Richard Teltschik, and Anga Timilsina, *The UN's Role in Nation-Building: From the Congo to Iraq* (Santa Monica, Calif.: Rand Corporation, 2005).

Doyle, Michael W., *UN Peacekeeping in Cambodia: UNTAC's Civil Mandate* (Boulder, Col.: Lynne Rienner, 1995).

Doyle, Michael W. and Nicholas Sambanis, *Making War & Building Peace: United Nations Peace Operations* (Princeton: Princeton University Press, 2006).

Evans, Gareth, "Cooperative Security and Intrastate Conflict," *Foreign Policy* 96 (1994): 3–20.

—— "Achieving Peace in Cambodia," in *A Century of War and Peace*, ed. T.L.H. McCormack, Michael Tilbury, and Gillian D. Triggs (The Hague: Kluwer Law International, 2001), 235–46.

Franck, Thomas M., "The Emerging Right to Democratic Governance," *American Journal of International Law* 86, no. 1 (1992): 46–91.

Goulding, Marrack, *Peacemongers* (London: John Murray, 2002).

Hawkins, Darren G. and Wade Jacoby, "How Agents Matter," in *Delegation and Agency in International Organizations*, ed. Darren G. Hawkins, David A. Lake, Daniel L. Nielson, and Michael J. Tierney (New York: Cambridge University Press, 2006), 199–228.

Hawkins, Darren G., David A. Lake, Daniel L. Nielson, and Michael J. Tierney, eds, *Delegation and Agency in International Organizations* (New York: Cambridge University Press, 2006a).

——"Delegation under Anarchy: States, International Organizations, and Principal-Agent Theory," in *Delegation and Agency in International Organizations*, ed. Darren G. Hawkins, David A. Lake, Daniel L. Nielson, and Michael J. Tierney (New York: Cambridge University Press, 2006b), 3–38.

Hiebert, Heidi, "On Stage: Agent, Structure, and Improvisation: A Review," *International Studies Review* 9, no. 3 (2007): 457–67.

Howard, Lise Morjé, *UN Peacekeeping in Civil Wars* (New York: Cambridge University Press, 2008).

International Court of Justice, *Legal Consequences for States of the Continued Presence of South Africa in Namibia (South-West Africa) Notwithstanding Security Council Resolution 276 (1970)*, Advisory Opinion, ICJ Reports 16, 1971.

Johnstone, Ian, "The Secretary-General as Norm Entrepreneur," in *Secretary or General? The UN Secretary-General in World Affairs*, ed. Simon Chesterman (New York: Cambridge University Press, 2007), 123–38.

Karl, Terry Lynn, "El Salvador's Negotiated Revolution," *Foreign Affairs* 71, no. 2 (1992): 147–64.

Karns, Margaret P., "Ad Hoc Multilateral Diplomacy: The United States, the Contact Group, and Namibia," *International Organization* 41, no. 1 (1987): 93–123.

Klotz, Audie, ed., "Moving Beyond the Agent-Structure Debate," *International Studies Review* 8, no. 2 (2006): 355–81.

Klotz, Audie and Cecelia Lynch, "Translating Terminologies," in Audie Klotz, ed. "Moving Beyond the Agent-Structure Debate," *International Studies Review* 8, no. 2 (2006): 356–62.

Knight, W. Andy, "Democracy and Good Governance," in *The Oxford Handbook on the United Nations*, ed. Thomas G. Weiss and Sam Daws (New York: Oxford University Press, 2007), 620–33.

Krasno, Jean, "The Quiet Revolutionary: A Biographical Sketch of James S. Sutterlin," ACUNS publication, 1998.

Leatherman, Janie, William DeMars, Patrick D. Gaffney, and Raimo Väyrynen, *Breaking Cycles of Violence: Conflict Prevention in Intrastate Crises* (West Hartford: Kumarian Press, 1999).

Lyne, Mona, Daniel L. Nielson, and Michael J. Tierney, "Who Delegates? Alternative Models of Principals in Development Aid," in *Delegation and Agency in International Organizations*, ed. Darren G. Hawkins, David A. Lake,

Daniel L. Nielson, and Michael J. Tierney (New York: Cambridge University Press, 2006), 41–76.

Marcoux, Christopher S., "Autonomous Actors or Faithful Agents? A Review," *International Studies Review* 9, no. 2 (2007): 262–64.

Paris, Roland, "Broadening the Study of Peace Operations," *International Studies Review* 2, no. 3 (2000): 27–44.

——*At War's End: Building Peace after Civil Conflict* (New York: Cambridge University Press, 2004).

——"Post-Conflict Peacebuilding," in *The Oxford Handbook on the United Nations*, ed. Thomas G. Weiss and Sam Daws (New York: Oxford University Press, 2007), 404–26.

Peou, Sorpong, "Implementing Cambodia's Peace Agreement," in *Ending Civil Wars: The Implementation of Peace Agreements*, ed. Stephen John Stedman, Donald Rothchild, and Elizabeth M. Cousens (Boulder, Col.: Lynne Rienner, 2002), 499–530.

Pérez de Cuéllar, Javier, *Anarchy or Order: Annual Reports 1982–1991* (New York: United Nations, 1991).

——*Pilgrimage for Peace: A Secretary-General's Memoir* (New York: St Martin's Press, 1997).

Pollack, Mark A., "Creeping Competence: The Expanding Agenda of the European Community," *Journal of Public Policy* 14, no. 2 (1994): 95–145.

——"Delegation and Discretion in the European Union," in *Delegation and Agency in International Organizations*, ed. Darren G. Hawkins, David A. Lake, Daniel L. Nielson, and Michael J. Tierney (New York: Cambridge University Press, 2006), 165–96.

Power, Samantha, *Chasing the Flame: Sergio Vieira de Mello and the Fight to Save the World* (New York: Penguin, 2008).

Stedman, Stephen John, Donald Rothchild, and Elizabeth M. Cousens, eds, *Ending Civil Wars: The Implementation of Peace Agreements* (Boulder, Col.: Lynne Rienner, 2002).

Sutterlin, James S., *The United Nations and the Maintenance of International Security: A Challenge to be Met* (Westport, Conn.: Praeger, 2003).

Thornberry, Cedric, *A Nation is Born: The Inside Story of Namibia's Independence* (Windhoek, Namibia: Gamsberg Macmillan, 2004).

United Nations, *The Blue Helmets: A Review of United Nations Peace-Keeping* (New York: UN Department of Public Information, 1996).

United Nations Secretary-General, *An Agenda for Peace—The Report of the Secretary-General*, unpublished excerpts related to specific recommendations and/or chapters of the report, from the statements made in the General Debate at the forty-seventh session of the General Assembly, 21 September–8 October 1999a.

——*An Agenda for Peace—The Report of the Secretary-General*, unpublished excerpts from the statements made in the forty-seventh session of the General Assembly debate on agenda item 10: Report of the Secretary-General on the Work of the Organization, 9, 14, 26–27 October 1999b.

United Nations Security Council, *Principles Concerning the Constituent Assembly and the Constitution for an Independent Namibia* (UN document S/15287), 12 July 1982.

——*Statement by the President of the Security Council* (UN document S/23500), 31 January 1992.

——*Statement by the President of the Security Council* (UN document S/PRST/2001/5), 20 February 2001.

Urquhart, Brian, "The Tragedy of Lumumba," *The New York Review of Books* 48, no. 15 (2001): 34–35.

Weinberger, Naomi, "Civil-Military Coordination in Peacebuilding: The Challenge in Afghanistan," *Journal of International Affairs* 55, 2 (Spring 2002): 245–74.

Wendt, Alexander, *Social Theory of International Politics* (New York: Cambridge University Press, 1999).

Young, Oran R., *The Intermediaries: Third Parties in International Crises* (Princeton, NJ: Princeton University Press, 1967).

Part II
Intergovernmental organizations

3 The anatomy of autonomy
The case of the World Bank
Susan Park and Catherine Weaver

- Explaining IO agency: bridging the rationalist-constructivist divide
- The tale of Wolf I: greening the bank and the "cancer of corruption"
- The tale of Wolf II: integrating the environment and crusading on anticorruption
- Conclusion

Nowhere is the debate over the meaningful role of international organizations (IOs) more hotly debated than in relation to the World Bank (hereafter "the bank"). From the very beginning of environmental consciousness within international relations in the 1970s, the World Bank has been considered both a leader and a laggard in establishing environmentally sustainable development. Meanwhile, the bank has been prominent in current debates amongst development theorists and practitioners over the relationship between corruption and socioeconomic development. The indisputable leader in the provision of global development aid and the production of development knowledge, the bank's leadership in the IO community in articulating and implementing the sustainable development and anticorruption agendas has been subject to extensive analysis and criticism, both external and internal to the organization. The aim of this chapter is to unpack the World Bank's ability to act independently in devising approaches to these development issues. Both agendas were firmly championed and radically revised by the bank's past two presidents, James Wolfensohn (Wolf I in bank parlance) and Paul Wolfowitz (Wolf II). Comparing the bank's troubled efforts to promote and operationalize the sustainable development and anticorruption agendas provides meaningful comparison for exploring the complex nature of IO autonomy and agency. In particular, the chapter reveals how any notion of an IO's autonomy and agency that treats the IO as a unified actor is prone to incomplete and inaccurate conclusions regarding how we discern and describe an IO's "self-directed action."

In short, in order to understand the limits to and the contours of the bank's ability to mainstream its sustainable development and anticorruption agendas, we must examine what the introductory chapter of this volume describes as the internal workings and the international forces shaping IO autonomy and agency. Just as international organizations are "open systems" invariably driven by the resource dependencies and political relationships with actors and forces in their external environments, they are also (especially in instances of large service organizations) complex bureaucracies whose intended actions are often impeded by all kinds of internal collective action problems and other sundries related to organizational histories, structures, staff dynamics and cultures. A pragmatic approach to understanding IO autonomy and agency must thus be willing to forego theoretical parsimony and be ready to delve into empirically rigorous work that unpacks multiple levels of analysis. The focus on specific organizational cases embraced in this volume is therefore not only appropriate, but necessary, in this endeavor.

In the context of this book's objective to explain the "self-directed" actions of IOs, we use the case study of the World Bank and its sustainable development and anticorruption agendas to investigate the opportunities and constraints on autonomy and agency. More specifically, we take the point made in the Introduction to this volume, regarding the role of individuals in organizations. As it points out, "IOs are made up of individuals, and both a PA approach and a constructivist one show us the importance of understanding the interests, beliefs, and roles of the individuals who make up IOs. When we talk, then, about IOs 'acting' or showing a level of independence, we are of course talking about decisions made by the staff of those IOs, or, at other times, state delegates, acting in ways not foreseen by those who had sent them there." Indeed, this argument is consistent with prior insights regarding the influence of "executive heads" within IOs (Cox 1969) and their ability to carve out room for autonomy and agency and to determine courses of action in the IO as a whole. Significantly, unlike most studies of IO autonomy that focus on the conditions for IO discretion vis-à-vis external principals (namely member states), we wish to examine the opportunities and constraints on the autonomy and agency of an IO's executive head vis-à-vis *both* the external environment of the IO and the internal bureaucracy.

This "mid-level" analysis is critical to solve the empirical puzzles faced by large service organizations like the World Bank. This chapter seeks to explain how and why James Wolfensohn was able to *successfully* promote sustainable development and to introduce and champion the anticorruption agenda during his 10 years at the bank (1995–2005) compared to the limited reorientation of the sustainable development agenda under Paul Wolfowitz and his largely *failed* attempts to aggressively mainstream the anticorruption agenda (July 2005–May 2007). In the case of James Wolfensohn (Wolf I), the story is one of an executive head navigating between Scylla and Charybdis in his attempt to promote sustainable development and anticorruption in relatively hostile external and internal environments. Wolfensohn, with an important cadre of internal staff advocates, ultimately managed to make significant strides in integrating both agendas into bank discourse, where sustainable development became fully operationalized and as the anticorruption rhetoric vaulted from "prohibition to prominence." Yet he simultaneously faced several constraints on his ability to mainstream his preferred policies and shortfalls in operational mainstreaming persisted.

In comparison, Paul Wolfowitz (or Wolf II) entered the bank at a moment when the sustainable development agenda had lost momentum while the anticorruption rhetoric had, by and large, been fully embraced in Bank research and operational policy but had yet to be put into practice in a meaningful way. Eager to effect change, Wolfowitz sought to speed up the mainstreaming of both agendas. He collapsed the vice-presidencies of environmentally sustainable development and infrastructure to create a one-stop shop for sustainable development mixing environmental overseers with infrastructure staff. Environmentalists cried foul over the structural weakening of the bank's internal environmental advocates. More damagingly, Wolfowitz used heavy-handed loan cancellations and ratcheted up internal investigations of fraud and other unethical behavior amongst the World Bank staff to mainstream anticorruption. The external and internal backlash was immediate: principal member states, donors and borrowers alike suddenly started to exercise much more oversight and control over the bank's anticorruption agenda to reign in Wolfowitz's behavior while a normally staid staff openly revolted, publicly opposing the new anticorruption policies.

The contrast could not be more profound. The World Bank had been the centre of the maelstrom of environmentally sustainable development under Wolfensohn, compared to the muted environmental challenge under Wolfowitz, despite the latter's actions. On anticorruption, what slow and uneven "self-directed action" the bank had achieved under the Wolfensohn era suddenly faced the threat of reversal or regression in response to Wolfowitz's efforts to accelerate the bank's anticorruption work. In these instances, what we clearly observe are the *limits* of self-directed action in sustainable development and anticorruption at different points in time. As detailed throughout the chapter, this can only be understood through recognizing shifts in the external and internal environments in which the Wolfs were operating and their ability to effect change: Wolfensohn faced division between principals and environmentalists over sustainable development but was able to navigate agreement on environmental issues, while building support for his anticorruption agenda. In comparison, weakening external support for the sustainable development agenda muted opposition to Wolfowitz's dismantling of the bank's environmental apparatus while his lack of political skills squandered support for the anticorruption agenda, revealing the divisions between principals (and staff). As a result, while internal and external dynamics limit the ability of autonomous IOs, the political skill of the executive head is also central to explanations of independent IO action. Similarly it will be shown that the preferences of external principals are an important explanatory factor, as is the nature of the organizational culture and staff preferences—the executive head had to face these constraints, and success depended on his skill or lack thereof. These factors help to explain the level of success of self-directed adaptation in one case, and the relative failure in the other.

Explaining IO agency: bridging the rationalist-constructivist divide

To unpack the bank as an empirical case study, we employ insights from two approaches to contemporary IO theory: principal-agent models and constructivist organizational theory. There is a clear utility of these approaches with respect to the central question of the scope conditions for the "self-directed action" of an IO executive head. These are articulated below and are then applied in the empirical analysis in the following section.

The principal-agent model

The principal-agent (PA) model delineates relationships embedded in complex delegation chains that affect the ability of an IO leader to pursue their own agenda. Who is the principal and who is the agent is contingent on which part of the delegation chain is under examination. In most instances, scholars examine the IO as agent and the principal(s) as member state(s) (Hawkins *et al.* 2006; Pollack 1997, 2003). The degree of discretionary behavior enjoyed by the (assumed) self-interested rational agent is dependent upon four broad interrelated factors: 1 the proximity and strength of principal preferences regarding the substance and direction of the agent's behavior in a given issue area; 2 the degree of preference heterogeneity among collective or multiple principals (with greater heterogeneity allowing wily IO agents to play-off principals with competing interests); 3 the costs to principals of employing available oversight and control mechanisms to direct agent behavior (e.g. financial leverage, accountability mechanisms and the presence of third-party watchdogs who might provide effective oversight and fire alarm roles); and 4 the degree of information asymmetry, meaning the extent to which agents can effectively hide what they are doing from principals either due to the complex nature of the agent's activity (asymmetry derived from the agent's expertise), or weaknesses in accountability rules and oversight mechanisms.

At the same time, PA models can delve further down the delegation chain to examine principal-agent relationships within IOs that are particularly useful here in terms of explaining the extent to which executive heads may realize their preferences. For example, PA models may examine the question of how an executive head, as the principal, might reform an organization, by utilizing oversight and control mechanisms to direct the behavior of management and staff as the agents (Nielson et al. 2006). Once again, the ability of the principal to shape agent behavior to produce organizational outcomes in line with their preferences is contingent upon the degree to which organizational staff share the executive head's preferences or effectively take advantage of information asymmetries to escape oversight and control.

The PA model is useful for the purposes of discerning the scope for autonomous agency for the World Bank president. In the first instance, James Wolfensohn and Paul Wolfowitz, as bank presidents, are the agents. They are both empowered and constrained by the bank's relationship with its principal member states. The World Bank enjoys a considerable degree of autonomy from its political masters, but remains in part financially dependent upon donor states for capital subscription replenishments (especially in the bank's soft-loan agency of the International Development Association, or IDA) and upon borrower states for loan demand (endangered by the decline in middle income-country borrowing). As a result, the president, as the bank's primary interlocutor, must appear responsive to the preferences of the bank's diverse principals, although he might also enjoy some discretion, particularly when those principals are divided.

Simultaneously, however, we must look further down the delegation chain to understand room for autonomous agency. In terms of realizing preferences with respect to institutionalizing new agendas, the executive head faces the dilemma of redirecting the behavior of the bank's management and staff. The preferences of the president (here the principal) and the staff (the agents charged with operationalizing new agendas) may differ. Executive heads must assess the use of oversight and other sanctions to control staff particularly in complex bureaucratic hierarchical organizations like the World Bank which has nearly 15,000 staff members and an entrenched organizational culture.

Constructivist organizational theory

In contrast to the rationalist PA model, the constructivist organizational approach illuminates many of the "non-material" factors shaping the discretionary action of executive heads in IOs. Externally, this captures the influence of international norms or prevailing "logics of appropriateness" with respect to shifts in IO actions that accord with ideas such as sustainable development or anticorruption. These ideas exist beyond IOs such as the World Bank, but can only be understood within international development in relation to how they have been taken up by prominent IOs and enacted by them (Park and Vetterlein 2010).

Internally, the constructivist approach also draws attention to the limits to agency posed by organizational culture (Weaver 2008). This draws on the specific culture of each organization, and cannot be generalized in the way the PA model can. For example, when reforms pushed by President Wolfensohn on anticorruption and sustainable development ran up against the bank's "approval culture," he was unable to bring about swift changes to how the bank does business (Nielson et al. 2006). However, this does not mean that change is not possible. By the time of Wolf II's arrival in 2005, staff had largely added environmental concerns where required into their workloads (Park 2010) and the culture of the bank had moved from corruption as taboo to one where addressing corruption was embraced. Operationalizing the anticorruption agenda nonetheless remained a difficult task. Examining the importance of the bank's external environment and organizational culture is therefore crucial to understanding the potential for, and extent of, self-directed action within the World Bank. These are analyzed through the bank's two Wolfs, next.

The tale of Wolf I: greening the bank and the "cancer of corruption"

Greening the World Bank

By the time James D. Wolfensohn took over as the ninth president of the World Bank in 1995 the institution was facing large-scale opposition to its operations. There was growing discontent amongst many civil society actors—including nongovernmental organizations (NGOs), the United Nations (UN), and practitioners in developing countries—who focused on the way the bank's lending, and structural adjustment in general, was harming the environment of developing countries. While the three previous presidents, Alden Clausen, Barber Conable and Lewis Preston, had each been forced to take (limited) steps towards engaging with these critics as a result of high-profile opposition and powerful principal support (read US and European donors), it was President Wolfensohn who attempted to act as a "circuit breaker" halting large-scale opposition to the bank from environmental activists.

Wolfensohn's appointment was to revitalize the World Bank through what became known as the "Strategic Compact" (Nielson *et al.* 2006). Part of his agenda was to reconfigure the way the World Bank engaged with issues like sustainable development. One of the first and most important acts in this respect was his immediate decision in August 1995 to cancel the Arun III dam and road building project in Nepal. Opposition to the bank's funding of dams in developing countries was reaching its zenith and the bank was on the back foot in demonstrating the merits of any dam funding (McCully 2001). Arun III was significant in being the first complaint filed by concerned citizens with the bank's new accountability mechanism, the Inspection Panel (established under President Preston in the fall out from the Narmada dam campaign). Civil society, as well as bank donor and borrower principals watched anxiously to see how the Panel would operate. Precisely because of entrenched positions of environmentalists, staff and principals, Wolfensohn unilaterally decided to cancel the project before the Panel could announce its findings: politically a decision either upholding the bank's operations or finding bank staff wanting would be seen as either giving in to environmentalists or covering up for staff.

Wolfensohn's next move was to institute more farreaching changes into the bank's operations. Wolfensohn elevated the environment within the bank under a newly created Vice-Presidency for Environmentally and Socially Sustainable Development (ESSD), giving unprecedented power and visibility to the green agenda, as well as rapidly increasing loans for environmental projects and the number of environmental specialists within the bank (Wade 1997; Nielson *et al.* 2006). In 2001 this culminated with the bank-wide strategy paper for the environment, which aimed to mainstream environmental considerations throughout the bank's operations and set the bank's agenda for the next decade (World Bank 2001).

Under Wolfensohn the bank was scrutinized in terms of its attempts to incorporate environmental concerns within its operations. The 2001 strategy paper recognized three impediments to improving the bank's environmental practices: that the bank's environmental commitments often outpaced their ability to deliver; that environmental practices were yet to be mainstreamed throughout the organization; and that sustainable development was "still evolving" in borrowers (World Bank 2001: xix; Park 2010). Environmental reviews undertaken by the bank in 1997 and 2002 recognized improvements but a 2001 report by the bank's Operation Evaluation Department (OED) stated that the lack of environmental mainstreaming was "disturbing" in lagging behind the bank's compliance efforts (Liebenthal 2002: vii, 8, 13, 19–20). The report specifically blamed the bank's "culture and structure" as producing "an unnecessarily adversarial relationship between compliance with safeguards and the promotion of environmental sustainability" (Liebenthal 2002: xvi).

The upshot was the view by environmentalists that the bank was merely being greenwashed, while staff necessarily grappled with the additional burden of environmental compliance within the pressure to lend organizational culture. Further measures were introduced to ensure staff compliance and managerial oversight through the creation of the Quality Assurance Group (QAG) and a compliance unit (QACU). While recognizing the need for further mainstreaming, environmentalists and powerful principals (again the US and European donors) viewed the policy and compliance changes within the bank as positive. A 2008 Independent Evaluation Group (IEG, formerly the OED) investigation of the bank's environmental record between 1990 and 2007 now recognizes that the bank had a "better record" in relation to the environmental performance of projects from the mid-1990s to 2007 than in the pre-1995 period (World Bank 1997; Green and Raphael 2002: 8; World Bank 2003, 2008: 28, 155, f/n 32). Irrespective, environmentalists and donors continued to maintain pressure on the bank to further mainstream environmental issues as it had articulated in the 2001 environmental strategy paper.

What this sections shows, however, is that Wolfensohn was able to rapidly scale up the bank's environmental activities as well as institute new monitoring and oversight mechanisms for staff. This radical restructuring of the organization's environmental activities was able to be instituted because it was demanded by environmentalists and backed by powerful principals. Moreover, as a new executive head, Wolfensohn was able to act as a circuit breaker in halting the entrenched opposition of environmentalists to the bank's operations and bank recalcitrance to being more environmentally aware. Despite these significant achievements, however, his efforts remained constrained by the organizational culture of the World Bank that would continue to overshadow the bank's environmental reform efforts.

Cleaning the World Bank

Up to the early 1990s the bank was in a "prohibition era" regarding governance and anticorruption work (World Bank 2006a), largely due to perception of external opposition to the overtly political nature of fighting corruption as well as a deep clash with the apolitical and technical norms of the bank's economistic culture (Weaver 2008: 92–139; Miller-Adams 1999; World Bank Operations Evaluation Department 2001a). As a result, the anticorruption agenda essentially lay dormant until 1995, when James D. Wolfensohn was appointed. Staff members were not encouraged to address issues of corruption, and were sometimes discouraged from doing so (World Bank Operations Evaluation Department 2001b: 7). Wolfensohn unilaterally criticized management's previous resistance to tackling corruption. In a famous speech given at the bank's annual meeting in Hong Kong in 1996, Wolfensohn denounced the "cancer of corruption" and proclaimed governance and corruption problems a priority.

Foreshadowing Wolf II's challenges, Wolfensohn's desire to push the anticorruption agenda was constrained by contrary pressures from inside and outside the organization. In 1999, Wolfensohn confessed:

> When I came to the Bank nearly five years ago, I was told we did not talk about corruption. Corruption was political. It was the "C-word." ... But it soon became very clear to me corruption and the issue of press freedom, while they may have a political impact, are essential economic and social issues, both key to development. *So we redefined corruption, not as a political issue but as an economic and social issue* ... in redefining the issue in this way our shareholder countries reacted very favorably
>
> (Wolfensohn 1999: A39, emphasis added)

Wolfensohn's support appeared to be the tipping point for the anticorruption agenda. According to Sebastian Mallaby, Wolfensohn broke through the "intellectual dam" at the bank, and "before long the Bank's research machine was gushing with new literature acknowledging the link between corruption and development" (Mallaby 2004: 176). Systematic attention by senior management to broader issues of good governance, especially corruption, became evident after 1996. This was in large part due to Wolfensohn's appointment of Joseph Stiglitz as chief economist, a scholar famous for his work in institutional economics and an open critic of the bank's past structural adjustment policies (Stiglitz 2000, 2002). Stiglitz contributed to a dramatic shift in the research focus of the bank, including the hiring of many new specialist staff.

These internal staff changes in turn ushered in a series of major publications indicating that governance and anticorruption issues had become part of the bank's official discourse. In particular, the 1997 *World Development Report: The State in a Changing World* presented for the first time the bank's embrace of good governance within its most widely read publication. That same year, the bank published an official anticorruption strategy entitled *Helping Countries Combat Corruption: The Role of the World Bank*. By 1997, governance concerns had gained enough traction intellectually to gain entry into the bank's broader analytical and operational work. Governance was given an "institutional home" and an increase in the number of staff working on governance issues, thus setting the stage for mainstreaming.

During the 1997 Strategic Compact reorganization, a thematic group on Poverty Reduction and Economic Management (PREM) was created and endowed with a number of staff keenly interested in governance and anticorruption issues.[1] PREM includes a separate division for analytical and operation work on the public sector, headed by its own director and sector board. By 2001, the staff of this group (PRMPS) reached 15 specialists. In addition, the expansion of the legal department of staff helped to broaden the governance agenda. Management also planned to increase the number of financial managers and procurement specialists to help identify misuse of funds in projects (United States General Accounting Office 2000: 14).

The World Bank's 1998 *Assessing Aid* report provided a powerful economic rationale for the bank's governance and anticorruption agenda. It argued that the effect of aid on economic growth was neutral or even negative until countries with "good" economic management were statistically distinguished from those with "poor governance" (on good governance see Isham *et al.* 1995, 1997; Keefer and Knack 1997; Kaufmann *et al.* 2000; Burnside and Dollar 2000; Knack 2000; Collier and Dollar 2000, 2001; Kaufmann *et al.* 2003; World Bank 2000). This study represented a watershed moment for the governance agenda, which resonated strongly with external critiques of aid effectiveness, including from the US administration. *Assessing Aid* articulated a specific economic justification for allocating aid selectively on the basis of governance performance.

Also in 1998, Wolfensohn set up (at his own initiative) an internal investigative unit to audit loans for evidence of corruption and a 24-hour telephone hotline to allow staff and members of the public to report corruption. Simultaneously, the bank established a "sanctions committee" to respond to the hotline information and punish companies and individuals found guilty of bribery and graft. In 2000 Wolfensohn turned this committee into the Department of Institutional Integrity, the primary function of which is now to investigate allegations of corruption in bank-funded contracts (debarring guilty companies from future contracts) as well as suspected corruption inside the bank (United States GAO 2000: appendix 1; Finer 2003). By 1999 it appeared that the bank was firmly embracing the anticorruption agenda and taking the necessary steps to translate the agenda into action.

Yet the anticorruption agenda faced incongruent goals, impeding the translation of Wolfensohn's 1996 commitment to "zero corruption" into a clear set of enforced policies and practices. Most notably, attention to corruption challenged the bank's apolitical mandate. Managers feared that if they raised issues of graft and bribery, they would provoke client governments' opposition during a key period in which demand for loans (especially in middle-income countries, or MICs) was already in decline (Pound and Knight 2006). Also, operational staff lacked effective tools for actually implementing Wolfensohn's plans for fighting corruption. In some instances, management and staff thought that corruption and poor governance were in fact defining attributes of underdevelopment. Therefore, withholding or canceling loans to countries that failed to meet standards for good governance and corruption seemed counter to the bank's very purpose. According to Dennis de Tray, the bank's former country director for Indonesia, canceling or withholding projects and loans out of concerns about corruption would "hurt those the Bank is supposed to be helping … If we are not careful in the way we deal with corruption, we will set up even sincere and committed leaders for failure … " (de Tray 2006).

In short, political opposition from borrowers, cultural fissures within the bank, and pragmatic concerns prevented the full embrace of Wolfensohn's anticorruption agenda. Meanwhile, there was a noticeable shift from relatively diffuse to more concerted external efforts to monitor and shape the bank's anticorruption activities. On a systemic level, the political and normative environment by the late 1990s changed to favor addressing corruption aggressively. Major international organizations, such as the Organisation for Economic Co-operation and Development (OECD), the UN, the Council of Europe, and the Organization of American States (OAS) were passing anticorruption conventions. International NGOs started to focus their multilateral development bank (MDB) campaigns around high-profile cases of corruption, especially in very visible and symbolic infrastructure and extractive industry projects. These NGOs likewise continued to lobby the US Congress, as they had done consistently (and successfully) in the past to push the environmental agenda. This time, the NGOs engaged the US power of the purse to push for new legislation that would more carefully monitor and sanction MDB activities to counter corruption.

Public statements by former bank insiders cast further doubt on the ability and willingness of the bank to act upon the new anticorruption mandates. In July 2003 Peter Eigin, a former World Bank staffer and founding president of Transparency International (the corruption watchdog organization with which the bank works closely) stated that, "It's very hard to change a large organization like the World Bank, and they're still working through this ... They were pretty bad, and allowed [corruption] to become a major problem. There's been a total change in policy, but to change from policy to total implementation is a long way to go" (Finer 2003). Former insider William Easterly further maintained that "if the client is important enough geostrategically or one they want to cultivate in the long run, [the World Bank] will continue lending to them, despite long histories of corruption. They continue forcing loans down that pipe" (quoted in Finer 2003).

The Government Accountability Project (GAP), an NGO, then published a report (2004) on the bank's internal whistleblower policies that expressly contradicted Wolfensohn's rhetoric about the effectiveness of bank mechanisms for reporting corruption in project lending and internal operations. In one case President Wolfensohn personally retaliated against a whistleblower in the financial sector vice-presidency and convinced the vice-president to withdraw his complaints (Government Accountability Project 2004: 25).

GAP lambasted what it saw as the "Trojan horse whistleblower laws" and a pervasive "culture of secrecy" that contradicted the bank's image as an open, transparent, and accountable institution. In the same period, the US Senate Foreign Relations Committee, chaired by Senator Richard Lugar (R-Ind.), launched a series of hearings on corruption in the MDBs, which included testimonies from academic experts, NGOs, and the US executive director to the World Bank (Rich 1994; Bapna 2004; Boswell 2004; Brookins 2004). As a result, Congress passed the Leahy-McConnell Amendment as part of the Consolidated Appropriations Act of 2004 (Section 581). The amendment requires the US Treasury Secretary to report to Congress on the MDBs' progress toward greater transparency and accountability.

However, critics remained unconvinced that these new laws had compelled substantial change in the bank's behavior, particularly in its internal whistleblower policies. GAP, for instance, notes that "MDB whistleblowers still proceed at their own risk ... [US] Treasury praises long-pending Bank promises of still-secret plans to create whistleblower policies. Secret transparency reforms are an oxymoron" (Government Accountability Project 2005). By the end of Wolfensohn's presidency in May 2005, doubt still lingered about the sincerity with which the bank pursued the identification and punishment of corruption. On the surface, the evidence was encouraging. In February 2005 the bank claimed that more than 2,000 cases of fraud and corruption (internally and in bank-funded projects) had been investigated and closed since 1999 (World Bank 2005). Public-sector lending took over the largest share of bank loans, at over 20 percent in 2006, and the bank's governance indicators were prominently used in new performance-based aid allocation systems (World Bank 2006b). Between 2002 and 2004 all Country Assistance Strategy (CAS) papers were reported to "explicitly or implicitly" recognize corruption concerns. By 2005 governance assessments were mandated in PRSPs and the diagnosis section of all CAS reports (World Bank 2006c).

At the same time, groups within the bank were beginning to talk quite bluntly about the ineffectiveness of governance and anticorruption reforms. A Sector Strategy Implementation Update came to a sobering conclusion about the all-important CAS papers:

> ... while all CASs comply ... the majority of CASs deal with governance in a perfunctory manner and still do not adequately assess the developmental or fiduciary risks or corruptions ... [T]hree reasons for this are weak commitment of governments to governance reform, disincentives for Bank country teams to analyze more fundamental institutional and political drivers of corruption and poor governance, and the tendency to compartmentalize and treat governance as a sector rather than as a cross-cutting theme.
> (World Bank 2006d: 29)

Likewise, the bank's Independent Evaluation Group reported limited changes in the governance perception indicators in countries where the bank had been funding public-sector reforms since the mid-1990s (World Bank Independent Evaluation Group 2006: 34).

To conclude, Wolfensohn was able to introduce the anticorruption agenda into the bank through framing it as an economic development issue, thus moving the organization into previously prohibited areas of development lending and research. This demonstrates the "self-directed" action of an executive head of an IO. Wolfensohn promoted the anticorruption agenda with new staff, institutional resources and high-profile research on the effects of corruption on development. However, even with evidence of organizational learning inside the bank, and increased support throughout Wolfensohn's tenure for more stringent policies on corruption from donor principals and other sources outside the bank, staff interviewed in Washington in mid-2005 still perceived significant bureaucratic resistance and cultural inertia to mainstreaming the anticorruption and governance agenda. Resources remained thin, and staff who report directly to country directors still believed that they faced conflicting priorities in an institution that espoused commitment to punishing corruption while continually rewarding "client responsiveness" and large loans.[2] Thus, by 2005, despite a seeming convergence in external pressure and an observable effort internally to develop feasible mainstreaming strategies, there continued to be critical goal incongruence inside the bank that inhibited genuine mainstreaming.

The tale of Wolf II: integrating the environment and crusading on anticorruption

In examining the limits to and the contours of the World Bank's autonomy and agency, this chapter has thus far examined the ability of the executive head, the bank's president, to integrate sustainable development and to introduce an anticorruption agenda. The chapter identified how President Wolfensohn was able to create a new dynamic in the bank's response to improve its environmental practices, and was able to introduce anticorruption as an acceptable area of Bank research and lending. Powerful donor and NGO support, along with tacit client state acceptance was crucial for the progress of both agendas. While Wolfensohn elevated both agendas through his 1997 Strategic Compact reorganization of the bank (providing both areas with new funding and staff), the organization's culture continued to inhibit the full realization of sustainable development and the mainstreaming of the anticorruption agenda.

In comparison, the tale of Paul Wolfowitz is significantly different from that of Wolf I. Despite bold changes undertaken by both presidents across both environment and corruption arenas, Wolfowitz's actions were seen as damaging to the organization, its staff, and its member states. Specifically, Wolfowitz reshuffled the bank's environmental operations and attempted to ramp up the bank's anticorruption efforts. While NGOs opposed the former, the latter was roundly criticized by donor and client states as well as NGOs, where Wolfowitz's specific actions were seen as ideologically driven and hypocritical. As demonstrated below, it was as much the (lack of) political skills of the President, as well as external and internal resistance that removed Wolfowitz from office and left the bank in a state of suspended animation in its sustainable development and anticorruption agendas. These are detailed next.

Greenwashing the World Bank?

Two prominent issues were already evident prior to Wolfensohn's departure: the rise of MICs, which were increasingly able to borrow from private capital markets specifically for infrastructure and development projects (with high demand for energy production), and the emphasis on "owner-driven" development by donor principals which emphasized developing country ownership of programs and projects to improve their outcomes (Hunter 2008: 477; World Bank 2006a: 21). The World Bank's sustainable development agenda rapidly became one of the areas identified by management as requiring reform to meet these new challenges.

First, President Wolfowitz aimed to improve the bank's bottom line, which had been hit by a decline in income formerly generated by repayments from MIC loans. Middle-income countries, it was perceived, could finance development projects from private capital markets without the red tape and lengthy project timelines associated with the bank (Birdsall 2006). Inside and outside the bank many began to argue that the "hassle factor" associated with complying with the World Bank's safeguard policies, along with the lengthy wait and cost of bank loans, made bank loans increasingly unattractive (Birdsall 2006). As a result, the bank began to review whether the mandatory suite of safeguard policies introduced under Wolfensohn should remain the basis for the bank's environmental strategy.

Second, and integral to bank management debates over the role of the bank in sustainable development, was the dramatic increase in energy needs for developing countries. The rise of MICs was associated with booming economies and a thirst for energy production. The World Bank saw this as a return to infrastructure development, at which it excelled but from which it had shied away in the late 1990s. By early 2006, there was a noticeable push back by the World Bank against northern based NGOs that had been so successful in pushing through the environmental agenda in the first place.[3] The signal to environmentalists and borrowers was clear: the bank was committed to infrastructure lending above all. Robert Calderisi, a former World Bank staff, suggested that Wolfowitz was under pressure from the United States to cut the bank's environmental work (Calderisi 2006). As noted in the section on anticorruption below, Wolfowitz sealed himself off from the bank's senior management and appointed a cadre of former US government Republican advisors. Ideologically, at least, there was a correlation between Wolfowitz and the US administration in opposing environmental issues.[4]

In response to perceived borrower interests, Wolfowitz instituted new changes within the bank's environmental apparatus. He merged the ESSD network with Infrastructure (INF) in June 2006 to create the Sustainable Development Network (SDN), under the INF vice-president, Katherine Sierra (Powell 2006). The merger aimed to streamline operations in order to improve the bank's responsiveness to borrowers. Significantly, the merger removed the bank's senior management environmental specialist (Seymour 2006). Environment staff also noted how two of the largest groups within the bank, with completely distinct internal cultures, were merged.[5] The restructure was unsuccessfully challenged by Washington-based NGOs, as it was clear that changes were needed to improve the bank's activities and it was not automatically the case that integrating compliance and operation efforts would undermine the integrity of the bank's environmental work.

As a result, despite Wolfowitz's short tenure at the helm of the bank, one might consider that he had little impact on the sustainable development agenda, merely allowing the unfolding of programs already in train. In some respects this is accurate. However, his decision to restructure the ESSD into the SDN and to return to "high-risk, high-reward" lending remains significant because it revealed the circumscribed power of environmentalists to challenge the bank's behavior. Further, it demonstrated that the bank under Wolfowitz was more willing to return to previous practices in funding traditional, environmentally risky development projects rather than grappling with finding sustainable alternative energy sources in light of the threat of climate change.[6] If anything, Wolfowitz's bank revealed a lack of leadership in helping developing countries shift to low-carbon economies while accelerating economic growth and reducing poverty.[7] In this respect, despite acting with the support of the bank's principals, Wolfowitz left an unfavorable imprint on the bank's sustainable development agenda.

Staining the World Bank?

In comparison to his limited efforts on sustainable development, Wolf II, much like his charismatic predecessor, immediately signaled his commitment to championing the anticorruption agenda when he took over the reins in May 2005. His first acts were dramatic. Between November 2005 and the end of June 2006, he canceled or withheld loans on at least nine major loans or debt-relief packages due to concerns over corruption or poor governance in the recipient countries.[8] He openly critiqued weaknesses in the Department of Institutional Integrity under the previous administration, revealing a large number of backlogged cases and promising resolutions as quickly as possible. Wolfowitz also espoused a commitment to allocating more staff resources toward governance and anticorruption work, both in project lending and in internal oversight functions such as financial disclosure and auditing of staff activities.

Nonetheless, in February 2006, the sincerity of Wolfowitz's commitment to weeding out corruption was called into question by external critics, once again over internal bank oversight and whistleblower protection policies. The controversy concerned a report written by American University law professor Robert Vaughn and commissioned by Wolfensohn. The report, submitted in June 2005, was intended to address previously identified weaknesses in existing whistleblower protections. Yet Wolfowitz refused to release it to the public despite repeated calls to do so by NGOs and the US Senate Finance Committee chairman, Charles Grassey.

In February 2006 the Global Accountability Project leaked the report with scathing statements regarding the bank's rhetoric about transparency and accountability (Bretton Woods Project 2006b; Mekay 2006; Pound and Knight 2006). In late March 2006 the Senate Foreign Relations Committee launched another set of hearings, with testimonies from development experts from think tanks, NGOs, and the US Treasury. In April 2006 Edward Pound and Danielle Knight published an article in *US News & World Report*.[9] They reiterated many points of prior critics on the lack of transparency, pervasive secrecy, under-resourced anticorruption units, and pressures to lend. Yet the bureaucratic hesitancy to follow Wolfowitz's lead may also have stemmed from something else, according to Pound and Knight: "Inside the Bank ... Wolfowitz has a bit of a rebellion on his hands. Internal critics complain that he is focused only on corruption. Development, not corruption busting, they say, is the principal mission of the Bank. The resentment runs deep" (Pound and Knight 2006; Williamson 2006).

On 11 April 2006 Wolfowitz delivered his most prominent speech on anticorruption, in Indonesia, where he had formerly served as US ambassador. The speech was reminiscent of Wolfensohn's cancer-of-corruption speech, but it was remarkable in two ways. First, it directly accused the Indonesian government, once a darling of the aid community for its economic growth record, of high levels of corruption. Breaking with the clientelistic culture of the bank, Wolfowitz clearly implied that even the most important borrower governments would not be immune from criticism. Second, Wolfowitz gave a strong public endorsement to the governance and anticorruption agenda as key priorities for the bank. He implicitly admitted that the gap between rhetoric and action still persisted, and outlined a clear plan for mainstreaming the agenda. Wolfowitz proclaimed that the bank would invest in more professional expertise to address corruption and hire more governance specialists to work directly in operations. He also discussed the construction and deployment of "anticorruption" teams to country offices and changing project design procedures to make them better equipped to address "the incentives and opportunities to fight corruption right from the start."

After the speech, in comments to reporters, Wolfowitz made a third notable remark. He announced his intention to take on directly the bureaucratic environment of the bank, where vested interests, incentive structures, norms, and operational habits had previously stymied efforts to enforce the governance and anticorruption agendas. Wolfowitz specifically targeted the bank's disbursement imperative and approval culture, arguing that he wanted managers to know that they would be rewarded "as much for saying no to a bad loan as for getting a good one out the door" (quoted in Dugger 2006). In making this statement, Wolfowitz set himself up for tackling one of the most daunting challenges facing any leader of a large organization: changing its culture.

One of the most remarkable results of Wolfowitz's aggressive push for the anticorruption agenda in 2006 was the visible pressure from numerous sources to pull back. At heart was not a rejection of the agenda itself, but a widespread discontent with the seemingly punitive and arbitrary methods employed by Wolfowitz (Marquette 2003, 2007). Contrary pressures also came from borrower governments, which resisted governance-based conditionality as an intrusion on their sovereignty, and also from a core group of European donor states, which objected to Wolfowitz's heavy-handed methods for pushing the anticorruption agenda. In particular, the European donors perceived Wolfowitz's choice of loan cancelations or suspensions (decisions largely made without consultation with the staff or board) to be suspiciously aligned with US geopolitical objectives and selectively applied without due process (Stiglitz 2007: 82). European donors and several borrowing member states also questioned the bank's mandate in this area, and (like staff) the desirability of punishing corruption through withdrawing funds (Benn 2006).

These growing concerns resulted in a formal request in April 2006 by the Board of Executive Directors for a new governance and

The case of the World Bank 109

anticorruption (GAC) strategy paper, to be presented at the 2006 annual meetings in Singapore. Most saw the insistence on a new GAC strategy as a desire on the part of the member states to "see the method in [Wolfowitz's] meddling" and to exercise greater board oversight (Behar 2007a). The "bruising" reception received by the GAC strategy paper during the September 2006 annual meetings in Singapore reflected the growing divide on the bank's board between the major donor states (European states versus the United States and Japan). The Development Committee's six-hour debate signaled that essential disagreements on the means of pursuing the GAC agenda had not been resolved by the new strategy paper (Bretton Woods Project 2006b).[10] China, backed by other important Asian borrowers, threatened to halt future borrowing if Wolfowitz did not rein in his anticorruption investigations or his plan to circumvent corrupt governments by developing direct relations with civil society (Behar 2007b, citing an internal email written by Hsiao-Yun Elaine Sun, the bank's China manager).

Under certain circumstances, a divide among principals like the one above would increase the room for maneuver of the president of an organization like the World Bank, but Wolfowitz faced other challenges. Inside the bank, rebellion was also brewing. Increasingly, operational staff were noting the hypocrisy of Wolfowitz's crusade, reflecting sentiments widely expressed by nearly half of the 3,200 participants in the external consultation surrounding the draft GAC strategy paper between November 2006 and February 2007. The ability of the staff to promote good governance and anticorruption reforms was undermined by the widespread perception that Wolfowitz (and by association, the bank) failed to practice what he so ardently preached. Wolfowitz himself attained the presidency through a US-controlled selection process completely lacking in transparency, meritocracy, and accountability. Moreover, Wolfowitz was not only a product of cronyism, but a perpetuator of it. Since coming to office, he had appointed, awarded generous salaries, and granted unprecedented authority to several "special advisors" from a narrow pool of conservative Republican loyalists.[11]

For staff, the worst offense was the appointment of Susan Rich Folsom to the directorship of the Department of Institutional Integrity (INT). Folsom was selected by Wolfowitz for the job despite an open search for the position that produced a short list of highly qualified candidates (she was not seen as qualified by the selection committee). Once in the position, staff members note, she used the INT to engage in an "internal witch-hunt" to root out corruption among staff, as opposed to investigating corruption in procurement contracts and in countries.[12] This contributed to the growing distrust and resentment of staff and management toward Wolfowitz. Thus, even before the scandal broke regarding Wolfowitz's involvement in the secondment, promotion, and salary deal for Shaha Riza, there was already a clear sense that Wolfowitz did not have the moral high ground from which to push the good governance and anticorruption agenda.

The governance and anticorruption strategy paper was formally approved by the board on 21 March 2007. The final draft reflects several of the concessions Wolfowitz was forced to make, thus demonstrating the limits of his ability to realize his preferences regarding bank actions (World Bank 2007; Bretton Woods Project 2007). Specifically, the GAC paper made it clear that the bank would remain engaged in countries with serious corruption problems, suspending loans only in "exceptional circumstances" with board approval. This was more in keeping with the practices of the bank, and unlike the rapid and dramatic suspensions Wolfowitz had enacted during his short tenure.

Conclusion

What emerges from this comparison of two presidents and two very different agendas within the World Bank? Most prominently, the comparison shows a sense of the limits on the self-directed action of IOs at the level of the autonomy and agency of executive heads. In large service organizations such as the World Bank, executive heads have a degree of autonomy that enables them some independence of decision-making. In the case of the World Bank, what we observe is a relatively high degree of success by Wolfensohn in introducing a new way to integrate the environment within the bank, and for introducing the previously taboo topic of tackling corruption. For sustainable development under Wolfensohn, this meant introducing new organizational units with a high degree of visibility and power, underpinned by a bank-wide strategy, additional special staff and earmarked resources. This compares to the limited but significant changes implemented by Wolfowitz, which attempted to reorganize sustainable development to fit new agendas promoted by donor and borrower principals (owner-driven development) while doing little to grapple with the energy requirement of developing countries for the twenty-first century.

In terms of anticorruption, both Wolf I and Wolf II were able to engender a strong consensus about the importance of fighting corruption for overall socioeconomic development. While Wolf I was able to commit intellectual and staff resources to the anticorruption agenda to make it one of the main platforms of the bank, Wolf II's actions quickly undermined principal and staff support for widely held views that corruption was a significant hurdle for developing states to achieve socioeconomic development. What we therefore observe are the clear constraints on the president's ability to select and use chosen methods for implementing their preferred agendas. In particular, the case of the World Bank illuminates the scope, autonomy and agency of the executive head stemming from two significant sources: the preferences of external principals and non-state actors, and the preferences and organizational culture of staff within the bank.

The World Bank's sustainable development agenda has significantly changed over the decades. The most profound shift took place under President Wolfensohn. Charged with reinvigorating the World Bank, he was able to signal early in his presidency a commitment to incorporating environmental concerns into the bank's operations. With the support of powerful member states, backed by the heightened influence of environmental NGOs, Wolfensohn oversaw the inclusion of environmental staff, lending and a suite of environmental and social safeguards to protect the natural environment and communities in development operations. The 2001 Environment Strategy was key to identifying ways to operationalize and mainstream the bank's environment work, despite an organizational culture built around a pressure to lend. In comparison, Wolfowitz too had the support of powerful states such as the United States in furthering changes to the sustainable development agenda to meet the bank's financial challenges and borrower needs. Yet the two most dramatic changes Wolfowitz enacted, merging ESSD and INF and resuming high-risk, high-reward energy lending, indicate that Wolfowitz had no intention of making the bank the driving authority on sustainable development among the IO community. The World Bank's future engagement with sustainable development is currently being debated as it reviews its environment strategy for the next decade (World Bank 2010), while real innovation on devising a new energy strategy has been lost.

In comparison, governance and anticorruption issues have come a long way in the bank from "prohibition to prominence," with significant evidence of mainstreaming and growing compliance with new mandates. Wolfensohn was able to achieve this through building internal and external consensus around anticorruption as a socioeconomic development issue and provide resources to undertake the necessary intellectual work to back this up. Yet there remain significant gaps in anticorruption mainstreaming related to the bank's organizational culture and pragmatic concerns around implementation. The more immediate dilemma will be reestablishing the bank's legitimacy in the wake of President Wolfowitz's own hypocrisy. For Robert Zoellick, Wolfowitz's successor, getting the bank's anticorruption agenda back on track will be one of his most important and difficult tasks, *if* he should choose to continue to champion the cause. More importantly for Zoellick is his ability to establish self-directed action after the unrest from both principals and staff: pushback from member states was already evident when Zoellick took office in July 2007. Nine of the bank's executive directors wrote to Zoellick to protest the bank's role in publishing the new 2007 governance indicators. The countries, which included China, Russia, Mexico, and Argentina, disputed their governance rating and argued that "the Bank should reconsider whether it should be in the business of producing this kind of analysis at all." In reaction, according to the story in the *Financial Times*, "some Bank officials see the letter as the beginning of an attempt by developing countries, in particular those with authoritarian governments, to capitalize on the ouster of Wolfowitz to roll back the Bank's governance agenda" (Guha and McGregor 2007). This could substantially weaken the ability of the executive head to direct the agenda of the bank. Furthermore, according to the October 2007 Volcker Commission investigation of the Department of Institutional Integrity, perceived resistance on the part of important borrowers (particularly the middle-income countries that have become so critical to the bank's long-term strategy) will reinforce the bank staff's resistance to the anticorruption agenda (Volcker *et al.* 2007: 8). In light of the observable limits to what Wolfensohn and Wolfowitz were able to accomplish in terms of championing the anticorruption agenda, it is perhaps not terribly surprising that in his first year Robert Zoellick did not make fighting corruption the focal point of his development agenda.

Notes

1 Interview with Rick Messick, April 2000, Washington, DC.
2 Interview with bank staff members, Washington, DC, July 2005.
3 Interviews with two NGO activists, 15 February 2006.
4 Wolfowitz was accused of keeping the bank back from addressing climate change when it became known that a Wolfowitz appointee had removed references to climate change in the bank's new *Clean Energy Investment Framework* strategy paper on how the organization could mitigate climate change (Nakhooda 2008). In April 2007 the Global Accountability Project discovered that the references to climate change in the strategy paper were removed by Wolfowitz's office. The incident raises serious questions as to the role of the bank in helping developing countries shift to low-carbon economies while accelerating economic growth and reducing poverty (Gumbel 2007).

The case of the World Bank 113

5 Interview with two Environment staff, World Bank, 21 February 2007.
6 Nakhooda 2008.
7 Gumbel 2007.
8 This list includes the well-known Chad–Cameroon oil pipeline case. Under the previous agreement with the bank, the Chad government was supposed to allocate most of the oil export revenues to social and human development programs. In late 2005 the Chad government announced that it would not comply but would instead use the oil profits to purchase arms. In response, Wolfowitz froze the bank account in Britain where Chad's oil revenues were being held. Other major loan cancellations or delays involved Argentina, Bangladesh, Cambodia, Congo, India, Kenya, Uzbekistan, and Yemen.
9 In the same month, a coalition of 74 civil society organizations and NGOs from around the world presented a petition accusing the bank of knowingly employing corrupt corporate contractors in its lending projects (Eurodad 2006; Food & Water Watch 2006).
10 The Development Committee is the principal advisory board to the Board of Executive Directors, made up of government ministers from member countries.
11 This included Kevin Kellems (former communications director for Dick Cheney), appointed to Directors of Strategy for External Affairs, and Robin Cleveland (former associate director of the Office of Management and Budget), appointed as special counselor to Wolfowitz.
12 Interview with Alison Cave, president of the World Bank Staff Association, July 2005. Suzanne Rich-Folsom resigned in January 2008.

Bibliography

Bapna, Manish, *Testimony before the U.S. Senate Foreign Relations Committee*, Hearing on Combating Corruption in the Multilateral Development Banks, 13 May 2004. Available at www.senate.gov/~foreign/hearings/2004/hrg040513a.html. Accessed 26 January 2008.

Behar, Richard, "Wolfowitz vs. the World Bank Board: It's Trench Warfare," Fox News, 31 January 2007a. Available at www.foxnews.com. Accessed 1 February 2007.

——"World Bank Anticorruption Drive Blunted as China Threatens to Halt Loans," Fox News, 27 March 2007b. Available at www.foxnews.com. Accessed 29 April 2007.

Benn, Hilary, "Improving Governance, Fighting Corruption," speech to Transparency International, 14 September 2006, London. Available at www.dfid.gov.uk/news/files/Speeches/fighting-corruption.asp. Accessed 17 May 2007.

Birdsall, Nancy, ed., *Rescuing the World Bank: A Centre for Global Development Working Report and Selected Essays* (Washington, DC: Centre for Global Development, 2006).

Boswell, Nancy Zucker, *Testimony before the U.S. Senate Foreign Relations Committee*, Hearing on Combating Corruption in the Multilateral Development Banks, 13 May 2004. Available at www.senate.gov/~foreign/hearings/2004/hrg040513a.html. Accessed 26 January 2008.

Bretton Woods Project, "World Bank Corruption Fight Drags On," Bretton Woods Project Update 53, 23 November 2006b. Available at www.brettonwoodsproject.org. Accessed 18 September 2007.

———"Bank Approves Anticorruption Strategy: Back to Where We Started?" Bretton Woods Project Update 55, 2 April 2007. Available at www.brettonwoodsproject.org. Accessed 15 October 2007.

Brookins, Carole, "Anticorruption Efforts of the MDBs," Testimony before the US Senate Foreign Relations Committee, Hearing on Combating Corruption in the Multilateral Development Banks, 13 May 2004. Available at www.senate.gov/~foreign/hearings/2004/hrg040513a.html. Accessed 26 January 2008.

Burnside, Craig, and David Dollar, "Aid, Policies, and Growth," *American Economic Review* 90 (4) (2000): 847–68.

Calderisi, Robert, "The Worst Man in the World?" *The New Statesman*, 15 May 2006.

Collier, Paul, and David Dollar, "Can the World Cut Poverty in Half? How Policy Reform and Effective Aid Can Meet International Development Goals," Policy Research Working Paper 2403, Washington, DC: World Bank, 2000.

———*Development Effectiveness: What Have We Learnt?* (Washington, DC: World Bank, 2001).

Cox, Robert D., "The Executive Head: An Essay on Leadership in International Organization," *International Organization* 23(2) (1969): 205–30.

de Tray, Dennis, "More Lessons from the Trenches: From Indonesia to Vietnam to Central Asia," Retirement speech, 23 February 2006, at the Center for Global Development, Washington, DC. Available at www.cgdev.org. Accessed 9 October 2007.

Dugger, Celia W., "World Bank Chief Outlines a War on Fraud," *The New York Times*, 12 April 2006: A7.

Eurodad, "Low-Down on the World Bank/ IMF Spring Meetings 2006," 27 April 2006. Available at www.eurodad.org. Accessed 15 October 2007.

Finer, Jonathan, "World Bank Focused on Fighting Corruption: Graft and Bribery, Once Tolerated, Punished by Blacklisting," *Washington Post*, 4 July 2003.

Food & Water Watch, "World Bank Finances Corporate Corruption," online report, 20 April 2006. Available at www.foodandwaterwatch.org. Accessed 15 May 2006.

Government Accountability Project, *Challenging the Culture of Secrecy: A Status Report on Freedom of Speech at the World Bank*, 2004. Available at www.whistleblower.org. Accessed 18 September 2007.

———"GAP Responds to Treasury Report on Multilateral Development Banks," News Release, 29 March 2005. Available at www.whistleblower.org. Accessed 6 October 2007.

Green, K., and A. Raphael, *Third Environmental Assessment Review (1996–2000)*, The Environment Department, Document 25577, The World Bank, 2002. Available at www.worldbank.org. Accessed 2001.

Guha, Krishna, "Wolfowitz Deputy Under Fire Over Climate," *Financial Times*, 24 April 2007.

Guha, Krishna and Richard McGregor, "World Bank Directors Test Zoellick," *Financial Times*, 12 July 2007. Available at www.ft.com. Accessed 12 July 2007.

Gumbel, Andrew, "Wolfowitz Tried to Censor the World Bank on Climate Change," *The Independent*, 14 August 2007.

Hawkins, Darren G., David A. Lake, Daniel L. Nielson, and Michael Tierney, eds, *Delegation and Agency in International Organizations* (Cambridge: Cambridge University Press, 2006).

Hunter, David, "Civil Society Networks and the Development of Environmental Standards at International Financial Institutions," *Chicago Journal of International Law* 8, no. 2 (2008): 437–77.

Isham, Jonathan, Daniel Kaufman, and Lant H. Pritchett, "Governance and Returns to Investment: An Empirical Investigation," World Bank Policy Research Working Paper 1550, Washington, DC: World Bank, 1995. Available at www.worldbank.org. Accessed 18 September 2007.

——"Civil Liberties, Democracy, and the Performance of Government Projects," *World Bank Economic Review* 11 (2) (1997): 219–42.

Kaufmann, Daniel, Aart Kraay, and Pablo Zoido-Lobaton, "Governance Matters: From Measurement to Action," *Finance and Development* 37(2) (2000): 10.

Kaufmann, Daniel, Aart Kraay, and M. Mastruzzi, "Governance Matters II: Governance Indicators for 1996–2002," World Bank Policy Research Paper 3106, Washington, DC: World Bank, 2003.

Keefer, Philip, and Stephen Knack, "Why Don't Poor Countries Catch Up? A Cross-National Test of an Institutional Explanation," *Economic Inquiry* 35(3) (1997): 590–603.

Knack, Stephen, "Aid Dependence and the Quality of Governance: A Cross-Country Empirical Analysis," Policy Research Working Paper 2396, Washington, DC: World Bank, 2000.

Liebenthal, Andres, *Promoting Environmental Sustainability in Development: An Evaluation of the World Bank's Performance* (Washington, DC: World Bank, 2002).

McCully, Patrick, *Silenced Rivers: The Ecology and Politics of Large Dams* (London: Zed Books, 2001).

Mallaby, Sebastian, *The World's Banker: A Story of Failed States, Financial Crises, and the Wealth and Poverty of Nations* (New York: Penguin, 2004).

Marquette, Heather, *Corruption, Politics, and Development: The Role of the World Bank* (Basingstoke, UK: Palgrave Press, 2003).

——"The World Bank's Fight Against Corruption," *Brown Journal of World Affairs* 13(2) (2007): 27–39.

Mekay, Eman, "IPS News—World Bank Slammed," News release, 13 February 2006. Available at www.whistleblower.org. Accessed 16 June 2006.

Miller-Adams, Michelle, *The World Bank: New Agendas in a Changing World* (London: Routledge, 1999).

Nakhooda, Smita, "Correcting the World's Greatest Market Failure: Climate Change and the Multilateral Development Banks," World Resources Institute Issue Brief, June 2008.

Nielson, Daniel, Michael Tierney, and Catherine Weaver, "Bridging the Rationalist-Constructivist Divide: Re-engineering the Culture of the World Bank," *Journal of International Relations and Development* 9 (2006): 107–39.

Park, Susan, *The World Bank Group and Environmentalists: Changing International Organisation Identities* (Manchester: Manchester University Press, 2010).

Park, Susan and Antje Vetterlein, eds, *Owning Development: Creating Policy Norms in the IMF and the World Bank* (New York: Cambridge University Press, 2010).

Pollack, Mark, *The Engines of European Integration: Delegation, Agency and Agenda Setting in the EU* (New York: Oxford University Press, 2003).

——"Delegation, Agency and Agenda Setting in the European Community," *International Organization* 51, no. 1 (1997): 99–134.

Pound, Edward T., and Danielle Knight, "Cleaning Up the World Bank," *U.S. News & World Report* 24 March 2006: 40–44, 46–48, 50–51.

Powell, Jeff, "Beware the Big, Bland Wolf: The First Year of Paul Wolfowitz at the World Bank," Bretton Woods Project article, 5 June 2006.

Rich, Bruce, *Mortgaging the Earth* (Boston: Beacon Press, 1994).

Seymour, Frances, "Sustaining the Environment at the World Bank," World Resources Institute Policy Note, September 2006.

Stiglitz, Joseph, "The Insider," *New Republic* 17–24 April 2000: 56.

——*Globalization and Its Discontents* (New York: W.W. Norton, 2002).

——"Democratizing the World Bank," *Brown Journal of World Affairs* 13(2) (2007): 79–86.

United States General Accounting Office, *World Bank: Management Controls Stronger, but Challenges in Fighting Corruption Still Remain*, Report to Congressional Committees. GAO/NSIAD-00-73, 2000. Available at www.gao.gov. Accessed 9 October 2007.

Volcker, Paul A. (chair), Gustavo Caviria, John Githongo, Ben W. Heineman, Jr, Walter Van Gerven, and Sir John Vereker, *Independent Panel Review of the World Bank Group Department of Institutional Integrity*, Washington, DC, 13 September 2007. Available at www.independentpanelreview.com/release02.shtml. Accessed 12 October 2007.

Wade, Robert, "Greening the Bank: The Struggle over the Environment 1970–95," in *The World Bank: Its First Half Century*, ed. Devesh Kapur, John Lewis, and Richard Webb (Washington, DC: Brookings Institute, 1997), 611–734.

Weaver, Catherine, *The Hypocrisy Trap: The World Bank and the Poverty of Reform* (Princeton: Princeton University Press, 2008).

Williamson, Hugh, "World Bank's Anti-graft Drive 'Needs Resources'," *Financial Times* 6 March 2006. Available at news.ft.com/cms/s/2593c052-ad55-11da-9643-0000779e2340.html. Accessed 7 March 2006.

Wolfensohn, James D., *A Proposal for Comprehensive Development Framework*, Discussion draft presented to the Board, Management, and Staff of the World Bank Group, 21 January 1999. On file with author.

World Bank, *Environment Strategy 2010: Consultations* (Washington, DC: World Bank, 2010).

——*Environmental Sustainability: An Evaluation of World Bank Group Support* (Washington, DC: World Bank, 2008).
——*Strengthening Bank Group Engagement on Governance and Anticorruption*, Final report, approved by the World Bank Group Board of Executive Directors, 21 May 2007. Available at web.worldbank.org/WBSITE/EXTERNAL/TOPICS/EXTGOVANTICORR/0,contentMDK:21096079~pagePK:210058~piPK:210062~theSitePK:3035864,00.html. Accessed 21 May 2007.
——*Annual Report* (Washington, DC: World Bank, 2006a).
——"Strengthening Bank Group Engagement on Governance and Anticorruption," draft report prepared for the Development Committee Meeting, Singapore, 8 September 2006b.
——*Integrating Anticorruption and Governance Elements in Country Assistance Strategies: A Suggested Framework for Use by Staff*, produced by the Public Sector Governance Unit, PREM, 6 January 2006c.
——*Sector Strategy Implementation Update, FY05*, Washington, DC: World Bank, 21 March 2006d.
——*Annual Report on Investigations and Sanctions of Staff Misconduct and Fraud and Corruption in World Bank-Financed Projects, Fiscal Year 2004* (Washington, DC: World Bank, 2005).
——*Putting our Commitments to Work: An Environment Strategy Implementation Progress Report* (Washington, DC: World Bank, 2003).
——*Making Sustainable Commitments: An Environment Strategy for the World Bank* (Washington, DC: World Bank, 2001).
——*2001 World Development Report: Attacking Poverty* (Washington, DC: World Bank, 2000).
——*The Impact of Environmental Assessment: The World Bank's Experience, Second Environmental Impact Assessment Review* (Washington, DC: World Bank, 1997).
World Bank Independent Evaluation Group, *Annual Review of Development Effectiveness* (Washington, DC: World Bank, 2006).
World Bank Operations Evaluation Department, *OED Review of the Bank's Performance on the Environment* (Washington, DC: World Bank, 2001a).
——*Governance—The Critical Factor, IDA10-12* (Washington, DC: World Bank, 2001b).

4 UNHCR, autonomy, and mandate change[1]

Alexander Betts

- Mandate change in UNHCR
- Explaining mandate change
- Conclusion

The Office of the United Nations High Commissioner for Refugees (UNHCR) was created by states in the aftermath of World War II. Its purpose was to work with states to ensure that refugees would receive access to protection and a durable solution to their situation. Its 1950 Statute established the basis of this mandate, giving it responsibility for supporting states to meet their obligations under the 1951 Convention on the Status of Refugees and a supervisory responsibility for overseeing states' implementation of the Convention (Loescher 2001; Betts *et al.* 2012).

Over time, UNHCR's original mandate prescribed in the Statute has changed. Its "mandate" can be understood to comprise the legitimate scope of the Office's work at any given point in time. This legitimacy comes from both explicit and implicit acceptance by states of the scope of the Office's work. Originally, the mandate was coterminous with the Statute, but today the mandate is much broader than what is described in the Statute, as the mandate has been subject to a range of formal and informal adaptations over time. UNHCR's mandate has changed in this period along two main dimensions: 1. "who to protect"—the scope of its so-called population of concern; and 2. "how to protect"—the scope of its activities.

UNHCR's original mission focused only on refugees, its activities were primarily about offering legal advice to states, and it worked exclusively in Europe. Today, however, its population of concern has expanded to include a range of forced migrants including refugees, internally displaced persons (IDPs), and victims of natural disaster. Its work is not just in Europe but is global in scale, and its activities include material assistance, humanitarian emergency response, and repatriation, etc. The question is: why and how has it been able to change and expand its mandate to such a significant degree during its 60-year existence?

One of the challenges in answering this question is that international relations (IR) lacks a compelling theory of international organization (IO) mandate change. Mainstream IR theories would predict that international organizational change would be primarily state-led. As creations of states, IOs would only be expected to adapt significantly if powerful states requested them to do so. At the margins, their principal-agent relationships with states might leave a degree of agency slack or "organizational pathology" to enable some degree of autonomous decision-making. While a range of critiques of this position have begun to emerge, not least from constructivist IO scholars, most mainstream IR would predict that major IO mandate shifts would be predominantly state-led rather than IO-directed.

At times, UNHCR mandate change has certainly been strongly influenced by states. A significant part of mandate change has been the result of explicit UN General Assembly Resolutions or resolutions of the Office's state-led Executive Committee (Excom). This state-led element is unsurprising given that states created UNHCR and exert significant controls over the organization: its funding has depended on a small group of states' annual voluntary contributions and Excom closely supervises the Office's work. However, the history of UNHCR mandate adaptation has not been exclusively state-directed. When one looks at particular episodes of mandate expansion a paradox emerges: change has sometimes taken place in spite of the absence of a clear demand for change by powerful donor states. Sometimes, adaptation has even taken place in areas in which core donor states have explicitly expressed opposition to mandate adaptation.

In other words, rather than its trajectory being exclusively determined by the choices and preferences of states, UNHCR's history of mandate expansion has sometimes been international organization-directed. The opposition of states shows that this expansion is more than merely delegated discretion. In order to unpack these claims, this chapter inductively examines the history of UNHCR mandate change over a 60-year period. Taking "mandate change" as the dependent variable, it examines five key turning points in mandate expansion: 1. prolonging its existence (1952–56); 2. geographical expansion (1957–67); 3. becoming a humanitarian relief agency (1990–2000); 4. assuming responsibility for IDP protection (1998–2006); and 5. protecting victims of natural disaster (2007–11).

In order to explain why mandate change took place at each turning point, the chapter assesses four competing explanations for mandate change, each derived from different bodies of literature on international institutions: 1. change in the preferences of states; 2. change in the nature of the problem; 3. change in the external institutional environment; and 4. change in the internal institutional environment. The chapter argues that the first two mainstream explanations of mandate change do not provide an adequate explanation either for UNHCR's decision to expand or the direction of its mandate change. Instead, the chapter suggests that a full explanation for UNHCR's mandate change needs to recognize not only the organization's vertical relationship to states but also its horizontal relationship with other organizations. Furthermore, it has exercised agency in how it has interpreted and responded to its structural environment.

As well as demonstrating the self-directed nature of much of UNHCR's mandate change, the chapter contributes to, and engages in dialogue with, Oestreich's framing piece in this volume in at least two respects. First, it highlights that alongside a concern for political context and the changing nature of forced displacement (as much of the existing principal-agent literature on IO autonomy would predict), UNHCR has also been concerned with the institutional context of its work. UNHCR has been part of wider networks of international organizations within the UN system. This network has served both as a motive for self-directed action, and as a mechanism through which it has been possible. As a motive, institutional proliferation over time has increased institutional competition and has created an incentive for the Office to seek to expand. As a mechanism, UNHCR's wider organizational network has at times served as a means to legitimate expansion into new areas, bypassing direct recourse to core donors. Second, as well as highlighting that wider institutional context is an important and neglected structural influence on IO behavior, the chapter also shows that at every turn in UNHCR's historical transformation, leadership has been a key factor in shaping exactly how structural pressures have been channeled into particular forms of organizational change. In particular, the personalities of successive UN High Commissioners for Refugees have mattered for defining the direction of the organization's mandate.

Mandate change in UNHCR

In order to examine the extent to which UNHCR has historically been self-directed, this chapter takes as its dependent variable UNHCR mandate change. The "mandate" of an IO can be understood to be the legitimate scope of its activities. Initially, in UNHCR's case this was set out in the 1950 Statute of the Office of the High Commissioner for Refugees, adopted by the UN General Assembly. However, over time, the mandate has been adapted and has expanded. Change in different organizations' mandates can be assessed along different dimensions. However, in the case of UNHCR, its mandate can be considered to encompass the questions of "who to protect" (its "population of concern") and "how to protect" (its activities). This section outlines the way in which UNHCR's mandate has changed, looking at the content of the Statute and outlining five main turning points at which the mandate has adapted.

UNHCR was a product of its time. It was conceived for a particular era and geographical context—post-War Europe—and its original Statute placed a range of restrictions on the Office's work, reflecting the interests of the more powerful states in the international system at the time. First, it was created exclusively to work with refugees, according to the 1951 Convention definition of a "refugee," rather than to protect other forms of forcibly displaced people. Chapter 1 explicitly gave it two specific functions: "providing international protection" to refugees, and "seeking permanent solutions to the problem of refugees." Second, it placed an initial temporal restriction on UNHCR's work. The Statute envisaged that UNHCR would protect refugees who were outside of their country of their nationality "as a result of events occurring before the 1 January 1951." While it also opened up the possibility to protect all other people "who had a well-founded fear of persecution for reasons of race, religion, nationality or political opinion," the emphasis was on protecting those displaced by the consequences of World War II. Furthermore, the General Assembly initially created UNHCR for a temporary (but renewable) period of just five years, after which it would be required to seek renewal of its term. Third, it was envisaged that UNHCR's work would be geographically focused on Europe. While this was not explicit in the statute, the statute explicitly connected the work of UNHCR to the 1951 Convention, and its geographical scope was originally confined to Europe.

The statute specifically tried to limit UNHCR's autonomy, requiring it to follow policy directives issued by the UN General Assembly, the Economic and Social Council (ECOSOC), or a future advisory committee established by ECOSOC, and to report annually to the General Assembly. Perhaps more significant, however, were the limitations placed on the financial autonomy of UNHCR. As specified in paragraph 20 of the statute, UNHCR was only to receive financial support from the

United Nations budget to cover administrative expenditures relating to the functioning of the Office, and that "all other expenditures relating to the activities of the high commissioner shall be financed by voluntary contributions." UNHCR thus became financially dependent on donor governments (Betts *et al.* 2012).

At its inception, UNHCR was therefore significantly restricted in the scope of its mandate. Its original population of concern focused just on refugees, its activities were primarily based on offering legal advice to states, it had limited resources of its own, and it worked exclusively in Europe. Yet, over the next 60 years it expanded its population of concern to include a range of other groups of forced migrants, and expanded its range of activities, becoming a large and expansive global humanitarian organization. It achieved these things in spite of—rather than because of—the preferences of states, and by demonstrating assertive and autonomous leadership. Five key turning points of "mandate change" can be highlighted to show how UNHCR engaged in self-directed mandate expansion.

Prolonging its existence

At its inception, UNHCR faced an inauspicious start. It was seen as a temporary institution and the United States, in particular, was not supportive of the work of UNHCR. It did not even fund UNHCR until 1955 and chose instead to support alternative humanitarian agencies, including its own refugee office, the US Escapee Program. Simply in order to survive and perpetuate its initially temporary mandate UNHCR therefore had to "prove its worth" to the United States, demonstrating that it could be relevant to the United States' emerging Cold War security interests in Western Europe.

The first high commissioner, Gerrit van Heuven Goedhart (1950–56), demonstrated assertive leadership to address these challenges head on. He successfully managed to identify resources, and began providing material assistance to refugees in Europe. With a Ford Foundation grant in 1952, which the Office distributed to nongovernmental organizations (NGOs) as assistance providers, UNHCR was able to play a broader role beyond its original legal assistance function. Furthermore, it was able to use this independently solicited funding to help address two early Cold War crises, in which it chose to become involved on the initiative of the high commissioner (Loescher 2001; Betts *et al.* 2012).

First, UNHCR got involved in addressing the West Berlin crisis of 1953, beginning to prove its usefulness and relevance to states beyond tidying up the immediate aftermath of World War II. In February, faced with a strike in East Berlin and a growing exodus to the West, UNHCR supported German and international voluntary agencies trying to help the influx of refugees passing through Berlin and integration of refugees in Western Germany. The plan enabled UNHCR to work in collaboration with a range of partner organizations, funded through the Ford Foundation Grant for Refugees, to highlight to states for the first time that it had a role to play in the Cold War context.

Second, UNHCR was proactive when, in 1956, the invasion of Hungary by the Soviet Army led to the mass exodus of nearly 200,000 refugees to neighboring Austria and Yugoslavia. Overwhelmed by the influx of refugees, Austria formally requested UNHCR to appeal to governments on its behalf for assistance in responding to the emergency. UNHCR established a coordinating group, comprising a number of leading intergovernmental organizations and NGOs. In both Austria and Yugoslavia, the high commissioner's local representatives chaired the groups that administered the emergency aid, thereby demonstrating that it was the only agency capable of coordinating both international refugee relief and the collection of funds for emergency material assistance. This paved the way for the General Assembly to designate UNHCR as the "lead agency" to direct the international emergency operation for Hungarian refugees in 1956. The second incoming high commissioner, Auguste Lindt (1956–60), demonstrated legal creativity to deal with the temporal limitations embedded in the refugee definition by arguing that the event in Hungary could be traced to events before 1951 and therefore action was within UNHCR's mandate.

These two events enabled UNHCR to demonstrate to the US government that it had a role to play in the Cold War context, which led to UNHCR's being able to extend its originally temporary existence, and expand its funding base. While these events involved UNHCR demonstrating its relevance to core donor states' interests, they were very much UNHCR-led, arising from the assertive leadership of the high commissioner, and his ability to draw upon wider networks beyond states for both funding and implementation partnerships. The outcome was that UNHCR won the confidence of the US government and the rest of the international community and with increased backing and funding was subsequently able to assume a greater role in providing material assistance in large-scale refugee crises.

Expanding its geographical scope

Having highlighted its relevance to states, and extended its existence, UNHCR faced the challenge of expanding the geographical scope of its work beyond Europe. As anti-colonial struggles and decolonization took place around the world, and Cold War proxy conflicts began in the so-called Third World, UNHCR gradually recognized opportunities to expand its work to other parts of the globe. However, throughout the process what was especially interesting for the purposes of this chapter was that the early stages of expansion were frequently in conflict with the preferences of some of the most powerful states. However, using its moral authority, UNHCR was able to overcome initial state resistance, and gradually expand its operations until UNHCR's wider role was so accepted that it was eventually endorsed by the UN General Assembly.

UNHCR's shift from a European organization to a global actor relied upon proactive leadership. Lindt used the concept known as "good offices," which involved the General Assembly granting UNHCR the authority to raise funds or to initiate assistance programs for operations outside its usual mandate. Yet, rather than the initiative coming from states, the areas in which UNHCR used "good offices" came from the proposals of the high commissioner, frequently in opposition to powerful states (Goodwin-Gill and McAdam 2007). In 1957, for example, it used the concept to respond to the Chinese refugees in Hong Kong and the Algerian refugees in Tunisia (Ruthström-Ruin 1993). What was remarkable about these moves is that UNHCR was able to confidently assume these roles despite resistance from two significant world powers, France and the UK, both permanent members of the UN Security Council and among the key states that helped establish UNHCR.

After Lindt, high commissioner Felix Schnyder built upon the legitimacy created in 1957 to identify opportunities in the changing nature of world politics to justify a more formal global role. In December 1961 the General Assembly gave UNHCR the authority to assist both "refugees within his mandate and those for whom he extends his good offices," thereby eliminating the legal and institutional barriers for future UNHCR action for non-mandate refugees. The distinction between "good offices" and mandate refugee operations was subsequently abandoned by the General Assembly in 1965, formally recognizing UNHCR's competence to provide protection and permanent solutions to both refugees within the UNHCR mandate and refugees covered by the high commissioner's good offices. In 1967 the Protocol to the 1951 Convention formally deleted the geographic and time limitations provisions from the 1951 Convention thereby bringing the Convention into line with the universal scope of UNHCR's Statute. The scope of the refugee regime was thereby expanded to the rest of the world.

What was interesting about this turning point was that while geographical expansion ultimately came from an inter-state agreement, based on the signing of the 1967 Protocol to the 1951 Refugee Convention, the process of how UNHCR's geographical mandate expanded was more complex than simply an inter-state bargaining process. The impetus for expansion had begun much earlier in 1957 and by 1967 UNHCR was a de facto global organization. The 1967 Protocol simply formalized a status quo which was significantly attributable to UNHCR, once again assertively staking out new areas of work—often in opposition to states' preferences—and then demonstrating those new areas of work to be compatible with states' interests.

Becoming a humanitarian relief agency

By the end of the 1980s UNHCR faced a challenge to redefine its identity. During the Cold War, UNHCR had a clear role in protecting people fleeing East–West or displaced by proxy conflict in the developing world. Life after the Cold War created new opportunities and challenges for the Office. The old certainties of East–West movements and the Cold War interests of Western states that had upheld the refugee regime were no longer present, requiring that UNHCR reinvent its role. In assuming the role of high commissioner, Sadako Ogata (1990–2000) sought to make the Office relevant to states. In order to do so, she proactively sought to expand the Office's work to address two emerging challenges: the end of old Cold War conflicts and the start of new post-Cold War conflicts known as the "new wars."

With the end of the Cold War, UNHCR took on an unprecedented role in repatriation. As proxy conflicts in Central America, the Horn of Africa, and South-East Asia wound down, a range of opportunities emerged for refugees to return to their countries of origin. In contrast, the Cold War assumption had been that those leaving Communism would have little prospect of returning home but would instead be resettled to a third country or locally integrated in the host country. "The decade of repatriation" saw UNHCR engage in large-scale return operations for Cambodians in Thailand, Mozambicans in Malawi, and Afghans in Pakistan and Iran, for example. Around the world, UNHCR estimates that more than 9 million refugees repatriated between 1991 and 1996. Barnett and Finnemore (2004) use exactly the case study of UNHCR adopting a role in repatriation to demonstrate that the behavior of international organizations simply cannot be explained by the preferences of states. They show how in the repatriation of Rohinga refugees it was bureaucratic institutional process, rather than the request of states, that defined how the organization became involved in repatriation and how it played out in practice.

There is no doubt that there was considerable pressure from states for repatriation. Host states wanted refugees to go home; donor states wanted a reduction in the humanitarian burden (Power 2008: 219). However, it was Ogata who chose to place UNHCR at the forefront of repatriation and to seize the opportunity to become *the* UN agency responsible for return (Ogata 2005). Many NGOs and activists expressed concern that UNHCR taking on such a role could conflict with its protection mandate, especially in contexts in which the "voluntariness" of return was questionable (Barutciski 1998). States could, theoretically, have used alternative agencies to provide support with repatriation. The International Organization for Migration (IOM), in particular, had been the main repatriation organization in the late 1980s. In its response to the situation of Indo-Chinese "boat people" only a few years earlier, UNHCR had refused to actively engage in returning people to Vietnam, leaving IOM as the operational agency (Betts 2009). Consequently, UNHCR had the discretion to take or leave a repatriation role, but it was Sadako Ogata who, faced with the need to compete for resources and institutional relevance, chose to pursue a role as a repatriation organization.

A similar story underlies UNHCR's growing involvement in responses to humanitarian relief during the 1990s. With the emergence of "new wars," the Office assumed responsibility for playing an assistance role in conflict zones, including Iraq, Bosnia, and former Zaire. Such involvement raised significant concerns about the integrity of UNHCR's mandate and about the consequences of providing assistance in the absence of a clear protection mandate. In Bosnia, UNHCR was accused of creating "safe zones" in which people were anything but safe (Weiss and Korn 2006). In Zaire, the provision of assistance to all those fleeing Rwanda led to accusations that UNHCR was effectively resourcing the *Interahamwe* genocidaires (Terry 2002). So why had UNHCR broadened its humanitarian assistance role? Did it need to because it was explicitly asked to by states? No. In both Bosnia and Zaire, a range of other humanitarian service providers were available to states. If UNHCR had refused to be involved, it would have had the normative authority to decline a role, albeit with the cost to its short-term humanitarian market share. Rather, it was Ogata who—led by the desire for UNHCR to be "relevant" and increase its funding base—expanded UNHCR operations in a way that was compatible with states' interests.

Assuming responsibility for IDP protection

During the 1990s there was growing recognition that a new population of forcibly displaced people was in need of international protection: so-called internally displaced persons (IDPs). IDPs are effectively people who are in a refugee-like situation but who have not crossed an international border. IDPs are defined by the international community as people "who have been forced or obliged to flee or to leave their homes or places of habitual residence in particular as a result of generalized violence, violations of human rights or natural or man-made disasters, and who have not crossed an internationally recognized state border" (Weiss and Korn 2006).

During the late 1990s the international community developed a normative framework to protect IDPs, the so-called Guiding Principles on International Displacement, completed in 1997. This document, developed outside of UNHCR, was a consolidation and application of existing human rights and humanitarian law standards to the situation of IDPs. The creation of a normative framework nevertheless left open the question of what the institutional framework for IDP protection should look like. Which organizations should assume responsibility?

What ensued was an interesting process. Initially, the institutional framework was based on a so-called "collaborative approach," within which a range of agencies shared responsibility for IDPs. UNHCR became the lead, coordinating agency within the collaborative approach. However, the collaborative approach left gaps (Phuong 2005; Weiss and Korn 2006). In 2000 Richard Holbrooke, the US Ambassador to the UN, proposed that UNHCR should assume responsibility for IDP protection, as he had also done during the 1990s, arguing that "co-heads are no heads." Despite having a request from UNHCR's biggest donor to assume responsibility for IDP protection, Ogata declined. One of the primary reasons for this was internal division within the organization. While UNHCR's Department of Operational Services (DOS) supported a greater role, the Department of International Protection (DIP) felt it would have a negative impact on refugee protection, and so Ogata said "no" (Freitas 2004).

Yet just six years later, High Commissioner Antonio Guterres (2005–) saw an opportunity and revisited the question. In the context of a wider process of UN humanitarian reform, international organizations negotiated a so-called "cluster approach" to divide responsibility for, among other areas, responses to IDPs. UNHCR assumed responsibility for IDP protection in 2006. Over the following five years this role expanded to leave UNHCR as the UN's IDP protection agency. For Guterres, assuming this role was an important part of ensuring that UNHCR remained relevant to states. However, for most commentators within the organization, Guterres' expansion owed more to his own personality and ambition than external pressure from states to take on an expanded role (Crisp 2009).

What was especially interesting was the mechanism used by Guterres to establish UNHCR as the UN's IDP protection agency. At no point has UNHCR's expanded role in IDP protection ever explicitly been examined or ratified by the UN General Assembly. Rather, in the context of UN humanitarian reform, an inter-agency body, the Inter-Agency Standing Committee (IASC), has assumed the role of developing and negotiating the inter-agency division of labor for different areas of humanitarian response. This inter-agency network of organizations has effectively enabled UNHCR to more than double its population of concern without ever seeking direct approval from states for its mandate expansion. Assuming responsibility for IDP protection on its own terms, UNHCR has been able to ring-fence its refugee budget and even insist that contributions from states for IDP protection include a 7 percent levy, which is reallocated to refugee protection (Betts *et al.* 2011).

Protecting victims of natural disaster

In the 2000s a debate has emerged on the potential impact of climate change on forced displacement, opening up questions of how the internationally community should respond to "climate refugees" or "environmentally displaced people." In numerous forums, Guterres expressed concern that UNHCR should engage with these issues, making several speeches on the topic and publishing a piece in *Foreign Affairs* called "Millions Uprooted" that discussed the issue at length.

However, a number of states, not least the United States, expressed a belief that UNHCR should not exceed its mandate. Consequently, in spite of Guterres' rhetoric, when the Office produced its first policy paper on the topic in 2009, it took a defensive stance; its immediate concern was to protect the unique "refugee status" and it argued strongly against the use of the term "climate refugee." The paper argued that those who were displaced internationally by climate change would not fall under its mandate (Hall 2011; UNHCR 2009).

Yet, alongside this, UNHCR was already gradually taking on a de facto role in responding to several natural disasters, including the Indian Ocean tsunami in early 2005, the South Asian earthquake later in 2005 and more recently the Pakistan floods and the Haiti earthquake in 2010. Many of UNHCR's early responses were motivated by the fact that natural disasters occurred in countries where it was already working with large refugee or IDP situations (Betts *et al.* 2012). Growing out of this practice of increasing involvement in natural disasters, the Office began to formalize its role in the area by the end of the decade. A 2010 evaluation of UNHCR's role in recent natural disasters outlined the organization's emerging practice, arguing that responsibility for the protection of victims of natural disasters was becoming an increasingly important area of UNHCR activity. In December 2010 the IASC approved a 12-month pilot program for UNHCR to assume the protection coordination role at a field level in response to natural disasters. By 2011, UNHCR had adopted a formal role in protecting victims of natural disaster, and Guterres was able to highlight them as a core part of UNHCR's "population of concern."

As with IDPs, UNHCR's role in protecting victims of natural disaster has never been formally recognized by the UN General Assembly. Instead, it is simply based on agreement through the IASC as a network of international organizations. UNHCR's ability to gradually build credibility over time through its de facto involvement in natural disasters, and its use of IASC, has therefore enabled Guterres to strategically place UNHCR at the forefront of responses to environmental displacement, despite the caution of core donor states.

Explaining mandate change

The question then is: how can we explain what has driven these key turning points within UNHCR's mandate change? Answering this is of potentially wider relevance because it can enable us to understand the extent to which it is appropriate to understand UNHCR's mandate adaptation as a primarily state-drive or IO-driven process. Furthermore, it can help us to identify whether the nature of UNHCR's position vis-à-vis states in the area of mandate change is most appropriately conceived as "autonomy," having some leeway within a delegated relationship to interpret state preferences, or as "independence," having the ability to make decisions and exert influence outside of a principal-agent relationship with states (McKittrick 2008).

In order to explain what has driven UNHCR mandate change, the following section assesses four competing explanations for the empirical story of adaptation outlined above. Each of the four competing explanations is derived from different bodies of existing theory on international institutions and they, deductively, represent the main set of plausible explanations for possible drivers of IO mandate change. The possible explanations for mandate change are as follows: 1. change in the demands of powerful *states* (liberal institutionalism); 2. change in the *nature of the problem* (neo-functionalism); 3. change in the *external institutional environment* (regime complexity); and 4. change in the *internal institutional environment* (constructivism). Each one is examined below.

Change in the demands of powerful states

Neo-Realists would argue that change could be explained only by a change in the interests of powerful states (Mearsheimer 1994–95). Most liberal institutionalists would agree that IO change would best be explained by a change in the demand for regimes by states (Keohane 1982), although some might recognize that the principal-agent problem at least allows some narrow degree of scope for IO autonomy (Hawkins *et al.* 2006).

On the surface it seems plausible that this explanation would apply. Some 77 percent of UNHCR's funding comes from just 10 donors, the most significant being the United States, the European Commission, and Japan (Loescher *et al.* 2008: 93). UNHCR also relies on annual voluntary contributions, a significant proportion of which are earmarked for specific countries or emergencies. Furthermore, UNHCR's governing body, its Executive Committee, comprises states, to which the high commissioner is accountable. Consequently, there are a range of structural reasons why one might anticipate that UNHCR mandate change would be driven by the shifting preferences of powerful states (Whitaker 2008). Indeed, Loescher and Scanlan (1998) demonstrate how the US in particular has been crucial to explaining the trajectory of UNHCR at key historical junctures. However, two forms of counterfactual evidence imply that the preferences of powerful states have been inadequate to fully explain UNHCR mandate change.

First, UNHCR has sometimes expanded its mandate in ways that have explicitly contradicted the immediate interests and requests of powerful states, or gone in a different direction from those interests. When Goedhart engaged in UNHCR's early expansion through responding to crises in Berlin and Hungary, it was in spite of rather than because of the influence of powerful states, and explicitly went against the initial vision the United States had had for the organization. When Lindt expanded UNHCR's work beyond the geographical scope of Europe to Hong Kong and Algeria in 1957, it was in direct opposition to China and France. When UNHCR took on responsibility for IDP protection, it initially declined a request from the US government to assume the role in 2000 and then took on the role later, when it fitted the agenda of the organization. When it took on responsibility for victims of natural disaster, it did so in spite of frequent suggestions by donor states in Excom that it should "stick to its mandate."

Second, at certain points, even when there has been observational equivalence between state interests and UNHCR mandate change, the sequencing of events suggests that the initiative has come from UNHCR, and that the specific direction of change would not have happened through purely state-led change. In the early Cold War it was the United States that extended UNHCR's existence by giving it financial and political backing; but it did so in light of UNHCR "proving its value" to the United States. In 1967 it was the UN General Assembly (and states) that agreed to formally extend the scope of the 1951 Convention (and, with it, UNHCR's supervisory responsibility) to the rest of the world. However, this was in the aftermath of UNHCR already de facto assuming a global role through its own innovation of "good offices." When Ogata extended UNHCR's role to repatriation, the request did not come directly from states, which could have gone to other organizations like IOM which had provided repatriation services in the late 1980s. Rather the initiative came from UNHCR.

Change in the nature of the problem

A second possible explanation for UNHCR mandate change is the idea that UNHCR's involvement in a wider range of activities was necessary simply in order to be able to fulfill its refugee protection mandate. In other words, the expansion was not expansion for its own sake. Rather it was based on the changing nature of the original problem requiring broader engagement in new areas—such as repatriation, IDP protection and natural disaster, as a means to ensure refugee protection. This explanation can be derived from *neo-functionalism*, which has been developed within attempts to explain regional integration in general and the European Union's (EU) expansion in particular (Haas 1958). The core concept in neo-functionalism is the idea of "functional spill-over," whereby involvement in one area of activity logically follows from another leading to a form of creeping expansion in bureaucratic mandates. In the case of the EU it offers a compelling account for how the logic of a common market has led to emerging levels of political unification over time.

Applied to UNHCR, this logic of functional spill-over would suggest that UNHCR became involved in new areas *in order to* protect refugees. In other words, there would be a clear causal link between the new areas of activity and the Office's ability to protect refugees. Empirically, in order to substantiate this argument it would need to identify that areas of expansion logically followed from the goal of refugee protection. A useful counterfactual for evaluating this is the question of whether UNHCR's expanded role into new areas reinforces or contradicts its ability to protect refugees.

Indeed, the most obviously "consistent" areas of mandate expansion are the early years of temporal and geographical expansion. Extending its existence and being able to work on a global scale were, of course, necessary in order to protect the world's refugees. Yet, even here, these expansions were not a classic case of functional spillover since the original mandate of UNHCR was to protect *Europe*'s refugees and to protect refugees resulting from the aftermath of World War II. So there was no necessity that, simply in order to fulfill this mandate, the early changes would need to logically follow.

The logic of functional spillover breaks down even further as an explanation when one looks at later mandate change. Many of the new activities of UNHCR, and new populations of concern, have at best a neutral impact on refugee protection and, in some cases, are potentially at odds with it. The roles assumed in repatriation, humanitarian relief, IDP protection, and natural disaster have each at times been seen to have a potentially detrimental effect on refugee protection. Even supporters of these mandate expansions have generally claimed their effects on refugee protection to be neutral, rather than clearly positive.

To take the example of IDP protection, UNHCR's role in this area does not have an obviously complementary relationship with refugee protection. During the 1980s and early 1990s UNHCR limited its involvement in IDP protection to situations in which there was a clear link to its core mandate of refugee protection. However, the adoption of a formal IDP protection role meant a change precisely because it implied UNHCR involvement when there was no such link. Furthermore, in many cases, UNHCR's involvement with IDPs appears to contradict rather than reinforce refugee protection. On an operational level, a number of authors have argued that at times UNHCR's involvement in IDP protection may have been used by states to indirectly "contain" IDPs within their country of origin to avoid them crossing a border and becoming refugees (Barutciski 1996; Dubernet 2003). Furthermore, in assuming protection responsibility under the cluster approach, UNHCR has received relatively limited additional staff or funding to support its new role, which some staff argue has led to a dilution of its capacity to focus on refugees.

While the nature of forced displacement has, of course, changed dramatically over the last 60 years, this does not provide an adequate explanation either for the fact of UNHCR's mandate change or for the direction of that mandate change. There was no inevitability that UNHCR should necessarily have assumed responsibility for those particular populations of concern or for the particular activities it has adopted.

Change in the external institutional environment

One of the least explored drivers of IO mandate change is the role played by the organization's wider institutional environment. A literature on regime complexity has emerged, highlighting how with institutional proliferation an increasingly dense network of institutions exist in parallel, overlap or are nested within one another. The effects of regime complexity on state behavior have been explored (Abbott and Snidal 2001; Alter and Meunier 2009; Busch 2007; Raustiala and Victor 2004; Mattli et al. 2008). However, the relationship between regime complexity and international organization adaptation has been left largely unexamined.

Yet, regime complexity has been important for UNHCR. At the time of its creation, the refugee regime was relatively isolated as an institutional framework. Subsequent to its creation a range of new international institutions have emerged—within and beyond the UN system—in areas including migration, human rights, humanitarianism, security, development, and peace-building, for example. Today, it makes more sense to speak of a "refugee regime complex" than simply a "refugee regime." Many of these new institutions have implications for refugee protection. In particular, some of them overlap with the refugee regime in the sense that they may have authority over related issues.

Some of the overlapping institutions have potentially complementary implications for refugee protection. For example, the emergence of the human rights regime offers sources of "complementary protection" that reinforce core areas of international refugee law. In contrast, others have potentially contradictory implications, enabling states to engage in forum shopping or regime shifting, in ways that allow them to potentially bypass either international refugee law or UNHCR. The emergence of regime complexity has played a role in explaining UNHCR mandate change at various stages—both as a motive for adaptation and as a means to enable adaptation.

As a motive, contradictory institutional overlaps have created a more competitive institutional context for UNHCR's work. Senior staff members have spoken of an emerging "humanitarian marketplace," in which other intergovernmental and nongovernmental organizations provide humanitarian services for states to groups that include refugees and displaced persons. The logic of this interorganizational competition was made clear to UNHCR in 2011 when the UK's Department of International Development (DfID) published a ranked assessment of different humanitarian partners as a basis for choosing between alternative humanitarian service providers (including UNHCR). Meanwhile, successive high commissioners such as Ogata, Lubbers and Guterres have explicitly referred to the need to ensure the "relevance" of UNHCR to states in a more competitive environment. Indeed this logic of seizing institutional opportunities that could have been filled by other UN or non-UN agencies has been especially present since the end of the Cold War. Each of UNHCR's roles in repatriation, humanitarian relief, IDP protection, and natural disaster relief could in theory have been taken on by NGOs or other international agencies. In each case UNHCR was not pressured to take on these roles; instead, it seized the initiative to fend off potential competition from other institutions (Crisp 2009; Guterres 2008).

Networks of organizations have also been used by UNHCR as a mechanism to enable its own expansion. Even early on in UNHCR's history, partnerships with other non-state actors were crucial to its independence from states. Goedhart used a Ford Foundation Grant in order to fund NGO partners to support the early interventions in Berlin and Hungary on which UNHCR's early expansion was built. It was the ability to use these partnerships, beyond the relationship with the state, which enabled UNHCR to act in a way that would not have been possible if it had been purely dependent upon a principal-agent relationship with its core donors. More recently, the IASC has served as a network of organizations through which UNHCR has been able to formally expand its mandate into new areas, without needing to seek direct approval from states. Indeed, IASC represents a fascinating example of how networks of organizations have independent effects in world politics. IASC has been the context in which UNHCR has negotiated its role in IDP protection and the protection of victims of natural disaster. Yet, no states are present in IASC, which is a body made up exclusively of IOs and NGOs, and IASC's highly influential role in determining inter-agency divisions of responsibility is never passed onwards to the UN General Assembly.

In summary, rather than simply being enabled or constrained by its vertical relationship to states, UNHCR has also been enabled and constrained by its horizontal relationship to other organizations. On the one hand, the increasingly competitive institutional environment has imposed new constraints on the Office. On the other hand, new networks of organizations have created political spaces, beyond the delegated state-IO relationship, which have enhanced UNHCR's independence.

Change in the internal institutional environment

Constructivist work has highlighted how, rather than being exclusively state-driven, internal organizational sociology and culture play an important role in defining IO behavior (Barnett and Finnemore 1999, 2004; Rittberger *et al.* 2006). Meanwhile, comparative politics literature on institutions has drawn attention to the "path-dependent" ways in which institutions may develop their own dynamics of adaptation (Mahoney and Thelen 2010).

Throughout UNHCR's history (Barnett and Finnemore 2004; Loescher 2001; Betts *et al.* 2012), leadership from within the organization has been a crucial part of adaptation. UNHCR has a directive leadership structure of having a single clearly identifiable head—the high commissioner (Gottwald 2010). At each turn in the Office's history of mandate change, leadership from the high commissioner has been crucial to explaining both change and the direction of change. Goedhart's early initiative brought in the Ford Foundation funding to engage in early crises, and it was his entrepreneurialism that impelled the organization to stake a claim for a wider and more enduring role within the UN system. Similarly, Lindt's legal creativity enabled UNHCR to justify use of "good offices" as a basis on which to work outside of Europe for the first time in defiance of some of the most powerful states in the world. It was Ogata's vision of the organization in the 1990s more than anything else that shaped its widening humanitarian role. UNHCR staff within the organization point to Guterres' personal interest in areas like climate change as an important reason for expansion into natural disasters.

In summary, although UNHCR has faced pressures from states and its changing institutional environment, structural pressures alone explain neither change nor the direction of change. Throughout the history of UNHCR, the person at its head—the high commissioner—has frequently directed the mandate along particular paths. Most of the adaptations in the Office's history would not have taken place without conscious choices by different high commissioners. Of course, as the initial rejection of full responsibility for IDP protection in 2000 highlighted, the decisions of high commissioners have been shaped by the internal preferences of the organization (Freitas 2004). However, crucially, it has been the organization—represented by the high commissioner—which has had significant control over the direction of its mandate.

Conclusion

UNHCR was created with a very clearly defined mandate: to support states in the provision of protection and solutions to refugees. Over the last 60 years its mandate has changed, both in terms of "who it protects" (its populations of concern) and "how it protects" (its activities). In that time it has gone from a small agency focused on providing legal support to refugees in Europe to protecting and assisting a range of forcibly displaced people around the world. This chapter has tried to explain that process of mandate change by looking at five key moments of mandate expansion in the organization's history. It has examined four competing explanations for mandate change, each derived from a different theoretical literature on international institutions.

This chapter has shown that UNHCR's mandate change cannot be understood as a purely state-led process. While UNHCR is undoubtedly constrained and influenced by its relationship to its core donor states, the changing preferences of those states are not sufficient to explain the ways in which UNHCR's mandate has adapted. At the key moments of adaptation, UNHCR's direction of change has frequently contradicted, rather than complied with, the preferences of major donors. Furthermore, process tracing reveals that, sequentially, even when the direction of mandate change has been consistent with states' interests, the initiative for change has often come from UNHCR, rather than donor states.

Rather than simply responding directly to states' changing interests, UNHCR has been proactive in shaping the path it has followed. At times this has been in response to the constraints created by needing to remain relevant to states' interests. However, it has also been in response to other structural concerns, such as the need to respond to competition from other international organizations in order to remain competitive. Ultimately, this concern with other organizations, of course, relates to the goal of remaining relevant to states but it is a motive that is not easily captured by a simple principal-agent view of the state-IO relationship.

Furthermore, in addition to responding to a range of structural constraints—changing state interests, the changing nature of forced displacement, and the changing institutional environment—UNHCR has had considerable agency to determine whether and indeed how it has adapted over time. In particular, successive high commissioners have played an important leadership role in interpreting structural constraints and innovatively defining the best response to the changing structural environment. In each case, different high commissioners have brought their own personalities and values to the role. Counterfactually, without the role of particular high commissioners, the specific changes that took place would not have occurred in the way that they did.

Conceptually, UNHCR's role in mandate change cannot be adequately understood through the lens of a relationship of delegation. The degree of influence it has had over whether and how to adapt to structural changes goes beyond the simple "agency slack" implied by a principal-agent relationship. Far from simply being a responsive actor, UNHCR has been proactive and pre-emptive in defining its mandate change, at times defying or bypassing powerful states in order to adapt in particular ways. In that sense, UNHCR needs to be understood as having a significant degree of independence in how it has defined its own identity.

One of the key mechanisms by which UNHCR has been able to independently expand its mandate has been through the use of networks of organizations. In its early years, it used foundation grants and NGO partners to define a resource space and degree of influence for itself that stood apart from state control. In recent years, it has used the IASC as an inter-agency coordination body to negotiate with other agencies its role in IDP protection and the protection of victims of natural disaster, without ever having to directly seek approval from an inter-state body such as the UN General Assembly.

The chapter highlights the need to reconceive the role of international organizations in world politics. Rather than simply being in a delegated relationship with states, they can better be understood to be independent actors involved in a range of political relationships and faced with a number of structural constraints, of which their relationship with states is just one. In addition to being in a "vertical" relationship with states, they are also in a "horizontal" relationship with other organizations, and need to respond to both competitive and complementary interaction with other institutions. Not only do IOs need to respond to the changing interests of states but, increasingly, also the changing competitive and complementary relationships they have with other organizations. In navigating between different sources of structural constraint and opportunity, UNHCR has shown that it has had considerable agency to define its own destiny.

Note

1 This chapter builds upon work developed in Alexander Betts, Gil Loescher and James Milner, *UNHCR: The Politics and Practice of Refugee Protection* (London: Routledge 2012). The author wishes to acknowledge the role of Gil Loescher and James Milner in contributing to the development of the research on which many of the ideas in the chapter are based.

Bibliography

Abbott, Kenneth and Duncan Snidal, "Why States Act Through Formal International Organizations," in *The Politics of Global Governance*, ed. Paul Diehl and Brian Frederking (Boulder, Col.: Lynne Rienner, 2001).

Alter, Karen and Sophie Meunier, "The International Politics of Regime Complexity," *Perspectives on Politics* (2009): 13–24.

Barnett, Michael and Martha Finnemore, "The Politics, Power, and Pathologies of International Organizations," *International Organization* (1999): 699–732.

——*Rules for the World: International Organizations and Global Politics* (Ithaca, NY: Cornell University Press, 2004).

Barutciski, Mickael, "The Reinforcement of Non-Admission Policies and the Subversion of UNHCR: Displacement and Internal Assistance in Bosnia-Herzegovina (1992–94)," *International Journal of Refugee Law* 8, no. 1/2 (1996): 49–110.

——"Involuntary Repatriation when Refugee Protection is No Longer Necessary," *International Journal of Refugee Law* 10, no. 1/2 (1998): 236–49.

——"Questioning the Tensions Between the Refugee and IDP Concepts: A Rebuttal," *Forced Migration Review* 4 (1999): 35.

Betts, Alexander, *Protection by Persuasion: International Cooperation in the Refugee Regime* (Ithaca: Cornell University Press, 2009).

Betts, Alexander, Gil Loescher, and James Milner, *UNHCR: The Politics and Practice of Refugee Protection* (London: Routledge, 2012).

Busch, Marc, "Overlapping Institutions, Forum Shopping, and Dispute Settlement in International Trade," *International Organization* 61, no. 4 (2007): 735–61.

Crisp, Jeff, "Refugees, Persons of Concern and People on the Move: the Broadening Boundaries of UNHCR," *Refuge* 26, no. 1 (2009): 73–78.

Department for International Development (United Kingdom), *Multilateral Institutions Review* (London: DfID, 2011).

Dubernet, Cecile, *The International Containment of Displaced Persons: Humanitarian Spaces without Exit* (Aldershot: Zed Books, 2003).

Freitas, Raquel, "UNHCR's Decision Making on Internally Displaced Persons," in *Decision-Making Within International Organizations*, ed. Bob Reinalda and Bertjan Verbeek (London: Routledge, 2004).

Goodwin-Gill, Guy and Jane McAdam, *The Refugee in International Law* (Oxford: Oxford University Press, 2007).

Gottwald, Martin, "Competing in the Humanitarian Marketplace: UNHCR's Organizational Culture and Decision-making Processes," UNHCR Working Paper, No. 190 (Geneva: UNHCR, 2010).

Guterres, Antonio, "Millions Uprooted," *Foreign Affairs* 87, no. 5 (2008): 90–99.
Haas, E., "The Challenge of Regionalism," *International Organization* Vol.12 (1958): 440–58.
Hall, Nina, "Greening Intergovernmental Organisations: Explaining UNHCR and UNDP's Response to Climate Change," paper presented at the second ULB-UGent WIRE (Workshop on International Relations), Workshop on Institutional Change in Intergovernmental Organizations, Belgium, 27–28 May 2011.
Hawkins, Darren G., David A. Lake, Daniel L. Nielson, and Michael J. Tierney, eds, *Delegation and Agency in International Organizations* (Cambridge: Cambridge University Press, 2006).
Keohane, Robert, "The Demand for International Regimes," *International Organization* 36, no. 2 (1982): 332–55.
Loescher, Gil, *UNHCR and World Politics: The Perilous Path* (Oxford: Oxford University Press, 2001).
Loescher, Gil, Alexander Betts, and James Milner, *UNHCR: The Politics and Practice of Refugee Protection into the Twenty-First Century* (London: Routledge, 2008).
Loescher, Gil and John Scanlan, *Calculated Kindness: Refugees and America's Half-Open Door* (Free Press, 1998).
McKittrick, Ann, "UNHCR as an Autonomous Organization: Complex Operations and the Case of Kosovo," *RSC Working Paper* no. 50 (Oxford: RSC, 2008).
Mahoney, James and Kathleen Thelen, *Explaining Institutional Change: Ambiguity, Agency, and Power* (Cambridge: Cambridge University Press, 2010).
Mattli, Walter, Duncan Snidal, and Joe Jupille, "Explaining Institutional Choice in Trade," paper presented at a seminar of the Oxford University Global Economic Governance Programme, 25 April 2008.
Mearsheimer, John, "The False Promise of International Institutions," *International Security* 19, no. 3 (1994–95): 5–49.
Ogata, Sadako, *The Turbulent Decade: Confronting the Refugee Crises of the 1990s* (New York: W.W. Norton, 2005).
Phuong, Catherine, *The International Protection of Internally Displaced Persons* (Cambridge: Cambridge, 2005).
Power, Samantha, *Chasing the Flame: Sergio Vieira de Mello and the Fight to Save the World* (New York: Allen Lane, 2008).
Raustiala, Kal and David Victor, "The Regime Complex for Plant Genetic Resources," *International Organization* 58, no. 2 (2004): 277–309.
Rittberger, Volker, Bernhard Zangl, and Matthias Staisch, *International Organization: Polity, Politics and Policies* (London: Palgrave MacMillan, 2006).
Ruthström-Ruin, Cecilia, *Beyond Europe: The Globalization of Refugee Aid* (Lund: Lund University Press, 1993).
Terry, Fiona, *Condemned to Repeat? The Paradox of Humanitarian Action* (Ithaca: Cornell University Press, 2002).

UNHCR, "Climate Change, Natural Disasters and Human Displacement," policy paper, August 2009.

Weiss, Thomas and David Korn, *Internal Displacement: Conceptualization and its Consequences* (Routledge: London, 2006).

Whitaker, B., "Funding the International Refugee Regime: Implications for Protection," *Global Governance* Vol. 14(2) (2008): 241–58.

5 Changing actors and actions in the global fight against AIDS

Christer Jönsson

- HIV/AIDS on the international agenda
- Early IO action and inaction
- WHO as "lead agency"
- From "lead agency" to public-private partnerships
- Conclusions

Evolving or threatening pandemics constitute dramatic manifestations of global interdependence, calling for coordinated action. The World Health Organization (WHO), a member of the United Nations (UN) family created in 1948, is the international organization we today expect to provide that coordinated action at the outbreak of new potential pandemics, such as bird flu, SARS or swine flu. Yet the first pandemic in the age of globalization, HIV/AIDS, illustrates that the "fit" between issue and organization is far from perfect.

This chapter will trace shifts in the organizational landscape concerning the international response to HIV/AIDS since the late 1980s and inquire into the kind of action taken. Unlike the other chapters in this volume, this one does not focus on one individual organization but rather on a sequence of organizations of different types, ranging from traditional intergovernmental organizations (IOs) to public-private partnerships. This chapter contrasts principal-agent (PA) explanations with constructivist accounts. PA theory views IO action as a result of delegation from principals (be they member states or other stakeholders) and addresses questions concerning the scope for independent IO action. Constructivism emphasizes the role of norms and institutional factors in accounting for specific IO actions.

Two sets of questions will guide the analysis. First, I will inquire into the "actorness" of IOs. To what extent can we speak of independent IO action? As I am looking at different organizations, how can we account for varying autonomy? The second, complementary set of questions concerns the kind of actions actually taken, or not taken. Why did IOs resort to this type of action or inaction, rather than other available alternatives?

It should be noted from the outset that HIV/AIDS differs from other health issues and previous epidemics in several significant respects. First, it represents a "long-wave event" where large-scale effects emerge gradually over decades (Barnett 2006). While more people have died from other epidemics in the past, the unabated continuation of a lethal epidemic for more than a quarter century is unprecedented (Lisk 2010: 5). As a result of the sexual nature of transmission, the long viral life cycle (it may take 10 years between infection and disease), and the high mutation potential, the full wavelength of the HIV epidemic curve is probably 50–120 years. Such long-term ramifications require long-term thinking, falling outside the normal time horizons of politicians (Barnett 2006: 302, 304; Panos 2003: 36–38).

Unlike the victims of earlier epidemics, HIV-infected persons are normally in their productive and reproductive age. This, in combination with the long incubation time, means that they are able not only to accelerate the spread of the pandemic, but also to organize in order to get their voices heard. For the first time in history, patients—people living with HIV/AIDS (PLWHA)—have been able to create effective pressure groups.

Whereas virtually every measure of disease control implies an element of social control, empowering the medical profession while reducing the diseased to the role of patients, the human rights aspects of AIDS are particularly prominent. Unlike other infectious diseases, AIDS has been associated with stigmatization, discrimination, persecution and a wide range of human rights abuses (Tomasevski 1992a; Csete 2007).

The complexity and sensitivity of HIV/AIDS as a policy problem should not be underestimated, as we inquire into the types of actors that have been and are involved on the global stage, and what kind of action has been taken or not taken. After a brief chronology of the international response to the pandemic, this chapter will analyze the actions and "actorness" of WHO in the early stage of the pandemic, and of the public-private partnerships emerging as WHO's successors around the turn of the millennium.

HIV/AIDS on the international agenda

The First International Conference on AIDS in Atlanta in April 1985, attended by scientists and health officials from 50 countries, constituted the beginning of a worldwide mobilization of the biomedical community. International AIDS conferences have since become annual events. Despite widening topics and participation, these remain primarily international forums for scientific exchange.

The reaction of the global political community to the HIV/AIDS issue was belated. A global offensive, involving governments and international organizations, was launched only in 1987, some five years after public health officials realized that a new disease was spreading. In May of this "year of global AIDS mobilization" (Panos 1988: 94) WHO initiated its Special Programme on AIDS, later known as the Global Programme on AIDS (GPA).

Governments and other international organizations promptly endorsed the WHO initiative. In October, AIDS was discussed by the UN General Assembly, the first time a specific disease was considered by that forum. Its resolution confirmed "the established leadership and the essential global directing and coordinating role" of WHO (Gordenker et al. 1995: 40).

Despite virtually universal endorsement initially and despite serious efforts at creating structures for coordinating UN agencies, donor countries and nongovernmental organizations (NGOs), GPA ran into a variety of problems in relation to other actors on the international scene. Whereas contributions to GPA increased significantly in the first few years, by 1991 they started declining, as donor governments started questioning the results of the program and shifted toward bilateral funding (Mann et al. 1992). As it became evident that HIV/AIDS was a problem with no medical solution in sight, other UN agencies, such as the UN Development Programme (UNDP) and the UN Children's Fund (UNICEF) claimed equally valid expertise and came to question WHO's role as lead agency. The World Bank had begun to make direct loans for health services, promoting "structural adjustment" measures, at the very time that the HIV/AIDS epidemic erupted. While controversial, the bank's loans for health surpassed WHO's total budget by 1990 (Brown et al. 2006: 67–68).

A critical external review of GPA, delivered in January 1992, recommended the establishment of a new global coordinative mechanism. After a series of interagency negotiations and donor country meetings, WHO and the UN Economic and Social Council (ECOSOC) in 1994 endorsed the launching of a new joint and cosponsored UN program by January 1996.

The Joint UN Programme on HIV/AIDS, known by the acronym UNAIDS, is designed to coordinate the HIV/AIDS-related programs of UN agencies. In addition to the cosponsors—the UN High

Commissioner for Refugees (UNHCR), UNICEF, the World Food Programme (WFP), the UNDP, the UN Population Fund (UNFPA), the UN Office on Drugs and Crime (UNODC), the International Labour Organization (ILO), the UN Educational, Scientific and Cultural Organization (UNESCO), WHO and the World Bank—representatives of 22 governments from all geographical regions and five NGO representatives, including associations of PLWHA, form its Program Coordinating Board (PCB). UNAIDS can be seen as a new kind of entity in the UN family, insofar as it unites several UN organizations—six at its creation, 10 at present—with the explicit objective to coordinate the UN system's response to the HIV/AIDS challenge (Kohlmorgen 2007: 136–37).

Initially UNAIDS lacked funding, staff and support from key states, such as the United States and Britain. By building a solid base of scientific studies of HIV prevalence and successful AIDS programs, UNAIDS managed to renew global interest in the pandemic. In January 2000 the UN Security Council, under US presidency, for the first time debated AIDS as a global security threat. In June 2001 the UN General Assembly held a special session on HIV/AIDS (UNGASS), which adopted, by consensus, a Declaration of Commitment entitled "Global Crisis—Global Action" (Patterson 2007: 208).

UNGASS concluded with a commitment to set up a global trust fund, as suggested by UN Secretary-General Kofi Annan at an African summit on HIV/AIDS in Abuja, Nigeria, in April. At their summit in Genoa in July, all G8 heads of state affirmed their support for the global fund and expressed their determination to make it operational as soon as possible. Malaria and tuberculosis were added to the mandate of the grant-making organization.

The Global Fund to Fight AIDS, Tuberculosis and Malaria (GFATM) was designed as a grant-making organization, funding proposals following technical review, with continued support tied to performance. At the insistence of some G8 countries, especially the United States and Japan, it was to stand apart from and operate outside the UN system, which was considered inefficient and bureaucratic (Bartsch 2007: 149; Lisk 2008: 149). A unique governance model was adopted: in addition to an equal number of government representatives from industrialized and developing countries, NGO representatives from developed and developing countries as well as private-sector representatives are included on the Fund's governing board. In January 2002 the Global Fund was constituted as an independent Swiss foundation with its secretariat in Geneva, and three months later the first round of grants were approved.

A major factor contributing to the renewed attention to HIV/AIDS around the turn of the millennium was the development in the 1990s of antiretroviral drugs (ARVs), which reduce the viral load and allow HIV-infected people to return to a healthier state. The pressure on pharmaceutical companies to reduce their prices to make these drugs available in poor countries mounted, and an access campaign "pitted a transnational network of NGOs against a transnational network of pharmaceutical firms" (Sell and Prakash 2004: 160). In May 2000 the UN-sponsored Accelerating Access Initiative (AAI) was launched, a partnership between five UN agencies—UNAIDS, WHO, UNFPA, UNICEF and the World Bank—and five, later seven, major ARV producers (Seckinelgin 2008: 27–28; Patterson 2007: 212). Unlike the previous public-private partnerships, the initiative for establishing AAI came from the pharmaceutical industry (Bull and McNeill 2007: 81).

Whereas the development of life-sustaining drugs for HIV/AIDS patients constitutes a major step forward, the search for a vaccine continues. This is another facet of the pandemic that has spawned public-private partnerships. The International AIDS Vaccine Initiative (IAVI), founded in 1996, engages in research, policy analysis, partnering with developing countries and advocacy (www.iavi.org). The Global HIV Vaccine Enterprise is an alliance of researchers, funders and advocates committed to accelerating the development of an HIV vaccine. Based on an initiative from researchers in 2003, the Enterprise is modeled in part on the Human Genome project, the alliance of scientific organizations that successfully mapped the human genetic code (www.hivvaccineenterprise.org). Both the Enterprise and IAVI have headquarters in New York.

As this (all too) brief overview indicates, there are two different types of IO actors to be discussed in the HIV/AIDS field. First, WHO functioned as "lead agency" during the first decade of the global response to the pandemic, following a traditional UN pattern. Second, the emerging public-private partnerships around the turn of the millennium represent a new breed of international organizations. To what extent can we speak of IOs as actors in these two different contexts? How can we account for their action and inaction?

Early IO action and inaction

WHO was very slow in acknowledging HIV/AIDS as a global problem. The first international organization to respond to the epidemic was not WHO, as one would have expected, but the Council of Europe. The WHO secretariat initially considered AIDS primarily as a problem of the rich world—a "disease of affluence," confined to the Western industrialized countries. A key component in WHO's ambitious "Global Strategy for Health for All by the Year 2000," launched in 1977, was the transfer of medical knowledge from the rich to the poor parts of the world. A 1983 internal WHO memorandum dismissed the need for WHO to become involved, because AIDS was "being very well taken care of by some of the richest countries in the world where there is the manpower and knowhow and where most of the patients are to be found" (quoted in Tomasevski 1992b: 8).

At the same time as medical experts agreed on a low-key WHO approach, the Parliamentary Assembly of the Council of Europe took a clear stand against discrimination towards homosexuals in the wake of the AIDS epidemic in Europe. In a November 1983 resolution, designed "to denounce the use of this disease as a pretext for campaigns against homosexuals," the Council of Europe called for "questionnaires and literature on AIDS to be worded in such terms as to avoid infringing, in any way, directly or indirectly, an individual's independence and privacy" (quoted in Gordenker *et al.* 1995: 39).

One crucial background factor accounting for this early action by the Council of Europe was a 1981 resolution affirming "the right to sexual self-determination" and calling upon WHO to delete homosexuality from its International Classification of Diseases, where at that time it figured among mental disorders. That resolution was "the first of its kind on this subject of homosexuality in a 'dignified' international forum," to quote the Dutch rapporteur, J.J. Voogd (Gordenker *et al.* 1995: 39). This early involvement by the Council of Europe conditioned its response to AIDS as a human rights issue in 1983. Both the 1981 and the 1983 resolutions involved lobbying from homosexual activists.

Only in 1985–86 did the full extent of the epidemic in the Third World become fully appreciated, and the realization grew that AIDS was a "disease of poverty" rather than wealth. This marked the beginning of more active WHO involvement. At a WHO African Regional Conference on AIDS in Brazzaville in November 1986, WHO Director-General Halfdan Mahler confessed that he had needed to be converted to the idea that AIDS was a problem which would affect the developing world (Gordenker *et al.* 1995: 40), and in 1988 he admitted: "I know that many people at first refused to believe that a crisis was upon us. I know because I was one of them" (Panos 1988: 3).

How, then, can we account for the long inaction by the most likely IO, WHO, and the early action by one of the least likely IOs, the Council of Europe? Neither can be readily explained in simple principal-agent terms. There is no indication that early WHO passivity was a response to government pressure. On the contrary, once WHO took on the AIDS issue, there was next to universal government endorsement, partly because it was convenient to assign the main responsibility for an issue that was surrounded by prejudices and taboos domestically to an international organization. By the same token, it was special-interest lobbying rather than government initiatives that prompted action by the Council of Europe, generally considered a conservative intergovernmental organization.

Institutional theory offers more plausible explanations. Institutions can be understood broadly as relatively stable collections of social practices consisting of easily recognized *roles* coupled with underlying *norms* and a set of *rules* or conventions defining appropriate behavior for, and governing relations among, occupants of these roles (Young 1989: 32; March and Olsen 1998: 948). These norms and rules "prescribe behavioral roles, constrain activity, and shape expectations" (Keohane 1988: 383).

Different branches of institutionalism point to different aspects of institutionalized behavior. Normative or sociological institutionalism emphasizes that organizations tend to develop norms of appropriate behavior; historical institutionalism directs our attention to path dependence, the fact that previous choices have a persistent influence over subsequent actions by eliminating alternative "paths" and creating lock-in effects. Both aspects are of relevance to the observed pattern of early responses to AIDS.

As support to developing countries in providing "health for all" was a mainstay of WHO's work, a combination of path dependence and appropriateness called for involvement only after the epidemic had been recognized as a North–South issue. Path dependence excluded action, as long as AIDS was seen as a disease of the rich part of the world; and the logic of appropriateness called for WHO assistance, once it was recognized as a disease of the poor. Whereas the early action by the Council of Europe on the AIDS issue cannot be explained by the logic of appropriateness, it was clearly path-dependent in terms of being conditioned by previous decisions concerning non-discrimination of homosexuals. In sum, the initial WHO inaction as well as the early Council of Europe action, both equally counterintuitive, can best be accounted for by institutional factors.

WHO as "lead agency"

Once WHO had been designated "lead agency" in the combat against AIDS in 1987, three types of action predominated: programmatic decisions concerning its overall strategy; operational decisions about its use of resources and provision of services; and boundary decisions relating to interaction with other actors on the global arena (cf. Cox and Jacobson 1974: 8–11).

Programmatic decisions

The Global Programme on AIDS rested on two premises: framing HIV/AIDS as a medical issue, and emphasizing its North–South aspects. WHO's "ownership" of HIV/AIDS as a global issue contributed to its "medicalization" in terms of framing the problem in medical terms, using medical vocabulary to discuss it, and mandating the medical profession to provide treatment (cf. Seckinelgin 2008: 72–73). A medical approach entails identifying the viral cause of the disease, managing it clinically, and finding a vaccine.

Yet orthodox medical solutions to epidemics long remained beyond reach in the case of AIDS. Despite considerable efforts, neither a drug that would cure the disease nor a vaccine that would prevent infection could be found. The main medical breakthrough remained the discovery of the human immuno-deficiency virus (HIV) in 1983–84, which ushered in the development of diagnostic tests, making it possible to identify infected but asymptomatic individuals. The availability of testing, in turn, facilitated exclusionary policies around the world, as governments adopted restrictions on entry for HIV-infected travelers or migrants either by law or in practice. Hence, paradoxically, medicalization tended to aggravate the problem, rather than providing a solution.

In fact, medicalization inevitably implies an element of social control. Virtually every measure of disease control has human rights implications. Public health responses to AIDS or other epidemics include restrictive measures, such as identification and surveillance of affected categories and individuals or safeguards against the spread of the epidemic.

GPA Director Jonathan Mann made repeated efforts at frame restructuring by referring to three epidemics. The silent and unnoticed spread of HIV infection beginning in the 1970s represents the first, the spread of AIDS cases the second epidemic. The third epidemic concerns the social, economic, political and cultural reactions to, and consequences of, the first two epidemics. According to Mann, this epidemic is "as central to the global AIDS challenge as the disease itself" and can be "as destructive as the preceding ones," threatening even "to overshadow and overwhelm the epidemics of HIV and AIDS" (quoted in Gordenker *et al.* 1995: 41).

The fact that the medical framing prevailed and Mann's idea of a third epidemic never took hold can be accounted for by a combination of principal-agent and institutional logics. For the original principals, the governments that endorsed the designation of WHO as "lead agency," the medical framing of AIDS was politically convenient, insofar as it transferred the chief responsibility for solving the problem from the political realm to the medical profession. Politically sensitive aspects of AIDS, such as stigmatization, human rights violations or poverty, were eclipsed by the search for a medical cure. Moreover, delegating AIDS to the medical profession offered a universalized language and pattern of thought and therefore held out the promise of a global consensus. Hence governments were happy to authorize WHO as an actor on the AIDS issue without too much interference. The second principal-agent link, between WHO as principal and GPA as agent, could only reinforce the medical framing. In WHO both governmental representatives and the international secretariat are drawn primarily from the biomedical and public health sectors.

At the same time, path dependence and the organizational culture of WHO preordained a medical framing of AIDS. Based on previous experiences of outbreaks of infectious diseases, WHO's response was medically and epidemiologically driven, spurred by a sense of emergency. WHO's campaign to eradicate smallpox, launched in 1967 and declared a success in 1980, was a precedent in targeting and eliminating a specific disease. Even if Jonathan Mann and others knew from field experience that there was more to AIDS than clinical interventions, "institutional inertia was hard to resist and directed policy and action firmly into the clinical-medical framework" (Barnett and Whiteside 2002: 76).

Just as the recognition of AIDS as a North–South issue was a precondition for WHO to get engaged, WHO's eventual involvement brought the North–South aspects of the pandemic into focus and pointed to development assistance as the principal kind of action in response to the problem. The earlier record of WHO supported this as a tenable approach. At the same time, this touched on the programs of several of the organizations of the UN system as well as those of national governments. As WHO's programmatic choice was translated into operational decisions, this would eventually prove to be problematic.

Operational decisions

For many governments that would normally prefer bilateral foreign aid, channeling assistance through WHO offered a convenient way out of a political quandary. Commenting on government willingness to contribute to GPA, WHO Director-General Halfdan Mahler stated in 1987: "A number of major political donors have stated clearly that their bilateral efforts to combat AIDS have been constrained by political sensitivities, and inadequate knowledge, expertise, experience and financial and human resources" (quoted in Gordenker et al. 1995: 74).

Again we can discern a combination of principal-agent and institutional logics. As principals, governments had good reasons to delegate responsibility to WHO. Since AIDS was an issue surrounded by moral and religious inhibitions and taboos, several governments were content not to take political responsibility themselves. If principals preferred "negative" delegation, the entrusted agent, WHO, was well prepared to deliver. The emphasis on transfers of resources from the rich to the poor parts of the world reflected appropriate and time-honored WHO behavior. Thus, GPA could draw on the previous experiences, expertise and organizational culture of WHO. By 1991, about one-half of all flows of assistance related to AIDS were directed to or through WHO (Mann et al. 1992: 519–21, 524).

However, no account of the increase of multilateral funding at the expense of bilateral aid would be complete without paying attention to the role played by the GPA secretariat, in particular Jonathan Mann. Beginning in mid-1986, Mann made frequent visits to prospective donor countries, talking with government leaders, senior officials in foreign aid agencies, scientists and national AIDS committees. His persuasive skills were instrumental in multiplying donor commitments to GPA from US$30.3 million in 1987 to $82.4 million in 1990 (Gordenker et al. 1995: 74).

In 1991 contributions to GPA began to decline, at the same time as all contributions for AIDS prevention and control in developing countries decreased (Mann et al. 1992: 511–12, 519). In addition to general "donor fatigue" and new demands for aid resulting from the collapse of the Soviet Union, dwindling reliance on multilateral assistance through GPA had to do with the strong opposition of major donor countries, led by the United States, to the reappointment in 1993 of WHO Director-General Hiroshi Nakajima as well as growing unease about the coordination within the UN system. Several UN agencies, such as UNICEF, UNESCO, UNFPA and especially the World Bank, developed programs that cut across GPA's efforts.

In addition, GPA encountered increasing difficulties within the WHO structure. GPA was criticized for its unwillingness to work within standard WHO procedures, for developing its own expertise in health education, laboratory technology and clinical support, and for choosing solutions not authorized by WHO. At the same time, there was, as the external review committee noted, "no doubt, resentment at the apparent ease with which GPA was raising substantial funds" (Gordenker *et al.* 1995: 77). The shrinking room for maneuver of GPA can be explained in principal-agent terms. As the initial fervor for multilateral approaches subsided, GPA as agent faced three categories of increasingly dissatisfied principals. Most importantly, donor governments turned their back on GPA and reverted to bilateral programs. Second, as designated "lead agency" WHO represented the UN family, and now other members of this family questioned WHO's mandate and developed overlapping, even competing, programs. Third, GPA was a branch of WHO, and WHO's leadership, as GPA's immediate principal, acted to limit the agent's autonomy.

Boundary decisions

As the branch responsible for WHO's "lead agency" role, GPA had to manage relations and interactions with two sets of actors: other members of the UN family, and the NGO community. Both proved to be problematic.

Lacking experience of coordinating the UN system, WHO officials had traditionally been effective in defining and protecting their organizational boundaries, claiming that the organization had unique expertise in public-health matters. Now they were to direct and coordinate the global fight against AIDS. The importance attached to managing interorganizational relations is indicated by Jonathan Mann's appointment of an experienced Canadian diplomat, Terry L. Mooney, to head external relations (Gordenker *et al.* 1995: 56).

GAP's coordinating role was complicated by the existence of parallel structures. Requested by the UN General Assembly resolution of 1987 to provide a coordinated response to AIDS, the Secretary-General formally designated the UN Department of International Economic and Social Affairs (DIESA) in New York to follow up the resolution. Reporting to the UN Administrative Committee on Coordination (ACC), DIESA organized a Steering Committee on AIDS which, in turn, created a Standing Committee on AIDS with little or no WHO presence. This elaborate structure accomplished little and was practically dormant by 1992 (Gordenker *et al.* 1995: 55–56).

The WHO GPA, for its part, established two structures to maintain system-wide leadership: an Inter-Agency Advisory Group (IAAG), made up of representatives of all agencies in the UN family interested in AIDS; and a GPA Global Management Committee (GMC), consisting primarily of representatives of all governments making unearmarked contributions to the GPA budget. IAAG included the World Bank, which did not participate in DIESA, and soon came to overshadow the New York structures when it came to stimulating AIDS programs in different agencies. GMC functioned as a reviewing body, reporting formally to the WHO director-general (Gordenker et al. 1995: 58–59).

In addition, the UNDP and WHO attempted to link their AIDS programs through a novel "Alliance to Combat AIDS." As attention to human rights gradually increased, WHO organized consultations on AIDS in Geneva in collaboration with the UN Centre on Human Rights. Participants from the two agencies discovered that they did not speak the same language and represented different organizational cultures (Gordenker et al. 1995: 64). In sum, overlapping efforts at IO coordination evinced different approaches to the AIDS issue rather than dovetailing of activities.

Coordination with NGOs proved even more problematic. As a unit of an intergovernmental organization, GPA could support governments but could not reach out to local communities, the necessity of which was emphasized both in WHO's global health for all policy and in UN resolutions on AIDS. Ministries of health, the traditional counterparts for WHO in member states, were notoriously weak and seriously constrained in confronting the AIDS pandemic in affected areas in the developing world. Thus, the GPA staff realized that the normal state-centered, sovereignty-based approach of WHO would be insufficient. While acknowledging the need to integrate various NGOs into coordinated global efforts to counter AIDS, GPA staff members had little experience in working with NGOs outside the public health sector. The AIDS epidemic had given rise to a new breed of NGOs, including so-called AIDS service organizations (ASOs) representing people living with HIV/AIDS.

No consensus existed within GPA concerning the proper role of NGOs. In the view of one group, the functions of NGOs were limited to assisting WHO in information gathering and program implementation. On the other hand, from the beginning of his tenure Jonathan Mann, who had directed a collaborative field research project on AIDS in Zaire prior to being recruited to WHO, demonstrated his conviction that NGOs needed to be included in all aspects of the policy process.

By the end of 1987, GPA recruited Robert Grose as NGO liaison officer. An experienced hand with NGO relations, Grose was seconded by the British Overseas Development Administration (Gordenker et al. 1995: 54, 90). Jeffrey O'Malley, from the Canadian Council for

International Co-operation, was hired as a consultant, helping Mann and Grose to develop a strategy of NGO involvement (Söderholm 1997: 160–61). A small network of NGO representatives that was formed around this trio prepared the ground for the First Meeting of ASOs in Vienna in early 1989. The meeting debated the idea of an umbrella organization or NGO forum, capable of channeling NGO input into GPA in a structured and coherent manner, but failed to reach consensus.

At subsequent international conferences of NGOs in Montreal in 1989 and in Paris in 1990, the establishment of an International Council of ASOs (ICASO) was discussed. The Paris conference revealed clashing ASO interests, overshadowing the general conference theme of "solidarity."

> Representatives of organized "sex workers" ... were angered, because they believed that they were being treated as a problem, not as a group that suffered from discrimination. From groups of male homosexuals, some of which confronted the conference with strident, largely sexual demonstrations, came similar complaints. The gay and lesbian caucus asserted that the plenary sessions failed to address their specific problems and issues sufficiently. The suggestion emerged from one of their caucuses that those gays or lesbians who were members of specialized panels should not talk about anything but gay issues. The women's caucus voted to exclude men from its meetings. This led to a partial walkout of other women from the remaining caucus sessions. The African caucus voted to exclude white Europeans from its meetings.
> (Gordenker *et al.* 1995: 97)

In the prevailing mood of discontent and conflict it came as no surprise that the intended ratification of the proposed ICASO failed. The predominance of American and European NGOs as well as the general difficulties of selecting a few organizations as representatives of the variegated NGO community eventually precluded the establishment of a formal coordinating body.

How can we account for GPA's failure to manage its external relations and establish effective coordination structures? The key word is complexity. There were simply too many stakeholders, with too diverse interests, claiming to be "principals" in the global fight against AIDS. Whereas the existence of multiple principals is generally considered to widen the leeway of agents (Lake and McCubbins 2006: 361), in this case it incapacitated GPA, as coordination—rather than individual action—was its key mandate. From a more constructivist viewpoint, the dramatic variety of organizational cultures among relevant actors precluded coordinated action. There was minimal interaction between "white coats, grey suits and T-shirts" (Gilmore 1992), that is, the medical profession, IOs/NGOs, and activists. Moreover, there were equally significant differences within each of these categories.

From "lead agency" to public-private partnerships

In addition to mobilizing donor countries to support a multilateral response to the pandemic and providing technical support to development countries, WHO GPA was successful in building consensual knowledge and establishing an international discourse around HIV/AIDS that increasingly emphasized empowerment and participation. By the mid-1990s no government or educated citizen was unaware of the complexity and severity of the pandemic. Moreover, GPA contributed to the recognition of the NGO community as legitimate participants in the fight against AIDS (Altman 1999).

The main criticism of GPA was that it failed to produce *coordinated* action. Despite all of its efforts, the gap between the rate of new infections and initial strategic expectations had grown ever wider (Altman 1999; Poku 2004: 98). Beginning in 1992, a series of inter-agency meetings and negotiations sought for a "multisectoral approach." In 1996 UNAIDS was established as the result of this drawn-out process. Thus a new type of international organization was born, which united several UN agencies in a non-hierarchical manner. By including representatives of NGOs, UNAIDS can be seen as a forerunner of the global public-private partnership format that in 1999 got a prominent manifestation in the UN Global Compact. The Global Fund to Fight AIDS, Tuberculosis and Malaria, initiated in 2002, is an even more pronounced example of this new organizational type, as it includes partners from the business sector as well.

The organizational changes in the HIV/AIDS field reflected a general trend in global public health governance. In the 1990s the realization grew that improved health conditions in poor countries constitute a precondition for economic growth (Hein *et al.* 2007: 226). Poverty reduction came back on the global agenda, culminating in the adoption of the Millennium Development Goals, one of which is to halt and reverse the spread of HIV/AIDS. This opened up for "multi-stakeholder diplomacy" (Lisk 2008: 147), allowing non-state actors—not only traditional NGOs, but also business, private donors and AIDS activists—into emergent new structures of global governance in public health.

A number of contextual changes paved the way for the emergence of public-private partnerships in international cooperation for health from the late 1990s (Buse and Walt 2000: 551–52). First, there was an ideological shift, insofar as the *neoliberal* focus on "freeing" the market gave way to *neocorporatist* notions of "modifying" the market and granting a variety of stakeholders a legitimate say in public policy-making. Second, growing disillusionment with the UN and its agencies created fertile ground for new organizational forms. Some observers saw public-private partnerships as a move away from the "big plans" of traditional international agencies toward "visible piecemeal steps" (Kickbusch 2005: 970). Third, a new perspective on health evolved, with increasing recognition that the determinants of good health are wide-ranging. Public health was increasingly framed in socioeconomic rather than purely medical terms. Hence, the global health agenda came to be regarded as too extensive for any single sector or organization to tackle alone.

As in other sectors, global health partnerships may take various forms. The common denominator is that they are hybrid organizations involving both public and private actors on a voluntary basis. In addition, they seem to share four characteristics: a common goal, an explicit division of labor, shared risks and benefits, and some form of joint decision-making (Buse 2005: 192).

Public-private partnerships, in short, are designed to handle the complexity that a single organization, such as WHO, cannot manage alone. To what extent, then, are composite partnerships capable of independent action? Can they behave as single actors? Let us discuss the "actorness" of UNAIDS and the Global Fund, in turn, and inquire into the kind of action taken.

UNAIDS

Whereas GPA put a lot of effort into mobilizing donor governments to support a multilateral response to the epidemic, the co-sponsoring UN agencies decided that UNAIDS would not be a funding agency but was to have a more pronounced advocacy role (Poku 2004: 98). In a sense, it is therefore more political than GPA. One example of coordinated action in this advocacy role is the process leading to UNGASS in 2001, when UNAIDS officials provided needed information to country delegations and built political support for the final Declaration of Commitment (Patterson 2007: 208).

> The process of convincing the General Assembly to call for the special session, negotiating the draft declaration before UNGASS,

and gaining unanimous support for the declaration at UNGASS required country delegates, UNAIDS officials, and NGO representatives to listen to each other and compromise ... UN civil servants, in conjunction with public health experts and AIDS NGOs, acted as knowledge brokers and intermediaries between member states.
(Patterson 2007: 211)

However, the process was probably more important and successful than the end product. A follow-up UN General Assembly High Level Meeting on HIV/AIDS in 2006 noted the lack of progress in the global response since the 2001 Declaration, which was attributed to governance-related factors, such as weak leadership and commitment (Lisk 2008: 146–47).

UNAIDS was designed to coordinate UN agencies. Yet its co-sponsors have continued to conduct their own policies and programs. As they have surrendered little of their autonomy, duplication and rivalry persist (Kohlmorgen 2007: 130). For example, the existence of a relatively large HIV/AIDS department in WHO parallels UNAIDS; the World Bank has run its Multi-Country HIV/AIDS Program (MAP) since 2000, and remains a leading single donor in the fight against AIDS; UNDP has a program seeking to integrate AIDS priorities in poverty reduction strategies; and UNICEF has launched its Unite for Children Unite Against AIDS campaign. In short, "the existence of UNAIDS has not abolished rivalries between UN organizations and has not solved the coordination and cooperation problems" (Kohlmorgen 2007: 138).

What kinds of action, then, has UNAIDS undertaken? Two notable examples concern its role, first, in monitoring national AIDS programs and improving coordination at the national level, and second, in setting standards and changing attitudes as norm entrepreneur.

UNAIDS' monitoring role is reinforced by the 2001 UNGASS Declaration of Commitment, which obliged UN member states to report progress in addressing the epidemic. In 2008 147 states reported a significant increase from previous reporting rounds, yet fewer than the total number of 192 UN member states (UNAIDS 2008: 3). In 2003 UNAIDS initiated its efforts to harmonize national programs by promoting the so-called "Three Ones" principle—one national AIDS authority, one national strategic framework, and one national monitoring and evaluation system (Kohlmorgen 2007: 140). Despite notable progress in implementing the principle, only 30 percent of the reporting governments fulfill all three criteria, and nearly half of them report that external partners fail to align their efforts with national HIV strategies (UNAIDS 2008: 29–30).

In assembling and disseminating information about HIV/AIDS UNAIDS functions as a knowledge-based epistemic community, with shared views of cause-and-effect relationships and common values (Haas 1992). As such, UNAIDS follows in the footsteps of WHO GPA. In its role as norm entrepreneur, promoting desirable behavior (Finnemore and Sikkink 1998: 896), UNAIDS has noted a measure of success in changing attitudes among stakeholders. For instance, one disputed issue at UNGASS in 2001 was whether or not to name specific groups, such as sex workers, male homosexuals or injection drug users, as particularly affected by and vulnerable to HIV. Early drafts of the declaration that included such references were resisted by the United States and a number of Middle Eastern states and had to be dropped despite the support of the European Union (EU) and several states (Altman 2006: 258; Csete 2007: 248). Gradually UNAIDS has managed to achieve more mutual recognition among civil society actors, including faith-based organizations. In follow-up UNGASS meetings, UNAIDS has been able to stage appearances by members of stigmatized groups (interview at UNAIDS, May, 2009).

The Global Fund to Fight AIDS, Tuberculosis and Malaria (GFATM)

Whereas advocacy is the primary purpose of UNAIDS, the Global Fund is a financial instrument, funding project proposals from applicant states. It functions in a similar way as research councils or foundations in the academic realm, insofar as proposals are subjected to peer review, grants are awarded to a fraction of the applicants for a limited period of time, and renewed grants are contingent on documented performance.

In formal terms, GFATM is a foundation registered under Swiss law. Yet it enjoys unique status as an international legal personality with privileges and immunities similar to those granted to IOs. Whereas the Fund is thus not a member of the UN family, the World Bank serves as its trustee, responsible for the collection, investment and management of funds, disbursement of funds to recipient countries and programs, and financial reporting (Panos 2003: 31).

The hybrid character of GFATM is reflected in the composition of its board. It consists of five types of constituencies: donor states, recipient states, civil society, private sector, and bilateral/multilateral agencies. These are sorted into two voting groups—a donor group and a recipient group—as well as one non-voting group. Eight representatives from industrialized states and two representatives from the private sector (one company, one foundation) constitute the donor group. In the recipient group are seven representatives from developing states and three civil society representatives (one north, one south, one affected communities). The non-voting group consists of three IO representatives from WHO, UNAIDS and the World Bank, as well as a Swiss member. Whereas government seats in the donor group are allocated on the basis of pledges to the fund, the selection of other members is left to their respective regionally defined constituencies.

Initially associations of affected communities belonged to the non-voting group, but eventually succeeded in their quest for voting status. To restore the balance between the two voting groups, the number of donor state seats then increased from seven to eight, thereby reducing the relative weight of developing states. The board normally operates by consensus; if this fails, a double majority, in absolute terms and within each voting group, is required (Bartsch 2007: 152).

The power imbalance is underlined by the fact that the two most important committees preparing board meetings, the Policy and Strategy Committee and the Finance and Audit Committee, are chaired by donor group representatives. The 35-member Technical Review Panel (TRP), the health and development experts reviewing grant applications, is another important body that has been accused of Western bias. African experts may be underrepresented in proportion to the level of funding going to African states, but the Board tries to strike a balance of gender, regional representation and multisectoral experience in appointing TRP members. "Although the empirical facts do not seem to support the claim of TRP bias, what is interesting is that there are a large number of stakeholders who believe that political and cultural bias is involved in the evaluation process" (Barnes and Brown 2009: 9).

As a global public-private partnership, the Global Fund strives to encourage similar consensus-building and dialogues between civil society, the private sector and government representatives in applicant countries. To apply for grants, a country must set up a Country Coordinating Mechanism (CCM), composed of representatives from governments, NGOs, multilateral and bilateral donor agencies, and business (Patterson 2007: 215–16). The CCM is regarded as an essential structure of the Fund's architecture, designed to reflect its commitment to local ownership, recipient-driven strategies and broad participation (Panos 2003: 30; Lisk 2008: 149; Brown 2009: 172–74).

While taking different forms in recipient states, CCM structures have typically run into a number of problems. They tend to be government-dominated, with token civil society representation. Even when formal representation is given to civil society organizations, practical constraints often inhibit their full participation. The role of CCMs is well defined in the preparation of a proposal, but is more ambiguous in the implementation phase after a grant is given (Bartsch 2007: 156). Because of limited resources and capacities, many CCMs seek outside assistance from international organizations, such as WHO, UNAIDS and the World Bank, in developing and writing proposals to the Fund (Panos 2003: 31; Bartsch and Kohlmorgen 2007: 132), which tends to dilute notions of local initiative and ownership.

How, then, can we characterize the Global Fund as an actor? Its demand-driven model means that funding is in line with country needs and priorities, and performance-based funding has promoted learning and improved program management. GFATM does not hesitate to publish data concerning grants with poor performance and lessons learned from them (see Global Fund 2009: 100–1). In the words of one outside observer: "What is impressive about the Global Fund is its ability to learn from critical evaluation and to rethink its institutional practice" (Brown 2009: 174).

Two characteristics of the approved funds are noteworthy. First, they target the poorest and most vulnerable countries and populations, with about 60 percent going to sub-Saharan African countries. For instance, 3.7 million orphans have been provided with medical services, education and community care. Second, access to ARV treatment has been a priority, and today 2.3 million people are receiving it as a result of Global Fund grants (www.theglobalfund.org).

Public-private partnerships as actors

Partnerships like UNAIDS and the Global Fund are "meta-organizations," insofar as they have other organizations rather than individuals as members (Ahrne and Brunsson 2008: 2). Instead of letting specialized agencies interact in complex issue-areas, public-private partnerships bring these diverse actors together under the same organizational umbrella.

> Creating meta-organizations entails the reduction of environment and an increase in organization—transforming part of what was once the members' environment into organization. Instead of constituting each other's environment, the organization's members become members in the same organization. Parts of a possibly troublesome environment are replaced by an organization with more or less troublesome co-members.
>
> (Ahrne and Brunsson 2008: 56–57)

The "actorness" of the new creation depends on the balance between cooperation and conflict within the partnership. The Global Fund seems to enjoy less intra-partnership conflict than UNAIDS. Compared to the task of coordinating UN agencies—which has been likened to walking cats on a leash (Jonathan Mann, quoted in Poku 2004: 98)— and the advocacy role of UNAIDS, the actions expected from the Global Fund are more concrete, better defined, and more easily implemented.

While it makes sense to turn the organizational environment into partnerships in order to manage such multifaceted issues as AIDS, the global response to the pandemic continues to be characterized by fragmentation, duplication and overlap. The fight against AIDS requires coordination both horizontally (between different actors at the global level) and vertically (between actors at the global and the national or local level). Whereas UNAIDS and the Global Fund have contributed to improved horizontal coordination, critics argue that this has led to bureaucratization, homogenization (search for "one size fits all" solutions) and incentives to underplay project difficulties and exaggerate benefits.

> Donors' interest in hasty demonstrable "results" reinforces this homogenised approach favouring interventions that can be easily measured (such as number of condoms distributed, training workshops organised, and number of people counselled). These concentrate on inputs rather than outcomes measuring, for example, changes in sexual behaviour. Interventions are usually short-term and the long-term benefits of these actions beyond a program or budget cycle are rarely considered.
> (Doyle and Patel 2008: 1934)

Vertical coordination has proved to be even more difficult. Several observers have pointed to the lack of congruence between global programs and local implementation.

> The global NGO order certainly presses its understanding of gender equality, human rights and community participation, but these interact on the ground with local understandings in ways that often differ from the paper trail international organizations leave in their mission statements.
> (Swidler 2006: 273)

The response to the pandemic "is broadly planned at the international level while implementation relies on a set of fragmented organisations"

(Seckinelgin 2008: 42). The CCMs, created at the behest of the Global Fund, were designed to replicate the coordination potentials of global partnerships at the national level. While improving, CCM consultations can still be poorly structured, and NGO participation has been uneven. In addition, UNAIDS and the World Bank, for their part, have encouraged the creation of National HIV/AIDS Councils (NACs) at the national level. The establishment of an NAC is a precondition for receiving loans and grants through the World Bank's MAP. Reviews of MAP have concluded that NACs "are not providing consistent leadership and oversight" (Kohlmorgen 2007: 139). Moreover, there is a lack of coordination between CCM public-private partnerships and government-based NACs, as well as considerable uncertainty as to which should be the leading body in the national response to AIDS (Kohlmorgen 2007: 139).

How, then, can we account for the paradox that public-private partnerships that were designed to facilitate coordination have been less than successful in producing a coordinated response? Principal-agent theory suggests that multiple principals in combination with long chains of delegation make it more difficult for principals to control agents (Lake and McCubbins 2006: 361–67). This would seem to give the secretariats of public-private partnerships more leeway to carry out their own agenda. However, the lack of vertical coordination has more to do with the multitude of actors—at various levels and with different agendas—that are *not* in any principal-agent relationship with the partnerships. In addition, to the extent that we can regard them as principals, the partners have never ruled out unilateral action by entering the partnerships.

The composite nature of UNAIDS and the Global Fund raises the question whether they can be regarded as unitary actors. Members of the secretariats are the only individuals who identify exclusively with the organization. Both organizations have started with a limited number of staff and expanded gradually. They have not existed long enough to have developed distinct organizational cultures of their own. Nor have they displayed charismatic leadership that compares with that of Jonathan Mann in WHO GPA. To be sure, Peter Piot, the first executive director of UNAIDS, is a highly respected leader with medical expertise and close relations with the UN Secretary-General, but he has had a more circumscribed mandate than Mann. In the Global Fund, the Bill & Melinda Gates Foundation can be said to play an informal leadership role. It is a major contributor to, and has a seat on the board of, the fund. The Gates Foundation is influential not only because of the magnitude of its grants, but also by virtue of its less bureaucratic, "hands on" management style and its concern to bring new technology to developing countries. These features make the partnership more attractive to the main proprietors of new technology, the big pharmaceutical companies. Thus, the Gates Foundation has been instrumental in bringing different parties together (Bull and McNeill 2007: 89).

Conclusions

The three organizations treated in some detail in this chapter—WHO GPA, UNAIDS and the Global Fund—must all be considered actors in the global governance of HIV/AIDS. They have been engaged in advocacy as well as service delivery, and they have entered into relationships with other actors at various levels. Their secretariats have built up a unique expertise in the complexity of the issue, going beyond the narrow medical realm, which has given them authority and facilitated independent action. Different types of leadership have been a significant component of their "actorness"—consider, for example, the charismatic role of Jonathan Mann as compared with the behind-the-scenes management of the Bill & Melinda Gates Foundation.

In accounting for the actions of these organizations, I have probed principal-agent and institutional theory. These are often posited as alternative, mutually exclusive explanations. However, my findings indicate that they may be complementary. Theories can be likened to floodlights that illuminate one part of the stage but, by the same token, leave other parts in the shade or in the dark. They sensitize us to certain aspects of a phenomenon or problem while desensitizing us to others.

This chapter has described two different patterns of IO agency and actions in one specific issue-area. The "lead agency" model, which has been the traditional UN response to new global problems, entrusts one organization with leadership and coordination. As it rests on expertise, this model assumes well-defined and delimited issue-areas. If the issue at hand proves to be more multifaceted than initially expected, affecting and being affected by different policy sectors, this model invites turf wars, as the HIV/AIDS case illustrates.

The public-private partnership model, by contrast, proceeds from the assumption that most contemporary policy issues are complex and multifaceted. Their solution requires the mobilization of different types of expertise and action that are not limited to the public sector. While eschewing outright turf wars, public-private partnerships face intricate internal bargaining and balancing processes among partners with different interests and backgrounds.

It is impossible to tell which model is better. Both, as we have seen, have a mixed record of partial successes and failures to act independently. One common denominator concerns the difficulty of achieving coordinated action, which is needed in order to solve global problems that cut across sectors and organizational domains. Efforts at coordination normally inject an element of hierarchy, which will be resisted by autonomous organizations. Everyone wants coordination, but no one wants to be coordinated.

One thing that the IOs have accomplished in the HIV/AIDS field is to have granted and legitimized civil society involvement and agency. This is a process that was initiated by WHO GPA and has been continued by UNAIDS and the Global Fund. The gradual incorporation of civil society into governance structures has been facilitated by the fact that "the first generation of AIDS activists have been replaced by professional international activists ... creating a much more professional civil society activism which is also technically competent to be a part of the international discussion" (Seckinelgin 2008: 35). In the Global Fund and elsewhere, civil society actors play a particularly important role in the implementation of programs. "NGOs, in fact, constitute the largest implementation component of the governance structure" (Seckinelgin 2005: 358–59).

In terms of halting the pandemic, what have the IOs achieved that could not have been attained by states and other actors in their absence? First of all, they have contributed to global awareness and improved knowledge of the pandemic, established an international discourse around HIV/AIDS, and formulated norms concerning treatment and non-discrimination. Without the constant reminders from IOs, the sense of urgency could easily have been lost, and AIDS activists around the world rely on information and statements from IOs as support and legitimation of their activities.

Technical assistance from IOs has, in particular, contributed significantly to access to ARVs among populations that could not otherwise afford them, and to treatment of vulnerable groups, such as women, orphans, sex workers and drug users. In response to growing criticism that concentration on one disease may drain resources and take attention away from other public health concerns, technical assistance increasingly invests in building health systems.

These undeniable accomplishments notwithstanding, the epidemic is becoming generalized in many developing countries, the incidence of new HIV transmissions remains high, and still only a fraction of PLWHA get adequate care and sustainable ARV treatment (Strand 2007: 217–18). Only one-third of adults who need treatment are currently getting it, and barely 10 percent of children in need are today getting treatment. The majority of people in the world who are HIV positive are unaware of their HIV status (All-Party Parliamentary Group on AIDS 2009: 6–7). We are still far away from the Millennium Development Goal of halting and reversing the spread of HIV/AIDS by 2015, and we are, in the words of a recent report, "sitting on a treatment timebomb," insofar as the predictable treatment needs of PLWHA in the coming decade are not compatible with treatments and prices available today (All-Party Parliamentary Group on AIDS 2009: 5). As no breakthrough seems imminent in the search for a vaccine, only prevention can ensure a reversal of the spread of HIV. While continuing, prevention programs have so far had limited success.

IOs alone cannot change this bleak picture. Without political will among governments in donor and recipient states alike, IOs can only make marginal contributions. At the same time, fragmentation and duplication in the IO community in the fight against AIDS needs to be replaced by improved coordination.

Bibliography

Ahrne, Göran and Nils Brunsson, *Meta-organizations* (Cheltenham: Edward Elgar, 2008).
All-Party Parliamentary Group on AIDS, "The Treatment Timebomb," a report of the Inquiry of the All Party Parliamentary Group on AIDS into long-term access to HIV medicines in the developing world, 2009, www.aids-kampagne.de/filead min/Downloads/Universal_Access/Treatment_Timebomb.pdf.
Altman, Dennis, "UNAIDS: NGOs on Board and on the Board," Montreal International Forum paper, 1999, www.fimcivilsociety.org.
——"Taboos and Denial in Government Responses," *International Affairs* 82, no. 2 (2006): 257–68.
Barnes, Amy and Garrett Wallace Brown, "The Global Fund to Fight AIDS, Tuberculosis and Malaria: Expertise, Accountability and the Depoliticisation of Global Health Governance," paper prepared for International Studies Association (ISA) 50th Annual Convention, New York, 15–18 February 2009.
Barnett, Tony, "A Long-Wave Event. HIV/AIDS, Politics, Governance and 'Security': Sundering the Intergenerational Bond?" *International Affairs* 82, no. 2 (2006): 297–313.
Barnett, Tony and Alan Whiteside, *AIDS in the Twenty-first Century* (Basingstoke: Palgrave Macmillan, 2002).
Bartsch, Sonja, "The Global Fund to Fight AIDS, Tuberculosis and Malaria," in *Global Health Governance and the Fight Against HIV/AIDS*, ed. Wolfgang Hein, Sonja Bartsch and Lars Kohlmorgen (Basingstoke: Palgrave Macmillan, 2007).

Bartsch, Sonja and Lars Kohlmorgen, "The Role of Civil Society Organizations in Global Health Governance," in *Global Health Governance and the Fight Against HIV/AIDS*, ed. Wolfgang Hein, Sonja Bartsch and Lars Kohlmorgen (Basingstoke: Palgrave Macmillan, 2007).

Brown, Garrett Wallace, "Multisectoralism, Participation, and Stakeholder Effectiveness: Increasing the Role of Nonstate Actors in the Global Fund to Fight AIDS, Tuberculosis and Malaria," *Global Governance* 15, no. 2 (2009): 169–77.

Brown, Theodore M., Marcos Cueto, and Elizabeth Fee, "The World Health Organization and the Transition from International to Global Public Health," *American Journal of Public Health* 96, no. 1 (2006): 62–72.

Bull, Benedicte and Desmond McNeill, *Development Issues in Global Governance: Public-Private Partnerships and Market Multilateralism* (London: Routledge, 2007).

Buse, Kent, "The Commercial Sector and Global Health Governance," in *Global Change and Health*, ed. Kelley Lee and Jeff Collin (Maidenhead: Open University Press, 2005).

Buse, Kent and Gill Walt, "Global Public-Private Partnerships: Part I—A New Development in Health?" *Bulletin of the World Health Organization* 78, no. 4 (2000): 549–61.

Cox, Robert W. and Harold K. Jacobson, *The Anatomy of Influence: Decision Making in International Organization* (New Haven: Yale University Press, 1974).

Csete, Joanne, "Rhetoric and Reality: HIV/AIDS as a Human Rights Issue," in *The Global Politics of AIDS*, ed. Paul G. Harris and Patricia D. Siplon (Boulder, Col.: Lynne Rienner, 2007).

Doyle, Cathal and Preeti Patel, "Civil Society Organisations and Global Health Initiatives: Problems of Legitimacy," *Social Science & Medicine* 66 (2008): 1928–38.

Finnemore, Martha and Kathryn Sikkink, "International Norm Dynamics and Political Change," *International Organization* 52, no. 4 (1998): 887–917.

Gilmore, Norbert, "Who's in Charge Here?" paper presented at symposium on Transnational Networks in Response to AIDS, Lund University, 13–14 January 1992.

Global Fund, *Scaling Up for Impact: Results Report* (Geneva: The Global Fund to Fight AIDS, Tuberculosis and Malaria, 2009).

Gordenker, Leon, Roger A. Coate, Christer Jönsson, and Peter Söderholm, *International Cooperation in Response to AIDS* (London: Pinter, 1995).

Haas, Peter M., "Introduction: Epistemic Communities and International Policy Coordination," *International Organization* 46, no. 1 (1992): 1–35.

Hein, Wolfgang, Sonja Bartsch, Lars Kohlmorgen, and Jan Peter Wogart, "Conclusion: Global Health Governance and the Fight Against HIV/AIDS in a Post-Westphalian World," in *Global Health Governance and the Fight Against HIV/AIDS*, ed. Wolfgang Hein, Sonja Bartsch and Lars Kohlmorgen (Basingstoke: Palgrave Macmillan, 2007).

Keohane, Robert. O., "International Institutions: Two Approaches," *International Studies Quarterly* 32, no. 4 (1988): 379–96.

Kickbusch, Ilona, "Action on Global Health: Addressing Global Health Governance Challenges," *Public Health* 119 (2005): 969–73.

Kohlmorgen, Lars, "International Governmental Organizations and Global Health Governance: The Role of the World Health Organization, World Bank and UNAIDS," in *Global Health Governance and the Fight Against HIV/AIDS*, ed. Wolfgang Hein, Sonja Bartsch and Lars Kohlmorgen (Basingstoke: Palgrave Macmillan, 2007).

Lake, David A. and Mathew D. McCubbins, "The Logic of Delegation to International Organizations," in *Delegation and Agency in International Organizations*, ed. Darren G. Hawkins, David A. Lake, Daniel L. Nielson, and Michael J. Tierney (Cambridge: Cambridge University Press, 2006).

Lisk, Franklyn, "Toward a New Architecture of Global Governance for Responding to the HIV/AIDS Epidemic," in *Global Governance and Diplomacy: Worlds Apart?* ed. Andrew F. Cooper, Brian Hocking and William Maley (Basingstoke: Palgrave Macmillan, 2008).

——*Global Institutions and the HIV/AIDS Epidemic* (London: Routledge, 2010).

Mann, Jonathan M., Daniel J.M. Tarantola, Thomas W. Netter, and Joel Finlay, "Funding the Global AIDS Strategy," in *AIDS in the World*, ed. Jonathan M. Mann, Daniel J.M. Tarantola and Thomas W. Netter (Cambridge: Harvard University Press, 1992).

March, James G. and Johan P. Olsen, "The Institutional Dynamics of International Political Orders," *International Organization* 52, no. 4 (1998): 943–69.

Panos, *AIDS and the Third World* (London: The Panos Institute, 1988).

——*Missing the Message? 20 Years of Learning from HIV/AIDS* (London: The Panos Institute, 2003).

Patterson, Amy S. (2007) "The UN and the Fight Against HIV/AIDS," in *The Global Politics of AIDS*, ed. Paul G. Harris and Patricia D. Siplon (Boulder, Col.: Lynne Rienner, 2007).

Poku, Nana K., "The Global AIDS Fund: Context and Opportunity," in *Global Health and Governance: HIV/AIDS*, ed. Nana K. Poku and Alan Whiteside (Basingstoke: Palgrave Macmillan, 2004).

Seckinelgin, Hakan, "A Global Disease and Its Governance: HIV/AIDS in Sub-Saharan Africa and the Agency of NGOs," *Global Governance* 11, no. 3 (2005): 351–68.

——*International Politics of HIV/AIDS* (London: Routledge, 2008).

Sell, Susan K. and Aseem Prakash, "Using Ideas Strategically: The Contest Between Business and NGO Networks in Intellectual Property Rights," *International Studies Quarterly* 48, no. 1 (2004): 143–75.

Söderholm, Peter, *Global Governance of AIDS: Partnership with Civil Society* (Lund: Lund University Press, 1997).

Strand, Per, "Comparing AIDS Governance: A Research Agenda on Responses to the AIDS Epidemic," in *AIDS and Governance*, ed. Nana K. Poku, Alan Whiteside and Bjorg Sandkjaer (Aldershot: Ashgate, 2007).

Swidler, Ann, "Syncretism and Subversion in AIDS Governance: How Locals Cope with Global Demands," *International Affairs* 82, no. 2 (2006): 269–84.

Tomasevski, Katarina, "AIDS and Human Rights," in *AIDS in the World*, ed. Jonathan M. Mann, Daniel J.M. Tarantola and Thomas W. Netter (Cambridge: Harvard University Press, 1992a).
——"Unfinished Agenda: Shifting from AIDS-Rights (Back) to Human Rights," paper presented at symposium on "Transnational Networks in Response to AIDS," Lund University, 13–14 January 1992b.
UNAIDS, *2008 Report on the Global AIDS Epidemic: Executive Summary* (Geneva: UNAIDS, 2008).
Young, Oran R., *International Cooperation: Building Regimes for Natural Resources and the Environment* (Ithaca, NY: Cornell University Press, 1989).

6 Disaggregating delegation
Multiplying agents in the international maritime safety regime

Kendall W. Stiles

- PA theory and regulatory agencies
- The initial principal-agent contract in the IMO: 1949–72
- The IMO contract in transition: 1972–92
- IMO accretion: 1992–present
- The results: the maritime safety regime in operation
- Conclusions

International regulatory organizations have generated relatively little attention in the academic literature on international institutions. This is true even with respect to the principal-agent (PA) literature.[1] This, in spite of the fact that regulatory agencies in general have developed considerable autonomy from the states that instigated them, and have instead developed interesting and significant ties to non-state actors. PA concepts and propositions can therefore be tested directly.

In particular, I will consider whether delegation chains are clearly understood in the PA literature, especially where principals have created mechanisms that deliberately limit the autonomy of agents through the creation or empowerment of alternative agents. I will show that in the case of maritime safety rules, principals have empowered the International Maritime Organization (IMO) in recent years. Principals have approved a procedure that makes new staff-generated regulations automatically binding on all members, thereby increasing the credibility and uniformity of state commitments, as well as an audit scheme that will put the IMO in a position to "name and shame" non-compliant member states. At the same time, principals have obstructed the IMO's monitoring and enforcement powers in areas such as anti-piracy and port safety. They organized various "Memoranda of Understanding" (MOU) to exercise control over port safety issues and empowered the International Maritime Bureau (IMB) to monitor and assess anti-piracy measures. They also have tended to delegate much of the enforcement of ship safety rules to private non-state actors such as insurance companies. We will see that clarifying the nature of principals' options with respect to their choice of agents provides important insights to explain the ebb and flow of a particular agent's autonomy and influence.

With respect to the volume's framework, this chapter will focus on two types of decisions: rule-creating and rule-supervisory. Further, it will disaggregate the first category into rule advocacy and rule adoption. By rule advocacy, I mean the conceptual and framing activities that actors do to persuade principals and other agents to adopt certain rules and regulations. Rule adoption is the formal articulation and ratification of those rules. Many of the framework's hypotheses are confirmed in this study, a few of which will be articulated here. To begin, the executive head of the IMO (the secretary-general) has become increasingly influential with respect to rule-creating decisions. This is particularly true with respect to rule advocacy. The forum structure of the IMO plays a key role in both dimensions of the rule-creation process. Powerful states play a key role in rule supervisory decisions, as predicted. Further, with respect to the nature of the issues, increased salience is correlated with increased major power engagement. We will see that this explains in large part the weakness of the IMO with respect to the anti-piracy regime. The lack of agreement between principals is also correlated with increased opportunities for the IMO, particularly as the open registry flag states gained in importance during the 1970s (see Table 6.1). The more technical the issue, the more the IMO has been able to establish its influence, although the link is not as strong as might be expected.

Finally, with respect to international organization (IO) characteristics, most of the predictions are borne out. The IMO's lack of influence overall correlates with its small size and an institutional culture that discourages

Table 6.1 Disaggregation of agent functions

Policy initiation	Policy ratification	Policy implementation	
X			International Law Commission
	X		UN General Assembly Plenary
X		X	International Labour Organization
X	X	X	International Monetary Fund

staff creativity and policy initiation in favor of technical service provision. The IMO's relatively weak integration in the UN system has also hampered its autonomy. The existence of networks is examined here although the results are not exactly what one would expect given the hypotheses in the opening chapter. On the other hand, as the organization has matured and its staff increased its expertise relative to other agents, its influence and autonomy have increased. A point that was not brought out in the theoretical overview to this volume is the interaction between these factors, specifically the fact that it was the staff's impartiality and technocratic culture that allowed its maturity to eventually become an asset: states felt confident that the staff would not abuse its new powers based on these many years of self-denial.

With an eye towards what has come in previous chapters, I will begin with an overview of some relevant aspects of the principal-agent approach in order to more clearly articulate the uniqueness of the approach that disaggregates the agent's roles and places multiple agents in a competitive environment with respect to principal delegation. The role of the IMO becomes clearer when placed in this competitive environment stemming in large part from conflicts between principals' aims and their desire to delegate different facets of agent roles to different agents at different times.

PA theory and regulatory agencies

Delegation of responsibility to an international organization is an embodiment of a "contract," whether explicit or implicit, and which may be modified over time. Both the principal and the agent are assumed to be rational actors with discrete and identifiable (although often obscured) interests that do not perfectly coincide. It is this lack of coincidence of interest that warrants the development of a theory of delegation. Principals are assumed to seek control over agents, but the realization of this control is limited in large part by the fact that delegation is prompted by the potential benefits to the principal of ceding control to the agent. Were the principal willing to expend the level of resources required to exercise complete control over the agent, it would no longer require the services of an agent. So some degree of agency loss (referring to the costs of an agent acting in ways that diverge from the principals' interests) is inevitable (Hawkins *et al.* 2006: 9). According to Hawkins *et al.*, limiting independence may be accomplished with monitoring and reporting requirements, institutional checks and balances, and sanctions. Another mechanism may be instituted as well. Principals may limit the autonomy of an agent by separating policy initiation and approval on the one hand from policy implementation on the other.

It is useful to disaggregate the role of agents into three discrete categories: policy initiation, policy ratification, and policy implementation and enforcement (see Table 6.1). Policy initiation refers to the range of actions agents may take to generate policy options to address a particular problem. This may include problem identification exercises as well as policy ranking. Many international organizations are heavily engaged in policy initiation, and for some this occupies the bulk of their time. The International Law Commission (ILC), for example, is tasked with the "progressive development" and "codification" of international law on a wide range of issues. Its efforts have resulted in 26 international conventions covering everything from the law of the sea to consular relations. Its most recent effort was the draft statute of the International Criminal Court (ICC) (Alvarez 2005: 304). For all its effort, however, the ILC stops at the level of proposing and leaves to General Assembly committees the task of disposing. The ILC is nonetheless an agent, albeit one with limited autonomy since it lacks the capacity to implement any of its proposals.

Yet another phase of policy-making by agents involves gaining the explicit or implicit approval of principals for its proposals. Most UN specialized agencies not only have staff who draft proposals, but also governing bodies composed of state representatives that explicitly sign off on them. In most cases, the agent simply provides a forum for debate—including agent advocacy—and it is left to the principals to "opt in" or "opt out" of the proposals. The International Labour Organization (ILO), for all its considerable autonomy, lacks the capacity—by rule of procedure—to force states to accept its proposals. In many cases ILO codes are left unratified by numerous ILO members. In a few cases, such as the IMO and the European Commission, states lack the option of "opting out" and the proposals put forward by the staff become binding law.

As we will see, by considering the last stage of delegation—policy implementation and enforcement—as a discrete phase, it is easier to measure how principals exercise control over agent actions. Principals may opt to give considerable power to agents to enforce rules, as is the case with the UN Environment Programme's Implementation Committee over the Non-compliance Procedure of the Montreal Protocol or the Counter-Terrorism Committee of the UN Security Council (Stiles 2007; Stiles and Thayne 2006). In these cases, the agent may be tasked with gathering information to measure compliance that forces the hands of states to carry out pre-ordained sanctions. In the case of the International Monetary Fund (IMF), the staff act as judge, jury and executioner and the principals play a relatively passive role (Stiles 1991). These situations have arisen largely in cases where the most powerful principals find that the preferences of the agent virtually coincide with their own, but where this is not the case principals may opt to retain control of implementation and enforcement—or delegate that set of tasks to still another agent over which they exercise greater control.

The international regime governing maritime security is an example of divided principals instituting a separation of authority between policy-initiating and -ratifying agents on the one hand and a series of policy-implementing agents on the other. This separation of roles was prompted by port states as a means of exercising control over flag-of-convenience states under an umbrella of international legitimacy. The IMO has received additional powers due to the increased efforts by secretaries-general to take the initiative, the well-established reputation of the staff as neutral facilitators, and the increased complexity of the issues in play. On the other hand, powerful states—especially traditional maritime powers—have held back from the IMO many of the enforcement measures that deal with the most salient problems, and instead have continued to delegate these to themselves, to new IOs over which they have considerable control, and to certain private non-state actors.

The initial principal-agent contract in the IMO: 1949–72

States were very cautious about delegating powers to an international organization that addressed maritime issues. Maritime law had historically been managed primarily as a private matter between ship owners, insurance companies, classification societies and so forth. British Admiralty law covered the remainder (Steinberg 2001). The dominant norm until World War II was freedom of navigation and minimum interference with commerce (Zacher 1996). Ship safety and piracy were the exception, as we will see later.

When proposals were made to create an international organization to address maritime issues, specific efforts were made to minimize the powers of the organization. To begin, the Secretariat was given limited powers of a clerical nature. According to the IMO Convention's article 21, the Secretariat's role is limited to maintaining records, preparing documents and financial statements, and providing updated information for the member states. Further, the original version of the organization was designed to be a "consultative one only" (International Court of Justice 1960: 14). The original name of the institution made this clear: the Inter-governmental Maritime Consultative Organization. Even with this very limited autonomy, governments were reticent about ratifying the Convention, and the organization did not open its doors formally until 1959, more than 10 years after the negotiations were concluded (Rosenne 1999: 256). In terms of our volume's overarching theoretical framework, the IMO was created as a strictly "forum" institution, tasked with enabling governments to engage in "rule-creating decisions." As we will see, even though the staff was very professional and skilled, it was simply denied the opportunity to inject itself in the decision-making process in these early years.

As an additional assurance that the organization would carry out the preferences of the major maritime states, the Council—a diplomatic executive committee—reserved one-half of its seats for states with a strong interest in maritime shipping services and transport or navigation (the other half were meant to go to other countries on the basis of geographic representation) (Anianova 2006: 80). The Maritime Safety Committee (MSC) was also set up to allow traditional maritime powers to shape rules on maritime safety.

The IMO staff and secretary-general were at first true to their assigned roles and limited their involvement to clerical activities and limited technical advice. Initiatives for new regulations and laws instead come primarily from traditional maritime powers such as the United Kingdom and France, either in committees or in the Council. Governments would identify a deficiency in the rules (usually after some maritime catastrophe) and work up a proposal informally, then submit it to other member states for their consideration. Since governments generally do not organize in voting blocs at the IMO (Anianova 2006: 87), deliberations are often slow and methodical, with most major shipping countries wielding a de facto veto (Gaskell 2003: 170).

The IMO had no enforcement powers at the outset. The staff size was limited to fewer than 300, and the budgets kept quite low, relatively speaking. Until the 1960 revision of the IMO's benchmark treaty—the Safety of Life at Sea (SOLAS) Convention—governments were not even required to submit reports on fleet characteristics or casualty statistics. Even after 1960 such reports were voluntary and rarely submitted (Wiswall 2007). Enforcement of conventions falls on the flag state, first and foremost (Horrocks 1999: 197). Lloyd's of London played the key role of gathering statistics on ship safety and in turn rewarded or penalized companies by raising or lowering insurance premiums. Even now, the staff at Lloyd's outnumbers that of the IMO by a factor of 10 to 1. Further, classification societies—organized as the International Association of Classification Societies—play the role of assessors of ship safety in order to classify them for the sake of calibrating insurance premiums and coverage (Campe 2009: 158). Of course, the shipping companies themselves are responsible for ensuring the safety of their own vessels. It is understandable that these states were reluctant to delegate beyond this tried and true network of agents.

Returning to our theoretical framework, it is clear that traditional maritime states sought to control the activities of the IMO from the outset, providing it with clerical and conference-hosting duties only. Member states could make use of the organization to draw up conventions and other regulations, but kept final ratification and enforcement powers for themselves. This stemmed from their united perception that shipping issues were highly salient and not suitable for delegation to a global public institution. Particularly with respect to enforcement, states retained the bulk of the power, and delegated only to private non-state actors that they trusted.

The IMO contract in transition: 1972–92

During the 1960s it became clear that something was amiss in the area of maritime safety. A series of catastrophes involving open registry ships prompted traditional maritime states to seek means to strengthen international regulations. The United States was in part to blame since it encouraged the emergence of Panama's open registry (which allowed ship owners without direct national ties to fly their flag) as a way for American shippers to save money on registration costs and thereby reduce the charges (Zacher 1996: 63). European states followed suit and even helped some of their former colonies to set up their own open registries. Open registry states were willing to lower the legal requirements that these companies applied in order to attract more ships to their flag (Güner-Özbek 2006: 123; DeSombre 2006). Ironically, this stemmed not only from the fact that a financial crisis in shipping was squeezing profits, but also because the new IMO standards that had been approved were driving up the cost of outfitting ships registered to traditional maritime powers (Boisson 1998: 505).

The result was a dramatic increase in the number of ships that did not meet safety standards. Traditional flag states sought a way to increase the political commitment of the open registry states to the new rules. While negotiating amendments to the International Regulations for Preventing Collisions at Sea in 1972, delegates opted for a radical new approach. Rather than waiting for two-thirds of states to ratify before activation, a convention could become binding so long as one-third of member states did not openly object (IMO 2009). This procedure was included in a number of new agreements and proved to be far more effective. Within a period of 18 months, several conventions and amendments became active—sometimes even where the original agreement was still pending (Wiswall 2007). Of particular importance was the International Convention for the Prevention of Pollution from Ships of 1973 (MARPOL), which expanded the enforcement powers of coastal states, something which became pivotal to changes in the IMO's contract in the next phase.

In addition to the tacit approval mechanism, the IMO member states and even staff sought alternatives to the convention approach by adopting not only resolutions but also "circulars"—technical codes and standards designed to clarify more broadly worded conventions. These notes and rules typically short-circuited the tedious and time-consuming processes and reached governments very quickly, although they were generally thought to be non-binding—at least in principle, although we will see that efforts were later made to make these more binding.

One important implication of the "tacit approval" mechanism is that some governments began to argue that a wide range (perhaps even all) of IMO's Conventions and even some Assembly Resolutions and other regulations and guidelines might be automatically binding on the entire membership, regardless of whether a state has endorsed them or how it may have done so. Later on, once the UN Convention on the Law of the Sea (UNCLOS) came into effect, they could fall under its "applicable" or "generally accepted" rules which by implication become binding on UNCLOS (Wolfrum 1999: 231). The implications are explained by Campe: "[T]he IMO secretariat staff has reported that this opportunity has been used quite frequently to update regulations. The tacit acceptance procedure has thus increased the secretariat's ability to influence conventions" (Campe 2009: 155).

Meanwhile, the IMO's Convention had altered the name and status of the organization to give it full international governmental organization characteristics. As staff members were assigned to support various new committees, it increased in size and competence.

This approach to IMO rules influenced a decision on the part of European port states to take a far more proactive approach to protecting their waters. In 1978 several European maritime powers gathered to begin outlining what would become the Paris MOU, an informal agreement (not a treaty) to standardize and promote the inspection of foreign vessels seeking to dock. In 1967 the British government had attempted to arrest the crew of the *Torrey Canyon* on the high seas for its spillage of oil without international protest (Boisson 1998: 607).

Further, the 147th International Labour Organization's Convention authorized port states to inspect ships to ensure labor standards were being upheld. The sense was that all ships, regardless of flag, owed it to the international community to comply with these fundamental rules, and should therefore be subjected to inspection (Güner-Özbek 2006: 122). The IMO staff was naturally concerned about this unilateral enforcement of international law represented by port state action. It feared that as they interpreted, applied, and enforced these IMO agreements, port state authorities would expand their original meaning and begin applying stricter and stricter standards. Once it became clear that this was not the intent of the MOU, it decided to reluctantly endorse the move as a welcome means of "filling the gap" (Güner-Özbek 2006: 124; Wolfrum 1999: 233). Oddly enough, the IMO did not seem especially uncomfortable with the message that the creation of the Paris MOU sent to the international community, namely that the multilateral regulatory system was broken and that powerful states would have to take the law into their own hands. This was reflective of a somewhat passive approach on the part of the IMO as a receiver of delegated authority rather than an initiator.

At roughly the same time, the International Chamber of Commerce established its own maritime safety monitoring station in Kuala Lumpur, Malaysia. The International Maritime Bureau, a purely private initiative, began collecting reports of incidents at sea—in particular those involving pirate attacks—and disseminating them to their subscribers (mostly shipping firms and national associations of shipping). In time these reports were transmitted to the IMO, which collated and posted them for public viewing (Zacher 1996: 56). While the IMO had little to do with their creation, it eventually began consolidating the reports and uploading them on its website for easy consumption. Again, we see that the IMO has been largely passive with respect to many key enforcement mechanisms, choosing instead to allow public and private ventures instigated by the traditional maritime powers to monitor and rate compliance and afterwards providing its seal of approval. This allows the IMO to at least appear engaged in rule-supervisory decisions without actually expending resources or taking political risks.

Returning to our theoretical framework, it is clear that delegation is selective on the part of the principals of the IMO. While they are willing to give powers to advocate and adopt new policies—particularly with respect to technical regulations regarding which it is perceived to have considerable expertise and credibility—they are not only unwilling to delegate rule-supervisory powers but will even go out of their way to create new bodies to fill these roles. The IMO, for its part, has opted to give its blessing to these efforts rather than challenge them. We will see that this has helped confirm its reputation as a reasonable and supportive agent that is unlikely to challenge the prerogatives of the traditional maritime states and the major non-state private players (Carlin 2001: 341; Campe 2009: 144).

IMO accretion: 1992–present

The IMO staff asked and answered a central question in 2007: shouldn't the IMO have some sort of police function? This seems to imply the creation of a team of inspectors and a fleet of patrol boats crewed by officials with the right to board any ships they suspected of contravening IMO regulations. In practice, the creation of such a force would be financially enormous—it would mean recruiting thousands of people—and politically impossible: most governments would never agree to allow ships flying their flag to be boarded in international waters and any attempt to introduce a system of penalties and punishments would be even more unacceptable (IMO 2007a).

This sums up better than most commentaries the inherent obstacles to IMO enforcement, but in spite of these considerable constraints, conditions on the world's oceans continued to deteriorate. In 20 years, from 1970 to 1989, open registry flags increased their share of global gross tonnage from 22 percent to 35 percent, while the share of Organisation for Economic Co-operation and Development (OECD) flags fell from 65 percent to 32 percent. Liberia and Panama alone controlled roughly 30 percent of the world's gross tonnage (Zacher 1996: 37). Most conventions were endorsed by most countries by this point, but total losses on the oceans were still high, hovering around 5.5 losses per 1,000 ships per year until the second half of the 1980s (Cowley 1999: 424). These trends reinforced the sense that traditional enforcers of maritime law were failing at their job. Flag states lack either the capacity or the will to adopt and enforce strict safety rules, flag states and shipping companies were content to work with lax classification societies, and even captains and crews shirked their duties in order to lower prices (Boisson 1998: 513). Those remaining states and private organizations that took their responsibilities seriously complained of being over-regulated and getting priced out of the market (Horrocks 1999; Kurz 1999).

This situation prompted states—particularly traditional maritime powers—to revisit the role of the IMO in the area of enforcement during the 1990s and the 2000s. As we will see, the institution was asked to take "rule-supervisory" decisions and move even more deliberately in the direction of becoming a service organization. In general, the staff did not seek out this role, although it gradually came to embrace it. Foremost among the advocates for increased powers in every aspect of delegation discussed in this paper was Secretary-General William O'Neil (1990–2003). O'Neil injected himself into negotiations over passenger ship safety, minimizing bulk carrier accidents, and especially putting the "human element" at the heart of IMO efforts. Specifically, he was the first secretary-general to utilize his powers to introduce a resolution to the IMO Assembly (on bulk carrier safety) (IMO 2003). He also emphasized the importance of seafarer training after a number of accidents in the early 1990s made it clear that improvements to ships' physical safety would only go so far (Dirks 2004: 201). In the process he was able to bring together an increasing number of non-state actors, traditional maritime powers, open registry flag states, and the IMO staff to design an agreement on training standards (*Standards of Training, Certification and Watchkeeping for Seafarers*, 1995), which allows various entities, including the IMO, to monitor and evaluate training programs around the world (Dirks 2004: 206). The secretary-general not only influenced the substance of the agreement but also the pace of ratification, by skirting ordinary committees and procedures. He assigned much of the preparatory work to an ad hoc expert committee, over which he "had a strong influence ... , instead of having the work carried out by the Maritime Safety Committee itself" (Dirks 2004: 210). The convention was approved two years earlier than normally would have been the case as a result. The IMO was given considerable powers to monitor and assess state performance—the first time such powers were delegated (Dirks 2004: 210).

The principal cause for this breakthrough seems to be increased assertiveness by the secretary-general, which succeeded, one could argue, in large part because his predecessors had been so pliant. After providing technocratic, impartial, pro-shipping advice for 30 years, the IMO's credibility was high enough that it could begin to push states on selected issues and could be trusted to pass judgment on their performance. Further, there were increasing problems with traditional agents such as shipping companies and classification societies since it was becoming increasingly clear that they were not demanding enough of themselves and their clients—hence the frequent accidents. On the other hand, in part by virtue of its relative passivity, the IMO had no stains on its reputation. Finally, one can add the fact that since even the weakest states in the IMO believed the agency was accessible and legitimate, there was no direct opposition to the granting of more power. In a sense, the IMO was everyone's second-best option, which gave it preeminence once other agents became tainted and the organization demonstrated a willingness to take on new tasks.

In general, both the principals and the IMO staff reached a new consensus during the 1990s that it was not enough to continue to approve new and more specific regulations. Rather, efforts should be made to improve compliance, albeit without necessarily moving too aggressively into an enforcement mode (Birnie 1999: 379). The mood indicated a gradual shift toward an emphasis on both capacity building and even punitive measures in the hope of ensuring that all flag states will comply with the rudimentary regulations (Anianova 2006: 98). In 1993 the Flag State Implementation Committee (FSI) issued guidelines to allow flag states to assess their own compliance in the hope that a straightforward checklist would remove any confusion or uncertainty about standards (Roach 1999: 153).

From the beginning, the IMO staff's approach has been to promote consensus, and so when it came to assessment, it promoted a facilitative and supportive approach focused on helping countries identify deficiencies and providing technical support and training to fix them (IMO 2006). The reports would not be disseminated and no public commentary would take place. Even the most delinquent countries would receive no public reprimand. On the contrary, they would likely receive the most assistance. The Technical Co-operation Committee formally endorsed this approach in the late 1990s, at least for the time being (Edwards 1999).

Not content to wait for the results to come in, developed countries pressed forward with their own assessment programs. The European Union (EU), in particular, viewed itself as the bastion of maritime law. In 1995 it issued European Commission (EC) Directive 95/21/EC and established the European Maritime Safety Agency in 2002 and, among other steps, began ranking individual ships as "high risk" (Güner-Özbek 2006: 132–33). The United States had already established its own tough inspection regime by this time, and so virtually all of the OECD states presented a united front in favor of increased accountability.

The accountability involved not only tough inspections and "naming and shaming," but states also claimed and acted upon the right to protect their ports by denying entry to deficient ships or requiring that repairs be made or procedures set in place before they could sail on to other ports. Detentions and relays are imposed for a variety of infractions, including the lack of proper certificates, lack of safety equipment, unsafe equipment, and so forth. The checklists are extensive and detailed, and the results of each ship's inspection are made public (they are now available online without charge). More will be said about what these reports tell us.

Returning to the voluntary self-reporting at the IMO, after a few years, governments took stock of the program and found it sorely wanting, as of March 2003 only 50 countries had submitted reports (Sasamura 2003). To say that the results were disappointing would be an understatement. As early as 2002, the FSI developed a new approach based loosely on the International Civil Aviation Organization's on-site country audits (Sasamura 2003; Roach 1999: 153). The early versions of the IMO Audit Scheme were debated in the MSC as a result of a Council assignment. They required states to assess their own performance on safety, security, and pollution control measures, consistent with a wide array of IMO Conventions and other provisions.

The scheme is by far the most intrusive measure ever adopted by the IMO and pushes the organization in the direction of policy implementation. It involves three steps, as outlined in Assembly Resolution A.974(24). To begin, governments are invited to complete an exhaustive questionnaire designed to take stock of whether flag states have the laws, policies, and institutional arrangements required in the IMO Conventions. These reports are submitted to the IMO secretary-general who passes them along to the staff for review and comment. At the next stage, the secretary-general appoints a chief auditor for the country, who assembles a team of assistant auditors who will carry out a site visit to the country. These auditors may have already visited the country, since governments are encouraged to carry out a "dry run" early on. Once they arrive, they meet with all the key maritime policy officials, ranging from transportation officials to coast guard and port authority figures—always in the company of a member of the government. After the week-long visit, the auditors provide the government with preliminary findings to which the government may respond in writing. These responses are added to a final report which is submitted to the secretary-general for analysis and comment. In the final phase, a summary of the report is circulated to other member states.

The scheme stops short of a full "naming and shaming" model since the final results are internal documents not for public viewing. Further, the program is voluntary and therefore does not infringe on the sovereignty of states. In fact, the IMO staff have tried to persuade governments to support the program on the grounds that this will serve to balance the actions of MOUs and may help improve the reputations of open registry flags (Barchue 2006: 5). While it is too early to know what effect the program will have, it is interesting to note that of the countries that have already submitted to the audit, none has come away without some criticism. The United Kingdom and Denmark were among the first to volunteer, no doubt confident that they are models for the rest of the world. Indeed, the

Disaggregating delegation in maritime safety 181

reports—made public to help increase the educational value of the exercise—pointed out some deficiencies with respect to organizational structures, currency of legal codes, and so forth (IMO 2007c).

The net effect of the introduction of the Audit Scheme will be a significant increase in the secretary-general's powers and the role of the IMO as a policy implementation agent. As put in an IMO document, "The Voluntary IMO Member State Audit Scheme is an initiative that will transform the character of monitoring the implementation of IMO Conventions" (IMO 2006). The secretary-general controls the constitution of the audit team, draws up the terms with governments, receives and interprets the final reports, and disseminates its summary to member states. Since a great deal of judgment will be involved in all of these actions, this dramatically increases the secretary-general's discretion in a new and vital area.

This is not the only way member states have allowed the secretary-general an expanded role in recent years. Following the *Achille Lauro* incident involving the seizure of a cruise ship by terrorists in 1985, then Secretary-General Efthimios Mitropoulos urged members to adopt an anti-terrorism convention, which culminated in the Convention for the Suppression of Unlawful Acts against the Safety of Maritime Navigation of 1988 (Balkin 2006: 32). After the 11 September 2001 terrorist attacks on the United States, Secretary-General William O'Neil was the prime initiator of a new ship security code, the International Ship and Port Facility Security Code of 2002 (Anianova 2006: 96). He also played a central role in creating and designing the Audit Scheme, pushing to make it voluntary as opposed to mandatory (as favored by traditional maritime powers) (Plaza 1999: 203). Finally, successive secretaries-general have been central to the adoption of new measures on fighting piracy. Recognizing this influence, the Council specifically assigned him the task of developing a coordinated approach to fighting pirates in the Malacca Straits and encouraging countries in other pirate-prone regions to adopt similar arrangements, which he did through a series of successful meetings (Balkin 2006: 33). Finally, secretaries-general have been central in the creation of IMO institutes and universities to improve training for maritime authorities from developing countries (Lloyd's List 2008: 13).

Secretaries-general have earned increasing respect from member states, as evidenced by their growing influence over policy as well as their longevity. From 1971 to 2003 only two men held the office (Lloyd's List 2008: 5). In ways both formal and informal, then, the IMO staff and its leadership have been accumulating greater influence over policy initiation, ratification, and implementation.

182 Kendall W. Stiles

This is not to say that the IMO's powers are expansive. They are still fewer than those of the ICAO or the ILO. The IMO still understands that it is not able to punish governments for reasons both financial and political, as pointed out at the beginning of this section. Instead, the IMO has enthusiastically endorsed the efforts of the MOUs, albeit after the fact (Brandt 2006). For several years it has been engaged in an effort to multiply the number of MOUs to cover the entire planet. There are now such arrangements in the Indian Ocean, Caribbean, Mediterranean, South Atlantic, Middle East, and around parts of Africa. While developing countries have more modest aims with respect to the number of inspections they can carry out, if these are targeted at the most delinquent ships we should expect to see some results (Plaza 1999: 210–19). Already the casualty ratio has begun to fall (Cowley 1999: 424).

As far as the theoretical framework is concerned, it is clear that changes are taking place to the basic principal-agent contract at the IMO. Specifically, the secretary-general and the staff have been given more opportunities to express opinions regarding both the agenda of issues and the type of standards to be adopted. Through the broader use of circulars, the staff has become more heavily involved in ratifying these policies, although the bulk of the work in this area is still reserved for states. Through its numerous publications aimed at both the professional and lay audiences, one could argue that the IMO is shaping attitudes and values regarding shipping safety (Dirks 2004: 209). Its efforts to enhance training and even to take on some of this training directly means that an increasing number of maritime officials in the developing world will have been shaped by the IMO in years to come, thereby spreading its influence indirectly. Most important, the secretary-general has a front-row seat at the gathering of compliance data, although the actual enforcement appears to be relegated to port states. However, even there the IMO has attempted to appear engaged by enthusiastically endorsing the MOUs and disseminating IMB piracy data.

Figures 6.1, 6.2, and 6.3 summarize these points, showing the relative primacy of six major actors over time.

These changes appear linked to both a glaring need for more enforcement as well as an increase in member state confidence in the IMO staff. The need increased in part because of initial moves by traditional maritime powers to allow widespread use of open registry, combined with the obvious lack of capacity by these states and private actors (with the exception of the insurance industry generally) to regulate ship safety and the overpowering financial incentives to lower standards. On the other hand, the alternative of letting the powerful states unilaterally

Disaggregating delegation in maritime safety 183

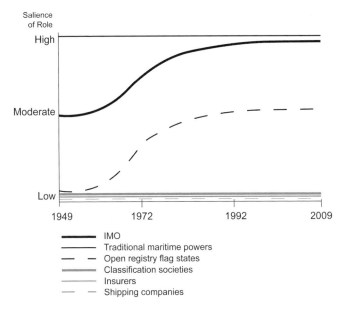

Figure 6.1 Actor powers in policy advocacy

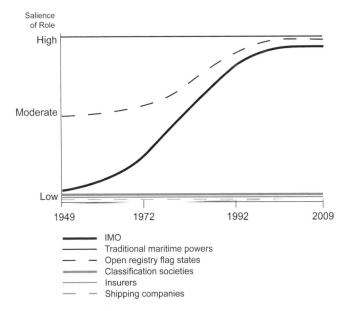

Figure 6.2 Actor powers in policy adoption

184 Kendall W. Stiles

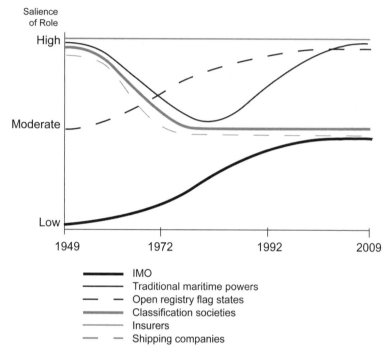

Figure 6.3 Actor powers in rule supervision

create and enforce maritime regulations gave these open registry states strong incentives to empower the IMO—a move the powerful states had already endorsed.

This account confirms the argument that agents' roles can be and are disaggregated. Agents can be tasked with very specific functions—such as rule-creation—and nothing else, while other tasks are assigned to other agents. This can pit the agents against each other, as we have seen in the case of the enforcement ship safety regulations, or it can simply create a division of labor, as in the case of anti-piracy measures. As for why the IMO has been given an increasing number of powers, much of this stems from the many years of goodwill fostered by the staff's neutral, technical, and pro-shipping culture. Although not spelled out explicitly in the Introduction to this volume, it appears that it was the passivity of the agency that, while weakening it in the short run, set the stage for its eventual limited empowerment. The implication is that IO characteristics, such as staff size, organizational maturity, and culture, should be seen as interactive traits that sometimes reinforce each other over long periods of time. It is also clear that the increasing disagreements between the principals created an opening for a "second-best" agent such as the IMO. The implication is that were this disagreement to resolve itself, principals might opt to turn to one of their first choices again.

The results: the maritime safety regime in operation

In this final section, we will review compliance with IMO Conventions in the areas of ship safety and anti-piracy measures, two areas of central importance today, and examine what they tell us about IO effectiveness in this case.

Piracy

Pirates have been a surprisingly persistent feature of maritime shipping, to the point that from antiquity to the Napoleonic era they could only be defeated by states with large fleets and more often than not were accommodated with payments and contracts to serve as privateers—navies for hire (Gottschalk and Flanagan 2000: 17). So long as they operated for personal gain, attacking ships on the high seas from aboard ship, they were subject to arrest by any navy, however, a rule actively enforced by the British Navy from the 1820s until the emergence of steel-hulled ships, which gave states a supreme advantage over pirates (Stiles 2007; Pérotin-Dumon 2001: 9; Randall 1988: 791).

International law on piracy was formally codified at a time when it was perhaps least necessary, in 1958 (Garmon 2002: 262), and repeated in the 1982 Third Convention on the Law of the Seas (LOS III). The definition excludes politically motivated acts, violence on board ship, and acts within territorial waters where states are expected to enforce domestic law. States have at different times—most recently in 1998—rejected expanding the definition of piracy (Keyuan 2005: 119). After the PLO attack on the *Achille Lauro* in 1985, although states agreed to outlaw terrorism at sea (the 1988 Convention on the Suppression of Unlawful Acts, SUA), they kept the definition of piracy limited to non-political acts (Balkin 2006: 7).

Piracy has experienced a resurgence since the end of the Cold War, peaking in the 2000's at a rate of one attack reported per day, which may only represent one-tenth of the total, due to under-reporting (Mukundan 2005: 40). A typical attack involves a handful of lightly armed locals scrambling on board a container ship, making off with rope and paint barrels; however, numerous attacks involve murder, hijacking, and even sinkings (Luft and Korin 2004; Dragonette 2005). While most attacks have been in Southeast Asia, they have occurred off the coasts of 69 different countries since 2000 according to the IMB, which receives and compiles reports.

The IMO stresses states' duties to police their own waters and to collaborate with neighboring states to ensure that maritime jurisdictional issues are addressed (IMO 1999, 2000; Goodman 1999: 158). The IMO has also enjoined states to pursue more vigorously pirates who attack ships in port and within territorial waters (IMO 1983). States, however, have resisted efforts to make these measures legally obligatory. The provision in the LOS III regarding enforcement of anti-piracy law on the high seas has ambiguous wording by design. On the one hand it enjoins states to pursue and apprehend pirates and grants them universal jurisdiction to try them; on the other hand a false arrest generates liability (articles 100, 105, 106).

States have limited the IMO's enforcement powers (Goodman 1999: 156; Wiswall 2007), have resisted creating an internal piracy court or placing piracy under the jurisdiction of the ICC, and continue to object to states pursuing pirates into another state's territorial waters. As yet the IMO does not even require regular reports from member states to declare the status of their efforts to implement the treaties (Marisec 2004: 5, 17). At the same time, states generally accept a duty to prosecute pirates who fall into their hands, and all accept the principle of universal jurisdiction over pirate attacks that occur on the high seas (although only India has appeared to have exercised it in recent years—see *Cargo Security International* 2003).

States have resisted granting the IMB or the IMO anything more than record-keeping powers with respect to piracy. Anti-piracy law has likewise provided little by way of multilateral enforcement. However, other agents have been enlisted. For example, Lloyd's of London, with the blessing of principals, increased premiums in the high-piracy area of the Malacca Straits. Within weeks, Jakarta and Kuala Lumpur began to reconsider their relatively nationalistic and intransigent policies regarding anti-piracy enforcement.

In recent years maritime piracy has become endemic off the coast of Somalia. However, rather than involving the IMO directly, the international community acted through the United Nations Security Council and the North Atlantic Treaty Organization (NATO). The IMO did take some small steps, for example, to urge states to cooperate with the UN on operations in Somalia (Maritime Security Primer 2008: 16), but these measures were small in comparison to UNSC Resolution 1816, which invoked the UN Charter's Chapter VII collective security provisions and revoked the traditional territorial water jurisdiction of the provisional Somali government for a renewable six-month period. As explained by a senior US official, Somalia's territorial waters are to be treated as the high seas (Bellinger 2008). UN Security Council resolution 1838, passed in October 2008 amid a new flare-up of attacks, reiterated and underscored these provisions, prompting NATO, India, and China to deploy naval vessels to the Gulf of Aden with the express mission of intercepting and arresting (and if necessary killing) pirates in the area.

It is perhaps not surprising that a pattern found across a wide range of issues is repeated here: where questions of national security and criminal law are concerned, states have been particularly reluctant to delegate authority to international agents. This has been the case, in spite of the fact that the IMO staff have repeatedly tried to weigh in on the issue and have access to key sources of information and intelligence. Rather, when the problem reached crisis proportions, states acted through the one body where the major powers are most likely to be able to protect their interests and sovereign rights: the UN Security Council.

Ship safety

The rules governing the next area of maritime safety—safe ships and safe command of vessels—have a comparable pedigree, emerging during the late 1800s. The International Convention for the Safety of Life at Sea, originally drafted in 1913 following the *Titanic* disaster, has seen multiple iterations, the most recent in 1974, and numerous amendments and two Protocols, all designed to expand, clarify, and strengthen regulations governing ships. As put by Zacher (1996: 50), "Damage control is the one general shipping issue where it is easiest to make the case that the regulatory regime is regarded as serving the interests of virtually all states." While all states favored accident prevention and other basic safety standards, poorer states resisted mandatory regulations that raised construction and operation costs, which reduced their competitiveness, so most standards were made voluntary and flexible.

Following the *USS Cole* attack and the events of 11 September 2001, both by Al Qaeda elements, developed states demanded stricter compliance with various safety standards for both ships and developing country ports. In 1998 IMO members adopted the International Safety Management Code, which required states to supervise the refitting of ocean-going vessels to ensure that they would conform to a long list of safety standards. Compliant ships would receive a certificate that could be displayed in foreign ports. The International Ship and Port Facility

Security (ISPS) code was adopted in 2002, and made mandatory on all 148 SOLAS signatories, requiring all ships to obtain the ISM certificates and authorizing port authorities to bar, detain or expel non-compliant vessels (*ISPS Code* 2003). We have already seen that various MOUs are the most engaged in enforcing these regulations.

Taken together, the anti-piracy and ship safety regimes have the potential to minimize mishaps at sea. They share the normative commitment to safe, free navigation under decentralized management. Both require states to expend considerable resources for the sake of a collective good. However, there are interesting differences. Anti-piracy measures have conflicted with traditional state sovereignty, prompting weaker states to resist their expansion and strengthening, while the principal objections to expanding ship safety rules have related to questions of cost and their implications for competitiveness. Anti-piracy measures are almost entirely under the purview of states, as opposed to ship safety which has a strong reciprocal element. Failure to enforce anti-piracy measures is generally not met with automatic or clear penalties for states, whereas the MOUs provide almost immediate consequences for flag states that do not enforce ship safety rules on their respective fleets. Anti-piracy rules, for all their seniority, still lack the precision of ship safety regulations.

It is perhaps not surprising that compliance rates vary considerably across these two regimes since the differences between them are among those hypothesized to matter a great deal (see especially Raustiala and Victor 1998). Based on a survey of two datasets—one drawn from the IMB's pirate reports covering 2000–07 and the other drawn from the Paris and Tokyo MOUs covering 2003–07—compliance rates are roughly reversed across the two areas. Of 1,440 successful pirate attacks recorded by the IMB, states undertook an active response (meaning that they at least began an investigation into the incident) in only 16 percent of the cases (the rate is roughly the same whether the attacks were in the territorial waters or beyond). This represents 84 percent non-compliance with the rule. On the other hand basic compliance with the ship regulations hovers around 96.5 percent—almost a mirror image of the situation with anti-piracy compliance.

Conclusions

Port states and open registry flag states share power in the IMO, but they rarely see eye to eye on issues of ship safety. Whereas port states seek to maximize security, others seek maximum flexibility in order to attract more shipping companies and thereby more government revenue. This is especially clear with respect to the ISPS and SOLAS regulations, which were largely imposed upon flag-of-convenience states by a coalition of port states and other IMO members. This said, enforcement of these measures was delegated to states, which quickly formed MOUs (particularly the Paris and Tokyo MOUs, which are dominated by port states) in order to coordinate information-sharing and standard-setting. The result is that port states now have far greater leverage—above and beyond market forces—to compel flag-of-convenience states to impose stricter guidelines on their fleets.

Likewise, anti-piracy measures, while less vigorously promoted, are enforced through yet another agent whose interests coincide with those of port states. The principal of these is the IMB, affiliated with the International Chamber of Commerce. Its accountability to states is mediated through a variety of public and private channels, but because its interests so clearly coincide with port states—many of which are also home to the world's great commercial shipping fleets—it is given considerable latitude to define piracy and collect data on its occurrence, as well as advocate reforms and regulations. Further, a set of private actors—namely international insurance companies based in the West—have considerable sway over states that fail to apprehend pirates. Although control over Lloyd's of London and other firms is not directed by states, the coincidence of interests allows states to take a hands-off approach to the issue.

A key point of this research is that agents should not be viewed as isolated institutions, but as actors playing one or more of three agent roles. For delegation to succeed, all three roles—policy initiation, policy ratification, and policy implementation—must be filled, but there is no reason these roles cannot be carried out by separate agents where principals are motivated to assert control over the delegation process.

With respect to this volume's overall approach, the case of the IMO's accretion of authority and autonomy can be linked to the factors discussed in the Introduction. Specifically, we can see that the IMO's size and complexity have grown, albeit tentatively, as its powers have expanded. It seems from our story that changes in the latter were the impetus for changes in the former, but now that both have expanded, the institution is poised for new responsibilities. Next, it seems clear that as the institution has aged and matured, governments find themselves more at ease with delegating powers to it. As we have seen, the IMO demonstrated considerable skill in implementing almost every task, and in some cases was actually ahead of the curve. Secretaries-general were able move diplomatic debates forward, the staff was able to gather and interpret large amounts of data, and develop and disseminate cogent and appropriate standards. It is perhaps no surprise that given this record, the staff has now been tasked with the Audit Scheme. It is interesting to note that, in reference to our model, staff expertise and professionalism was apparently not enough to prompt states to delegate powers. Instead, it also had to prove itself over a long period of time. It also mattered that other agents that were supposed to carry out key enforcement roles had gradually demonstrated their inability to do so. In some ways, the IMO was a fall-back for states—but at least it provided an option. Finally, it is interesting to see that the IMO was increasingly networked with other agencies—both public and private—but that this was probably not a key element in its accretion of powers. On the contrary, the IMO seems to have helped undermine some of its potential allies by pointing out in vivid terms their failures. Thus, while the IMO and the various classification societies should have increased their links and collaboration, they seem to have emerged as rivals. Likewise, as the IMO's rules have become more complex and strict, shipping companies no longer see it as a friend. On the other hand, various advocates for seamen and port security are more committed to the IMO's work than ever. In sum, then, it would seem that the key factor is the organization's maturation and the increasing confidence placed in it by the principals.

A final thought would be that the principals have been willing to cede authority to the IMO only on issues that do not cut too close to their national security interests, as predicted in the model. Where issues of anti-piracy (and by implication anti-terrorism) are concerned, states have delegated relatively few powers to any agent. Only the IMB has data-gathering powers, although most experts agree that the vast majority of pirate attacks go unreported, so even the IMB's efforts are weak. It is doubtful that any degree of confidence in the IMO's technical skill and impartiality will change this.

Notes

1 Note, for example, that they do not figure in Hawkins *et al.* 2006, while the work provides three studies of the International Monetary Fund.

Bibliography

Alvarez, Jose, *International Organizations as Lawmakers* (Oxford: Oxford University Press, 2005).
Anianova, Ekaterina, "The International Maritime Organization—Tanker or Speedboat?" in *International Maritime Organizations and their Contribution*

towards a Sustainable Marine Development, ed. Peter Ehlers and Rainer Lagoni (Hamburg: LIT, 2006), 77–103.

Balkin, Rosalie, "The International Maritime Organization and Maritime Security," *Tulane Maritime Law Journal* 30, Winter/Summer (2006): 1–34.

Barchue, L.D., Sr, "Making the Case for the Voluntary IMO Member State Audit Scheme," (London: IMO Headquarters, 2006).

Bellinger, John B., III, "The United States and the Law of the Sea Convention," *Berkeley Journal of International Law Publicist* 1, Article 2 (5 November 2008): 7–17.

Birnie, Patricia, "Implementation of IMO Regulations and Oceans Policy Post-UNCLOS and Post-UNCED," in *Current Maritime Issues and the International Maritime Organization*, ed. Myron Nordquist and John Norton Moore (The Hague: Kluwer Law International, 1999), 361–90.

Boisson, Philippe, *Politiques et Droit de la Securité Maritime* (Paris: Bureau Veritas, 1998).

Brandt, Wioletta, "Does the EU Constitute a 'Maritime Superpower'?" in *International Maritime Organizations and their Contribution towards a Sustainable Marine Development*, ed. Peter Ehlers and Rainer Lagoni (Hamburg: LIT, 2006), 259–84.

Campe, Sabine, "The Secretariat of the International Maritime Organization: A Tanker for Tankers," in *Managers of Global Change: The Influence of International Environmental Bureaucracies*, ed. Frank Biermann and Bernd Siebenhüner (Cambridge: MIT Press, 2009), 143–68.

Cargo Security International, "India: Court Jails Pirates in Breakthrough for Maritime Security," 28 March 2003, www.cargosecurityinternational.com/print.asp?id=853.

Carlin, Elaine, "Oil Pollution from Ships at Sea: The Ability of Nations to Protect a Blue Planet," in *Environmental Regime Effectiveness: Confronting Theory with Evidence*, ed. Edward Miles, Arild Unterdal, Steinar Andresen, Jørgen Wettestad, Jon Birger Skjærseth and Elaine Carlin (Cambridge: MIT Press, 2001), 331–56.

Cowley, James, "Commentary" in *Current Maritime Issues and the International Maritime Organization*, ed. Myron H. Nordquist and John Norton Moore (Boston: Martinus Nijhoff, 1999), 421–28.

Cox, Robert and Harold Jacobson, *The Anatomy of Influence* (Cambridge: Cambridge University Press, 1973).

DeSombre, Elizabeth, *Flagging Standards: Globalization and Environmental, Safety, and Labor Regulations at Sea* (Cambridge: MIT Press, 2006).

Dirks, Jan, "Decision Making in the International Maritime Organization: The Case of the STCW 95 Convention," in *Decision Making within International Organizations*, ed. Rob Reinalda, Bertjan Verbeck (London: Routledge, 2004), 201–13.

Dragonette, Charles N., "Lost at Sea," *Foreign Affairs* 84, no. 2 (2005): 231–33.

Edwards, David, "Technical Assistance: A Tool for Uniform Implementation of Global Standards," in *Current Maritime Issues and the International*

Maritime Organization, ed. Myron H. Nordquist and John Norton Moore (Boston: Martinus Nijhoff, 1999), 391–416.

Garmon, Tina, "International Law of the Sea: Reconciling the Law of Piracy and Terrorism in the Wake of September 11th," *The Maritime Lawyer* 27, Winter (2002): 257–75.

Gaskell, Nicholas, "Decision Making and the Legal Committee of the International Maritime Organization," *International Journal of Maritime Law* 18, no. 2 (2003): 155–214.

Goodman, Timothy H., "'Leaving the Corsair's Name to Other Times': How to Enforce the Law of Sea Piracy in the 21st Century through Regional Agreements," *Case Western Reserve Journal of International Law* 31 (1999): 139–68.

Gottschalk, Jack A. and Brian P. Flanagan, *Jolly Roger with an Uzi: The Rise and Threat of Modern Piracy* (Annapolis, Maryland: Naval Institute Press, 2000).

Güner-Özbek, Meltem Deniz, "Paris Memorandum of Understanding—an Example of International Co-operation and its Perspectives," in *International Maritime Organizations and their Contribution towards a Sustainable Marine Development*, ed. Peter Ehlers and Rainer Lagoni (Hamburg: LIT, 2006), 105–34.

Hawkins, Darren, David A. Lake, Daniel L. Nielson, and Michael J. Tierney, "Delegation under Anarchy: States, International Organizations, and Principal-Agent Theory," in *Delegation and Agency in International Organizations*, ed. Darren Hawkins, David A. Lake, Daniel L. Nielson, and Michael J. Tierney (New York: Cambridge University Press, 2006), 3–37.

Horrocks, Chris, "Thoughts on the Respective Roles of Flag States and Port States," in *Current Maritime Issues and the International Maritime Organization*, ed. Myron H. Nordquist and John Norton Moore (Boston: Martinus Nijhoff, 1999), 191–98.

International Court of Justice, "Constitution of the Maritime Safety Committee of the Inter-Governmental Maritime Consultative Organization," Advisory Opinion, 8 June 1960.

International Maritime Organization (IMO), "Conventions," 2009, www.imo.org/about/conventions/Pages/Home.aspx.

———"FAQs," 2007a, www.imo.org/About/mainframe.asp?topic_id=774.

———"ISPS Code," 2007b, www.imo.org/About/mainframe.asp?topic_id=897.

———"Audit of Denmark, 18–25 September 2006: Final Report 9 February 2007," 2007c.

———"Briefing 22, 23 June," 2006.

———"Voluntary IMO Member State Audit Scheme and Draft Code for the Implementation of Mandatory IMO Instruments," 2005, www.imo.org/Newsroom/mainframe.asp?topic_id=110&doc_id = 4834.

———"International Maritime Prize Awarded to IMO Secretary-General Emeritus, Mr. William A. O'Neil," 2003, www.imo.org/Newsroom/mainframe.asp?topic_id=848&doc_id = 4443.

———"Focus on IMO," January 2000.

—— "Piracy and Armed Robbery Against Ships: Recommendations to Governments for Preventing and Suppressing Piracy and Armed Robbery against Ships," IMO MSC/Circ. 622/Rev.1, 16 June 1999.

—— "Measures to Prevent Acts of Piracy and Armed Robbery Against Ships," IMO resolution A.545(13), 17 November 1983.

ISPS Code, International Ship and Port Facility Security Code and SOLAS Amendments, adopted 12 December 2002 (London: IMO, 2003).

Keyuan, Zou, "Seeking Effectiveness for the Crackdown of Piracy at Sea," *Journal of International Affairs* 59, no. 1 (2005): 117–34.

Kurz, G.E., "Implementing IMO Regulations and Oceans Policy," in *Current Maritime Issues and the International Maritime Organization*, ed. Myron H. Nordquist and John Norton Moore (Boston: Martinus Nijhoff, 1999), 353–59.

Lloyd's List, "IMO Celebrates 60 Years—Special Report," 7 November 2008.

Luft, Gal and Anne Korin, "Terrorism Goes to Sea," *Foreign Affairs* 83, no. 6 (2004): 156–73.

Marisec, *Pirates and Armed Robbers: Guidelines on Prevention for Masters and Ship Security Officers* (London: International Chamber of Shippers/International Shipping Federation, 2004).

Maritime Security Primer, "Global Maritime Security Cooperation in an Age of Terrorism and Transnational Threats at Sea," Multilateral Planners Conference VI, Denmark, 13–15 May 2008.

Mukundan, P., "The Scourge of Piracy in Southeast Asia: Can any Improvements be Expected in the Near Future?" in *Piracy in Southeast Asia: Status, Issues and Responses*, ed. Derek Johnson and Mark Valencia (Singapore: Institute of Southeast Asian Studies, 2005), 34–44.

Pérotin-Dumon, Anne, "The Pirate and the Emperor: Power and the Law of the Seas, 1450–1850," in *Bandits at Sea: A Pirates Reader*, ed. C.R. Pennell (New York: New York University Press, 2001), 25–54.

Plaza, Fernando, "The Future for Flag State Implementation and Port State Control," in *Current Maritime Issues and the International Maritime Organization*, ed. Myron H. Nordquist and John Norton Moore (Boston: Martinus Nijhoff, 1999), 199–219.

Randall, Kenneth C., "Universal Jurisdiction under International Law," *Texas Law Review* 66, March (1988): 785–841.

Raustiala, Kal and David Victor, "Conclusions," in *The Implementation and Effectiveness of International Environmental Commitments: Theory and Practice*, ed. David Victor, Kal Raustiala, and Eugene Skolnikoff (Cambridge: MIT Press, 1998), 659–707.

Roach, Cpt. J. Ashley, "Alternatives for Achieving Flag State Implementation and Quality Shipping," in *Current Maritime Issues and the International Maritime Organization*, ed. Myron H. Nordquist and John Norton Moore (Boston: Martinus Nijhoff, 1999), 151–71.

Rosenne, Shabtai, "The International Maritime Organization Interface with the Law of the Sea Convention," in *Current Maritime Issues and the*

International Maritime Organization, ed. Myron H. Nordquist and John Norton Moore (Boston: Martinus Nijhoff, 1999), 251–68.

Sasamura, Yoshio, "Development of Audit Scheme in ICAO and IMO," seminar on Model Audit Scheme, London, 27 May 2003.

Steinberg, Philip E., *The Social Construction of the Ocean* (New York: Cambridge University Press, 2001).

Stiles, Kendall, "Testing Theories of International Law Compliance: The Montreal Protocol" unpublished manuscript, 2007.

——*Negotiating Debt: The IMF Lending Process* (Boulder, Col.: Westview Press, 1991).

Stiles, Kendall and Adam Thayne, "Compliance with International Law: International Law on Terrorism at the United Nations," *Cooperation and Conflict* Vol. 41, No. 2 (July 2006): 153–76.

Wiswall, Frank L. (Vice-President h.c. of the Comité Maritime International and Chairman of the Joint International Working Group), e-mail to author, 17 January 2007.

Wolfrum, Rüdiger, "IMO Interface with the Law of the Sea Convention," in *Current Maritime Issues and the International Maritime Organization*, ed. Myron H. Nordquist and John Norton Moore (Boston: Martinus Nijhoff, 1999), 223–36.

Zacher, Mark, with Brent A. Sutton, *Governing Global Networks: International Regimes for Transportation and Communications* (New York: Cambridge University Press, 1996).

7 Not just states or the Secretary-General, but also staff
The emergence of UNOPS as a new UN organization

Dennis Dijkzeul

- A complex, salient issue: how to do development cooperation
- UN reform: the proposed merger with DDSMS
- Another staff initiative: the leaky boat strategy
- On its own
- Conclusion

The volume asks whether international organizations (IOs) have the ability to perform independently in international politics. This chapter looks at the United Nations Office for Project Services (UNOPS) and how it became a separate UN entity. Most of this process occurred in the early 1990s. Contrary to most international relations (IR) theory, which expects states and, in a more limited way, the UN Secretary-General, to play a central role in establishing such an organization, this chapter shows that actually staff members and the bureaucratic logic of decision-making processes in UN bodies drove forward the haphazard process of making UNOPS an independent UN organization. While previous chapters—most notably those in the first section, on the UN Secretariat—have emphasized the importance of leadership by a single person or small group of people in creating and pushing for new ideas, this chapter sees bureaucratic logic as having an effect over outcomes. UNOPS staff, concerned about their careers and the resources and influence available to their organization, were driven by bureaucratic logic in pushing for desired outcomes. Interestingly, they resisted both state pressure and pressure from other parts of the UN Secretariat.

The staff members—who are often neglected in the literature on IOs—acted on their own by engaging in internal lobbying, actually circumnavigated both member states and the UN Secretariat in order to protect their jobs, organization, and UN ideals of peace and development. They could because member states cared about service delivery by UNOPS in the area of development cooperation. In other words, in this case (and contrary to the predictions made in Chapter 1) the salience of the issue to member states actually increased, rather than decreased, IO independence. Clever lobbying by UN staff actually used the salience of the issue to their advantage. They were able to do that because another factor—the complexity of development delivery— did work in their favor, once they had convinced member states of their expertise in this area. They were also able to manipulate differences among multiple principals and, more importantly, different overseeing bodies. This chapter shows that staff members' strong operational expertise in the complex issue of development cooperation and knowledge of decision-making processes in the UN system became the (unexpected) basis for a decision to remake OPS into UNOPS. Such a decision to officially name and establish a UN entity is not part of the framework by Cox and Jacobson, as elaborated in the Introduction of this volume.

This chapter will first discuss which type of organization UNOPS actually is. Then it lays out the organizational and issue factors, as well as the type of decisions, it will examine. Then it will tell the history of the organization, which is closely linked to the search for more effective modes of international development cooperation. Next, it will tell the story of the process in which UNOPS became a separate entity. The conclusion analyses the organizational and issue factors, the type of decisions made, and it will discuss both the contributions and shortcomings of principal-agent (PA) and constructivist theory. It will argue that they still focus too much on states as central actors and do not have a sophisticated understanding of the diversity of the actors involved, their bureaucratic interests (as well as personal motivations), and the internal organizational processes. These theories should focus both more on path-dependent and garbage-can decision- and policy-making processes and their implementation.

A complex, salient issue: how to do development cooperation

As its name indicates, UNOPS is a quintessential "service" organization as defined in Chapter 1. It is unique as the organization within the UN system that is exclusively demand-based. It is designed as a businesslike organization that focuses on management and provision of services within the broader UN context, for example by executing development and relief projects. UN organizations and member states are under no obligation to assign projects to UNOPS. It thus continuously competes

The emergence of UNOPS as a new UN organization 197

on the market in order to be financially self-reliant. As a consequence, UNOPS needs to pay careful attention to the relevance, costs and quality of its services on an ongoing basis. Otherwise it runs the risk of going out of business. At the same time, the behavior of UN organizations is largely determined by the member states, and it is to a large extent dependent on government action. Hence, UNOPS shares both international private and public organizational characteristics. This chapter can be read as an analysis of the impact of financial self-reliance in a state-based UN system.

UNOPS grew out of one of the most influential UN reforms, which was based on the 1969 *Study of the Capacity of the United Nations Development System*. Informally referred to as the Jackson Report, it provided a trenchant criticism of the functioning of the UN system. After the two successive waves of decolonization in respectively Asia and Africa, the report addressed the question of how to make Third World countries more stable and prosperous. In the bipolar world of the 1960s it was clear that development cooperation shared components of both "high" and "low" politics. Development also meant a considerable expansion of the tasks of the UN system. The persistent question that arose was whether and how such development could be carried out successfully.

The traditional model of UN development cooperation was a state-based tripartite system. Three partners were involved: a funding agency, such as the UN Development Programme (UNDP), the United Nations Children's Fund (UNICEF), etc.; an executing agency (traditionally one of the specialized agencies) to provide technical expertise and inputs; and a coordinating agency from the national government, to recognize national sovereignty.

When the Jackson Report was commissioned, it was clear that the operational capacity of the UN system for development cooperation needed to be strengthened. Hence, the report studied the capacity of the UN development system in a far broader perspective than just UNDP or the tripartite system. The report noted that the UN system had become slow and unmanageable and that it lacked a central "brain" for policy development. The report proposed a wide-ranging set of recommendations for UNDP, the Economic and Social Council (ECOSOC) and interagency coordination. UNDP was supposed to become the central funding agency that would, through the sheer size of its resources, have the leverage to coordinate other UN organizations, including the specialized agencies. It would thus dampen inter-agency rivalry. The report also paid some attention to UNDP's role in project execution. UNDP's central coordinating role implied that it would have to pick up the slack if other UN organizations did not recognize the changing environment for development agencies (United Nations 1970, A/2688 (XXV), Vol. II).

The report continued that execution by UNDP "would be an exceptional case," the most probable example being "multi-disciplinary projects where delays now often occur when a conflict of jurisdiction arises over the major responsibility among the Specialized Agencies" (United Nations 1970, A/2688 (XXV), Vol. V: chap. 5, para. 128; see also United Nations 1984b, A/39/80: 2–3). This attention to UNDP's role in executing development cooperation provided the embryonic form of its role in the management of project services and execution. Many proposals of the report found their way into General Assembly resolution 2688 (XXV) of 1970—the so-called Consensus Resolution—which delineated the roles and accountability of the different UN organizations, and provided the official green light that UNDP could use to establish its own executive arm.

Internally many UNDP staff members wanted to seize this opportunity, because they were highly critical of specialized-agency execution in the tripartite system. First, UNDP staff noticed that the UN system was overlooking some of the main sources of knowledge in development, such as the private sector, nongovernmental organizations (NGOs), and universities. "Tapping the private sector with subcontracts or other arrangements was a completely revolutionary concept, which none of the other agencies had" (confidential interview, henceforth "IV"). It would be a new way of "getting the best available product to the market" (IV). Second, staff felt that there were development needs that the agencies did not cover. Third, specialized-agency execution was sometimes too slow and too cumbersome. In particular, UNDP staff found that in the tripartite system some projects were basically floating with no specific person really responsible with clear oversight. UNDP staff felt that this resulted in unclear accountability, which caused delays, and they started seriously looking for alternative ways of project implementation. Of course, UNDP-based execution could also strengthen the competitive position of their organization and help create interesting jobs.

Still, UNDP was walking on eggs. It knew that the specialized agencies would vehemently oppose UNDP moving towards project execution, out of fear of competition. The UNDP Administrator—the executive head of the organization—established a Project Execution Division (PED) in February 1973. Significantly, it had to earn its own income from project execution. It was hoped that this financial self-reliance would prevent at least some criticism from the specialized agencies. The classes of projects envisaged for execution by UNDP covered the following:

- Interdisciplinary and multi-purpose projects;
- Projects that did not fall within the competence of any individual agency;
- Individual projects that required general management and direction rather than expert sectoral guidance; and
- Projects to which UNDP could bring special assistance in the form of particular financing or investment follow-up arrangements.

As a result of PED's work, UNDP was combining several roles. UNDP was a funding organization. Its regional bureaux shaped development policies, and designed and supervised development programs. In consultation with the bureaux, PED could take on the role of an implementing/executing organization. The UNDP Resident Representatives often preferred this UNDP in-house option and started writing development project proposals that fitted the four PED categories. As a result, the specialized agencies felt that their position was being weakened and started to protest.

In 1975 the Projects Execution Division had already grown to the point where it could no longer "be conveniently accommodated, as a division, within any of the ... existing larger organizational entities" within UNDP (United Nations 1988, DP/1988/INF. 1: 1; IV). It was moved under the direct supervision of a higher ranking official. In addition, PED was also renamed and upgraded as the Office for Projects Execution (OPE) and continued to grow.

The specialized agencies, however, perceived OPE as an unfair competitor. In their eyes, UNDP played judge and jury, as well as chief beneficiary, in the allocation of projects to OPE (United Nations 1989, DP/1989/75: 2). They argued that OPE was encroaching upon their terrain (United Nations 1989, DP/1989/75: 2). Moreover, it was argued that the accountability of the administrator suffered, because he was now responsible "to himself for the efficacy with which any particular project or the UNDP-executed program as a whole is conducted" (United Nations 1984b, A/39/80: 22). There was, in other words, considerable bureaucratic infighting among UN agencies, which strongly affected their approach to development service delivery.

Although OPE's opponents were able to voice their opinions, they were never able to really limit the powers of OPE. Recommendations from a Joint Inspection Unit (JIU) report (United Nations 1984a, JIU/REP/83/9), a UN auditing body, to phase out OPE, on the arguments mentioned above, were not followed up by the General Assembly. Instead, the Secretary-General noted that there were also organizations in the system that recognized "OPE's versatility and flexibility in responding to a variety of assistance requests from developing countries" (United Nations 1984c, A/39/80/Add. 1: 3). Moreover, UNDP's Governing Council reaffirmed "that there was a need for the Administrator to have at his disposal an appropriate instrument for providing direct project services to Governments" (United Nations 1989, DP/1989/75: 2). As a result, a government's needs would provide the criteria for selecting the executing agency, which could imply either specialized agency or OPE execution.[1] In the end, UNDP also issued new guidelines that involved the specialized agencies in determining which projects should be executed by OPE.

OPE also increasingly redefined its activities as a different type of work, distinct from specialized-agency execution. It downplayed the importance of its technical projects and focused more and more on the managerial aspects of project design, implementation and service delivery. It argued that:

> [t]echnical work performed by subcontractors could ... be supervised without great difficulty, the *essential function of OPE being that of management or service intermediary, setting in motion and controlling the project actors and the needed inputs of expertise and equipment*. A rural water supply project, for example, may demand a technical effort, but the role of OPS would consist of the service of procuring the capital equipment used in the project. At times, such services embrace full responsibility for project management. Thus, feeder road construction in the Sahel must be able to draw on engineering expertise, with OPS acting not as a consultant in its own right but as management contractor on behalf of the entity funding the project and using the best specialists available to it, normally from the private or non-governmental sector.
> (United Nations 1989, DP/1989/75: 4, italics by the author)

Subcontracting of "institutions and firms within and outside the UN system" became a central feature of OPE's work.

Within UNDP, OPE was able to expand. During its first six years, OPE experienced a growth surge. "Project disbursement grew rapidly to a level of $50–60 million, reaching a peak of $79 million in 1981" (United Nations 1989, DP/1989/75: 22). Gradually, it appeared that OPE's subcontracting skills were also of use to organizations other than UNDP. "The involvement of [OPE] in an executing or service capacity on behalf of trust funds and special funds began in earnest in 1978" (United Nations 1989, DP/1989/75: 10). Most of these funds, such as the United Nations Capital Development Fund (UNCDF) and the UN Sudano-Sahelian Office (UNSO), were actually administered by UNDP.

A third funding category, management service, made its first appearance in 1983. In 1983 expenditure under management services projects was a mere 2.2 percent; by 1988 they made up 33.6 percent of the total project expenditure of OPE. The management services modality accentuated OPE's service character. With the management service agreements, OPE was engaged on behalf of governments receiving loans from international development banks or grants from bilateral donors.

The traditional two funding categories, UNDP and trust funds, although declining in relative importance, continued to grow in absolute financial amounts. "From 1984 to 1988, OPE experienced a second growth surge, when overall program expenditures more than tripled" (United Nations 1989, DP/1989/75: 9–12, 22–23). From 1985 to 1990 project acquisition showed a sevenfold increase.

Through its focus on managing service delivery, OPE was able to distance itself from the original criticism that it was not a real technical expert in development cooperation. In order to preempt further criticism, its name was changed again. The new name had to be a more "adequate reflection of the distinction that exists between the management and service-oriented nature of direct execution on the one hand, and the technical emphasis of project execution by the Specialized Agencies on the other" (United Nations 1988, DP/1988/INF.1: 1–2). OPE thus wanted to avoid confusion with the technical specialized agencies. In 1988, the new name became Office for Project Services (OPS).

Through its focus on managerial services and subcontracting, OPS distinguished itself from the specialized agencies and their expertise in functional sectors, such as health or agriculture. OPS thus enabled itself to ward off criticism from these specialized agencies by stressing its managerial skills in managing development cooperation. Still, the Agencies resented the ability of OPS to grow, diversify, develop its expertise and discretion, and earn income as part of UNDP. At the same time, the UN system as a whole received regular criticism that its development activities were not up to par.

The evolution of the three modes of delivering development cooperation show a slow but discernible movement away from states towards other actors, such as universities and private enterprises, and more businesslike methods. At the same time, the discussion of the best ways of executing development cooperation often became narrowed into a technical discussion about the best methods of service delivery (and the concomitant competitive tensions among UN organizations). The global structural factors limiting the possibilities and impact of development cooperation received less attention. As a result, the issue of how to make the Third World countries more stable and prosperous remained difficult to answer, and anxiety continued among member states on what would be the best way to execute development cooperation.

UN reform: the proposed merger with DDSMS

When Boutros Boutros-Ghali became UN Secretary-General in 1992, he inherited a UN system that operated in an international context differing considerably from the one his predecessor originally faced. In particular, the end of the Cold War opened up new opportunities for low politics, with greater involvement of non-state actors, such as NGOs and other civil-society initiatives. It also refocused interest on issues such as good governance, international conflict resolution, and cooperation (Boutros-Ghali 1992: 89).

His reforms started in earnest in 1992. One proposal would strongly affect OPS: the Secretary-General wanted to transfer it to the UN Secretariat a Department for Development Support and Management Services (DDSMS). It would carry out two related functions.

> The first [was] to serve as a focal point for the provision of management services for technical cooperation. The second to act as an executing agency in selected cross-sectoral areas, with emphasis on the twin concepts of institutional development (including institution building, institutional reform and enterprise management) and human resources development (including activities aimed at human capital formation and at enhancing the contribution of different social groups to development).
> (United Nations 1992: 4, A/47/753)

The Secretary-General also "noted that the new arrangement would require a significant reallocation of existing programs within the economic and social sectors" (United Nations 1992: 8–9, A/47/753).

Kenneth Dadzie, at the time the Secretary-General of the United Nations Conference on Trade and Development (UNCTAD), became the "Special Advisor and Delegate" to address these issues. In his report on the reform of the economic and social sectors, commonly referred to as the Dadzie Report, he argued that the new DDSMS should incorporate OPS "as a semi-autonomous entity." One of the main reasons for this organizational change was the desire to strengthen UNDP's core mandate as the central funding and coordinating body for operational activities. In this respect, Dadzie argued that the relocation of OPS would assist in focusing UNDP's activities on this core mandate (Dadzie 1993: 8–9). This in turn would prevent duplication in service delivery and foster "the creation of a more unified and collaborative" UN system (United Nations 1993a, A/C.5/47/88: 21).

For OPS the news of the proposed merger came completely out of the blue. A few people, gathered in the office of the Executive Director, Daan Everts, assumed that the Secretariat had made a mistake. After all, OPS was in good shape and growing. Nobody in OPS had asked for a transfer into DDSMS. They even called the Secretariat to ask whether some mistake had been made. The answer was negative. Several staff members were curious whether this change would offer new opportunities for OPS. Others felt more neutral. In any case, it is an unwritten rule in the UN system that you do not officially disagree with the Secretary-General (IV). Hence, at least publicly everybody supported the proposals; they could disagree, however, on the quality of their implementation.

The member states were hesitant, if not outright reluctant about this merger. Some member states felt that they had not been consulted properly. They also wanted assurances that OPS could remain successful under the new arrangements and that their influence would not be diminished. Development cooperation may not be as high on the international agenda as security concerns, but member states strongly care about finding or protecting ways to make it more effective. Although the Governing Council member states took care not to be negative about the reform proposals, they diplomatically indicated that they did not just want to let go of OPS. Within UNDP, many felt that UNDP was being intentionally hamstrung, because it was becoming too powerful by combining coordinating, funding, program design, and implementing roles. Yet, the incoming Administrator of UNDP, James (Gus) Speth, and other top UNDP officials went along with the changes.

The exact modalities of the integration of OPS into DDSMS were supposed to be hammered out by a joint task force in 1993, so that at the start of 1994 OPS could separate from UNDP (United Nations 1993a, A/C.5/47/88: 2).

A bureaucratic decision-making process on reform implementation

The Advisory Committee on Administrative and Budgetary Questions (ACABQ) reviews biennial budgets of the UN system, which are also affected by reforms. Its members are directly elected by the General Assembly in their personal capacity, and can thus freely form their own independent judgment. The ACABQ essentially fulfills an external reviewer's function. It advises the Fifth Committee of the General Assembly on budget and management questions. As part of its responsibilities, the ACABQ reviewed the impact of Boutros-Ghali's reform proposals on the revised 1992–93 budget. In its report to the General Assembly the ACABQ gave biting criticism on the overall proposals. Noting that the Secretary-General's report was submitted too late to be reviewed properly, the ACABQ stated that:

> A major difficulty the Advisory Committee had in considering the report was that it lacked a context, a long-term concept or framework for the whole process of restructuring and information on how the restructuring of the Secretariat fitted into that process. The Committee believes that there is a need for a clear statement of an overall restructuring plan ... a time-frame for its implementation ... and how the restructuring would achieve the management aim of "a more responsive cost-effective, streamlined Secretariat."
>
> (United Nations 1993b, A/47/7/Add. 15: 67)

Concerning OPS, the ACABQ noted that the incorporation of OPS into the Secretariat would strengthen the primary purpose of UNDP as a central coordinating and funding mechanism. In addition, the incorporation would address concerns about duplication (United Nations 1993b, A/47/7/Add. 15: 71).

However, in its meeting of 18 June 1993, the Governing Council remained skeptical. Although, in principle, it accepted the modalities proposed in the report, it also wanted steps to protect OPS' autonomy, OPS' links with UNDP, and OPS' financial self-reliance. The council further asked for more information on the timetable for integration and staffing arrangements. In this respect, it stated that its understanding was that:

> the modalities will be clarified further and solutions reached prior to the transfer taking place and that the date of 1 January 1994 should be regarded as a target date pending review by the General Assembly, taking into account the views expressed by the ACABQ ...
>
> (United Nations 1993c, decision 93/42)

The emergence of UNOPS as a new UN organization   205

In August 1993 the executive director, Daan Everts, left OPS for a position at the World Food Program (WFP). Some OPS staff members felt betrayed by his departure during this insecure period. Yet his position would have been very difficult had he stayed. It became increasingly clear that pursuing the merger as proposed created an impossible situation in which preservation of the successful OPS characteristics, such as its financial self-reliance and operational management discretion, was incompatible with carrying out the specific proposals of the Secretary-General, DDSMS, the Department of Administration and Management, and the new Administrator of UNDP. OPS staff members felt uncertain whether their jobs would continue under the new structure. When would a new Executive Director be appointed? Most staff members also increasingly doubted whether a merger with DDSMS would add value to the operations of OPS. Would becoming part of the Secretariat improve OPS' functioning? Dissatisfaction was rising, especially in the task force preparing the merger. OPS staff, as well as others, felt more and more that instead of making the Secretariat more flexible, the merger would stifle OPS and make it more bureaucratic (IV). Moreover, clients demanded to know whether and how OPS would continue.

Instead of going along with all the proposed changes, some staff members informally started sharing their concerns with some ACABQ and Governing Council members. This was done only in a very discreet, hidden way. Five years later, staff members were still secretive about the ways in which they indirectly—and often anonymously—approached the ACABQ and Governing Council members during this period. They feared harming their own positions or those of the diplomats who shared their views.

In the absence of an executive director, Ivo Pokorny, an old OPS hand, became Officer in Charge. During this period OPS staff also continued working on the "Proposed Program Budget for the Biennium 1994–95," which focused on the "Institutional and administrative arrangements governing the integration of UNDP/OPS in the Department for Development Support and Management Services." This report was discussed in the ACABQ in November 1993. The ACABQ was not convinced that all arrangements had been worked out satisfactorily. Its members responded by recommending that "the date of integration be [changed to] 1 January 1995" (United Nations 1993d, A/48/7/Add. 1). The committee further recommended that the Secretary-General should re-submit a "report … when all pending issues are resolved at the inter-organizational level." The report also had to include an operational budget and information on the projected size of the portfolio of OPS and its internal organization.

In contrast to the ACABQ, top officials in UNDP and the Secretariat did not want such a postponement. Instead they tried to push ahead more rapidly. At this point in time, OPS staff felt so concerned that they decided to take their fate into their own hands. They felt that the official documents and statements sketched too rosy a picture of the merger and its probable consequences. For only the second time in UN history, staff presented its concerns directly to the ACABQ. Ms Deanna Gomez, chairperson of the UNDP/United Nations Population Fund (UNFPA) Staff Council, delivered a speech on behalf of OPS staff. It indicated the main areas of staff concern. The speech had an enormous, crippling effect on the merger process. Gomez expressed the nervousness of the OPS staff, particularly its concern that drastic change would shrink its client base and thus lead to job reductions. OPS staff, she said, did not believe that staffing issues had been adequately resolved. She also pointed out structural challenges to the merger, such as the difficulty of combining computer systems, and incompatible management cultures.

Ultimately, the ACABQ did not complete its review, officially saying it lacked time to do so properly. When the Governing Council assembled on 16 December 1993, OPS staff also decided to jointly attend that meeting. The unusually large number of OPS staff underscored the high degree of concern they felt about the outcome of the deliberations. As a result of the staff's earlier activities, and with many of them quietly sitting in the conference room, it was impossible for member states to say that all was well with the merger. Finally, the Governing Council recommended that OPS:

> should remain within the United Nations Development Programme until 1 January 1995 and decide[d] to review the modalities for its transfer to the Department for Development Support and Management Services.
>
> (United Nations 1993e, Governing Council Decision 93/46)

The Governing Council also wanted the OPS Management Board to further clarify the arrangements for transfer. Likewise, it requested the Secretary-General to report as soon as possible on the follow-up to its decisions. In other words, OPS and its staff had another year of breathing space to review the merger and arrange the transition properly. In addition, the member states increasingly doubted the merits of the merger.

Business impact: financially self-reliant for how long?

On the business front, the insecurity surrounding the proposed merger also started to have a profound impact on project acquisition. Clients

The emergence of UNOPS as a new UN organization 207

were reluctant to give projects for implementation to an OPS unsure of its continuation. Even if OPS remained active, the clients reasoned that the organizational changes could negatively impact the implementation of projects. In addition, the income of OPS had been small for the last few years, which made the organization financially vulnerable.

For OPS staff the proposed merger meant a considerable increase in workload. First, they had to keep the day-to-day operations running while the customers wanted clarity on the future of OPS. Second, they had to produce a financial surplus to secure their jobs. Third, they had to negotiate and prepare for the merger. This caused a fair degree of insecurity. After all, OPS jobs were on the line. Owing to this increasing pressure, OPS implemented some quality improvement measures, such as Total Quality Management, limited decentralization, and the establishment of Project Implementation Assistants to help the Project Management Officers on hold.

Starting 1 January 1994, a new executive director, Reinhart Helmke, was appointed. He had already gained a reputation as an innovative Resident Representative in Haiti, where he had strongly supported the democratization process that led to the election of Bertrand Aristide. Still, most OPS staff members were apprehensive. The umbilical cord with UNDP had not yet been cut, but the future relationship with UNDP (their largest client) remained unclear. The merger with DDSMS was not desired, and the practical arrangements for transfer, or the lack thereof, instilled fear. Yet, as the (internally) unexpected proposal for the merger showed, UN reform had its own bureaucratic dynamic, which was not easily influenced. OPS staff asked itself: Would a formal UNDP Res Rep be the right person for leading OPS out of UNDP? What about the relationships with the other UN organizations? Would OPS staff team up with each other or would the merger become a survival of the fittest? Would Reinhart Helmke have a personal agenda about his and OPS' future? Could the slow-down in project acquisition be a temporary dip, or was it worse?

Another staff initiative: the leaky boat strategy

OPS now also faced many new challenges in the delivery of aid and development. For multilateral organizations the age of entitlement was ending; increasingly donors tried to tie funding to performance. Funding sources were either declining or subject to increasing competition. OPS had to focus on its own functioning to be able to respond to a changing world. At the start of 1994, Norman (Sandy) Sanders, then a consultant with OPS, sat down to write his views on these strategic changes in an informal paper. He likened OPS to a leaky boat and identified key issues that were important "irrespective of what happened with the DDSMS restructuring proposal" (Sanders 1994). On the positive side, the informal paper noted that OPS' delivery was still growing and that during the merger discussions "staff had gained a collective self-confidence. The relatively participatory and open OPS management practices—sharing information and drawing on all available talents—reinforced staff's pride in the people and managerial culture of OPS." The paper continued: "This confidence and energy can, if harnessed skillfully, be redirected back into other challenges and opportunities that now face OPS" (Sanders 1994).

To address the issues raised by the paper, a simple exercise was set up. Over the course of a week staff listed and weighed what they considered OPS' internal strengths and weaknesses, as well as its external threats, and opportunities—a "SWOT analysis." In addition, the specific priorities for the next 12 months had to be identified. This analysis was carried out without interruption of daily work and gave a quick insight into what people in the organizations believed to be crucial issues for OPS' survival.

Although OPS was still part of UNDP, the process also reflected the considerable mental distance that staff had already taken from UNDP. OPS saw a possibility to diversify into new programming areas, such as peacekeeping and peacebuilding, and to be more proactive in terms of finding new clients with which to work. In response, working groups were assigned specific tasks in this diversification process, and they used simple standard forms for reporting. In this way, reform was initiated by providing proposals that followed a similar reporting format, were ready for action, and assured accountability. Through the proposals, OPS was able to identify its priorities. All the steps away from OPS' traditional functioning also implied threats, some typical to the UN system. The proposals took great care not to compete with or antagonize other UN parties. OPS staff felt that living within UNDP would, in all likelihood, become impossible, but it also knew that living with UNDP would remain a necessity. Other UN organizations could become clients as well as competitors. Doing substantive work with one UN organization could antagonize another. Hence, developing these relations would require in-house consensus for a start and careful execution to find a way through the inter-organizational UN sensitivities. Still, it was difficult to move ahead, because the future relationships with DDSMS and UNDP needed to be worked out.

On its own

After the last Governing Council meeting, the Secretariat and the government representatives were keenly aware of the problems surrounding the merger. They knew that it was necessary to make a decision on the status of OPS soon.

A sea change

In May 1994—after the leaky boat exercise—the Secretary-General submitted a response to the Executive Board (United Nations 1994a, DP/1994/27). The merger was still on. This report was written by the task force that had also written the other reports. The report outlined the "Institutional and administrative arrangements concerning the Office for Project Services" and was sent to the Executive Board. By this time, however, the OPS members of the task force felt that they were just there to correct the grammar of the reports. OPS staff was also afraid that DDSMS had designs on the positions at OPS, which led to more hidden opposition. The board, still cautious, did not accept the new arrangements. Instead it deferred their consideration until its Annual Session, scheduled to take place in Geneva in June.

Before this Annual Session, the Secretary-General, or more accurately staff members of the Secretariat, made an about-face. Resistance from member governments spurred on by OPS staff, and fears about loss of OPS' flexibility, had grown too much. In addition, some Security Council members were increasingly dissatisfied with Boutros-Ghali and as a signal they became more critical about the merger that he proposed (IV). In a new report, the Secretary-General restated his intention that UNDP should fulfill its coordinating role for the operational activities of the UN system in an impartial manner. OPS, as part of UNDP, posed an inherent conflict in this respect, because of its implementation function. However, the Secretary-General was "extremely concerned by the continuing uncertainty, which [he understood, was] shared by the member states" (United Nations 1994b, DP/1994/52: 2). He therefore proposed a new solution, namely:

> to establish the Office for Project Services as a separate identity headed by an Assistant Secretary-General as the responsible manager under the authority of the Secretary-General ... [Its] Executive Director would report on the activities of OPS to the UNDP Executive Board.
>
> (United Nations 1994b, DP/1994/52: 2)

The proposal also provided a broad outline for the new relationship with UNDP and other UN bodies.

> Administrative support for OPS would continue to be provided by UNDP, as a reimbursable service. The existing financial and personnel regime would be maintained. OPS would continue to work at country level through the field network of UNDP ... The UNDP Executive Board would serve as the governing body for OPS in the same way as it serves, for example, as the governing body of UNFPA ... The role of the member states *vis-à-vis* OPS operations would remain unchanged.
> (United Nations 1994b, DP/1994/52: 3)

As a result, OPS now entered a whole new ballgame: it would become a separate UN organization and OPS staff had only about half a year left to prepare their organization for its new role.

A flurry of activity

In the Executive Board, the reactions of the government representatives to the proposal varied. "Some favored its acceptance, while others expressed reservations ... Several delegations opposed the creation of a new United Nations agency and emphasized their support for a close association with UNDP" (United Nations 1994c, DP/1994/L.4/Add.4).

The Executive Board decision

The subsequent decision laid down the legal basis for the separation from UNDP. It also showed how the concerns of member states and the UN system shaped the opportunities of OPS to fill in its new roles in the UN system.

The Executive Board decision began by recognizing UNDP's central coordinating role, as well as the fears of the specialized agencies that OPS would be a competitor in funding and technical expertise; it reiterated the distinction between funding and implementation and made it clear that the role of a new OPS was the latter. It further declared that OPS would be self-financing, meaning that it would be a hybrid between a UN agency and a private corporation. It hoped that this (through the need to operate according to sound business principles) would provide some assurance of project quality and efficiency. The Executive Board "stress[ed] the importance of OPS continuing to operate within the United Nations development system" rather than

The emergence of UNOPS as a new UN organization

breaking away to create a new specialized agency. Finally, it recommended that OPS become a separate entity (but not a new agency), in a relationship with UNDP and operating through its field offices. It directed OPS to make recommendations, through the ACABQ, on how it could move forward in a responsible way with the creation of a separate entity.

This Executive Board decision set the stage for a whole range of papers that provided the framework for OPS' independent role and functioning. The main issue in writing these reports was OPS' hybrid form. On the one hand, OPS had to become as businesslike as possible. On the other, it had to be a part of the UN system, which was not geared toward providing free-enterprise opportunities.

Establishing the office as a "separate and identifiable entity"

On 26 July 1994 ECOSOC recommended that the General Assembly approve this decision. In response, the General Assembly decision stated:

> At its 105th plenary meeting, on 19 September 1994, the General Assembly, on a proposal by Australia and on the recommendation of the Economic and Social Council, decided that the Office for Project Services should become a separate and identifiable entity in accordance with United Nations Development Programme Executive Board decision 94/12 of 9 June 1994.
> (United Nations 1994e, GA/48/501)

The Executive Director detailed the establishment of OPS as "a separate and identifiable" entity and introduced OPS' new name: the United Nations Office for Project Services (UNOPS) (United Nations 1994d, DP/1994/62). With this name the report intended to distinguish UNOPS as different from OPS, while "retaining its image of a client-focused, responsive organization with more than twenty years' experience in service delivery" (IV). Besides, this name sounded better in the other official UN languages. UNOPS saw itself as a demand-driven, client-oriented entity that provides a variety of services:

- Comprehensive project management, including contracting for technical expertise and backstopping;
- Implementation of components of projects under execution by other organizations of the United Nations system or by national institutions;

212   Dennis Dijkzeul

- Project supervision and loan administration on behalf of international financial institutions; and
- Management services for multilateral, bilateral, and beneficiary-financed projects.

UNOPS saw itself as being "unlike Specialized Agencies, which possess institutional technical competence." UNOPS, instead, functioned "as a management contractor on behalf of the client, setting in motion and managing the project actors and the needed inputs of expertise and equipment" (United Nations 1994d, DP/1994/62: 3). In all these respects, UNOPS repeated arguments that OPS had already used to protect its activities, discretion, and flexibility. The remainder of the report described the structure and management mechanisms.

In October, the Executive Board convened. Reinhart Helmke addressed the meeting and stated that, in addition to the ACABQ, the UN Legal Counsel had reviewed UNOPS' documentation and that it saw no real problems. Yet UNOPS was still in a hurry, because it needed Executive Board approval to be ready for 1995. UNOPS, however, did not get complete approval (United Nations 1994g, decision 94/32). The board did authorize the Administrator and Executive Director to take all steps necessary to establish a self-financing UNOPS. The board also took note of the proposed financial regulations of UNOPS and decided to review them at its first regular session in 1995.

Once again, UNOPS staff prepared the necessary paperwork—often in unpaid overtime—responding to the board and refining its financial rules and regulations. The ACABQ reviewed the documents, and suggested that UNOPS, as a separate, businesslike organization, should provide information on how it was going to deal with its new risks and liabilities as well as with its surplus income. The Executive Board met on 10 January 1995 to discuss the latest documentation. Finally, board decision 95/1 concluded more than two years of deliberations on the status and role of OPS. UNOPS was established, as of 1 January 1995, as a separate and identifiable entity.

From now on, UNOPS could report to the Executive Board at two regular meetings a year, normalizing its reporting process. Instead of creating new rules and regulations, it could focus on making them work. However, as a separate, businesslike entity UNOPS still had to prove itself.

Conclusion

The whole process towards the creation of an independent UNOPS came about in a very tangled and haphazard way. Originally, there was

The emergence of UNOPS as a new UN organization 213

no discussion about separation at all. The real impetus came from political decision-making in the complex intergovernmental bureaucratic supervisory structure of the UN system. This was fueled by a perceived need for UN reform, by inter-agency competition, and by the Secretariat's desire to respond to the political needs of member states. Another factor was the complex, and highly salient, issue of development cooperation. OPS' financial self-reliance, also, was an influential factor.

Looking at bureaucratic factors, it is noteworthy that OPS staff played a crucial role in shaping the process. Their agenda (and evolving interests) differed from those of the member states and the Secretary-General. After OPS staff members had overcome their initial surprise, and began to confront the uncertainty they felt, they decided to act in their own best interests and to set their own agenda. Moreover, their opposition to the merger grew as the process unfolded, because they feared that OPS would lose its speed and flexibility—and, hence, an important part of its own identity. They had to act as quickly as possible because their organization had to be financially self-reliant. Moreover, as their interests became clearer, it was not just saving their jobs and organization that concerned them, but also the innovative character of their organization's modes of execution in development cooperation and rebuilding—organizational culture was a driving factor in interest formation. They cared about UN ideals of peace and development and also used those to their own advantage. Self-interested and altruistic motivations simultaneously played a role. Subsequently, they also contacted informally the representatives of UN decision-making bodies and some member state diplomats, which had the effect of changing the course of the organization, so that it ultimately became a separate entity. As the concept is used in this volume, staff acted independently and, if not exactly against state interests, then in a way that bent those interests to their own will.

Two elements provided some structure to this process. First, OPS staff themselves, concerned about their jobs and the future of their organization, did not assume that things would somehow turn out all right in the end. They brought forward their own proposals and changed their stance from reactive to proactive. They had some leeway as states were concerned, if not a bit anxious, about the modes—and forms of service delivery—for international cooperation (originally mainly in development, but later also in other areas). Member States certainly did not want to rock the boat by dissolving an organization that had been innovative and financially self-reliant in this respect.

Second, the UN decision-making process, while often slow and impersonal, did provide some decision points and evaluation forums. There was a rhythm in the Executive Board decisions and ACABQ reviews—and for OPS, to a lesser extent in ECOSOC and the General Assembly decisions—that slowly kept pushing processes forward. Member state diplomats never meaningfully questioned these processes, and OPS staff members informally used these processes to make their objections to the merger clear. In other words, they were able to use the bureaucratic logic of UN decision-making processes to further their interests. The rules and regulations of the UN, formulated long ago, created a path-dependent process which had as much to do with the outcome as any decision taken by specific people.

It is remarkable how little the official legal documentation of Executive Board decisions, proposals and reviews refers to staff initiative. It is almost completely absent. The leaky boat strategy was not considered either, because it was an internal—and informal—event that ran parallel only in the very last year of the merger-cum-separation process. Thus one problem in understanding these official UN decision-making processes is that the official documentation is more about giving a green (or red) light than about the actual driving. Put differently, the main decisions are taken, but it is not always clear who initiated this decision-making process, how these decisions are going to be executed, nor how they will impact upon the actors involved. The focus is on what should be done, not on how it could be done. As a self-financing entity that needed continuity, OPS had a hard time accommodating this decision-making process, although it simultaneously facilitated independent staff initiative.

The UNOPS case points out some interesting shortcomings of both PA and constructivist theory. They are both too much "broad brush" techniques for understanding intergovernmental organizations. IR scholars do a better job at understanding security issues than modes of execution for international cooperation. Their theories often fail to do justice to the diversity of actors (e.g., the positions of the different UN specialized agencies on OPS execution) and differing modes of execution. The quality of these modes in terms of speed, knowledge transfer, efficiency, and impact was a salient issue for member states. Yet little scientific research was done into these issues. At the same time, however, the UN organizations involved did develop a strong institutional interest in certain modes of execution. More projects simply meant more money for them—and they responded to the bureaucratic imperative to increase resources and influence.

Without an understanding of the diversity of actors, their evolving interests, and the (internal) bureaucratic processes, rules and regulations in which these actors are embedded, PA and constructivist theory lack explanatory power. PA usually does not pay enough attention to altruistic motives, or to how staff members creatively combine more selfish interests (their jobs were on the line as the organization had a hard time ensuring its financial self-reliance) with the UN ideals of peace and development. Constructivist IR theorists generally do a better job at explaining changing interests, but still fail to take the effect of staff members seriously. This chapter has shown that staff capacities and knowledge of the bureaucratic logic of decision making shape the ways in which international organizations are (unexpectedly) formed and evolve. Without attention to bureaucratic factors and personal interests, these theories fail to link either state or staff interests with (unexpected organizational) action, and do not explain sufficiently how staff can act independently from state interests.

Both PA and constructivist scholars, as discussed in the introduction of this volume, still focus too much on state-based decision-making and official policy. They should also focus more on the internal workings of these diverse organizations, and how they implement, and therewith often change, these policies and decisions. Both IR constructivist and PA scholars should incorporate more complex management theory. In this way, the study of these organizations can foster more interdisciplinary social science debates. Both theories are already steps in this direction, but they can and should go further if we want to understand better the actual behavior did impact international organizations.

Note

1 An additional argument to maintain OPE was that the Administrative Committee on Coordination's (ACC) Consultative Committee on Substantive Questions concerning Operational Activities (CCSQ(OPS)) had concluded that "it was not possible to arrive at a clear and definitive assessment of the utilization of subcontracting by the executing agencies" (United Nations 1984c, A/39/80/Add. 1: 5). Information on cost effectiveness, knowledge transfer and promotion of self reliance was too scarce. It was also pointed out that "other, non-UNDP sources of funding ... directly available to some agencies [had] grown substantially" (United Nations 1984c, A/39/80/Add. 1: 7).

Bibliography

Boutros-Ghali, Boutros, "Empowering the United Nations," *Foreign Affairs* (1992): 89–102.

Dadzie, K., *Report of the Special Advisor and Delegate of the Secretary-General on the reform of the economic and social sectors*, 7 February 1993.

Dijkzeul, Dennis, *Reforming for Results in the UN System: A Study of UNOPS* (London: Macmillan, 2000).

——*The Management of Multilateral Organizations* (The Hague: Kluwer Law International, 1997).

Sanders, N., *Informal Working Paper – A Management Agenda for OPS* (Leaky Boat Memorandum), 18 January 1994.

United Nations, *The Capacity of the United Nations Development System*, also known as the Jackson Report or Capacities Study (UN document A/2688, XXV), 11 December 1970.

——*Office for Project Execution of the United Nations Development Programme*, report circulated to the General Assembly with A/39/80 (UN document JIU/REP/83/9), 28 February 1984a.

——*Operational Activities for Development: United Nations Development Programme, Joint Inspection Unit*, Office for Projects Execution of the United Nations Development Programme, Note by the Secretary-General (UN document A/39/80), 28 February 1984b.

——*Operational Activities for Development: United Nations Development Programme, Joint Inspection Unit*, Office for Projects Execution of the United Nations Development Programme, Comments of the Secretary-General (UN document A/39/80/Add.1), 26 April 1984c.

——*Change of name of the Office for Projects Execution to Office for Project Services, Note by the Administrator*, Governing Council of the United Nations Development Programme (UN document DP/1988/INF.1), 3 February 1988.

——*Role and Functions of the Office for Project Services, Report of the Administrator*, Governing Council of the United Nations Development Programme (UN document DP/1989/75), 4 May 1989.

——*Secretary-General's Note on Restructuring and Revitalization of the UN in the Economic, Social and Related Fields* (UN document A/47/753), 3 December 1992.

——*Revised Estimates of the 1992–93 Programme Budget*, Report of the Secretary-General (UN document A/C.5/47/88), 4 March 1993a.

——*First Report of the Advisory Committee on Administrative & Budgetary Questions on OPS* (UN document A/47/7), 24 March 1993b.

——*Governing Council Decision 93/42*, 18 June 1993c.

——*Second Report of the Advisory Committee on Administrative & Budgetary Questions on OPS* (UN document A/48/7/Add.1), 4 November 1993d.

——*Governing Council Decision 93/46*, 16 December 1993e.

——*Report of the Secretary-General on institutional and administrative arrangements concerning OPS* (UN document DP/1994/27), 4 May 1994a.

——*Report of the Secretary-General on OPS* (UN document DP/1994/52), 6 June 1994b.

——*Draft Report of the Annual Session* (UN document DP/1994/L.4/Add.4), 9 June 1994c.

——*OPS Executive Director's Report on OPS* (UN document DP/1994/62 + Add.1–3), 16 August 1994d.

The emergence of UNOPS as a new UN organization 217

——General Assembly Decision endorsing E/1994/284 and EB 94/12 (Decision 48/501), 19 September 1994e.
——ACABQ report on DP/1994/61 & 62 (UN document DP/1994/57), 4 October 1994f.
——Executive Board Decision 94/32, 10 October 1994g.
——Administrator's and OPS Executive Director's Report on Financial Regulations for UNOPS, and the proposed UNOPS Annex to UNDP Financial Regulations and Rules (UN document DP/1995/7 & Add.1), 22 November 1994h.

Part III
Expanding the argument

8 ASEAN as an informal organization

Does it exist and does it have agency? The emergence of the ASEAN secretariat

Bob Reinalda

- ASEAN as a regional security regime 1967–2007
- ASEAN as a regional economic regime 1970–2008
- Genesis and evolution of the ASEAN secretariat
- Conclusion: a formal organization with an active secretariat

The main issue attributes of the Association of Southeast Asian Nations (ASEAN) are distrust among members (and with other states) and lack of agreement over economic cooperation. The main organizational attribute is its informality. ASEAN, established in 1967, is known as a regional organization that is barely bureaucratic, given the salience of "Asian values" and the consensus-oriented "ASEAN way of working." It is described as "a loosely structured association rather than a formal organization" (Thambipillai 1994: 105). Others even claim that "informal integration" is the major form of regional cooperation in Asia (Eliassen and Monsen 2001: 121). Because ASEAN's member states, or "principals," are dominant and have adequate means for overseeing the actions of their "agent," the ASEAN secretariat and its secretary-general are considered weak and scarcely present. Given these issue and organizational attributes it is difficult to expect the ASEAN secretariat to play a role of its own, either externally by being a recognizable entity with initiatives or organizational preferences, or internally by pursuing its own interests in terms of functions or careers.

This chapter will explore whether ASEAN is as informal as is claimed. Formal organizations in international relations are purposive entities, capable of monitoring activity and of reacting to it, deliberately set up and designed by states. They are bureaucratic, with explicit rules and the specific assignment of rules to individuals and groups (Keohane 1989: 3–4). The article will first look at ASEAN's two major regimes (security and economics) to see to what extent governments have built a formal organization. It does so from a perspective that focuses first on governments and their cooperation. The article then includes the internal workings of ASEAN in its perspective, by tracing the emergence and evolution of its secretariat in order to find out what role it has played in the regimes described earlier and to see to what degree ASEAN is bureaucratic and has (potential) agency through its secretariat. While *regimes* are characterized by explicit rules agreed upon by governments, the term *institutionalization* is used as an indication of organization building, in particular by providing continuity and assigning this task to a specific body, which in international organizations (IOs) is usually the permanent secretariat. The conclusion is that the informality claim is no longer valid, as by now ASEAN has a clearly described organizational set-up and the ASEAN secretariat has shown (unforeseen) agency as a global negotiator representing ASEAN.

This article presents empirical data needed to understand how ASEAN slowly, and hardly noticed, grew into a regional security and economic organization with an active international secretariat without which the 10 Asian member states can no longer manage all important issues in international relations. Various developments resulted in a window of opportunity in which the secretariat, on its own volition, created for itself a function that member states had not originally intended. For this analysis official documents and literature on ASEAN are used (see Appendix 1 for the agreements on the ASEAN secretariat concluded between 1967 and 2007; all ASEAN documents are in English and available at www.aseansec.org).

ASEAN as a regional security regime 1967–2007

It makes sense to start from a realist regime perspective, since ASEAN's cooperation began as a security issue and resulted in a climate of trust among members and with other states. Öjendal (2001: 165) calls ASEAN a "soft security organization" with successes and limitations. Its decisions have been taken by the foreign ministers and, after a while, the heads of government. Overcoming the issue attribute of distrust among neighboring states was a gradual process, as the 40 years of this (mainly informal) security regime show.

ASEAN was created against the background of strained relations in Southeast Asia. When in July 1961 Malaya, the Philippines, and Thailand established the Association of Southeast Asia, other states in the region regarded this as too Western-oriented. Conflicts in the region, such as the formation of Malaysia, the 1965 military coup in

Indonesia and the secession of Singapore from Malaysia, added to the tensions, but also to discussions about more friendly intra-regional relations. The replacement of Sukarno by Suharto as Indonesian president in early 1967 ended the Indonesia–Malaysia confrontation over the future of the island of Borneo and allowed Indonesia to become the group's *de facto* leading state or "regional hegemon" (Webber 2003: 134). The efforts resulted in the issuing of the ASEAN Declaration in August 1967 in Bangkok by the foreign ministers of Indonesia, Malaysia, the Philippines, Singapore and Thailand. These five states established ASEAN, with the aim of common action to promote regional cooperation in a spirit of equality and partnership and thereby contributing towards peace, progress and prosperity in the region.

The Bangkok Declaration is not a traditional international treaty that binds the parties, but rather an impetus for voluntary cooperation, describing in a general way the aims and purposes of the association, with a fairly light organizational structure in which the states ("nations") had to learn how to cooperate and find solutions for Asian issues. The foreign ministers were inspired by the Non-Aligned Movement, set up in 1961 with a limited organizational structure and based on traditional "Westphalian" principles such as mutual respect for each other's territorial integrity and sovereignty, mutual non-aggression and non-interference in domestic affairs. The later term *ASEAN way of working* characterizes the practice and observance of a set of principles and norms of interstate conduct and modes of cooperation and decision-making. In ASEAN the formal vote is not used, as political will and general consensus are preferred to strict rules of procedure (Caballero-Anthony 2003: 199). Although all members need to agree to support a particular issue, some dissent is allowed and expressed in the concept of "five minus one" (Thambipillai 1994: 120).

Given the intensification of conflicts and the threat from communism in the region, the ASEAN states began to discuss their foreign policies from a *regional* rather than a nationalist perspective. They used the first decade to explore the possibilities of the Association and to learn to feel at ease with each other. In 1971 the foreign ministers signed the *Declaration on the Zone of Peace, Freedom and Neutrality*, in which they expressed their wish to keep the region free from any form or manner of interference by outside powers. They also stated that the states in the region should make concerted efforts to broaden the areas of cooperation. It was not until the Vietnam War was over and the three states in Indochina had come under communist rule that ASEAN began to define further ways of cooperation. In February 1976 ASEAN's first Summit was held in Bali, where the heads of government also began to play a role. This resulted in the *Treaty of Amity and Cooperation in Southeast Asia*, with principles for their relations and rules for cooperation and peaceful settlement of disputes, and the *Declaration of ASEAN Concord*, which contained a program of action as a framework for ASEAN cooperation. Their cautious cooperation created a climate of trust among the governments, which watchfully approached problems that were prepared by civil servants in committees with the purpose of reaching consensus.

The members gradually grew towards common foreign positions. This became apparent during the late 1970s, when as a result of regional instability caused by the end of the Vietnam War, "boat people" and refugees from the states in Indochina were looking for help. ASEAN's common position meant that these refugees found only temporary shelter in its member states and were then resettled in states such as Australia, France, and the United States. In 1982 the ASEAN members also prevented the Cambodian regime installed by Vietnam after its intervention to expel Pol Pot from taking over the Cambodian seat at the UN. Brunei Darussalam joined in 1984 and Vietnam acceded in 1995, Laos and Myanmar (formerly Burma) in 1997, and Cambodia in 1999.

In 1992 ASEAN decided that more cooperation was needed in the interest of security in the region, partly influenced by the new global relations after the end of the Cold War. In 1991 the Japanese foreign minister had proposed that official regional security dialogues be held under the auspices of the ASEAN Post-Ministerial Conferences (PMCs). Pressure to start such security consultations also came from Australia and the United States (Johnston 1999: 292). An advantage of using the PMCs was that the Dialogue and Consultative Partners could be involved without too much difficulty. These developments led to the 1993 decision to launch the ASEAN Regional Forum (ARF), which has virtually no formal organizational structure.

What the ASEAN states wanted was to preserve economic prosperity while being able to plan what they should do if things went wrong in security relations. They regarded the usual mechanisms for this, such as an arms program and alliance building, as too costly and preferred a cautious type of organization. The state presenting the greatest danger in the region seemed to be China, and if they wanted more information about its intentions in order to reduce uncertainty they needed China to cooperate in the ARF. However, China should also not feel threatened, a consideration that equally underlay the decision to keep the "organization" of the "forum" as weak as possible. This proved acceptable to most of the states. By 1997, however, the ARF had in place "a series of intersessional governmental working groups examining everything from templates for defence white papers, to military observers at military exercises, to the South China Sea, to nuclear weapons free zones, to peacekeeping standby arrangements" (Johnston 1999: 290).

By the late 1990s, however, ASEAN was also confronted with a loss of authority due to the Asian financial crisis (see next section), a military coup in Cambodia (just before its accession to ASEAN), and the cross-border environmental problems that were caused by forest fires. These last were started deliberately every year by Indonesian farmers trying to expand the land available for agriculture, and occurred on such a scale that other states were faced with smog problems. ASEAN proved unable to influence any of these crises (Webber 2003: 135). Other matters included the continuing violations of human rights in Cambodia and Myanmar, where opposition leader and Nobel Prize winner Aung San Suu Kyi was kept under house arrest or severely restricted in her movements. As a result of foreign demands ASEAN appealed for her release in 2003, and in 2005 it put pressure on Myanmar not to take up its rotating chairmanship in 2006. Both actions went against its principle of non-intervention in the domestic affairs of its members. Furthermore, ASEAN did not play a role in East Timor, a former Portuguese colony occupied by Indonesia, after Indonesia's 1999 decision to allow East Timor a referendum on its future status. Neither ASEAN nor the ARF succeeded in responding to the unfolding humanitarian disaster in their midst or in taking part in the political solution found by the United Nations (UN). It was not until September 2007 that the secretaries-general of ASEAN and the UN—the latter had criticized ASEAN for its weak role in peacekeeping—signed a Memorandum of Understanding (MOU) to establish a "partnership for closer cooperation." ASEAN thus opted for a weak form of agreement, rather than the usual observer status.

Conclusion about the security regime

This short history of security relations shows that ASEAN has been successful as an ongoing regional security regime for its members and as the ARF initiator. The issue attribute of distrust among states was solved not by the usual (but costly) security mechanisms of alliance-building and an arms program, but rather by steady consensus building and an informal forum format which also allowed consulting with other states. However, as East Timor and other crises show, the security regime also has its clear limitations. These include the lack of support institutions, the preference of most ARF members for bilateralism rather than multilateralism and ASEAN's limited potential and capabilities for setting the agenda to address major issues such as nuclear non-proliferation in the Korean peninsula and competing claims in the South China Sea (Caballero-Anthony 2003: 204). External factors played an important part in forging ASEAN into a regional entity. The potent threat of communism in China and the Indochinese peninsula, with China as a potential aggressor, helped to identify common interests and develop common policies. Although institutionalization can be observed, the security entity seems informal rather than bureaucratic, with roles for governments and apparently no role for the organization.

ASEAN as a regional economic regime 1970–2008

ASEAN is also a regional economic regime, with decisions taken by the heads of government and foreign ministers as well as the trade and finance ministers. Still, it was not until the early 1990s that the economic regime began to function, mainly in reaction to external influences. This section shows the rise of Southeast and East Asia as regional players in the world economy and describes the history of the economic regime, again from a state-centric perspective.

Initially, economic cooperation seemed relevant because of the threat of communism in the region. Soon after ASEAN's establishment the UN, which had made "development" its priority goal of the 1960s and 1970s, proposed that ASEAN should coordinate industrial activities as a way towards development and regional cooperation. As with security, ASEAN took its time in establishing economic cooperation. This was necessary, given some serious obstacles. Whereas Singapore was in favor of free trade, Indonesia was strongly opposed. Another problem was that the larger states' products were fairly similar. By 1976 states began to embark on a coordinated set of development "national projects," referred to as ASEAN Industrial Projects (AIP) (Thambipillai 1994: 113).

Economic cooperation as a "drive" continued, but remained weak in the 1970s and early 1980s (Thambipillai 1994: 114). However, the world economy of the 1980s, in particular the recession of 1985–86 and the change in the dominant economic paradigm from Keynesianism towards neoliberalism, left less room for ASEAN's restricted free trade policy and pushed toward a change. Webber discerns two external factors that supplied the momentum behind this change. The first was the so-called Plaza Accord of 1985, when the United States in the G7 (a group of the finance ministers from seven industrialized nations) context abandoned its opposition to international monetary management and relinquished its laissez-faire policy by approving interventions in the exchange markets. The Plaza Accord included more active participation by Japan, which led to a massive appreciation of the Japanese yen in the late 1980s and in Southeast Asia to a big increase in the volume of foreign, in particular Japanese, direct investment.

The second factor promoting trade liberalization was the economic rise of China, which became an increasingly serious competitor of ASEAN states as a location for foreign direct investment (FDI) and for low-cost manufactured goods. "For the following decade, Chinese competition for FDI continued to be a major source of pressure on the ASEAN governments not to 'backslide'" on their free trade commitments (Webber 2003: 135). Webber attributes ASEAN's u-turn in the early 1990s to Suharto's government. Until the late 1980s Indonesia, the regional hegemon, was most hostile to the idea of intra-ASEAN trade liberalization and had the least open economy in ASEAN. However, after "a precipitous fall in oil prices, a worsening balance of payments position and economic recession in the mid-1980s" (Webber 2003: 134), it began to shift towards a more liberal economic and trade policy stance.

At the Singapore ASEAN Summit in January 1992 this took the form of a Common Effective Preferential Tariff (CEPT) scheme to reduce import levies, a decision taken by the economic ministers who now gained prominence, and a proposal for an ASEAN Free Trade Area (AFTA) by 2008, with a framework agreement on enhancing ASEAN economic cooperation signed by the heads of government. In 1997 ASEAN's economic fortunes began to reverse when it was hit by the already mentioned "triple challenge" of the Asian financial crisis, the coup in Cambodia and the smog crisis (Webber 2003: 135). ASEAN was also faced with a leadership void, as Indonesian President Suharto was forced to resign in 1998 and his successors were preoccupied with domestic stability. An erosion of ASEAN's underpinnings took place, with members looking for individual solutions. "Unilateralism, not regionalism, reigned supreme under the watchful eye of the [International Monetary Fund]," according to Weatherbee (2009: 104).

In November 1997, in response to the Asian financial crisis, new preventive measures were discussed within the wider Asia-Pacific Economic Cooperation (APEC), resulting in the so-called Manila Framework, which let the International Monetary Fund (IMF) role remain central but included enhanced regional surveillance in South and East Asia itself. In October 1998 ASEAN announced a stronger ASEAN Surveillance Process, which all members should support. Its work was facilitated by a growing sense of regional identity. "A number of ASEAN countries, notably Indonesia, Malaysia and to some extent the Philippines, have, by rejecting certain stipulations in IMF packages, focused on the importance of Asian alternatives to what are perceived as Western interventions" (Eliassen and Monsen 2001: 129). The regional identity was firmly enhanced by a clash with the IMF, which at the 1998 APEC meeting first agreed that an Asian monetary fund should be set up, but afterwards, and to the astonishment of the Asian states, publicly rejected this (Webber 2003: 140–41).

The ASEAN Summit in Hanoi in December 1998 adopted the *Hanoi Plan of Action*, with a six-year timeframe, in which ASEAN recognized the need to address the current economic situation in the region by implementing "initiatives to hasten economic recovery" and by taking measures which "reaffirm ASEAN commitments to closer regional integration." In 1997 ASEAN had contacted China, Japan and South Korea with the aim of expanding its relations to include the whole of East Asia. At an equally informal summit of this expanded ASEAN, ASEAN Plus Three (APT), which immediately followed the ASEAN Summit in November 1999, it was decided to work more closely together within this group of states and in IOs such as the UN and the World Trade Organization (WTO). This led to bilateral trade agreements between ASEAN and China and Japan, opening up the prospect of an East Asia Free Trade Area (EAFTA).

In early 2003 ASEAN's economic ministers adopted a Protocol to once again adjust the CEPT and AFTA plans, achieving substantial tariff reductions. By 2007 there was a well-advanced free trade area within ASEAN, certainly within ASEAN-6. Weatherbee (2009: 105) calls 2003 the year in which ASEAN was "reinvented," because Indonesian President Megawati Sukarnopruti began to play a leadership role in shaping the region's future, and the Summit in Bali decided to create an integrated ASEAN Community by 2020. ASEAN would henceforth consist of three "pillars": the ASEAN Security Community (ASC), ASEAN Economic Community (AEC) and ASEAN Socio-Cultural Community (ASCC). The goal of the first pillar is for the member states to "live at peace with one another and with the world at large in a just, democratic and harmonious environment," the second aims to expand the free trade area into a broad internal market, and the third pillar intends to expand the partnership into a community of caring societies based on a common regional identity. In 2005 ASEAN decided to draft a constitution. The ASEAN Charter is a codification of previous principles, standards and procedures. It was adopted in November 2007, came into force in December 2008 and made ASEAN a legal entity.

Conclusion about the economic regime

The issue attribute of lack of agreement over economic cooperation remained dominant until the early 1990s. ASEAN as a regional economic regime strongly depended on external actors and policies (the UN, Plaza Accord and IMF), as well as on economic and financial crises (1985–86, 1997–98) which required an answer by ASEAN. In addition to the foreign ministers and heads of government, the trade and finance ministers played their roles. The economic ministers' part remained restricted until 1992, when they introduced a soon successful free trade policy. Then the finance ministers added to this by initiating ASEAN's monetary surveillance as a contribution to solving the financial crisis of the late 1990s. ASEAN's economic regime was widened to APT by including the three major economies in East Asia. In spite of its informal way of working, ASEAN used written agreements and legal codification when it promoted and expanded its trade regime and its institutionalization. These are indications of formal rather than informal cooperation in this economic regime.

Genesis and evolution of the ASEAN secretariat

The article now moves from a state-focused perspective to one that includes ASEAN's internal workings. It opens up its "black box" and investigates the role of the secretariat in the intergovernmental developments described above. There are three time periods: 1967–76, when ASEAN did not have a secretariat, 1976–92, when a permanent secretariat was created, and 1992–2007, when this secretariat was restructured and enhanced. During the first period a new position was given to the trade ministers, who in reaction to the global economic pressures of the 1980s began to play a larger role in ASEAN's second period. Their role and some inter-organizational developments (between ASEAN, the European Union (EU) and the General Agreement on Tariffs and Trade (GATT)), which promoted a stronger position of the ASEAN secretariat, created a window of opportunity for the secretariat to claim a trade-related role of its own as ASEAN's "global negotiator." This section shows how the secretariat came into being and later began to play an active role in both economic and organizational developments.

1967–76: no ASEAN secretariat, but a role for the trade ministers

During the first period ASEAN did not meet the official definition of an intergovernmental organization as no permanent international secretariat had been created. It did meet two other conditions: a written agreement between governments, and three or more member states. The 1967 ASEAN Declaration provided for an annual meeting of foreign ministers (the Ministerial Meeting), a Standing Committee under the (rotating) chair of the foreign minister of the host country, plus national secretariats in each member state. Thambipillai regards this agreement as "influenced by politics" but "camouflaged in socioeconomic terms": "it was more a response to geopolitics, the external environment and bilateral regional relations than a desire to coordinate national political issues" (Thambipillai 1994: 116). Weatherbee explains the simple machinery devised by the founders as reflecting the low expectations of the initiators (the foreign ministers) for a decentralized consultative grouping (Weatherbee 2009: 100), while Öjendal argues that ASEAN came into being because of internal conflicts, in particular the communist threat. He regards the national elites as the agents of regional rapprochement, because ASEAN became an "integral part of the various states' nation-building strategies," which explains why terms such as "integration" or "supranationality" are not used in the Declaration (Öjendal 2001: 156).

ASEAN's actual engagement with economic policies resulted from independent external stimulus. Trade as a basis for regional cooperation, however, was problematic within ASEAN, because attempts at preferential trading during the period preceding ASEAN's formation had led to the disruption of peace in the region and discord between Singapore, Malaya (later Malaysia) and Indonesia (Panagariya 1998: 83). The issue also arose in 1974–75, when Singapore called for a more liberalized intra-ASEAN trading system, whereas Indonesia opposed this as it would be damaged most by it. This controversy brought an urgency to reaching consensus on some of the means to regional cooperation at the already agreed-upon informal 1976 summit. Although ASEAN immediately began to proceed with trade liberalization (Thambipillai 1994: 112), the room for maneuver on this new path remained restricted due to Indonesia's protectionist stance until the end of the 1980s. Nonetheless, the new position of the economic ministers was underlined at the 1977 follow-up summit in Kuala Lumpur, where their status became co-equal with that of the foreign ministers, with their reporting line going directly to the heads of government (Weatherbee 2009: 102). It should be kept in mind, however, that during ASEAN's first three decades the political demands of the regional security regime diverted most political resources away from ASEAN's non-political tasks (Weatherbee 2009: 99).

1976–92: a secretariat to keep the paperwork flowing and inter-organizational developments

The 1976 Declaration of ASEAN Concord adopted in Bali comprised a section on the "improvement of ASEAN machinery," including the signing of an agreement on the establishment of the ASEAN secretariat by the foreign ministers, a regular review of the ASEAN organizational structure and a study on the desirability of a new constitutional framework for ASEAN. That this Summit agreed to establish a permanent ASEAN secretariat (the start of the second period) was the result of "rapidly growing activities" and the "need for a central administrative organ to provide for greater efficiency in the coordination of ASEAN organs and for more effective implementation of ASEAN projects and activities." The secretariat consisted of three bureaux: economic; scientific and technological; and social and cultural. It comprised a head, known as "secretary-general," a "staff," and some locally recruited "clerical staff." The secretariat's premises were inaugurated in May 1981 in Jakarta, Indonesia.

The secretariat was not given a role of its own. It was a coordination office rather than a decision-making body, as it could not act independently. It remained responsible to the Ministerial Meeting and the Standing Committee (Thambipillai 1994: 109). "The post had no executive or policy role. Its charge was to keep the paperwork flowing" (Weatherbee 2009: 101). Most of the work relating to ASEAN was done by the national secretariats, which coordinated the work at the foreign ministry of the member states.

The ASEAN secretariat was not an "international secretariat" as can be found in the UN and many other IOs, because there were no provisions for the recruitment of a corps of secretariat bureaucrats independent of national governments. On the contrary, the ASEAN secretary-general, bureau directors and other staff officers "were seconded from national governments to carry out the functions of the secretariat" (Thambipillai 1994: 122). This went as far as the first secretary-general, who was an Indonesian national, being dismissed by Indonesia for domestic political reasons (Weatherbee 2009: 102). As the secretariat merely coordinated the soon numerous meetings and activities, it remained mainly an observer of the new ASEAN bureaucrats. Most policies had their origins in working groups and senior officials' meetings before they were brought up to the ministerial level for decision-making.

New agreements by the foreign ministers (see Appendix) further regulated the privileges and immunities of the ASEAN secretariat (1979), the use and maintenance of the headquarters (1981), the creation of a new category of economic staff officers which the Standing

Committee might deem necessary (1983), the increase in the term of duty of the secretary-general from two to three years to provide more continuity (1985), and the creation of the posts of deputy secretary-general and assistant bureau directors (1989). These agreements did not affect the general position of the secretariat, but added to its further institutionalization. The economic ministers also began to meet regularly and to create committees dealing with issues such as trade, energy, finance and tourism in addition to committees for the non-economic topics of the secretariat's bureaux. Below the level of each of these committees various sub-committees and working groups, as well as *ad hoc* groups, were established that would meet several times in a year (Thambipillai 1994: 122).

That the economic ministers began to play a larger role in ASEAN during the 1980s was caused by the global economic pressures which in 1992 resulted in ASEAN's move to trade liberalization. Their slowly increasing role was paralleled by some inter-organizational developments, which added to the position of the secretariat, despite ASEAN's modest internal economic accomplishments. In 1972 ASEAN had formed an ASEAN-Brussels Committee to coordinate negotiations with the European Community. This coordination was continued under the 1980 Cooperative Agreement between the two groups of states to encourage increased trade. Eventually it gave the ASEAN secretariat a position similar to that of the European Commission as the actual representative of the regional entity in the negotiations. A similar development took place within the GATT. Over the years ASEAN members have increasingly had a unified voice towards the GATT. During the 1980s the ASEAN secretariat became the interlocutor for this cooperation in foreign economic matters. Its success within the GATT gave the members a stronger voice in the international arena than they could have hoped to exercise individually and created a sense of cohesion, according to Stephenson (1994: 440).

The secretariat began also to play a monitoring role. By 1987 the ASEAN secretariat served as the surveillance body responsible for monitoring the adherence to the obligations and commitments made to liberalize trade. These developments gave the secretariat a sense of importance, as it wanted to be recognized formally in order to be a stronger negotiator in international forums.

1992–2007: an enhanced ASEAN secretariat with a trade-related role of its own

The economic ministers' Agreement on the Common Effective Preferential Tariff Scheme for AFTA, signed in January 1992 at the summit in Singapore as an answer to the global developments, laid down an additional role both for themselves and for the secretariat. Article 7 on institutional arrangements stipulated that the ASEAN secretariat was to provide the support to the ministerial-level council (comprising one representative from each member state plus the secretary-general) for "supervising, coordinating and reviewing the implementation of the Agreement" and assisting the ASEAN Economic Ministers (AEM) in all matters relating thereto. Member states entering into bilateral arrangements on tariff reductions had to notify the other members and the ASEAN secretariat of such arrangements. The secretariat was required to monitor and report on the implementation of the agreement to the Senior Economic Officials' Meeting (SEOM), which also supported the ministerial-level council. In addition, member states had to cooperate with the secretariat in the performance of its duties. This monitoring of the CEPT agreement's implementation gave the secretariat a role of its own and provided it with regular information about domestic economic developments.

The position of the ASEAN secretariat was officially enhanced in July 1992 through restructuring of the secretariat. It addressed the problem of continuity and direction within ASEAN itself and strengthened the secretariat further by increasing its role and the size and quality of its staff. The secretary-general of the ASEAN secretariat was redesignated "secretary-general of ASEAN" (which covers more than the secretariat) and accorded ministerial status to add recognition to the position, with a five-year term in office and an enlarged mandate to "initiate, advise, co-ordinate and implement ASEAN activities" (Article 3.4). The secretary-general was also allowed to coordinate ASEAN dialogues with international and regional organizations (Article 3.5.c). Furthermore, the secretariat staff was increased and professionalized, although it was still relatively small.

In addition to its wider mandate, the new role established by the economic ministers soon strengthened the secretariat in practice in line with the developments of the late 1980s. The creation of CEPT as a reaction to global economic developments implied a reduction in the national room for maneuver, which had previously been unthinkable in ASEAN. It had become acceptable because the major dynamics did not come from increased intraregional trade, but rather from adapting to global markets in order to attract FDI (in particular from Japan), and to increase the international competitiveness of ASEAN industry (in particular vis-à-vis China).

These goals required regional coordination and transformed ASEAN into a "global negotiation club," with its secretariat representing and articulating ASEAN's interests in the world economy in order to approach Japan, compete with China and get access to the European and US markets (Öjendal 2001: 157–58). While the United States in 1993 signaled a greater willingness for ASEAN to participate in multilateral forums (Foot 2000: 242), the ASEAN secretariat sought collective strength where the benefits were associated with a unified stand, in particular in trade negotiations in GATT and the agricultural CAIRNS pressure group (Thambipillai 1994: 124). In the Asia Europe Meetings (ASEM), with regular biennial meetings from 1996 onwards, both the ASEAN secretariat and the European Commission are full participants together with the member states.

The new situation required an adequate amount of internal coordination to reach consensus on international policies (Weatherbee 2009: 98, 103). A large part of the required internal coordination was provided by the newly revamped secretariat and its secretary-general. The secretariat's new role as global negotiator implied a new division of labor, with the national secretariats taking care of ASEAN's many intergovernmental sessions and the ASEAN secretariat focusing on macroeconomic international policies, representation in multilateral forums and the related internal coordination.

The active part played by ASEAN's finance ministers during the Asian financial crisis brought another role to the secretariat in 1998, when the ASEAN Surveillance Coordinating Unit was based there (Eliassen and Monsen 2001: 128). In the context of countering the crisis, the Hanoi Plan of Action of December 1998 became the starting point for a further step-by-step strengthening of the ASEAN secretariat, with the active engagement of the secretariat's high-level staff (the directors-general). In September the Standing Committee had already established a "Special Directors-General Working Group on the Review of the Role and Functions of the ASEAN Secretariat." In April 1999 the Standing Committee agreed that the secretariat should function as a "coordinating Secretariat to help facilitate effective decision-making within and amongst ASEAN bodies." The new division of labor with the national secretariats was confirmed: the secretariat "would emphasize more on substantive matter, while its tasks on servicing the various meetings would be precisely defined" (www.aseansec.org/11856.htm). In July 1999 the foreign ministers agreed on a more responsive secretariat, given the new demands that had been placed on it. The ASEAN Plus Three finance ministers looked forward "to the study by the ASEAN Secretariat on other appropriate mechanisms that could enhance the ability to provide sufficient and timely financial support to ensure financial stability in East Asia" (www.aseansec.org/921.

htm). As ASEAN reacted to new developments, staff members of the secretariat began to express their views on substantial issues—a new development in itself. Furthermore, the ministers and heads of governments accepted initiatives by the secretariat. These are indicators here of important self-direction by the secretariat, even if decisions are ultimately made by the ministers and heads of governments.

In July 2001 the foreign ministers stressed ASEAN's continued interest in boosting closer cooperation with the UN and other IOs, and welcomed "the ASEAN Secretariat's efforts to coordinate closer cooperation with these organizations" (www.aseansec.org/3045.htm). At their Summit in November 2001 the heads of government agreed to review the secretariat's terms of reference, so as to strengthen its function and role. They recognized the presence of the secretary-general in summit meetings and also proposed establishing an APT secretariat (which in December 2003 resulted in the ASEAN Plus Three Unit of the ASEAN secretariat). When in June 2003 a new secretary-general was appointed, the foreign ministers welcomed "his initiatives to streamline and strengthen the ASEAN secretariat and to enhance its role in line with the changing political and economic environment and regional priorities" (www.aseansec.org/14834.htm). In June 2004 they directed the secretary-general and directors-general to complete "their study on ASEAN's institutional framework to determine how the ASEAN structure could be further strengthened to facilitate the realization of an ASEAN Community" (ASEAN 2005: 103, Article 67). This was followed by the heads of government in November agreeing to further strengthen the secretariat, "particularly in undertaking policy analysis and providing recommendations to ASEAN Member Countries in carrying out ASEAN cooperation" (ASEAN 2005: 3, Article 23).

Among the institutional changes decided upon in November 2007 were a further enhanced mandate and role for the secretary-general in monitoring progress of implementation of Summit decisions and ASEAN agreements, ensuring compliance with economic commitments, reporting to the ASEAN summits on important issues requiring decisions by ASEAN leaders, interpreting the ASEAN Charter if and when required, interacting with entities associated with ASEAN, representing ASEAN's views in meetings with external parties and advancing the interests of ASEAN and its legal personality. The Charter also underlined the *international* character of the ASEAN secretariat, as it stipulated that secretariat officials are responsible only to ASEAN and that member states should respect the exclusively ASEAN character of the responsibilities of the secretary-general and the staff.

Conclusion about the secretariat

This section, based on a perspective that included ASEAN's internal workings, showed that the idea of ASEAN as an informal organization was confirmed by the first period, when a secretariat was absent, and also to a large extent by the second period, when a permanent secretariat was established but without having any executive role. This changed by the end of the 1980s, when the ASEAN secretariat built up a trade-related role of its own. Within a very short time the secretariat evolved into an active player, externally representing ASEAN's interests and internally acting as the required coordinator of the international policies. The secretariat's functions cover various phases of the policy cycle: deliberation and decision-making (assisting the ministers), and monitoring and reporting on implementation. The secretary-general's mandate to initiate ASEAN activities also covers agenda-setting.

The secretariat's new role did not result from the original purpose of increasing intra-ASEAN trade, but rather from adapting to global market developments and to global monetary and financial crises. The window of opportunity for ASEAN's secretariat to play a role of its own hence depended strongly on *external* factors, in particular on inter-organizational developments, such as negotiation processes with the EU or within the GATT/WTO, IMF and APEC, and on global economic hardships. The secretariat's agency did not only become visible in its *external* role as global negotiator, but also *internally* in the activities and initiatives of high-ranking staff members during the process of enhancing ASEAN's bureaucratic machinery, which helped them to improve their function and position.

Conclusion: a formal organization with an active secretariat

Threatened by national and regional instability the ASEAN member states, all of which were engaged in their own process of nation-building, slowly built a security regime upon which they all agreed. They took their time to reach consensus and developed a cautious common style known as the ASEAN way of working. This style favored informal organization, with much of the work remaining at the foreign ministries. However, it did not prevent its institutionalization. Although it looks informal, both ASEAN and the ASEAN Regional Forum in their regular functioning have strongly institutionalized. Here a constructivist-oriented, rather than a state-centric, explanation may help. The process of ARF institutionalization, according to Johnston, illustrates how institutions become more valued over time because they provide information about identities, which permits a re-evaluation of a state's definition of interests. The weakly institutionalized structure also helped to clarify the environment and to create conditions for dialogue, persuasion and socialization that led to higher levels of institutionalization. Johnston therefore calls the ASEAN way of working "mythic" in the sense that it did not prevent further institutionalization: "its elements allowed states to converge on an agreement that established an extremely low level of institutionalization with a very non-intrusive agenda. These institutional features, in turn, created a process of social interaction that appears to have allowed further institutional movement" (Johnston 1999: 324).

Rather than calling it an informal organization, by now it is clearly better to describe ASEAN as a formal organization with its own bureaucracy, explicit rules and specific assignments at both the international and national level. We may then ask, does ASEAN have an independent identity and ability to act, and if so, who is "acting," and on whose behalf? The three time periods discussed in the previous section show that the secretariat did not play an active role until the late 1980s. ASEAN's main actors have been the foreign ministers and the heads of government. Intergovernmentalism and leadership by the regional hegemon, as stressed by realism, explain the founding of ASEAN (1967), its major policy shift towards trade liberalization (late 1980s) and also ASEAN's "reinvention" (2003). However, by the end of the 1980s and between 1998 and 2003 ASEAN was faced with a leadership void, due to Indonesia's domestic problems. That ASEAN during these periods of crisis and lack of leadership survived and strengthened cannot be attributed to the revival of the regional hegemon alone. The role of other actors should also be taken into account. These include the economic ministers, who at an early moment were charged with a task they could barely fulfill, and the ASEAN secretariat. The economic ministers eventually succeeded in playing an active role once trade liberalization had become acceptable to all members, including the regional hegemon.

Having understood the crucial role of single negotiator in international forums through its European Community and GATT experience, the secretariat played its role in this time period when leadership was weak and a common answer to adapt to global economic developments was required. Using this window of opportunity, the secretariat became ASEAN's "face" internationally and also within ASEAN—another player alongside the ministers and the heads of government. The economic ministers then strengthened the secretariat formally by giving it an additional role in the 1992 CEPT agreement, soon recognized by the foreign ministers. The hegemon's absence between 1998 and 2003 confirmed the secretariat's new position. In the formal strengthening of the secretariat and secretary-general by the foreign ministers and heads of government after 1998, the secretariat's high-ranking staff members themselves played an active role to promote the interests of their secretariat. They were present at the procedures, presented studies, provided expertise, and took initiatives.

Neither the secretariat's active role as global negotiator and supervisor nor its internal ability to strengthen its position was expected. Here a principal-agent explanation may help to understand the divergence, or "slack," between the ASEAN members and their secretariat. The principals among themselves were divided in vision and economic development. They had not foreseen a role of ASEAN as an economic unity in international forums and in global crisis situations, or predicted a role of the secretariat as global negotiator, let alone as internal coordinator of national policies. However, it was the secretariat that understood those roles and succeeded in building up both of them. Hence, developments were not pushed by the principals, but rather by the agent. When oversight is lax and organizations are not well designed, as is argued in the Introduction to this volume, slack may occur, with bureaucrats furthering their own careers and strengthening the position of their unit. This process turned ASEAN into an IO in which the secretariat successfully promoted its own agency. Those wishing to understand ASEAN must definitely include the role of its secretariat.

Appendix

ASEAN agreements regarding the ASEAN secretariat 1967–2007

Place and date	Document (signed by)	ASEAN secretariat
Bangkok, 8 August 1967	The ASEAN Declaration (foreign ministers)	No ASEAN secretariat
Bali, 24 February 1976	Declaration of ASEAN Concord (heads of government)	
Bali, 24 February 1976	Agreement on the Establishment of the ASEAN Secretariat (foreign ministers)	Permanent ASEAN secretariat created
Jakarta, 20 January 1979	Agreement Between the Government of Indonesia and ASEAN Relating to the Privileges and Immunities of the ASEAN Secretariat (foreign minister of Indonesia)	

(continued)

Place and date	Document (signed by)	ASEAN secretariat
Jakarta, 25 November 1981	*Agreement on the Use and Maintenance of the Premises of the ASEAN Secretariat* (secretary-general Department of Foreign Affairs)	
Bangkok, 27 January 1983	*Protocol Amending the Agreement on the Establishment of the ASEAN Secretariat (Economic Officers)* (foreign ministers)	
Kuala Lumpur, 9 July 1985	*Protocol Amending the Agreement on the Establishment of the ASEAN Secretariat (Term-of-Duty of the Secretary General)* (foreign ministers)	
Bandar Seri Begawan, 4 July 1989	*Protocol Amending the Agreement on the Establishment of the ASEAN Secretariat* (foreign ministers)	
Jakarta, 5 November 1991	*Agreement on the Temporary Use of Part of the Premises of the ASEAN Secretariat*	
Singapore, 28 January 1992	*Agreement on the Common Effective Preferential Tariff (CEPT) Scheme for the ASEAN Free Trade Area* (economic ministers)	Additional role for the Secretariat
Manila, 22 July 1992	*Protocol Amending the Agreement on the Establishment of the ASEAN Secretariat* (foreign ministers)	Restructuring of the Secretariat
Subang Jaya, 23 July 1997	*Protocol Amending the Agreement on the Establishment of the ASEAN Secretariat* (foreign ministers)	
Hanoi, 15 December 1998	*Hanoi Plan of Action* (heads of government)	Starting point of a continuous strengthening of the Secretariat
Singapore, 20 November 2007	*Charter of the Association of Southeast Asian Nations* (heads of government)	Enhanced mandate and role plus international character

Bibliography

ASEAN, *ASEAN Documents Series 2004* (Jakarta: ASEAN Secretariat, 2005).

Caballero-Anthony, Mely, "The Regionalization of Peace in Asia," in *The United Nations & Regional Security: Europe and Beyond*, ed. Michael Pugh and Waheguru Pal Singh Sidhu (Boulder: Lynne Rienner, 2003), 195–211.

Eliassen, Kjell and Catherine Monsen, "Comparison of European and Southeast Asian Integration," in *European Union and New Regionalism: Regional Actors and Global Governance in a Post-Hegemonic Era*, ed. Mario Telò (Aldershot: Ashgate, 2001), 111–33.

Foot, Rosemary, "Pacific Asia: The Development of Regional Dialogue," in *Regionalism in World Politics: Regional Organization and International Order*, ed. Louise Fawcett and Andrew Hurrell (Oxford: Oxford University Press, 2000), 228–49.

Johnston, Alastair I., "The Myth of the ASEAN Way? Explaining the Evolution of the ASEAN Regional Forum," in *Imperfect Unions: Security Institutions over Time and Space*, ed. Helga Haftendorn, Robert Keohane, and Celeste Wallander (Oxford: Oxford University Press, 1999), 287–324.

Keohane, Robert, *International Institutions and State Power: Essays in International Relations Theory* (Boulder: Westview Press, 1989).

Monte Hill, B., "Community Formation within ASEAN," *International Organization* 32, no. 2 (1978): 569–75.

Öjendal, Joakim, "South East Asia and a Constant Crossroads. An Ambiguous 'New Region'," in *Regionalization in a Globalizing World: A Comparative Perspective on Forms, Actors and Processes*, ed. Michael Schulz, Fredrik Soderbaum, and Joakim Öjendal (London: Zed Books, 2001), 147–72.

Panagariya, Arvind, "Preferential Trading in Asia," in *Regional Integration and Multilateral Cooperation in the Global Economy*, ed. Jan J. Teunissen (The Hague: FONDAD, 1998), 77–92.

Stephenson, Sherry M., "ASEAN and the Multilateral Trading System," *Law and Policy in International Business* 25, no. 2 (1994): 439–48.

Thambipillai, Pushpa, "Continuity and Change in ASEAN: The Politics of Regional Cooperation in South East Asia," in *The Political Economy of Regional Cooperation: Comparative Case Studies*, ed. W. Andrew Axline (Madison, Wis.: Fairleigh Dickinson University Press, 1994), 105–35.

Weatherbee, Donald, *International Relations in Southeast Asia. The Struggle for Autonomy* (Lanham: Rowman & Littlefield, 2009).

Webber, Douglas, "Two Funerals and a Wedding? The Ups and Downs of Regionalism in East Asia and Asia Pacific after the Asian Crisis," in *Comparative Regional Integration: Theoretical Perspectives*, ed. Finn Laursen (Aldershot: Ashgate, 2003), 125–57.

9 New types of organizations and global governance in the twenty-first century
The case of ICANN

James P. Muldoon, Jr

- The ICT revolution and challenge of Internet governance
- Building and operationalizing a global network of computer networks
- Administration and management of the Internet
- The ICANN experiment
- Evolution of ICANN
- Conclusion

At the turn of the twenty-first century, a new generation of international organizations started to emerge in response to the changing character of the international system and demands for a more representative, effective and responsive governance system. These new and innovative "hybrid" international organizations vary widely in size, composition and functional capacity and go by a variety of names—global public policy networks, inter-organizational networks, public-private partnerships, and (ad hoc) global alliances and coalitions. They represent a new approach to solving or managing the complex issues and problems currently on the global agenda and a significant departure from the traditional form of international organizations and conventional understanding of their role(s) in the governance of the international system.

This new generation of international organizations differs in a number of ways from organizations established in the latter half of the twentieth century. In particular, they are designed to be inclusive of all relevant "stakeholders" of the international system, not just states and governments, to institutionalize the participation of non-state actors such as nongovernmental organizations (NGOs) and transnational corporations (TNCs) in authoritative decision-making, and are imbued with the capabilities or capacity of self-directed action on a range of global issues and problems. Predominantly structured as public-private partnerships (PPPs), these multistakeholder arrangements "emerged at the beginning of the 1990s as the preferred form to organize cross-sectoral alliances that could build on the comparative advantages of NGOs, governments, and corporate actors" (Forman and Segaar 2006: 215). They reflect a shift from the traditional "top-down" or hierarchical structures of governance to "bottom-up" or horizontal forms of collective decision-making and global policy-making.

As "hybrid governance forms" these partnership arrangements are a relatively new phenomenon and range "from loose forms of cooperation to legally binding contracts for the implementation of specific projects" (Schäferhoff et al. 2009: 453). Many global PPPs are set up to address specific problems or development needs and/or to implement "intergovernmental commitments, such as the Millennium Development Goals (MDGs) and the Johannesburg Plan of Implementation" (Schäferhoff et al. 2009: 459), and operate through the policies and procedures of existing international organizations. Others are set up as private non-profit corporations with their own offices, staffs and budgets and have decision-making and policy-making procedures and processes largely independent of existing intergovernmental organizations (Forman and Segaar 2006: 220). What institutional design or organizational form they take varies according to the situation structure, the complexity of the issue or problem, and/or governance need that is being addressed. In many if not most cases, these factors lead to largely informal structures that supplement or enhance the ability or capacity of existing international organizations to manage and/or solve complex international issues, such as development or humanitarian crises. However, there are a few instances of new formal organizations being created, particularly in issue areas that arise from new technologies such as the Internet, which do not comport with traditional intergovernmental structures or processes (Fukuyama and Wagner 2000; Kruck and Rittberger 2010).

There is a lively debate on the effectiveness, legitimacy and accountability of this new generation of international organizations, particularly legally independent partnership entities like the International AIDS Vaccine Initiative or the Global Fund to Fight AIDS, Tuberculosis and Malaria. As relatively new governance mechanisms, many of these organizations are still evolving in terms of their authority, purpose or function, and independence, and still developing the organizational resources and institutional competence that is considered necessary to fulfil governance tasks or to provide public goods. As Tanja Börzel points out:

> The collective self-organization of society has been discussed as an alternative to the provision of common goods by government. Yet,

like governments, non-governmental actors must have the necessary action capacity and autonomy to engage in governance with/out government. On the one hand, they need sufficient personnel, information, expertise, money and organizational resources to make strategic decisions, to act as reliable negotiation partners and to offer each other and/or government something in exchange for becoming involved in the policy process. On the other hand, non-governmental actors have to have the necessary autonomy to act free from political control.

(Börzel 2010: 15)

The literature on transnational PPPs suggests that the inclusion of stakeholders brings in the necessary resources and information to increase the problem-solving capacity of governance; creates a sense of ownership of generated norms, rules, and regulations and thus stronger compliance with those norms, rules, and regulations; and that the network structure of PPPs encourages communicative action and deliberation which produces consensus on policies and solutions to global problems (Schäferhoff *et al.* 2009: 458–59; Forman and Segaar 2006).

This chapter focuses on one of the more prominent organizations of this new generation of international organizations, the Internet Corporation for Assigned Names and Numbers (ICANN), which is a private, non-profit, public benefit corporation created in 1998 to take over the centralized coordination and management of the Internet's domain name system (DNS) from the US government. Unlike the intergovernmental organizations (IOs) examined in this volume that were designed to be instruments of member governments, "ICANN was deliberately set up as a private sector, multistakeholder governance organization" that would operate independently of national governments and IOs (Mueller *et al.* 2007: 238). Its unique, novel organizational design and decision-making and "bottom-up" policy development processes were an "experiment" for "managing a global resource on a nongovernmental basis. Indeed, in its early days it was touted as a model for other issues that required unified action of numerous groups" (Cukier 2005: 10–11). Yet, as will be discussed below, ICANN's independence—its ability to formulate and carry out policies through internal processes and determined by endogenous rather than exogenous forces (as Oestreich wrote in the Introduction to this volume)—was in fact limited. The irony here is that ICANN was to a large extent created to be independent; there was a feeling among international actors that Internet governance had been too closely directed by the United States (where the Internet was "invented") and that its continued growth required an independent oversight body. There was also a feeling that the very nature of the Internet demanded greater independence. Thus, the failure of ICANN to act independently in the .xxx controversy described below turns the volume's model on its head: rather than an agency designed to be an agent but seeking autonomy, it is a case of an agency designed to be autonomous but failing in this role.

This chapter explores the cultural, technical and political issues of the Internet's development and governance that led to the creation of ICANN rather than creating a traditional IO or delegating the task to an existing IO like the International Telecommunication Union (ITU). This case study also highlights crucial factors that constrain ICANN's agency and undermine its independence. In this regard, the ".xxx controversy"—the first major policy problem for ICANN—is a case in point of the various limits on ICANN's autonomy and its ability to "act" independently. Among other factors generally discussed in the Introduction, the newness of ICANN, the small size of its staff, and the political salience of the issues involved hindered its ability to act autonomously in the way that had been foreseen.

The ICT revolution and challenge of Internet governance

The revolution in information and communications technology (ICT) is a powerful source of global change that is rapidly transforming the political, economic, and social landscape of the international system. As a driving force of globalization, ICTs, particularly the Internet, are dramatically changing the way people work, play, and interact, as well as the relationships between society, government and business. They have increased the number of actors on the world stage, disrupted (and undermined) traditional hierarchies, and spread power and authority more widely (see Sassen 1996; Knight 1999; Simai 2001; Brühl and Rittberger 2002; Kennedy *et al.* 2002; Grieco and Ikenberry 2003; Muldoon 2003; Benkler 2006).

The ICT revolution and the rapid spread of and growing access to the Internet around the world pose considerable challenges to the existing structure of international governance. The ubiquity of the Internet, particularly within the "advanced" information societies, has revolutionized the communications environment, creating a highly decentralized universal system of communications, information-sharing, entertainment, and commercial transactions that runs roughshod over the centralized vertically structured and territorially arranged governance system.

Obviously decentralized, horizontally linked global interactions and connections are at odds with the international system's organizational structures, which are designed to operate vertically, and undermine governmental authorities' ability to control or regulate society, making traditional "top-down" approaches to governance of ICTs and the Internet impractical and "creating new dilemmas for governance, particularly in relationships between nations" (Franda 2002: 3; Fukuyama and Wagner 2000).

According to William Drake:

> Since the mid-1990s, the globalization, commercialization, and mass popularization of the Internet have radically transformed the world of international communications. The technologies, transactions, and actors that are increasingly driving the worldwide restructuring of the sector emerged outside of the old communications industries and are not easily governed by traditional forms of national and international public authority ... At the same time, the Internet also has given rise to new and unique patterns of international cooperation ... Both governments and firms are collaborating—with varying degrees of success—in a diverse range of forums to devise shared rules on communications behavior and global electronic commerce conducted over that infrastructure.
>
> (Drake 2001: 26)

Governance of the Internet has become increasingly important and contentious. Issues of accessibility (digital divide), freedom of expression, security and stability, and a number of legal/jurisdictional questions have been the focus of intense debate over how the Internet should be governed and who should control it (Spar 1999). There is no simple, straightforward answer to who is in control. Indeed, as Cane (2006) points out, "The question is whether the Internet's existing informal, some say anarchic, controls are adequate or whether a formal governance structure will have to be imposed."

Building and operationalizing a global network of computer networks

The origins of the Internet can be traced to the work of J.C.R. Licklider of Massachusetts Institute of Technology (MIT) (and the first head of the computer research program of the US Defense Department's Advanced Research Projects Agency (ARPA)) in 1962 on his "Galactic Network" concept: "He envisioned a globally interconnected set of computers through which everyone could quickly access data and programs from any site" (Leiner *et al.* 2003). The ARPANET was born in

1969 when four host computers—University of California Los Angeles, Stanford University, the University of California at Santa Barbara, and University of Utah—were successfully connected, which then grew into the Internet. The Internet as we now know it embodies a key underlying technical idea, namely that of open architecture networking. In this approach, the choice of any individual network technology was not dictated by a particular network architecture but rather could be selected freely by a provider and made to interwork with the other networks through a meta-level "Internetworking Architecture" (Leiner et al. 2003).

Marcus Franda (2001: 21–23) points out that "a *worldwide* network of subsidiary computer networks and even individual computers" was made possible only after Robert Kahn, Vinton Cerf, and other leading computer scientists within the ARPA community, developed in 1972 the Transmission Control Protocol (TCP) and the Internetwork Protocol (IP) which "allowed a streamlined overall system in which the IP protocols passed individual packets between machines (from host to packet switch or between packet switches) while the TCP ordered the packets into reliable connections between pairs of hosts." The TCP/IP suite ultimately became the de facto global standard that all computer networks used, thereby establishing "wide acceptance of two principles: (1) that the authority for operationalizing the Internet would be decentralized internationally and (2) that the process for developing international technical standards would be inclusive rather than proprietary or government directed, and two norms: (1) that operation of the global Internet would be designed to handle diversity at all network levels and (2) that the Internet would be characterized by interoperability and heterogeneity both within and among networks" (Franda 2001: 28).

Hans Klein (2002: 195) points out that "The Internet really consists of two 'systems,' one for communications (the 'TCP/IP' protocols) and one for addressing (the DNS)." The communication system is the Internet as we commonly know it and is extremely decentralized. The DNS is centralized. Designed in 1983 by Paul Mockapetris of the University of Southern California, it has a database that includes pairs of domain names and IP numbers. The domain names are easy to read identifiers of various computers; the IP numbers are for use by other computers. The DNS takes domain names and looks up the appropriate IP number, thus allowing email or other communication to occur (Klein 2002: 195).

The DNS assigns a specific name—a unique numerical address—for each machine on the Internet and maintains a master list of them in what is called the Internet's name space. As the Internet grew, the name space was broken down into partial, separate databases on separate computers or zone files. Each zone is tied to a name server (a software program for name resolution) and a host computer (a dedicated machine for the name server and zone file). Zones are arranged in a hierarchy, with a root zone at the top, and various "subtrees," called "domains," below (Klein 2002: 197). "A domain consists of a zone and all zones beneath it in the hierarchy ... Domains beginning at top-level zones are *top-level domains* or TLDs; domains beginning at the next level are *second-level domains*, and so on ... The entire system constitutes the domain name system or DNS" (Klein 2002: 197). Within this hierarchy, the TLDs were organized into two categories—a group of six generic top-level domains (gTLDs: .com, .gov, .edu, .mil, and .net), and 244 two-digit domains for countries and territories called country code top-level domains (ccTLDs: .uk for United Kingdom, .jp for Japan, and so on).

The DNS is considered the "heart" of the Internet since the root server and the DNS servers for particular networks "are *single controlling points* that could be used to choke off access to the Internet" and "control of the root server and the system of domain name allocation could provide a mechanism for (1) collecting taxes (those who do not pay the fee or tax lose their domain name or have it suspended), (2) regulating behavior or collecting information, and (3) enforcing intellectual property rules and laws" (Franda 2001: 48; see also Cukier 2005; Goldsmith and Wu 2006; Mathiason 2009). For obvious reasons, control of the domain name system raised many concerns, especially the immense power of those administering and managing the system, and became the focal point in the debate over the structure of Internet governance.

Administration and management of the Internet

As the foregoing discussion suggests, the Internet emerged out of a technical research project of computer scientists based in the United States and underwritten by the US government. So, the Internet backbone that was developed by Kahn, Cerf, Roberts and others in the ARPA community from 1969 to 1986 was "directly owned and controlled by the U.S. Department of Defense (DoD) or its contractors ... During the next six years (1986–92) Internet governance and management functions became divided between DoD and NSF [National Science Foundation], with a number of private associations playing various roles" (Franda 2001: 45). In the early years, managing the development and implementation of protocols and network operations was in the hands of the Network Working Group (NWG), which consisted of a core group of computer scientists and engineers involved in the creation of ARPANET. "When the NWG was disbanded in the early 1970s, Cerf and Kahn set up an advisory group of network experts called the Internet Configuration Control Board (ICCB) to coordinate discussion of technical questions among government and private groups and to 'oversee the network's architectural evolution.' The ICCB was replaced in 1985 by the Internet Activities Board (IAB)"[1] (Franda 2001: 45).

In the early 1990s the Internet Society (ISOC)—a non-profit, non-governmental, international, professional membership organization—was created as a funding mechanism to support the Internet Engineering Task Force (IETF) and as the organizational home for groups responsible for Internet infrastructure standards and administration (see Cerf 1995). The establishment of ISOC in 1992 coincided with the formal transfer of management of the Internet backbone from the US government to private and public companies and the decision "to move the system's technical administration out of the U.S. government entirely, with the result that formal oversight of IAB and IETF was contracted to the Internet Society" (Franda 2001: 46).

The IAB has two primary components—the IETF and the Internet Research Task Force (IRTF). The IETF "has primary responsibility for further evolution of the TCP/IP protocol suite, its standardization with the concurrence of the IAB, and the integration of other protocols into Internet operation (e.g., the Open System Interconnection protocols). The Internet Research Task Force continues to organize and explore advanced concepts in networking under the guidance of the Internet Activities Board and with support of various [U.S.] government agencies" (Cerf 1992).

The US government contracted the University of Southern California's Information Services Institute under the direction of Jon Postel to administer the DNS.[2] Postel single-handedly assumed the functions of maintaining the root zone file, authorizing the addition of new top-level domain names, choosing zone file administrators to whom to delegate authority, and other administrative tasks. Postel created the Internet Assigned Numbers Authority (IANA)—an "informal" organization that was "accepted as a constituent organization of ISOC in 1992, but never had legal standing" (Franda 2001: 48)—through which he was able to exercise policy authority over the DNS (Klein 2002: 198). As the US government started to "privatize" the Internet's technical management and administration, the NSF had reached a five-year cooperative agreement with Network Solutions, Inc. (NSI) to manage the "A" root server and zone file and the DNS registry (known as InterNIC),

The case of ICANN 249

creating a monopoly and "a lucrative, multimillion-dollar revenue stream for NSI" (Franda 2001: 49; Weinberg 2000: 199).

The contract with NSI was not well received by ISOC, which "sensed that a key feature of its long stewardship of the civilian part of the Internet was being surrendered to NSI" (Franda 2001: 49). As Daniel Drezner (2004: 494) explains, ISOC formed a committee to seek alternatives to NSI. Several international organizations were involved, the ITU was particularly interested in participating, as it saw itself as a natural manager of these sorts of issues. However, many states, particularly the United States, were opposed (as they saw the ITU as acting without the approval of member states and their governments), as were many Internet activists (who worried about lack of accountability and corporate influence).

The Clinton administration moved swiftly to marginalize the proposed role of the ITU in the governance of the DNS. On 1 July 1997 President Clinton issued an Executive Order instructing the National Telecommunications and Information Agency (NTIA) of the US Department of Commerce (DoC) to get behind efforts that would make governance of the DNS private and competitive, creating a contractually based self-regulatory regime. As Ira Magaziner, a close Clinton advisor who was put in charge of the initiative, argued: "As the Internet grows up and becomes more international, these technical management questions should be privatized, and there should be a stakeholder-based, private international organization set up for that technical management. In the allocation of domain names, we should, where it is possible, create a competitive marketplace to replace the monopoly that now exists" (quoted in Drezner 2004: 494). On 3 June 1998 the NTIA released a White Paper entitled "Management of Internet Names and Addresses," which "advocated privatization of the DNS system based on four principles: stability, competition, private bottom-up coordination, and representation" (Drezner 2004: 495; also see Franda 2001: 52–54; Mathiason 2009: 56–58). This intervention by the US government was clearly reflective of the neo-liberal values that were guiding domestic and foreign commercial and economic policies of the Clinton administration and "a calculated attempt to promote further the US neoliberal trade agenda in the emerging online e-commerce by curtailing the participation of the world's governments and international [governmental] organizations" in the incipient governance structure of the Internet (Antonova 2008: 140–41).

Although there was no real opposition to privatizing the DNS, there was little "consensus" among the main stakeholders as to the model of self-regulation that would meet the four guiding principles outlined in the White Paper (Antonova 2008: 160–65). Through the White Paper process, the US government resolved the issue by selecting a proposal[3] for a new private non-profit corporation, ICANN, which IANA/ISOC had incorporated under US (California) law and established headquarters in Marina Del Rey, California. As Franda points out:

> The creation of ICANN was clearly the result of a negotiating process led by IANA/ISOC coalition in conjunction with Ira Magaziner and the U.S. Department of Commerce ... ICANN produced controversy in the way it was created and immediately faced downright hostility from critics who argued that ICANN—if legitimized by NTIA—would have tremendous powers with no accountability, would be soft on civil liberties issues, and especially did not represent the full spectrum of Internet users. The atmosphere among Internet users was particularly charged when Jon Postel died, at age fifty-five on October 18, 1998. Two days after Postel's death NTIA "tentatively" accepted the IANA/ISOC proposal, with the proviso that it be "refined" in consultation with "groups and others who commented critically on [it] to try and broaden the consensus." In response to NTIA's concerns, the ICANN interim board made a number of changes in its articles of incorporation and bylaws, committing itself to the creation of an open membership structure. With those changes, ICANN was accepted by the U.S. Commerce Department on November 25, 1998, as the private corporation that the Clinton administration would work with to build the governance aspects of the international Internet regime.
>
> (Franda 2001: 55)

With the formal designation of ICANN to oversee the technical management and development of the DNS, administration and management of the Internet's technical infrastructure was situated firmly in the private nongovernmental arena with shared responsibilities over Internet policy and governance with public authorities (see Figure 9.1). This arrangement reflected the Clinton administration's vision of a private sector-led governance system for the Internet that would rely more on market competition and decentralized authority than on regulation and governmental control. At the same time, the US government had promised to the business community that it would remain actively involved to ensure the stability of the Internet and protect trademark holders. As Mueller *et al.* (2007: 240) argue, "Thus, in the ICANN regime, the United States succeeded in establishing a governance regime dominated by itself and by nonstate actors. The US government

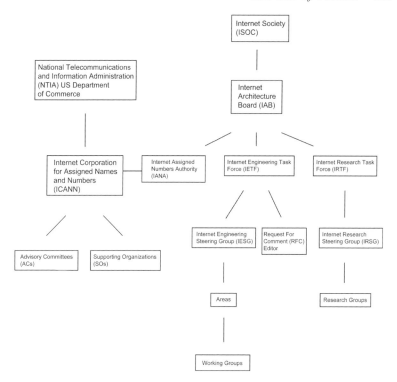

Figure 9.1 Network of Internet governance organizations
Source: Malcolm 2008: 39

privatized and internationalized key policymaking functions but retained considerable authority for itself" (see also Goldsmith and Wu 2006: 168–71; Antonova 2008: 169–72).

The ICANN experiment

The semi-corporatist organizational structure of ICANN reflects a conscious effort on the part of its designers to meet the demands of the US DoC and a number of Internet constituencies that ICANN "be structured in such a way that it would act much like a *public* organization while at the same time being incorporated as a *private* organization with private management virtues" (Franda 2001: 60), and remain true to the Internet's tradition of decentralization. Implementation of ICANN decisions and policies, as well as performing the day-to-day services and administrative functions, was the responsibility of a small staff led by a president and Chief Executive Officer.

Throughout the first four years ICANN struggled to resolve "controversial organizational, structural and procedural issues ..." (Antonova 2008: 164–65, 168). Its initial efforts to operationalize the multistakeholder, bottom-up governance model created a proliferation of committees, working groups, advisory bodies and other ad hoc entities which "led to criticism from some—especially business and government leaders—that due process and deliberation within ICANN often results in frivolous claims or concerns that tend to override serious policy considerations" (Franda 2001: 72). The criticism precipitated sweeping structural and procedural reforms engineered by ICANN's second CEO, M. Stuart Lynn, who had replaced Michael Roberts in 2001. In February 2002 Lynn issued a report entitled "ICANN—The Case for Reform," which detailed his proposals for ICANN's reorganization and operational reform.[4] The ICANN Board established the Committee on ICANN Evolution and Reform (ERC) to shepherd the process and to gather input from the different constituencies and interested parties of the organization. Over the next eight months the ERC facilitated the re-examination of ICANN's mission and values, structure and procedures, policy development process, and board composition and selection process. The committee's final recommendations came in the form of new bylaws, which the ICANN Board adopted in December 2002.

Although the new bylaws did not significantly alter the organization's basic structure (see Figure 9.2), they did create a distinctly different policy development process (PDP), which expanded the decision-making power of the ICANN Board and staff and was both more efficient and predictable. As Antonova argues:

> In 2002, the ICANN Management exploited the widespread dissatisfaction with the Corporation and initiated a reform benefiting particular stakeholders (i.e. the European Union and its membergovernments, and the registry/registrar operators community, as their voting power on the GNSO Council increased). The President, Lynn, acted on his belief that a more effective and predictable ICANN could persuade the U.S. government to follow up on its promise to transfer the authority over the legacy Internet root to ICANN. Therefore, the focus shifted from policymaking based on achieving stakeholder consensus to decision-making by a mighty Board, constructed of selected individuals. In addition, by *redefining ICANN as a public-private partnership*, where the perimeter of governmental participation was expanded, it was expected to close the gaps in the ICANN contractual web (achieving agreements

The case of ICANN 253

with the ccTLDs and RIRs [regional IP address registry]), which was a task left over from the original ICANN mandate.

(Antonova 2008: 277)

ICANN 2.0, the term commonly used for the corporation since the new bylaws came into effect at the end of 2002, operates much more like a business, emphasizing its administrative and managerial responsibilities and day-to-day services involved to perform the IANA functions and ensure the stability and security of the DNS and de-emphasizing its policy-making role. It has a much larger staff (from 12 in 2000 to 110 in 2009), a larger operating budget (US$52 million in 2009) based on revenues of $61 million, and has established new offices in Brussels,

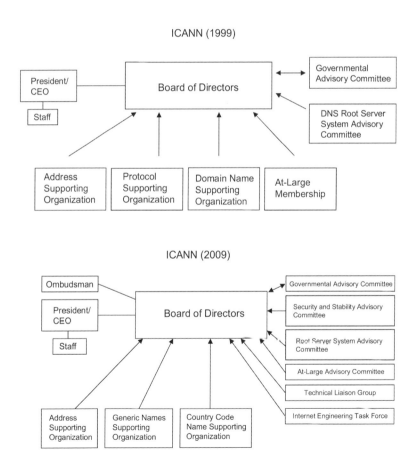

Figure 9.2 ICANN structure in 1999 and 2009

Sydney and Washington, DC. Under Paul Twomey's leadership (Twomey succeeded Stuart Lynn as ICANN President and CEO in 2003), the staff became more professional and since 2004 has been guided by a Strategic Plan—an annual process involving all ICANN stakeholders to determine the key priorities in rolling three-year periods for the organization. By most accounts, ICANN's operational performance did improve significantly under the new bylaws, which helped to salvage the credibility of both the corporation and the contractually based model of self-regulation of the DNS. More importantly, though, ICANN 2.0 provided a place for the key interest groups and established open and transparent procedures for achieving a balanced and "representative" Board of Directors "that reflects the main stakeholders"[5] of the corporation (Mathiason 2009: 83–84). This enabled greater international participation in the policy development process and strengthened the legitimacy of and compliance with Board decisions.

Evolution of ICANN

The bumpy road to autonomy

Over the course of 10 years ICANN has evolved into a truly unique international organization, a new hybrid form where a private-sector entity functions as a regulator of a global public resource with the ability to make national and international public policy decisions that are binding and independent of governments and intergovernmental (treaty-based) organizations (Mathiason 2009: 71; Brauer and Haywood 2010: 11). However, ICANN's authority and independence have never been total or unassailable since both relied on ICANN building "a worldwide consensus around the governance regime it has been assigned to create" and retaining US government support for its approach (Franda 2001: 76). In essence, ICANN needed to demonstrate that its "bottom-up" policy development process could produce consensus among the main interest groups on policies affecting them.

ICANN spent considerable energy in its early years developing a consensus process that would satisfy all stakeholders' interests and produce substantive policies of sufficient credibility and legitimacy with, and therefore compliance from, the diverse constituencies of the Internet community. However, as Antonova (2008: 206) points out, "ICANN was required by the U.S. DoC to produce consensus policies without an established process model to guide the participants in issue formation [or] leadership." The whole effort quickly became bogged down in prolonged discussions that were neither efficient nor productive, and could only produce agreement on broad general propositions. This situation threatened a fatal loss of confidence in and support of ICANN and the private-sector approach to managing the DNS. It was only after the reforms in 2002, which put in place a policy process similar to the IETF's "rough consensus" approach to protocol standards that was considerably faster and less contentious, that ICANN was able to restore confidence in its ability to develop appropriate and effective policies.

Many, if not most, of ICANN's problems in this regard stem from the fact that its policy authority over and management of the DNS was delegated to ICANN by the US government, which technically "owns" the DNS, and was conditionally granted through a Memorandum of Understanding (MOU). This meant that ICANN was contractually obligated to submit status reports on fulfilling the conditions of the MOU to the NTIA and to appear before the US Congress. "Initially, the United States promised that [its policy] authority [over the domain name system's root] was temporary; ICANN would become fully privatized and independent after two years" (Mueller *et al.* 2007: 240). However, this timeframe for completing the transfer of responsibility from the United States to ICANN was unrealistic, which became quite clear in ICANN's second status report of 30 June 2000, and that each status report "was followed by certain amendments [to the MOU] and, consequently, a year-long extension" (Antonova 2008: 172, n248). Although the US government stayed out of the day-to-day management of the DNS and was judicious in exercising its oversight role, ICANN's autonomy was clearly limited and other stakeholders, especially non-US groups, often questioned its actions.

The delay in bringing to an end US control of the root and oversight of ICANN reinforced growing suspicions that ICANN was nothing more than a tool of US hegemony. Moreover, it invited even more criticism of ICANN and calls for shifting oversight and control of the DNS to a multilateral intergovernmental body. According to Kenneth Cukier:

> All this came to a head in 2003, during the preparatory meetings for the World Summit on the Information Society ... Telecom-policy officials mildly supportive of ICANN were replaced by senior representatives from foreign ministries, officials less familiar with the details of Internet governance but more experienced in challenging U.S. power. Watching the United States go to war in Iraq despite global opposition, these diplomats saw ICANN as yet another example of American unilateralism ... Surely [they argued]

the Internet ought to be managed by the international community rather than a single nation. Governments worldwide sought to dilute the United States' control by calling for a new arrangement, and in November 2004 UN Secretary-General Kofi Annan appointed a 40-person working group to address questions of Internet governance. Washington had planned to grant ICANN autonomy from its oversight in 2006. But the more other countries clamored for power, the more the United States reconsidered its policy of relinquishing control. Ultimately, it came down to national interest: Washington, with so much at stake in the Internet's continuing to function as it had, decided it was not prepared to risk any changes. So, as the UN working group was preparing to release its report (which, unsurprisingly, favored transferring authority over the Internet to the UN), the U.S. government made a preemptive strike. In the brief Commerce Department statement [issued on 30 June 2005], Washington announced its decision: the United States would retain its authority over ICANN, period.

(Cukier 2005: 11–12)

Coincidentally, the United States in August of 2005 took the surprising step of intervening directly in a key ICANN function—the authorization of new gTLDs—thereby reversing the US government's position and policy of not interfering in ICANN policy decisions or processes with respect to domain names and Internet content.

The .xxx controversy

One of ICANN's core tasks was to develop and implement a process for expanding the number of gTLDs from the original seven—three gTLDs: .com, .org, and .net; and four limited-use TLDs: .edu, .gov, .mil, and .int. The new gTLDs policy that ICANN developed resulted in 13 new TLDs, all of which were non-controversial and added to the system without any objection from the United States or other governments active in the Governmental Advisory Committee (GAC). Mathiason (2009: 95) points out that, "While the designation of new domain names was always somewhat contentious, the first major problem that became controversial was when the Internet Content Management (ICM) Registry in 2000 proposed creating a top-level domain .xxx for providers of adult content ... This was immediately controversial, in part because what was considered adult content varied from country to country, in part because in some jurisdictions all adult content was considered pornography or obscene, and in part because of child pornography, which was globally prohibited under international conventions." The Board decided to pass over ICM's application and 39 others in the first "proof of concept" round for introducing new gTLDs, selecting only seven applicants to go forward into contract negotiations with ICANN staff.

In 2003 the ICANN Board adopted resolutions for the introduction of new sponsored TLDs (sTLDs) and posted a Request for Proposals (RFP) that detailed the application process and selection criteria that would be used for evaluating proposals. Ten sTLD applications were submitted, including that of ICM Registry for an sTLD .xxx, publicly posted on the ICANN website for comment from all stakeholders, and evaluated by an independent panel of experts. This time the .xxx application was allowed to go forward when "the ICANN Board in June 2005 authorized its staff to enter into negotiations [relating to proposed commercial and technical terms for] the .xxx domain name" (Mathiason 2009: 95). It was this decision that gave rise to comments expressing concerns about the ICM application from several members of the GAC at its meeting in Luxembourg of July 2005.

Within the United States, conservative groups led by Jim Dobson of the Family Research Council mounted a campaign against the .xxx proposal and began to put immense pressure on the DoC to stop the proposal from being approved. The email campaign in opposition to .xxx eventually convinced the US government to send a letter on 11 August 2005 to ICANN's Chairman of the Board, Vint Cerf, requesting that the ICANN Board delay a decision on the .xxx and expressing the US government's concerns about the opposition to the proposal that it had received. This was followed a day later by a letter from the Chairman of the GAC, Mohd Sharil Tarmizi, writing in his personal capacity, which also called for a delay on .xxx to "allow time for additional governmental and public policy concerns to be expressed." From mid-August until March 2006 the United States actively opposed the .xxx domain and urged other members of the GAC to do the same (IGP 2006: 4–5). Throughout this period ICM produced subsequent draft registry agreements in response to specific requests of ICANN staff for amendments. The third draft agreement was considered by the ICANN Board at a special meeting on 10 May 2006. The Board voted not to approve the agreement but did not reject ICM's application. Over the next year ICM prepared two more draft agreements before the ICANN Board at its meeting in Lisbon. On 30 March 2007 it finally decided by a vote of nine to five, with one abstention, to reject the proposed agreement (the fifth draft registry agreement) with ICM concerning the .xxx sTLD, and ICM's application request for delegation of the .xxx sTLD.

The long drawn out saga of the .xxx controversy is perhaps the most obvious example of US dominance of ICANN and the deleterious effects of domestic politics on US supervision of the Internet (IGP 2006: 5). Indeed, the actions of the NTIA in 2005–06 were clearly:

> ... stimulated by a cascade of protests by American domestic organizations, such as the Family Research Council and Focus on the Family. Thousands of email messages of identical text poured into the Department of Commerce demanding that .xxx be stopped ... [W]hile officials of the Department of Commerce concerned with Internet questions earlier did not oppose and indeed apparently favored ICANN's approval of the application of ICM, the Department of Commerce was galvanized into opposition by the generated torrent of negative demands, and by representations by leading figures of the so-called "religious right," such as Jim Dobson, who had influential access to high level officials of the US Administration. There was even indication in the Department of Commerce that, if ICANN were to approve a top level domain for adult material, it would not be entered into the root if the United States government did not approve. The intervention of the United States came at a singularly delicate juncture, in the run-up to a United Nations sponsored conference on the Internet—the World Summit on the Information Society—which was anticipated to be the forum for concentration of criticism of the United States over the Internet. The *Congressional Quarterly Weekly* ran a story entitled, "Web Neutrality vs. Morality" which said: "The flap over .xxx has put ICANN in an almost impossible position. It is facing mounting pressures from within the United States and other countries to reject the domain. But if it goes back on its earlier decision, many countries will see that as evidence of its allegiance to and lack of independence from the U.S. government."
>
> (ICDR 2010: 16–17)

Moreover, the .xxx problem awakened governments to the implications of their limited role in and power over ICANN and the management of critical Internet resources. It not only sensitized many governments to the "inevitable effects of unilateral oversight of ICANN by a single nation-state" (IGP 2006: 5), but also led to a more assertive GAC in the internal governance of ICANN and a more influential governmental role in ICANN's decision- and policy-making process. Hence, "ICANN's independence was fatally undermined" by the .xxx controversy, according to Mueller (2010), and its autonomy circumscribed by the GAC's pronounced influence on Board decisions.

Conclusion

On 1 October 2009 the ICANN/DoC Joint Project Agreement (formerly the MOU) was replaced by a long-term permanent agreement called "Affirmation of Commitments" (AoC) between ICANN and the DoC. The new agreement declares that the essential mechanisms, methods, and procedures for "the technical coordination of the Internet's domain name and addressing system (DNS), globally by a private sector led organization" (AoC, para. 1) are in place and that all the steps necessary to transfer management responsibility for DNS functions to ICANN have been taken. It loosens the US government's oversight of ICANN which "will become more self-governing, subject to advisory reviews by panels including one that represents 100 countries" (Menn 2009). The new review process as outlined in paragraph nine of the AoC will be conducted by teams of volunteers drawn from the Internet community and the recommendations arising out of the reviews will be posted for public comment. Although the US continues to have a guaranteed place in the review teams, the process shifts accountability of ICANN and its performance to the global Internet community.

The AoC simply recognizes the coming of age of ICANN and its autonomy as an international private sector, multistakeholder governance organization. At the same time, ICANN's "freedom" has come at a price, namely accepting the privileged role of the GAC. As the Internet Governance Project (IGP) pointed out in 2008:

> Despite its nominal status as an "Advisory Committee" within a private corporation, GAC is really an intergovernmental body with the potential to reproduce the alliances, coalitions and politics of the UN. Since 2002, it has been practically mandatory for ICANN to follow GAC's "policy advice." But unlike a "real" international organization, GAC's authority is not based on a formal treaty, and its rules and powers were never ratified by any democratically elected legislature. Moreover, unlike a formal treaty or negotiation process, which requires consensus agreement among all governments before it is effective across all jurisdictions, GAC is able to issue "policy advice" without obtaining a formal consensus of its members. Thus, as a vehicle for arbitrary governmental interference in DNS, GAC raises far more concerns than the UN, the

IGF [Internet Governance Forum], or unilateral actions by other governments.

(IGP 2008: 7)

Whether or not the GAC is the appropriate mechanism to involve the world's national governments in the ICANN process, its influence on the decisions and policies of the ICANN Board is obviously significant and certainly challenges the notion that ICANN's decisions are independent. It also compromises the multistakeholder, private sector-led, bottom-up policy development model, thereby constraining ICANN's autonomy.

ICANN is nonetheless an important institutional and organizational innovation that despite its flaws actually works. ICANN has developed over the past 12 years the capacity to "act" with considerable independence and to pursue its own agenda and policies for managing the DNS. Yet ICANN's evolution is far from over and this unique international organization will certainly face difficult and controversial problems and challenges in the years ahead. How well or poorly ICANN handles such challenges and problems will determine the fate of both itself and the new generation of international organizations.

Notes

1 The IAB changed its name to the Internet Architecture Board in 1992.
2 See a profile of Jon Postel in the 21 April 1997 issue of *Network World*, "Industry asks: Who is Jon Postel?" www.networkworld.com/news/0421postel.html (accessed on 20 October 2005).
3 The NTIA had received two other proposals for the new private corporation—one from the Boston Working Group and the other from the Open Root Server Confederation—but neither of these had as much support among major world government leaders and corporate interests as the ISOC-led coalition's proposal (Franda 2001: 54).
4 "President's Report: ICANN—The Case for Reform" (24 February 2002), www.icann.org/en/general/lynn-reform-proposal-24feb02.htm.
5 The one exception is the stakeholder group of governments (including intergovernmental organizations), which are not permitted to serve as a director under the bylaws (Article VI, section 4.1), though governments are represented via the Governmental Advisory Committee (GAC) non-voting liaisons to the board, the Nominating Committee, and the supporting organizations (SOs) Councils and Advisory Committees.

Bibliography

Anheier, Helmut, Marlies Glasius, and Mary Kaldor, eds, *Global Civil Society 2001* (Oxford: Oxford University Press, 2001).

Antonova, Slavka, *Powerscape of Internet Governance: How was Global Multi-stakeholderism Invented in ICANN?* (Saarbrücken: VDM Verlag Dr. Müller Aktiengesellschaft & Co. KG, 2008).

Benkler, Yochai, *The Wealth of Networks: How Social Production Transforms Markets and Freedom* (New Haven: Yale University Press, 2006).

Börzel, Tanja A., *Governance with/out Government: False Promises or Flawed Premises?* SFB-Governance Working Paper Series, No. 23 (Berlin: Research Centre (SFB) 700, March 2010).

Brauer, Jurgen and Robert Haywood, *Non-state Sovereign Entrepreneurs and Non-territorial Sovereign Organizations*, Working Paper No. 2010/09 (Helsinki: UNU World Institute for Development Economics Research (UNU-WIDER), February 2010).

Brühl, Tanja and Volker Rittberger, "From International to Global Governance: Actors, Collective Decision-making, and the United Nations in the World of the Twenty-first Century," in *Global Governance and the United Nations System*, ed. Volcker Rittberger (Geneva: United Nations, 2002), 1–47.

Cane, Alan, "It Ain't Broke Yet, But Might Need Fixing," *Financial Times*, 4 December 2006.

Cerf, Vinton G., "Computer Networking: Global Infrastructure for the 21st Century," Computing Research Association, 1997, www.cs.washington.edu/homes/lazowska/cra/networks.html.

——"IETF and ISOC," Internet Society, 18 July 1995.

——"A Brief History of the Internet and Related Networks," Internet Society, 1992, www.isoc.org/Internet/history/cerf.shtml.

Cukier, Kenneth Neil, "Who Will Control the Internet?" *Foreign Affairs* 84, no. 6 (2005): 7–13.

Cutler, A. Claire, Virginia Haufler and Tony Porter, eds, *Private Authority and International Affairs* (Albany, NY: State University of New York Press, 1999).

Drake, William J., "Communications," in *Managing Global Issues: Lessons Learned*, ed. P.J. Simmons and Chantal de Jonge Oudraat (Washington, DC: Carnegie Endowment for International Peace, 2001), 25–74.

Drezner, Daniel W., "The Global Governance of the Internet: Bringing the State Back In," *Political Science Quarterly* 119, no. 3 (2004): 477–98.

Forman, Shepard and Derk Segaar, "New Coalitions for Global Governance: The Changing Dynamics of Multilateralism," *Global Governance* 12, no. 2 (2006): 205–25.

Franda, Marcus, *Launching into Cyberspace: Internet Development and Politics in Five World Regions* (Boulder, Col.: Lynne Reinner, 2002).

——*Governing the Internet: The Emergence of an International Regime* (Boulder, Col.: Lynne Reinner, 2001).

Fukuyama, Francis and Caroline S. Wagner, "Information and Biological Revolutions: Global Governance Challenges—Summary of a Study Group," RAND Monograph Report MR-1139-DARPA, 2000, www.rand.org/pubs/monograph_reports/MR1139.

Goldsmith, Jack and Tim Wu, *Who Controls the Internet? Illusions of a Borderless World* (New York: Oxford University Press, 2006).

Grieco, Joseph M. and G. John Ikenberry, *State Power and World Markets* (New York: W.W. Norton, 2003).

International Centre for Dispute Resolution (ICDR), "Declaration of the Independent Review Panel," ICDR Case No. 50 117 T 00224 08, 19 February 2010, www.icann.org/en/irp/icm-v-icann/irp-panel-declaration-19feb10-en.pdf.

Internet Governance Project (IGP), "Review of Documents Released under the Freedom of Information Act in the .xxx Case," Internet Governance Project, Paper IGP06–003, 2006, www.internetgovernance.org/pdf/dist.sac.pdf.

——— "Comments of the Internet Governance Project on the Continued Transition of the Technical Coordination and Management of the Internet's Domain Name and Addressing System: Midterm Review of the Joint Project Agreement," 15 February 2008, www.internetgovernance.org/pdf/IGP-JPA-08-comments.pdf.

Kennedy, Paul, Dirk Messner, and Franz Nuscheler, eds, *Global Trends and Global Governance* (London: Pluto Press, 1992).

Klein, Hans, "ICANN and Internet Governance: Leveraging Technical Coordination to Realize Global Public Policy," *The Information Society* 18 (2002): 193–207.

Knight, W. Andy, "Engineering Space in Global Governance: the Emergence of Civil Society in Evolving 'New' Multilateralism," in *Future Multilateralism: The Political and Social Framework*, ed. Michael G. Schechter (Basingstoke: Macmillan, 1999), 255–91.

Kruck, Andreas and Volker Rittberger, "Multilateralism Today and its Contribution to Global Governance," in *The New Dynamics of Multilateralism: Diplomacy, International Organizations and Global Governance*, ed. James P. Muldoon, Jr, JoAnn Fagot Aviel, Richard Reitano, and Earl Sullivan (Boulder, Col.: Westview, 2010), 43–65.

Leiner, Barry M., Vinton G. Cerf, David D. Clark, Robert E. Kahn, Leonard Kleinrock, Daniel C. Lynch, Jon Postel, Larry G. Roberts, and Stephen Wolff, "A Brief History of the Internet," version 3.32, 2003, www.isoc.org/history/brief.shtml.

Malcolm, Jeremy, *Multi-Stakeholder Governance and the Internet Governance Forum* (Perth: Terminus Press, 2008).

Mathiason, John, *Internet Governance: The New Frontier of Global Institutions* (London: Routledge, 2009).

Menn, Joseph, "US eases grip on Internet oversight group," *Financial Times*, 1 October 2009.

Mueller, Milton, "Will Stonewalling on .xxx be Beckstrom's First Big Mistake?" *CircleID Blogs*, posted 22 February 2010, www.circleid.com/posts/20100222_will_stonewalling_on_xxx_be_beckstroms_first_big_mistake.

——— *Ruling the Root: Internet Governance and the Taming of Cyberspace* (Cambridge: MIT Press, 2002).

Mueller, Milton, John Mathiason, and Hans Klein, "The Internet and Global Governance: Principles and Norms for a New Regime," *Global Governance* 13, no. 2 (2007): 237–54.

Muldoon, James P., *The Architecture of Global Governance: An Introduction to the Study of International Organizations* (Boulder, CO: Westview Press, 2003).

Muldoon, James P., JoAnn Fagot Aviel, Richard Reitano, and Earl Sullivan, eds, *The New Dynamics of Multilateralism: Diplomacy, International Organizations, and Global Governance* (Boulder, Col.: Westview Press, 2010).

Naughton, John, "Contested Space: The Internet and Global Civil Society," in *Global Civil Society 2001*, ed. Helmut Anheier, Marlies Glasius, and Mary Kaldor (Oxford: Oxford University Press, 2001), 147–68.

Rittberger, Volker, ed., *Global Governance and the United Nations System* (Tokyo: United Nations University Press, 2002).

Sassen, Saskia, "The Spatial Organization of Information Industries," in *Globalization: Critical Reflections*, ed. James H. Mittelman (Boulder, Col.: Lynne Rienner, 1996), 33–52.

Schäferhoff, Marco, Sabine Campe, and Christopher Kaan, "Transnational Public-Private Partnerships in International Relations: Making Sense of Concepts, Research Frameworks, and Results," *International Studies Review* 11, no. 3 (2009): 451–74.

Schechter, Michael G., ed., *Future Multilateralism: The Political and Social Framework* (Tokyo: United Nations University Press, 1999).

Simai, Mihály, *The Age of Global Transformations: the Human Dimension* (Budapest: Akadémiai Kiadó, 2001).

Simmons, P.J. and Chantal de Jonge Oudraat, eds, *Managing Global Issues: Lessons Learned* (Washington, DC: Carnegie Endowment for International Peace, 2001).

Spar, Debora L., "Lost in (Cyber)space: The Private Rules of Online Commerce," in *Private Authority and International Affairs*, ed. A. Claire Cutler, Virginia Haufler, and Tony Porter (Albany, NY: State University of New York Press, 1999), 31–51.

Weinberg, Jonathan, "ICANN and the Problem of Legitimacy," *Duke Law Journal* 50 (2000): 187–260.

10 Conclusion

Joel E. Oestreich

This volume has taken theoretical approaches to the study of international organization (IO) behavior, and used them to interpret the contentious issue of IO independence. Our question has been, under what circumstances can IOs be meaningful actors in world affairs? We have posited a two-step approach to acting: first, having preferences independently of states; second, translating those preferences into actions that have a real impact on world politics. We have tried to do so by looking at a wide range of organizations and an equally wide array of topics, from the Secretary-General's office to the United Nations (UN) Office for Project Services, and from the high politics of international trade to the regulation of pollution discharged into the oceans.

One thing that emerges just from the previous paragraph, as well as from the volume as a whole, is an appreciation of the incredibly wide range of issues that the UN and other organizations are called on to regulate, legislate, coordinate, control, or monitor. There are multiple UNs, ranging from the talking shops of the General Assembly and its committees to the dogged, behind-the-scenes work being done by everything from the UN Development Programme to the World Meteorological Organization. It is a complex, wide-ranging, and evolving set of international organizations that seek to solve global problems, and they interact in ways that are not easy to predict.

Recap: issues and organizations

We have noted that one key factor identified as aiding in IO independence is the complexity of issues involved. It is important to note what complexity really means here; for example, Internet Corporation for Assigned Names and Numbers (ICANN) deals with very technical issues of Internet management, but the policy matters—for example, the creation of a .xxx domain—are actually fairly straightforward, and ICANN has a quite limited mandate compared to, say, the World Bank. Here we note that the complexity of the entire system of international regulation and problem-solving must also contribute to the independence we have observed. It might be a cliché to say that the globalized world means more complexity, and more problems of externalities that need to be controlled, and more interactions among states that require some structure if they are to be successful.

Another issue-oriented factor identified in the introductory chapter, issue salience (that is, its relation to the central interests of states), has figured more prominently in our chapters than complexity. Salience appears to be a central concept; states, not surprisingly, exert more control over issues they consider most important politically. We have seen how varying perceptions of salience can lead to varying levels of independence: for example, in Susan Park and Catherine Weaver's chapter on the World Bank, where different issues raised different concerns from member states. Dennis Dijkzeul has also charted the ups and downs of issue salience in respect to the UN Office for Project Services (UNOPS).

Finally, we noted that clever IOs can exploit lack of agreement among principals—states—around particular issues in order to gain a level of independence. Both Kendall Stiles and James Muldoon have specifically pointed to efforts by IOs to exploit this lack of agreement, although in both cases with limited results; indeed, in both cases the organization being studied was hampered by other factors, such as their small size and relative newness. Still, they were aware of these opportunities and tried to use them.

From our list of organizational variables, the role of leadership in particular has been particularly prominent in this volume. The frequency with which we have grappled with the importance of having strong, visionary leaders in an organization points to the obvious fact that these are human institutions, run by people who are key variables in themselves. We have seen cases both of visionary leaders taking their IO in a new direction—for example, the Secretary-General setting the democracy agenda—and leaders failing to do so, despite making their best effort. We have also looked at the role of other people below the top level of an organization and how their roles in the policy process have shaped outcomes, as in Margaret Karns' chapter on peacebuilding, and Dennis Dijkzeul's on UNOPS. It is not surprising that constructivist thought has informed much of our work in this area and that many of our findings comport well with the concepts from sociological theories of international relations. Humans make up these organizations and human nature, learning, and understanding inform their actions. It is worth noting, for example, that in Park and Weaver's chapter, we saw how effective leadership could overcome the problems imposed by issue salience: the work of the World Bank certainly seems important to states, but good leadership can still carve out a niche for an organization.

The size and complexity of organizations have also played an important role in the cases presented. Here, in some cases, the negative have been more telling than the positive cases; for example, the small size of the Joint United Nations Programme on HIV/AIDS (UNAIDS) has been a limiting factor, as has the relative smallness of the Association of Southeast Asian Nations (ASEAN) secretariat. Similarly, the maturity of organizations has been shown in both positive and negative ways; the well-established authority of the UN Secretary-General, in Kirsten Haack and Kent Kille's case for example, can be contrasted with the newness of ICANN from that of Muldoon. While one would not want to push a comparison between these cases too much (due to their extreme differences in organizational form) that's somewhat of the point here; they are very different, and they work differently in the international system. Age and maturity are power resources that can be used effectively in some situations.

Dijkzeul's case study of UNOPS, and Park and Weaver's study of the World Bank, each do a good job of bringing into focus the issue of staff characteristics, and particularly bureaucratic politics, in determining IO independence. Bureaucratic politics is an important function of IO independence, clearly, although one that works differently to other factors; bureaucratic politics introduces a level of unpredictability and even dysfunction in IO operations and it can be hard to predict which direction it will take an IO. At its worst, bureaucratic politics is responsible for much IO pathology, as described by Barnett and Finnemore, and mentioned in the introductory chapter.

Finally, the availability of networks of IOs, and the resources they give IO leadership, has also factored into several chapters. Alex Betts, in particular, has shown how the UN High Commissioner for Refugees (UNHCR) has expanded its mandate by exploiting its place in networks of actors. As Betts shows, this takes help from leadership as well: these networks are exploited by those in positions of authority, who actively seek them out as they further their own goals. Similarly, Christer Jönsson shows the ability of UNAIDS to leverage public-private partnerships and other transnational networks in its own quest to fight the HIV/AIDS pandemic.

We recognize that the interaction of these factors remains underspecified, although we hope that our case studies have been illuminating.

As we were at pains to point out in the introductory chapter, bureaucracies can't and shouldn't be thought of as unitary actors. There might be room to maneuver in one issue-area but not another, or at one time but not another. Issues and actors, we insisted during our initial roundtable, must be thought of together; it is not accurate to treat them as independent of each other, and we hope this has come through in our cases. In some places we have seen factors work against each other: for example, small organizations trying to exploit disagreement among principals. Which wins out? That question, it seems, can't be put so simply; you have to take the issue and the organization as a single problem to be solved, rather than looking for simple answers of the "this IO is showing independence, this one isn't" variety.

IR theory and IO action

As we stated in the introductory chapter, this volume is not intended to present a new theory of IO behavior, nor create some sort of synthesis or sorting out of existing theories. It should be clear from the cases presented that there is no single, simple explanation of IO behavior that can be taken away from it. Many of the chapters in this volume, indeed, felt free to borrow from a variety of perspectives in order to explain various aspects of IO agency. This might open the book to accusations of being inconsistent—how can multiple theories all be right?

We reject the notion, however, that theories can never be combined in this way. Of course, some approaches are incompatible with others, at least in certain areas. For example, we might say that a strictly Realist approach does not comport well with one that puts the emphasis on ideas in foreign policy, since "ideas" are used by sociological approaches as an alternative to pure power-seeking behavior. However, even this would be misleading. Many issues in international relations are not necessarily about national survival, even taken in the long term, and there is no necessary reason in Realist theory to assume that in such issues states would not cede some control to IOs; an example might be the refugee protection regime. The most powerful states would not want to see an organization like UNHCR establish too much independence (for fear of setting a precedent, perhaps) but also might not see their vital interests threatened if it did. Similarly, principal-agent (PA) theory, as we've seen, assumes rational self-interested actions on the part of actors, but acting as individuals, rather than as organizations. The insights of PA theory about how agents "shirk" can be combined with the insights of constructivist theory about the role of ideas, to create a useful lens into how IOs determine what their interests are and how they go about pursuing those interests.

On the other hand, we have been careful in this volume not to move back and forth between theories too blithely. It would be easy to believe that one can simply mix and match among the various approaches to IOs, without thinking about how they fit together. When an issue is extremely salient to a state (e.g., control of the Internet) and that state reins in an IO, we can say this comports with Realist predictions; when bureaucratic logic proves determinative (e.g., the case of UNOPS), we might see a more social process; but unless we are careful to explain why we see one in the first case and another in the second, and show how they don't contradict each other, then there is a loss of clarity. We hope we have not transgressed in that way with this volume.

Defining independence

It was noted already that defining independence—in particular, distinguishing it from delegated discretion—is a difficult thing to do, and one of the key questions with which the authors have grappled in this volume. That grappling began with the original roundtable in which many of us participated, at the genesis of this project. It remains a key question for us.

These cases suggest, it appears, that this is a deeper question than even we first thought. The main question we asked ourselves at first was, how do we distinguish "delegated discretion" from "true independence"? Surely, we knew, states don't expect to be consulted on every decision their creations take; an advantage of creating IOs is that they can handle the day-to-day or even medium-term unexpected questions and problems that come up, without involving states. However, we can also look at a much deeper level. Is it possible that states want their creations to have not just delegated discretion, but a level of "true independence"? Perhaps that, too, can be delegated in a way. When the Secretary-General sets out an agenda for post-conflict reconstruction, as unexpected as that might be, perhaps there was an intention all along to have a UN leader who could act beyond the obvious terms of his contract from the principals. What is the dividing line between discretion and independence? Even active resistance from states might not truly establish that line.

So at some point, the direction of this inquiry might have to return to a fundamental question, namely, What do states really want from international organizations? Is it purely to solve collective-action problems? Or is it something more? This question might lie at the edge of being purely philosophical—it turns on how you define terms like "want"—but it remains unresolved. It has a lot to say about how IOs are structured, and why. Chapter One began by suggesting that a lot of subtlety has been lost in international relations theory by the habit of grouping all IOs, and indeed all international institutions, in a single theoretical bucket. The real world turns out to be more difficult to classify. While we recognize a need for answers that don't lose too much parsimony (in the "every IO is a unique thing" vein), we do suggest that a certain amount of subtlety is essential.

Index

actor/agent, agency 214–15, 264–67; agency as part of an organization/ as individuals 21; HIV/AIDS, 'lead agency' 143, 145, 147–54; IOs as agents 77, 78; 'lead agency' model 162, 163; PA theory, role of agent 171–72; 'public-private partnership' model 162, 163; two-step definition 12, 13, 15, 264; types of IO action 14–15; What does it mean to act? 11–13; Who acts? 13–14; *see also* constructivism; independence; PA theory
AIDS *see* HIV/AIDS
Annan, Kofi 30, 31, 36, 73, 144, 256; democracy assistance 47, 49; democracy, institutionalization through practice 45–48; 'Kofi Doctrine' 46; MDGs 45, 48, 154, 164, 242; people-centered politics 48; 'quiet revolution' 46, 47; *see also* UN Secretary-General
ASEAN 221–40, 266; ARF 224–25, 226, 236; ASCC 228; ASEAN Charter 228, 235; ASEAN Concord 224, 231; ASEAN Declaration 223, 230; Asian financial crisis 225, 227, 229, 234; bureaucracy 221, 226, 236, 237; China 224, 226, 227, 228, 233, 234; constructivism 236; development 226; genesis and evolution 222–24, 230; informality/institutionalization 221, 222, 226, 229, 232, 236–37, 266; issue, agreement among states 221, 226, 229, 238 (distrust among members 221, 222, 225); Japan 227, 228, 233, 234; PA theory 221, 238; regional cooperation 222, 223–24, 230, 232, 235; security regime 222–26, 230, 236 (ASC 228); Summits 223, 227, 228, 230, 232, 235; weakness/ shortcomings 225–26; *see also* ASEAN, economic regime; ASEAN, secretariat
ASEAN, economic regime 226–29, 230, 231–36, 237–38; AEC 228; AFTA 227, 228, 232; APEC 227, 228, 236; economic cooperation 221, 226–27, 229, 230; GATT 229, 232, 234, 236, 237; IMF 227, 228, 229, 236; Plaza Accord 226–27, 229; trade liberalization 226–29, 230, 232, 237; *see also* ASEAN; ASEAN, secretariat
ASEAN, secretariat 222, 229–36, 237–38, 266; 1967–76 229–30, 236; 1976–92 229, 231–32, 236, 237; 1992–2007 229, 232–36; independence 222, 231, 235; institutionalization 232; organizational structure 231; restructuring 233; role 231–32, 233–35, 236, 237, 238; secretary-general 233, 234, 235, 236; weakness 221, 237; *see also* ASEAN; ASEAN, economic regime
authority 187; ICANN 250, 251, 252, 254, 255; IOs authority 8, 10,

18, 79–80, 187; moral authority 34, 50, 51, 124; UN Secretary-General 77–79; UNHCR 124
autonomy: Boutros-Ghali, Boutros 78; definition 77; HIV/AIDS 151; ICANN 244, 252, 254–56, 259; IMO 170, 173, 174; IOs autonomy 2, 5, 9, 10, 50, 76, 77–79, 130; IOs, staff 76, 77; Pérez de Cuéllar, Javier 77–78; UN Secretary-General, post-conflict peacebuilding 61, 72–73, 74, 75, 76, 77–79, 82; UNHCR 121, 129; World Bank 91, 93, 95, 110, 111

Barnett, Michael/Finnemore, Martha 8, 17; bureaucratization of world politics 8, 266; IOs as bureaucracies 8, 50, 79–80, 82, 266; *Rules for the World: International Organizations in Global Politics* 8, 50, 75–76, 82; UNHCR, repatriation 125–26
Betts, Alexander: UNHCR 118–40, 266
Boutros-Ghali, Boutros 30, 36, 38–42; *Agenda for Democratization* 40–41, 43–45, 79; *Agenda for Development* 40, 43, 79; *Agenda for Peace* 40, 41–42, 43, 60–61, 65, 71–73, 78, 79, 84; autonomy 78; OPE/DDSMS merging 202, 204, 209; peacebuilding concept 61, 72, 73, 74, 79–80; post-conflict peacebuilding 60, 61, 63, 71, 72, 73, 78, 79; *Supplement to Agenda for Peace* 40, 63; *see also* democracy; peace; UN Secretary-General; UN Secretary-General, post-conflict peacebuilding
bureaucracy 8, 16, 21, 215, 266, 267, 268; ASEAN 221, 226, 236, 237; bureaucratic behavior 7, 80; bureaucratic culture 9, 14; constructivism 10; decision-making 14; IOs as bureaucracies 8, 50, 79–80, 82, 92, 125–26, 221, 266; PA theory 6, 7; primary goal of 7;

Rules for the World: International Organizations in Global Politics 8, 50, 75–76, 82; state/IOs relationship 8; UNHCR, repatriation 125–26; UNOPS 195, 203–6, 213, 214, 268; World Bank 92, 93, 95–96, 99–101, 103–4, 106, 108, 109–10; *see also* IOs, staff

Cambodia 60, 64, 70–71, 74, 82, 224, 225, 227; UNTAC 70, 71
capacity: capacity for independence 16, 17, 19; UN post-conflict peacebuilding 60, 71, 73, 83
case studies 2, 13, 15–16; case selection 22–23; independence 2; IOs and issues 20–21; the story of a decision 21; structure of 15–16, 20–22
Central America 64, 67–70; Cuba 67; Nicaragua 37, 41, 68–69, 74, 81, 82; El Salvador 41, 69–70, 74, 79, 82; *see also* Pérez de Cuéllar, Javier
Chesterman, Simon: *Secretary or General? The UN Secretary-General in World Politics* 35
civil society 10; anticorruption agenda 113; environmental agenda 97–98; HIV/AIDS 157, 158, 163; *see also* NGOs
Cold War 39, 122, 123, 124, 125, 131, 134
constructivism 2, 265–66, 267–68; ASEAN 236–37; bureaucracy 10; HIV/AIDS 141, 147, 149, 150, 153–54, 162; independence 8–11, 12, 13; international institution 4; IOs as conduits for globalized/ globalizing ideas 9, 38, 40–41, 44–45; IR theory 4; norm entrepreneurship 36, 48, 50, 74, 79–80, 83; PA theory 8; shortcomings 214–15; UN Secretary-General 30, 36, 38, 50, 51; UN Secretary-General, post-conflict peacebuilding 61, 79, 83; UNHCR, mandate change 120, 130, 135–36; UNOPS 196, 215; World Bank 96; *see also* institutionalism

Index

Council of Europe 101, 145, 146, 147
Cox, Robert/Jacobson, Harold: *The Anatomy of Influence* 14–15, 74; see also decision-making

decision-making 2, 14, 241; boundary decisions 14, 15, 74, 148, 151–54; bureaucracy 14; Cox, Robert/Jacobson, Harold: *The Anatomy of Influence* 14–15, 74; ICANN 243, 252; operational decisions 15, 74, 148, 149–51; programmatic decisions 15, 147, 148–49; rule-creating decisions 15, 74, 169, 173; rule-supervisory decisions 15, 169, 176, 177, 184; see also independence
democracy: *Agenda for Democratization* 40–41, 43–45, 79; *Agenda for Peace* 42; Annan, Kofi 30, 45–48; Boutros-Ghali, Boutros 30, 38–42; democracy assistance 47, 49; development 37; election assistance 38, 41, 42, 47, 49, 81; election monitoring 42, 67, 68–69, 74, 81; good governance 42, 46–47, 49; human rights 37, 41, 47, 49 (right to democracy 37, 47–48, 81); ICNRD 37, 41; as ideology 37, 39, 44; institutionalization 45; Pérez de Cuéllar, Javier 39, 69; post-conflict peacebuilding 69, 73, 74, 81; self-determination 37, 41, 64; Third Wave of democratization 37, 41, 64, 81; triangulation of democracy, peace, development 40, 42, 49; UN democracy agenda 30, 37–51, 265
development 20; *Agenda for Development* 40, 43, 79; ASEAN 226; corruption/socioeconomic development relationship 91, 99, 103, 110, 111; democracy 37; development cooperation 196–202, 213; human development 48, 113; IOs 5; right to development 45; state 37; triangulation of democracy, peace, development 40, 42, 49; World Bank, environmentally sustainable development 91, 93, 96–98, 105–6, 111, 112; see also World Bank
Dijkzeul, Dennis: UNOPS 21, 195–217, 265, 266
discretion 7, 21; definition 77; delegated discretion 11, 21, 77–79, 268; factors determining discretionary behavior 94–95; UN Secretary-General, post-conflict peacebuilding 61, 70, 75, 77, 79, 80; World Bank 95

ECOSOC (UN Economic and Social Council) 121, 143, 197, 211, 214
enforcement: IMO, policy implementation/enforcement 169, 171–72, 173, 174, 175–76, 177, 179, 180, 181, 182, 186, 189; peace enforcement 65, 84
English School 3
environmental issues 19; civil society 97–98; climate change 106, 112, 128, 135; NGOs 97, 101, 106; UNHCR, victims of natural disaster 118, 119, 128–29, 131, 132, 134, 135, 137; Wolfensohn, James 96–98, 110, 111; Wolfowitz, Paul 105–6, 110, 112; World Bank, environmentally sustainable development 91, 93, 96–98, 105–6, 111, 112
epistemic community 9, 19, 157
EU (European Union) 131, 157, 179, 229, 236
EU Commission 82, 83
expertise 8, 9, 10, 79–80, 150, 162, 170, 176, 190, 196, 211; see also independence

Ford Foundation 122, 123, 134, 135

Gates Foundation 161–62
GATT (General Agreement on Tariffs and Trade) 229, 232, 234, 236, 237
GFATM (Global Fund to Fight AIDS, Tuberculosis and Malaria) 144, 154, 157–59, 160, 161–62,

163, 242; CCM 158–59, 161; a financial instrument 157; Gates Foundation 161–62; TRP 158; *see also* HIV/AIDS; PPPs
global governance: global health governance 154, 162, 163; Internet 244; IOs, new generation 241, 242; vertically structured 242, 244–45; *see also* governance
globalization 9, 141, 244, 245, 265
governance: democracy 42, 46–47, 49; good governance/governance support 42, 48, 49; good governance, principles of 47; Internet's governance 243, 244–45, 247–51, 256; peace 42, 48; World Bank 42, 99–100, 109, 112; *see also* global governance
GPA (Global Programme on AIDS) 143 148–54, 155, 157, 161, 162, 163; criticism/failure 143, 150–51, 153, 154; Mann, Jonathan 148–49, 150, 151, 152–53, 160, 162; success 150, 154; *see also* HIV/AIDS; WHO

Haack, Kirsten: UN Secretary-General 23, 29–59, 265, 266
HIV/AIDS 141–67, 266; civil society 157, 158, 163; constructivism 141, 147, 149, 150, 153–54, 162; coordination, lack of 150, 152, 153, 156, 160–61, 163, 164; Council of Europe 145–47; current assessment 160–61, 163–64; global health governance 154, 162, 163; human rights 142, 146, 148, 149; international agenda 142–45; IOs autonomy 151; IOs independency 141, 162; issue, complexity 141, 147, 148, 150, 162; 'lead agency' model 162, 163; medicalization 148; NGOs 143, 144, 151, 152–53, 154, 156, 160, 163; a North–South issue 147, 148, 149; organizational culture 149, 150, 152, 154, 161; PA theory 141, 149, 150, 151, 153, 161, 162; PPPs 145, 155–62, 163, 266; UN General Assembly 143, 144, 151, 156; UNDP 143, 144, 152, 156; UNGASS 144, 155–56, 157; UNICEF 143, 144, 145, 150, 156; World Bank 143, 144, 145, 150, 152, 156, 157, 158, 159, 161; *see also* GFATM; GPA; HIV/AIDS, treatment; UNAIDS; WHO
HIV/AIDS, treatment 145, 148, 149, 159, 163–64; antiretroviral drug 145, 159, 163; life-sustaining drugs 145; vaccine 145, 164; *see also* HIV/AIDS
human rights 45; democracy 37, 41, 47, 49 (right to democracy 37, 47–48, 81); HIV/AIDS 142, 146, 148, 149 (discrimination 146, 153); human rights-based approach 47; post-conflict peacebuilding 63, 67, 69–70; *see also* UNHCR

IASC (Inter-Agency Standing Committee) 128, 129, 134, 137
ICANN (Internet Corporation for Assigned Names and Numbers) 241–63, 264–65, 268; AoC 259; authority 250, 251, 252, 254, 255; autonomy 244, 252, 254–56, 259; criticism 252, 255–56; decision-making 243, 252; DNS 250, 253, 254, 255, 259, 260; GAC 256, 257, 258, 259–60; hybrid form 241, 242, 250–51, 254; IANA/ISOC coalition 250; ICANN Board 252, 254, 257, 259, 260; ICANN, evolution 254–56; ICANN, experiment 243, 251–54; ICANN, newness 244, 254, 266; independence 243–44, 254, 258–59, 260; issue salience 244, 265, 268; origins 243, 250; a public-private partnership 250–51, 254; staff 244, 251, 252, 253, 254, 257; state control 254–56, 257–58, 268; United States 250, 254–56, 257–58, 259; the '.xxx controversy' 244, 256–59, 264–65; *see also* Internet; PPPs
ICC (International Criminal Court) 171, 186

274 *Index*

IDPs (internally displaced persons) 118, 119, 127–28, 130, 131, 132, 134; definition 127; *see also* UNHCR
ILC (International Law Commission) 171
ILO (International Labour Organization) 144, 171, 176, 182; Thomas, Albert 33
IMB (International Maritime Bureau) 168, 182, 186, 188, 189, 190; *see also* IMO
IMF (International Monetary Fund) 11, 16, 172; ASEAN 227, 228, 229, 236
IMO (International Maritime Organization) 168–94, 265; 1949–72 172–74; 1972–92 174–77; 1992–present 177–85, 189; Audit Scheme 168, 180–81, 190; autonomy 170, 173, 174; characteristics 169–70, 184, 189; Council 173, 180, 181; expertise 170, 176, 190; IMB 168, 182, 186, 188, 189, 190; issue, nature of 169, 190 (agreement among states 169, 172, 185, 265; issue complexity 169, 172; issue salience 169, 172, 190); MOU 168, 175–76, 182, 188, 189; network 170, 174, 190; open registry flag states 169, 174, 177, 178, 180, 182, 184, 188; organizational culture 169–70; piracy 172, 176, 185–87 (anti-piracy 168, 169, 181, 186, 188, 189, 190); port safety 168, 175–76, 179, 187; private non-state actors 169, 172, 174, 176, 177, 189; rule adoption/advocacy 169, 183; rule-creating decisions 169, 173; rule-supervisory decisions 169, 176, 177, 184; ship safety 169, 172, 173–74, 177, 178, 179, 181, 182, 187–88; SOLAS 173, 188; state control 174; terrorism 181, 185, 187, 190; *see also* IMO, PA theory; IMO, staff
IMO, PA theory 168–69, 182, 189; disaggregate delegation of agent roles 170–72, 176–77, 184, 189; policy implementation/enforcement 169, 171–72, 173, 174, 175–76, 177, 179, 180, 181, 182, 186, 189; policy initiation 169, 170, 171, 172, 181, 189; policy ratification 169, 171, 172, 174, 178, 181, 189; *see also* IMO; IMO, staff
IMO, staff 170, 172, 173, 175, 178, 179, 181, 182, 184, 189–90; Mitropoulos, Efthimios 181; O'Neil, William 178, 181; secretary-general 169, 172, 173, 178, 180, 181, 182, 189; *see also* IMO; IMO, PA theory
independence 1, 2, 5, 22–23, 241, 264, 266, 268–69; approaches to 5–11, 20 (strengths/weaknesses of each approach 10–11, 20); constructivism 8–11, 12, 13; definition 11, 268; delegated discretion/independence distinction 11, 268; effectiveness 12; expertise 8, 9, 10, 79–80, 150, 162, 170, 176, 190, 196, 211; information 6–7, 10; institutionalism 20; IOs authority 8, 10, 18, 79–80, 187; IOs autonomy 2, 5, 9, 10, 50, 76, 77–79, 130; IOs power 9, 10, 79–80; limitations 13; PA theory 5–7, 10, 12, 13; realism 11, 20; slack 6, 7, 18, 20, 79, 119, 137, 198, 238; types of IO action 14–15; What does it mean to act? 11–13? Who acts? 13–14; *see also* decision-making; independence, case studies; independence, factors of; IOs and issues
independence, case studies 2; ASEAN 222, 231, 235; HIV/AIDS 141, 162; ICANN 243–44, 254, 258–59, 260; UN Secretary-General, independent leadership 29, 30, 31, 32–34, 35–36, 49–50–1, 76, 82; UN Secretary-General, post-conflict peacebuilding 61, 70, 71, 79; UNHCR 129, 131, 134, 135, 136–37 (High Commissioner 122, 123, 124, 126, 128, 134, 135–36,

Index 275

137, 266); UNOPS, staff initiative 195–96, 198, 206, 213, 265, 266 (independency 195–96, 213, 214; leaky boat strategy 207–8, 214); World Bank 91, 100, 103, 110, 265
independence, factors of 16–20, 264–67; organizational attributes 17–19, 184, 265–67 (IO maturity/ age 17–18, 75, 184, 244, 254, 266; IO networks 18–19; IO size and complexity 16, 17, 75, 169, 173, 184, 189, 233, 244, 265, 266; IO staff, personal characteristics 18); issue attributes 19–20; *see also* IOs and issues; IOs, staff; network; organizational culture
information 6–7, 10; asymmetric information 6–7, 20, 95; *see also* Internet
institutionalism 20; ASEAN, informality/institutionalization 221, 222, 226, 229, 232, 236–37; democracy, institutionalization 45–48; Internet, informality 245; IOs, institutionalization 222; IOs, new generation: informality 242; *see also* constructivism
international institution 3; definition 3–4; English School 3; institution as organization 3, 4
international politics 2, 4; constructivism 13; IOs, effect on international politics 4–5, 8; state 6; UN 83
Internet 242, 243–44; administration and management 243, 247–51; DNS 243, 246–47, 248–50, 253, 254, 255, 259, 260; global governance 244; a global network 245–47, 251; gTLDs/ccTLDs/ sTLDs 247, 253, 256–57; IAB 248, 260; IANA 248, 250, 253; IANA/ISOC coalition 250; ICT revolution 244–45; informality 245; International Telephone and Telegraph Union 17; Internet's governance 243, 244–45, 247–51, 256; ISOC 248, 249, 250; ITU 19, 244, 249; origins 245–47; 'TCP/IP' protocols 246, 248; United States 243, 245–46, 247, 248–51, 257–58; *see also* ICANN
intervention 40, 41, 47, 79; humanitarian intervention 46
IOM (International Organization for Migration) 126, 131
IOs 1–25, 264–67; as agents 77, 78; as bureaucracies 8, 50, 79–80, 82, 92, 125–26, 221, 266; as conduits for globalized/globalizing ideas 9, 38, 40–41, 44–45; effect on international politics 4–5, 8; hybrid form 155, 157, 210, 211 (ICANN 241, 242, 250–51, 254); institutionalization 222; international norms 4; international regulatory organizations 168; IR 1, 4, 29, 51–52, 221, 267–68, 269; limitations of 2, 8; ontology 3–5; 'open systems' 10, 19, 92; organizational attributes 17–19, 184, 265–67; *see also* decision-making; independence; IOs and issues; IOs, new generation; IOs, staff; IOs and the state; PPPs
IOs and issues 15–20, 77, 141, 147, 148, 150, 162, 264–65, 267; agreement among states over issues 20, 169, 172, 185, 221, 226, 229, 238, 265 (distrust among members 221, 222, 225); issue complexity/linkage with other issues 19, 141, 147, 148, 150, 162, 169, 172, 196–202, 213, 264–65; issue salience to states 19–20, 30, 49, 169, 172, 190, 196–202, 213, 244, 265, 268; 'lead agency' model 162, 163; 'public-private partnership' model 162, 163; *see also* independence
IOs, new generation 241–43; decision-making 241; global governance 241, 242; hybrid form 241, 242, 254; independence 241; informality 242; NGOs 241, 242; PPPs 241–43; *see also* ICANN; PPPs
IOs, staff 13–14, 20, 82, 92, 215, 265; agency as part of an

organization/as individuals 21; autonomy 76, 77; GPA, Mann, Jonathan 148–49, 150, 151, 152–53, 160, 162; ICANN 244, 251, 252, 253, 254, 257; IMO, secretary-general 169, 172, 173, 178, 180, 181, 182, 189 (Mitropoulos, Efthimios 181; O'Neil, William 178, 181); IMO, staff 170, 172, 173, 175, 178, 179, 181, 182, 184, 189–90; independent leadership 265–66 (High Commissioner 122, 123, 124, 126, 128, 134, 135–36, 137, 266; UN Secretary-General 29, 30, 31, 32–34, 35–36, 48–51, 76, 82); personal characteristics 18, 29, 92; Secretary-General as individual 34–35, 51–52, 61, 75, 77, 265; UNOPS, Helmke, Reinhart 207, 212; UNOPS, staff initiative 195–96, 198, 206, 213, 265, 266 (independency 195–96, 213, 214; leaky boat strategy 207–8, 214); World Bank, executive head 92, 93, 94, 95–96, 103, 104, 110–11, 112; *see also* Annan, Kofi; ASEAN, secretariat; Boutros-Ghali, Boutros; bureaucracy; Pérez de Cuéllar, Javier; UN Secretary-General; UNHCR, High Commissioner; Wolfensohn, James; Wolfowitz, Paul

IOs and the state 4, 8–9, 11, 268–69; bureaucracy 8; contract 5–6, 7, 11; created by the state 6, 8, 11, 119, 268; state control 2, 19, 22, 29, 174, 267, 268 (ICANN 254–56, 257–58, 268); state-led mandate shifts 119; state resistance 12, 45, 49, 65, 112, 209, 268; UNHCR 119, 130 (state control 119, 130, 267; state-led change 119, 130, 131; state resistance to change 124, 125, 130, 135, 136)

IR (international relations) 195, 214, 267–68; constructivist IR theory 4; IOs 1, 4, 29, 51–52, 221, 267–68, 269; IOs, mandate change 119; PA theory 7; states as actors 1; *see also* constructivism; PA theory; realism

ITU (International Telecommunication Union) 19, 244, 249

Jönsson, Christer 18; HIV/AIDS 141–67, 266

Karns, Margaret P.: UN post-conflict peacebuilding 60–88, 265
Kille, Kent J.: UN Secretary-General 23, 29–59, 265, 266

League of Nations 65; Drummond, Sir Eric 33
liberalism: ASEAN, trade liberalization 226–29, 230, 232, 237; IOs as loci of international cooperation 1, 13; neoliberalism 37, 155, 249; UNHCR, mandate change 120, 122, 130–31

maritime safety regime *see* IMO
Mathiason, John: *Invisible Governance: International Secretariats in Global Politics* 35–36
MDGs (Millennium Development Goals) 45, 48, 154, 164, 242
Muldoon, James P., Jr: ICANN 241–63, 265, 266

NATO (North Atlantic Treaty Organization) 1, 186, 187
neo-functionalism: UNHCR, mandate change 120, 130, 131–33
network 18–19, 266; IASC 128, 129, 134, 137; IMO 170, 174, 190; Internet, a global network 245–47, 251; NGO 19; UNHCR 120, 123, 128, 129, 134–35, 137, 266
NGOs 10, 241, 242; anticorruption agenda 101–2, 107, 113; environmental agenda 97, 101, 106; Government Accountability Project (GAP) 102; HIV/AIDS 143, 144, 151, 152–53, 154, 156, 160, 163 (ASOs 152, 153; ICASO 153); ISOC 248, 249, 250; network 19; UNHCR 122, 123,

126, 133, 137; *see also* civil society; ICANN
norm entrepreneurship 36, 48, 50, 74, 79–80, 83

OAS (Organization of American States) 67, 101
OECD (Organisation for Economic Co-operation and Development) 101, 177
Oestreich, Joel E. 1–25, 264–69
organizational culture 9, 184; bureaucratic culture 9, 14; HIV/AIDS 149, 150, 152, 154, 161; IMO 169–70; UNOPS 208, 213; World Bank 9, 92, 94, 96, 98, 103–4, 108, 111

PA (principal-agent) theory 2, 94–96, 170–72, 267; agent, role of 171–72; ASEAN 221, 238; bureaucracy 6, 7; constructivism 8; HIV/AIDS 141, 149, 150, 151, 153, 161, 162; independence 5–7, 10, 12, 13; IOs as agents 77, 78; IR 7; literature 168; principal-agent contract 5, 170; rationalism 8, 10, 96; self-interested actors 6–7, 9; shortcomings 214–15; UN Secretary-General 30, 51; UN Secretary-General, post-conflict peacebuilding 61, 75, 77, 79, 83; UNOPS 196, 215; World Bank 94–96; *see also* discretion; IMO, PA theory
Park, Susan 4; World Bank 91–117, 265, 266
path dependence 16, 147, 149, 196, 214
peace 5; *Agenda for Peace* 40, 41–42, 43, 60–61, 65, 71–73, 78, 79, 84; conflict, causes of 41; democracy 42; good governance/governance support 42, 48; 'Kofi Doctrine' 46; peace enforcement 65, 84; peacekeeping missions 41, 62, 73, 80, 82, 84; *Supplement to Agenda for Peace* 40, 63; triangulation of democracy, peace, development 40, 42, 49; UN Secretary-General 32; *see also* Boutros-Ghali,

Boutros; security issues; UN Secretary-General, post-conflict peacebuilding
Pérez de Cuéllar, Javier: autonomy 77–78; Cambodia 71; democracy 39, 69; ending conflicts in Central America 64, 67–70, 76; post-conflict peacebuilding 64, 67–70, 71, 74, 76, 77–78, 80–81; *Report on the Work of the Organization* 77, 80–81; UN decolonization process 37–38; *see also* UN Secretary-General, post-conflict peacebuilding
piracy 172, 176, 185–87; anti-piracy 168, 169, 181, 186, 188, 189, 190; UN Security Council 186–87; *see also* IMO
policy: IMO, role of agent 171–72 (policy implementation/enforcement 169, 171–72, 173, 174, 175–76, 177, 179, 180, 181, 182, 186, 189; policy initiation 169, 170, 171, 172, 181, 189; policy ratification 169, 171, 172, 174, 178, 181, 189)
PPPs (public-private partnerships) 241–44; HIV/AIDS 145, 155–62, 163, 266; hybrid form 155, 157, 210, 211 (ICANN 241, 242, 250–51, 254); IOs, new generation 241–43; meta-organizations 159; network 243; 'public-private partnership' model 162, 163; stakeholders, inclusion 241, 243, 254, 260; *see also* GFATM; ICANN; UNAIDS

rationalism 3, 8, 10, 21, 96; *see also* PA theory
realism 1, 2, 11, 267, 268; denial of IOs' importance 5, 12, 13; IR theory 4; neo-realism 12, 130; state as actor 1, 130
regime complexity: UNHCR, mandate change 120, 130, 133–35
Reinalda, Bob: ASEAN 221–40, 266

security issues 187, 190; ASEAN, security regime 222–26, 228, 230,

236; authority 187; humanitarian intervention 46; 'Kofi Doctrine' 46; Responsibility to Protect 46, 48; triangulation of democracy, peace, development 40; UN Secretary-General 32, 82; *see also* peace
self-determination 37, 41, 64; *see also* democracy
slack 6, 7, 18, 20, 79, 119, 137, 198, 238
state *see* IOs and the state; realism; state sovereignty
state sovereignty 42; anti-piracy 188; democracy 41; post-conflict peacebuilding 62, 68, 70, 73, 74; UN Charter 62, 68, 74; Westphalian principles 223
Stiles, Kendall W.: IMO 168–94, 265

terrorism 181, 185, 187, 190; *see also* IMO

UN (United Nations) 196–97; 'lead agency' model 162; state-based system 197; Sutterlin, James 72, 84
UN Charter 186; post-conflict peacebuilding 62, 68, 70, 74, 75; state sovereignty 62, 68, 74; UN Secretary-General 29, 31, 32, 36, 38, 50, 77
UN decolonization process 63, 64–67, 68, 83, 124, 197; Congo 61, 65, 82; Namibia 37, 41, 60, 64, 65–67, 71, 74, 79, 81, 82; West Irian 64–65
UN General Assembly 43, 68, 73; democracy agenda 37–38; HIV/AIDS 143, 144, 151, 156; UN Secretary-General 31, 32; UNGASS 144, 155–56, 157; UNHCR 118, 121, 123, 124, 129, 131
UN Secretary-General 16, 23, 29–59, 195, 203, 265, 266; Ban Ki-Moon 31–32; constructivism 30, 36, 38, 50, 51; democracy agenda 30, 37–51, 265; Hammarskjöld, Dag 34, 36, 76; independent leadership 29, 30, 31, 32–34, 35–36, 48–51, 76, 82; issue salience 30, 49; moral authority 34, 50–51; norm entrepreneurship 36, 48, 50; PA theory 30, 51; perspectives on the UN Secretary-General 30–36; role 29, 31, 32–33, 35, 50, 51, 76–77; Secretary-General as individual 34–35, 51–52, 61, 75, 77; Secretary-General as self-directed actor 35–36; secretary vs. general 31–34; state control 29; Thant 76; UN Charter 29, 31, 32, 36, 38, 50, 77; UNOPS 202, 203, 205, 209; Who acts? 29; *see also* Annan, Kofi; Boutros-Ghali, Boutros; democracy; Pérez de Cuéllar, Javier; UN Secretary-General, post-conflict peacebuilding
UN Secretary-General, post-conflict peacebuilding 60–88, 265; *Agenda for Peace* 40, 41–42, 60–61, 65, 71–73, 78, 79, 84; Ahtisaari, Martti 66, 74, 78–79, 80; authority/autonomy 61, 72–73, 74, 75, 76, 77–79, 82; capacity 71, 73, 83; constructivism 61, 79, 83; de Soto, Alvaro 67, 69, 72, 74, 75, 78–79, 80; democracy 69, 73, 74, 81; discretion 61, 70, 75, 77, 79, 80; human rights 63, 67, 69–70; independence 61, 70, 71, 79; international system changes 80–82; norm entrepreneurship 74, 79–80, 83; PA theory 61, 75, 77, 79, 83; peacebuilding concept 61, 62–63, 71–72, 74, 80; post-conflict peacebuilding tasks 63, 72; power/expert authority 79–80; preventive diplomacy 60, 71, 72, 75; roots and evolution 63–71 (UN decolonization process 63–67; UN in Cambodia 64, 70–71; UN in Central America 64, 67–70); state sovereignty 62, 68, 70, 73, 74; UN Charter 62, 68, 70, 74, 75; UN Security Council 60, 62, 67, 71, 73, 80; UNTAG 66, 71, 79, 81; *see also* Boutros-Ghali, Boutros; peace; Pérez de Cuéllar, Javier; UN decolonization process

Index 279

UN Security Council 43; 1992 Summit 60; anti-piracy 186–87; Cambodia 71; Namibia 65, 66; ONUCA 67, 68, 84; peacebuilding 60, 62; peacekeeping missions 41, 62, 84; Permanent Five 81, 124; post-conflict peacebuilding 60, 62, 67, 71, 73, 80
UNAIDS (UN Programme on HIV/AIDS) 143–44, 145, 154, 155–57, 159, 161, 162, 163, 266; role 155, 156, 157, 160; 'Three Ones' principle 156; *see also* HIV/AIDS; PPPs
UNCLOS (UN Convention on the Law of the Sea) 175
UNDP (UN Development Programme) 18, 47; good governance 42; HIV/AIDS 143, 144, 152, 156; UNOPS 197–211 (coordinating role 197–98, 204; execution role 197–200; Executive Board 209, 210–11, 212, 214; PED 198–99); *see also* UNOPS
UNESCO (UN Educational, Scientific and Cultural Organization) 1, 144, 150
UNFPA (United Nations Population Fund) 144, 145, 150, 206, 210
UNHCR (UN High Commissioner for Refugees)16, 118–40, 266; 1950 Statute 118, 121; 1951 Convention on the Status of Refugees 118, 121, 124; 1967 Protocol 124–25, 131; activities 118–19, 121, 122, 136; autonomy 121, 129; Cold War 122–23, 124, 125, 131, 134; Executive Committee 119, 130, 131; financial dependency 121–22, 130; Ford Foundation 122, 123, 134, 135; 'good offices' 124, 131, 135; IASC 128, 129, 134, 137; independence 129, 131, 134, 135, 136–37; network 120, 123, 128, 129, 134–35, 137, 266; NGOs 122, 123, 126, 133, 137; population of concern 118, 121, 122, 128, 129, 132, 136; purpose 118, 121, 136; state control 119, 130, 267; UN General Assembly 118, 121, 123, 124, 129, 131; United States 122, 123, 128, 130, 131; *see also* UNHCR, High Commissioner; UNHCR, mandate change
UNHCR, High Commissioner 120, 135–36, 137; assertive, autonomous leadership 122, 123, 124, 126, 128, 134, 135–36, 137, 266; Guterres, Antonio 127–28, 129, 134, 135; Lindt, Auguste 123, 124, 130, 135; Lubbers, Ruud 134; Ogata, Sadako 125, 126, 127, 131, 134, 135; Schnyder, Felix 124; Van Heuven Goedhart, Gerrit 122, 130, 134, 135; *see also* UNHCR; UNHCR, mandate change
UNHCR, mandate change 118–19, 121, 122, 136; explanations 120, 129–36 (constructivism 120, 130, 135–36; liberal institutionalism 120, 122, 130–31; neo-functionalism 120, 130, 131–33; regime complexity 120, 130, 133–35); self-directed nature 120, 122, 123; state-led change 119, 130, 131; state resistance to change 124, 125, 130, 135, 136; turning points 119, 122–29, 136 (geographical expansion 119, 123–25, 130, 132, 135; humanitarian relief/repatriation 119, 125–26, 131, 132, 134, 135; IDP protection 118, 119, 127–28, 130, 131, 132, 134; prolonging its existence 119, 122–23, 130, 132, 135; victims of natural disaster 118, 119, 128–29, 131, 132, 134, 135, 137); *see also* UNHCR; UNHCR, High Commissioner
UNICEF (UN Children's Fund) 17, 25, 197; HIV/AIDS 143, 144, 145, 150, 156
United States 179; Clinton administration 249, 250; ICANN 250, 254–56, 257–58, 259; Internet 243, 245–46, 247, 248–51, 257–58 (DNS 243, 246–47, 248–50, 253, 254, 255, 259, 260); UNHCR 122, 123, 128, 130, 131
UNOPS (UN Office for Project Services)195–217, 265, 266, 268;

ACABQ 203–6, 211, 212, 214; Boutros-Ghali, Boutros 202, 204, 209; bureaucracy 195, 203–6, 213, 214, 268; constructivism 196, 215; development cooperation 196, 201–2 (complex/salient issue 196–202, 213, 265); Executive Director (Everts, Daan 203, 205; Helmke, Reinhart 207, 212); expertise 196, 211; financial self-reliance 197, 204, 205, 210, 213, 215; hybrid form 210, 211; Jackson Report 197–98; merging with DDSMS 202–7, 209, 213, 214 (business impact 206–7; Dadzie Report 202–3); OPE 199–201, 215 (criticism 199, 201); OPS 196, 200, 201–11 (a separate UN entity 209–11); organizational culture 208, 213; PA theory 196, 215; staff initiative 195–96, 198, 206, 213, 265, 266 (independency 195–96, 213, 214; leaky boat strategy 207–8, 214); UN Secretary-General 202, 203, 205, 209; UNDP 197–211; UNOPS, a separate UN entity 211–12; *see also* UNDP

UNTAG (UN Transition Assistance Group) 66, 71, 79, 81

Weaver, Catherine: World Bank 91–117, 265, 266
WHO (World Health Organization) 141, 145–46, 147–54, 156, 159; autonomy 151; HIV/AIDS, 'lead agency' 143, 145, 147–54 (boundary decisions 148, 151–54; operational decisions 148, 149–51; programmatic decisions 147, 148–49; questioning of 143); Mahler, Halfdan 146, 150; Nakajima, Hiroshi 150; passivity 145–47; path dependence 147, 149; *see also* GPA; HIV/AIDS
Wolfensohn, James 91, 92–93, 95, 96–104; anticorruption agenda 99–104, 110; environmentally sustainable development 96–98, 110, 111; shortfalls 101–4; success 92–93, 94, 98, 110, 111; *see also* World Bank
Wolfowitz, Paul 91, 93, 95, 104–10; anticorruption agenda 106–11, 113; cronyism 109, 113; failure 93, 94, 104, 106, 107, 108, 111, 113; greenwashing the World Bank? 105–6, 110, 112; hypocrisy 104, 109–10, 112; lack of political skills 94, 104; restructuring ESSD into SDN 106, 111; resuming high-risk, high-reward energy lending 105–6, 110, 111; *see also* World Bank
World Bank 13, 91–117, 265, 266; anticorruption agenda 91, 93, 99–104, 106–12 (shortfalls/failure 101–4, 106, 107, 108, 111); *Assessing Aid* 100; autonomy 91, 93, 95, 110, 111; bureaucracy 92, 93, 95–96, 99–101, 103–4, 106, 108, 109–10; constructivism 96; corruption/socioeconomic development relationship 91, 99, 103, 110, 111; Development Committee 109, 113; discretion 95; environmentally sustainable development 91, 93, 96–98, 105–6, 111, 112; executive head 92, 93, 94, 95–96, 103, 104, 110–11, 112, 266; external dynamics 92, 93, 95, 96, 97–98, 101, 104, 105, 108–9; good governance 42, 99–100, 109, 112; HIV/AIDS 143, 144, 145, 150, 152, 156, 157, 158, 159, 161 (GFATM 157; MAP 156, 161); independence 91, 100, 103, 110, 265; organizational culture 9, 92, 94, 96, 98, 103–4, 108, 111; PA theory 94–96; Social Development approach 13; whistleblower policy 102, 107; Zoellick, Robert 112; *see also* Wolfensohn, James; Wolfowitz, Paul
WTO (World Trade Organization) 1, 15, 228, 236